NEW SOUTH AFRICAN KEYWORDS

NEW SOUTH AFRICAN KEYWORDS

edited by Nick Shepherd
and Steven Robins

Jacana / Johannesburg
Ohio University Press / Athens

First published 2008
In North and South America and the Pacific Rim by
Ohio University Press
The Ridges, Building 19
Athens, Ohio 45701, USA
www.ohioswallow.com

and in the rest of the world by
Jacana Media (Pty) Ltd
10 Orange Street, Auckland Park 2092, South Africa
(+27 11) 628 3200
www.jacana.co.za

ISBN 978-0-8214-1868-0 (Ohio University Press)
ISBN 978-1-77009-546-5 (Jacana Media)

Cover design by banana republic
Set in Adobe Garamond
Printed by CTP Book Printers
Job no. 000658

Library of Congress Cataloging in Publication data is available on request.

Contents

Introduction: New South African Keywords
Nick Shepherd and Steven Robins 1

AIDS *Deborah Posel* 13

CRIME *Jonny Steinberg* 25

CULTURE *Harry Garuba and Sam Raditlhalo* 35

DEMOCRACY AND CITIZENSHIP *Bettina von Lieres and Steven Robins* 47

DEVELOPMENT *Kees van der Waal* 58

EMPOWERMENT *Edgar Pieterse* 69

ETHNICITY *John L Comaroff and Jean Comaroff* 79

FAITH *Jean Comaroff and John L Comaroff* 91

GENDER *Helen Moffett* 104

HERITAGE *Nick Shepherd* 116

INDIGENOUS KNOWLEDGE Part I *by Kai Horsthemke* 129
                     Part II *by Lesley JF Green* 132

LAND *Thembela Kepe, Ruth Hall and Ben Cousins* 143

MARKET AND ECONOMY *Thomas Koelble* 157

RACE *Zimitri Erasmus* 169

RIGHTS *Steven Robins* 182

TRADITION *Emile Boonzaier and Andrew D Spiegel* 195

TRANSFORMATION *Thiven Reddy* 209

TRAUMA *Christopher J Colvin* 223

TRUTH AND RECONCILIATION *Fiona Ross* 235

WRITING AFRICA *Achille Mbembe in conversation with Isabel Hofmeyr* 247

XENOPHOBIA *Owen Sichone* 255

LIST OF CONTRIBUTORS 264

INDEX 265

INTRODUCTION:
NEW SOUTH AFRICAN KEYWORDS

Nick Shepherd and Steven Robins

ON MAY DAY 2007 thousands of demonstrators marched through the streets of Durban protesting against government proposals to rename close to 200 buildings, roads and other landmarks. The protest was led by the Zulu-dominated Inkatha Freedom Party (IFP). IFP spokespersons complained that the ANC-controlled city council had bulldozed the name changes through without adequate consultation. The names suggested were all heroes of the ANC's liberation struggle, which had culminated in the first democratic elections of 1994. Opposition to the proposed name changes also came from Afrikaners, the white descendants of European settlers who had systematically inscribed their names across the entire South African landscape. Perhaps the most vehemently contested of all the proposals was that to change the name of Umlazi's Mangosuthu Highway, named after the IFP leader Mangosuthu Buthelezi, to Griffiths Mxenge Highway in honour of a slain ANC activist and lawyer. IFP leaders warned of violence and bloodshed if this name change went ahead. Clearly, names, like language and culture, have become highly contentious aspects of the political transformation in South Africa.

One of the most compelling ideas to have come out of the humanities and social sciences is the idea that language, words and the names that we give to things play an active and determining role in constructing social realities. Far from being a passive process whereby we specify what is already known, the act of naming something becomes part of the process of its constitution, and an active site of social contestation. This is especially true of societies in transition (and what society is not in transition?). To say and to name is to know – but always to know in particular ways. In this book we set out to do two things. The first is to provide a guide to the keywords and key concepts that have become central to public and political discourses in post-apartheid South Africa. Our idea in this regard is a simple one. A significant aspect of the social, political and economic changes in South Africa in the post-1994 period has been the advent of a new terminology and a new conceptual apparatus through which to describe and imagine these changes. Some older terms have dropped out of circulation. Previously little-used terms have assumed a new prominence. In some cases existing terms have been renegotiated and have assumed new meanings.

It is part of the double nature of language itself that these new keywords and concepts are both enabling and disenabling, providing both wings for and shackles to the imagination. On the one hand, they open up fields of possibility and suggest daring new formulations of self and society. On the other hand, they set limits to this project, determine it in particular ways, and involve it in new combinations of power and interest. The same gesture that opens up some new horizons makes other formulations unthinkable, unsayable. Whatever happened to notions like 'tribe' and 'revolution', staples of apartheid and anti-apartheid discourses respectively? How have words like 'culture', 'race' and 'tradition' been renegotiated and re-interpreted? What exactly is implied by newly prominent words like 'rights' and 'transformation'? In each case it turns out that the answer is quite complex. At the same time, a close reading of this changing terrain of language provides one of the surest guides to the deeper nature and the contested contexts of the New South Africa.

The second thing that we set out to do in this book is to provide a compendium of current thinking on post-apartheid society. Here again, our approach was a simple one. We asked some of the most exciting current thinkers and commentators on post-apartheid South Africa to write essays on given keywords. We wanted the chapters to be short, punchy and accessible. At the same time, we wanted them to capture the complexity of current debates and the often ambiguous, unresolved senses in which these keywords circulate. Authors were asked to avoid academic circumlocutions, and to illustrate theoretical discussions with real world examples from post-apartheid contexts. The result is a concise and insightful guide to post-apartheid society which we hope will be useful to students, citizens, tourists, business managers, decision-makers – in fact, to anyone wanting to make sense of South African society today.

A vocabulary of culture and society

This book follows in illustrious footsteps. Most immediately, it acknowledges one of the most important books to come out of South Africa in the late 1980s, Emile Boonzaier and John Sharp's *South African Keywords: The Uses and Abuses of Political Concepts* (1988). For each of us, in different ways, this book was formative. As students, it provided us with an indispensable guide to the confusing, obfuscatory political discourse of apartheid. It is still a work that we recommend to colleagues, set as reading for courses, and dip into in the course of our own work. In their preface, Boonzaier and Sharp described their project as being 'to know how some of the key concepts of South African politics are used and abused in various arguments about the nature of society, and … to distinguish good sense from nonsense' (1988: ix–x), an admirably straightforward intention. In his introduction, Sharp suggested why this can be a complicated business: 'one cannot assume that any representation of … society is a straightforward description of its real nature, because each representation is a political statement which includes the assumptions and intentions of the people who make it' (2).

In the case of apartheid South Africa, he described the existence of a 'discourse of domination', which consists of 'a series of terms' that are 'related to each other by the manner in which they are understood'. Together they 'constitute a discourse about the nature of South African society, which reveals the logic and serves the interests of those who wield power' (6). Very briefly, he described a series of recognisable phases in the development of this discourse of domination. First organised around notions of 'race' and 'tribe', in the 1950s these were supplanted by a new vision of 'ethnic groups' and 'nations' as the building blocks of apartheid. In the 1980s, there was a shift to a developmentalist language, characterised by a 'two worlds' argument – that is, the notion that South Africa was a mix of 'first world' and 'third world' populations – and by the need for the 'development' and 'upliftment' of the 'backward' sectors.

In his account of the history of South African anthropology from 1920 to 1990, David Hammond-Tooke noted that the publication in 1988 of *South African Keywords* was a major contribution to South African anthropology. According to Hammond-Tooke, *Keywords* provided 'a critical examination of conventional beliefs about the nature of South African society, pointing out both the slippery nature of concepts such as culture, community, tradition, race, tribe, development, ethnic group and others, and demonstrating how they could be misused in political rhetoric and discourse' (1997: 180). Interestingly, only a few pages earlier on, Hammond-Tooke criticised the same 'University of Cape Town anthropologists' who participated in *Keywords* for endorsing a crudely materialist brand of Marxism in terms of which 'culture as an explanatory concept was rejected as idealist and encouraging false consciousness, and any investigation into ethnicity was similarly discouraged'. He challenged these anthropologists for embracing an orthodox Marxism that 'claimed to explain everything, but it did so at too high a level of generalisation, and thus explained very little' (1997: 176). Having roundly criticised this tendency, Hammond-Tooke nevertheless went on to claim that *Keywords* 'saved' South African anthropology from the clutches of a stultifying Marxist orthodoxy.

Notwithstanding Hammond-Tooke's criticisms, the *Keywords* project drew on the work of influential Marxist literary scholars and social historians such as Raymond Williams, EP Thompson and Shula Marks. In particular, it was inspired by Williams's classic *Keywords: A Vocabulary of Culture and Society* (1976). Williams's *Keywords* began as an appendix to his book *Culture and Society* (1956), which was cut from the final publication because it was too long. Williams wrote: '[but] the file of the Appendix stayed on my shelf. Over nearly twenty years I have been adding to it: collecting more examples, finding new points of analysis, including other words' (1976: 12). He spoke of the limitations of dictionary definitions of words, both in that they appear frozen in time, and in that they do not show the ideological struggle around keywords and their meanings.

Williams's *Keywords* was informed by a lively sense of the way in which conceptions of culture and society are both shaped by and reflected in the changing meanings of its key terms. Not only is language reflective of social and cultural formations, but struggles over meaning are a key component of struggles over the changing nature of society itself. In a central formulation, Williams referred to this as the notion of an 'active vocabulary'. In this sense, he described his project in *Keywords* as 'Notes on a list of words; analyses of a certain formation: these were the elements of an active vocabulary – a way of recording, investigating and presenting problems of meaning in which the meanings of *culture* and *society* have formed' (1976: 13).

In a similar fashion, Boonzaier and Sharp positioned their work as a polemic against apartheid state-centred discourse understood as a misuse of language. This was signalled in their sub-title: the 'use and abuse' of political language. Williams, though, has a more nuanced understanding of the relation between language, culture and society. For Williams, there is no neutral or value-free form of language which offers a stable alternative to this misuse. In a significant passage, he wrote of what it is that can be gained from an exercise in historicising and contextualising these key terms: 'What can really be contributed is not resolution but perhaps, at times, just that extra edge of consciousness' (1976: 21). He commented:

> This is not a neutral review of meanings. It is an exploration of the vocabulary of a crucial area of social and cultural discussion, which has been inherited within precise historical and social conditions and which has to be made at once conscious and critical – subject to change as well as continuity – if the millions of people in whom it is active are to see it as active: not a *tradition* to be learned, nor a *consensus* to be accepted, not a set of meanings which, because it is 'our language', has a natural authority; but as a shaping and reshaping, in real circumstances and from profoundly different and important points of view: a vocabulary to use, to find our ways in, to change as we find it necessary to change it, as we go on making our own language and history (1976: 21–2).

Drawing out this distinction a little further helps us to make a point about the particularity of a local tradition of research in anthropology. Boonzaier and Sharp's

Keywords, and a strand of South African anthropology through the 1980s, can be characterised by its desire to be politically relevant and interventionist. This response was not surprising, given the immediacy of the horrors of apartheid. A more general critique of anthropology's complicity in colonialism (see Asad 1973) no doubt also drove some South African anthropologists to articulate a clear political position vis-à-vis the apartheid state and its discourses. It may be argued that this contributed towards the privileging of action over thought, politics over theory, and applied over pure research (see Gillespie and Dubbeld 2008). For example, Steven Robins recalls discussing with fellow postgraduate students in the early 1980s how their Honours research projects on the devastating impact of forced removals in the South Sotho ethnic homeland of Qwaqwa would be useful to a democratic government some day in the future. In other words, it was the political relevance and utility of the research for a future democratic government that justified doing this research in the first place.

This activist orientation – so clear in Boonzaier and Sharp's project – continues to animate sectors of South African scholarship, and was one of the legacies that we needed to consider in positioning our own book. Complexity is never good for its own sake. What can we offer, if not a clear account of 'use' and 'abuse'? What is the role of critique, and how do we situate our own project in relation to a tradition of critical humanities scholarship? Above all, how can we render this complexity in a form that is genuinely useful, as a set of empowering ideas – tools to think with – rather than a kind of unravelling?

How 'new' is the New South Africa?

An important insight in Boonzaier and Sharp's *Keywords* was the manner in which the conceptual apparatus of modernity made itself available to apartheid ideologues, to the extent that it was concerned with embedded notions of culture and identity, with notions of racial difference, and with elaborating categories and hierarchies of classification. One way of understanding apartheid is as the outcome of a certain strand of thought in modernity itself, along with fascism, authoritarianism (as Hannah Arendt has argued), and racial slavery and colonialism (as Tony Bogues and others have argued). This suggestive formulation has been taken up by, for example, the French philosopher and poststructuralist theorist Jacques Derrida, who described events in South Africa as a 'concentration of world history'. Writing in the mid-1980s, he said: 'we might be tempted to look at this region of the world as a giant tableau or painting, the screen for some geopolitical computer. Europe, in the enigmatic process of its globalization and its paradoxical disappearance, seems to project onto this screen, point by point, the silhouette of its internal war, the bottom line of its profits and losses, the double-bind logic of its national and multi-national interests' (1985: 336–7).

The theme here is not the familiar and discredited notion of South African exceptionalism, but rather its opposite, the notion that South Africa presents an intensification of processes and relations seen elsewhere. The extreme forms taken by the development of racial capitalism under apartheid, the stark nature of its social contexts, the dramatic political transition of the 1990s: all work together to render South Africa in some ways exemplary, paradigmatic. It is not altogether fanciful to say that in getting a handle on the contested social, economic, political and cultural contexts of contemporary South Africa, we simultaneously gain insight into a far broader set of processes and relations, particularly in as far as they affect those parts of the world that have developed in the shadow of colonialism, on the flip-side of the global economy.

At the same time, there are significant continuities between pre-1994 and post-1994 contexts in South Africa. Broadly speaking, these follow two paths. Firstly, the continuing influence of development discourses, and their articulation with notions of globalisation and with neoliberal economic strategies (see Van der Waal, Koelble and Reddy, this volume). Secondly, the recycling of embedded notions of culture, tradition and identity, and their reappearance in public life via debates around notions of rights, entitlements, citizenship and heritage (see Garuba and Raditlhalo, Boonzaier and Spiegel, Robins and Von Lieres, and Shepherd, this volume). An exemplary instance of just how complex this play of conceptual continuity and difference has been, is the contemporary fate of the notion of 'ethnicity'.

In the first *South African Keywords* project, John Sharp focused on ethnicity as a primarily (apartheid) state-driven political and historical construction. In this book, John and Jean Comaroff draw attention to new forms of non-state-centred ethnic mobilisation and identity politics. The Comaroffs' chapter highlights the salience of 'Ethnicity Inc.' as a paradigmatic post-Cold War, neoliberal form of ethnicisation that reflects the legal expression of the commodification of culture and indigenous intellectual property. This contrasts sharply with John Sharp's analysis of the rise of Afrikaner ethnic nationalism and separate development (Bantustan or homeland) policy, a project that focused primarily on capturing the institutions of the nation-state, and stressed timeless and essential ethnic identities. Rather than seeking control of the state, or reacting against state forms of discrimination as ethnic minorities, 'Ethnicity Inc.', as exemplified in the case of the San ('Bushmen'), is concerned with legal struggles over access to land and intellectual property rights.

The San case reflects the emergence of new forms of ethnogenesis in terms of which identity and 'community' are reconstituted through the commodification of culture and intellectual property rights. These new forms of 'ethnic' mobilisation sometimes involve lucrative business empires. For example, in 1999, the Bafokeng Kingdom of North West Province won a ten-year legal battle for royalty payments from Impala Platinum Holdings (Implats). The Bafokeng have used these massive deposits of platinum, the largest outside Russia, to both reproduce 'tribal' traditions and build modern infrastructure including schools, clinics, hospitals, sports and recreation facilities, and a major Science and Technology Academy (see Comaroff and Comaroff, this volume).

Nor is it the case that these new forms of ethnogenesis have displaced prior, more embedded forms of ethnic mobilisation. Rather, it seems that both forms can coexist. While the changing fortunes of the notion of ethnicity reveal particularly interesting breaks and continuities with the apartheid past, the chapters in this book on tradition, race, gender, development and transformation are equally revealing in this regard. It is clear that some keywords have long shelf lives that may defy scholarly deconstruction and critiques. Popular understandings of race, gender and development are especially immune to scholarly deconstruction. Notwithstanding ongoing anti-essentialist critiques of the sort attempted in *South African Keywords*, essentialist understandings of race, gender and tradition are alive and well in the public sphere. No longer are timeless and essentialist ideas about San identity, for instance, simply imposed from 'the outside' but they are also reproduced 'from below' by indigenous peoples making claims to the state and the courts for access to land and political resources. Whereas during the anti-apartheid struggle, Left intellectuals and activists believed that outmoded ideas about ethnic and cultural difference would give way to modern, socialist understandings of working-class consciousness and solidarity, political life in post-apartheid South Africa continues to be animated by discourses on 'African tradition' and ethnic difference.

Some of the chapters in this book reveal that there have indeed been striking discontinuities and unanticipated new developments since the demise of apartheid. For example, the AIDS pandemic has opened up questions surrounding sexuality and sexual rights as never before, and has served to place the body at the centre of public and political discourses. Closely guarded taboos around gender and sexuality have been challenged, and patriarchal sexual ideas and practices have come under the gaze of public and scientific scrutiny. The Jacob Zuma rape trial in 2006, for example, was perceived by gender activists as a disturbing lens on to patriarchal culture in South Africa. The trial also revealed the profound tensions and contradictions between progressive, constitutionally mandated sexual rights and conservative, culturally embedded sexual cultures. This made for new public expressions of sexual politics that could not have been anticipated by the contributors to the original *Keywords* project.

The public debate around the causes and correct treatment of HIV/AIDS has also served to focus attention on questions of knowledge and epistemology. In quite surprising and surely unprecedented ways, discussions around science and society, and around 'Western' versus 'African' ways of knowing and being in the world, have become staples of media reportage. This has been due in part to the peculiar centality of this debate, emanating from the office of the President (see Posel in this volume). Perhaps more than any other, the public debate around HIV/AIDS has presented a nation in the process of thinking through a set of meanings and values, just as it has presented the world (and ourselves) with some of the most difficult and troubling material in thinking through the New South Africa.

The idea of critique

Boonzaier and Sharp's volume was characterised by its unity of approach. The authors, all of whom were anthropologists, had their sights set firmly on the political discourse of apartheid, and it was towards the end of deconstructing this discourse that the essays in that volume were directed. Our own approach is necessarily more interdisciplinary and heterodox. It has become a commonplace that the political transition in South Africa coincided with the intensified effects of globalisation. It also coincided with a fundamental reorganisation of global political and economic power, and with the end of a certain way of understanding global social dynamics. This was not Francis Fukuyama's 'end of history', but the end of a certain teleological view of history as being bound up with class struggles, state entities and the historical movement against a capitalist mode of production. Writing ten and more years after the first democratic elections in South Africa, we need to account for a more complex and ambiguous terrain, both with regard to social processes and with regard to notions of agency, history and teleology.

One example of this is the disappearance of a consensual political vocabulary of the Left which was available to Boonzaier and Sharp (although, arguably, they overestimated the extent of this consensus, even in the mid-1980s). Ours is a situation in which, for example, a radical feminist position competes for the label of 'progressive' in the realm of cultural politics with an Afro-centric position founded on essentialised notions of culture, tradition and knowledge, with decided views on the role of women in society. It is also a situation in which a broadly Marxist political economy, transmuted into the liberal democratic language of socio-economic rights, competes for the same label with a radical anti-globalisation position founded on notions of autarky and self-reliance. More prosaically, it is a situation in which political leaders whose personal histories lie in the struggle against apartheid can appear one day in suits at Davos, and the next in Communist Party T-shirts at a meeting of trade unionists, even as they endorse conservative economic strategies whose overwhelming effect has been to benefit 'new' as well as old elites.

What we offer here is not a single reading but a set of perspectives from which to make sense of these entangled contexts, based on a close account of their key terms and the social and intellectual contexts in which they have been used and articulated. This is not to say that there are no firm positions from which to view developments, decide between competing approaches, even make judgements and take sides. Rather, it is to say that the hopes of a single, encompassing narrative have been largely frustrated. Or that key questions of agency, causality and value now seem more complexly nuanced. Or that the binaries set up by colonial discourse and adopted and inverted by anti-colonial discourses – us–them, black–white, South–North, the Rest–the West – begin to break down in the face of more ambiguously interpenetrating social and political arrangements. We might say that there is no easy walk to enlightenment.

One of the threads running through the explication of keywords in this volume has to do with their 'protean' nature, whereby 'meanings tend to go in several directions at once' (Garuba and Raditlhalo, in this volume). Harry Garuba and Sam Raditlhalo are writing of culture as a postapartheid keyword, but the same might equally be said of 'tradition', 'ethnicity', 'heritage' or any number of other keywords. Each is situated at a complex juncture, pointing forwards and backwards, gesturing towards the fixed and essential even as they function as complex sites of cultural construction and self-stylisation. In our account, a starting point for critique is a willingness to hold this kind of doubleness in mind. It means resisting the pull of either a (self-defeating) search for authenticity, or a (defeated) relativism whereby all meanings become equally valid. It also means being prepared to occupy a slightly indeterminate middle ground, tacking backwards and forwards between seemingly contradictory sets of meanings, taking local contexts and histories of usage as appropriate reference points.

A second point is the realisation that it is precisely their protean and ambiguous nature that renders such terms available and attractive as sites of cultural construction and contestation. As Nick Shepherd argues in this volume in relation to the notion of heritage, it is its indeterminate nature – situated at a point of conjunction of past and present, the individual and the collective, rootedness and constructedness – which makes it available as a site where new subjectivities and notions of citizenship are negotiated and contested. In these terms, a notion of critique which thinks of itself as uncovering some essential logic or true meaning cancels the very quality that makes these terms critically interesting and significant.

A further point to be made in relation to such a conception of critique is that it implicitly demotes the role of the scholar-political activist. In the traditional notion of critique the high priests and priestesses of the academy or of the Party, appropriately conscientised and in touch with theory, rip aside the veil of language and customary usage to reveal the real conditions of existence. In contrast to this image, we would want to emphasise the often sure-footed manner in which citizens in the postcolony themselves negotiate a difficult and contradictory conceptual landscape. In this volume Steven Robins writes in relation to a conception of 'citizenship and rights', 'In the daily scramble for livelihoods and security, poor people tend to adopt several strategies and draw on multiple political identities, discourses and social relationships to navigate daily life'. We might extend this insight to a landscape of meanings, point to the irony and realism which allow people to enjoy the faux authenticity of GrandWest Casino's reconstructed District Six (from which people were forcibly removed under apartheid) even as they experience the unrequited pangs of forced removal, or wear global brand-name goods even as they retain allegiances to the local and distinctive.

Another thread running through these chapters is the question of what to do when discourses themselves become historically overdetermined, weighed down by a set of traumatic histories. More subtly, many chapters are haunted by an unfulfilled project of redemption. How does one evade or emerge from underneath these traumatic histories? What would it entail to achieve a full realisation of rights and personhood, to seize control of the alienated terrain of meaning and representation? In the case of Boonzaier and Sharp's *Keywords*, the answer took the form of a project of political liberation, but what does it mean to ask these same questions in the context of the postcolony? One of the contributions to this volume that breaks format is an interview with Achille Mbembe, which is constituted as an answer to this set of questions.

Achille Mbembe is an indispensable commentator on postapartheid South Africa and on the postcolony more generally. His considerable ingenuity and importance has been to locate himself at just the kind of critical juncture that we describe above, rejecting an easy set of binaries, suspicious of an inherited set of discourses of liberation, be they Marxist, nationalist or nativist. In an interview with Isabel Hofmeyr – herself a distinguished critic – reproduced here under the heading 'Writing Africa', he talks about the process of writing his landmark book *On the Postcolony* (2001). More generally, he discusses the politics of representation: as Hofmeyr puts it, 'the difficulties of writing about Africa in a field that has been overburdened by centuries of formulaic representation' (262); and as Mbembe has it, ways of evading 'the cul-de-sac of the many discourses on Africa ... means for escaping the trap of the name' (262–3).

In a formulation which takes us back to Raymond Williams's notion of an 'active vocabulary' in the original *Keywords*, Mbembe describes his project in *On the Postcolony* as being 'an attempt to experiment with a different dictionary of representation – a lexicon in which to pose different questions about the "now"' (258). In relation to a critique of 'certain strands of postcolonial theory or nativism', he says: 'any serious critique of freedom entails, of necessity, a revisiting of our fables and the various grammars that, under the pretext of authenticity or radicalism, prosaically turn Africa into yet another deadly fiction' (259). In his own work he points ahead, suggesting ways around the traps of discourse, combining modalities from music, poetry and the sensuality of lived experience, to allude to new ways of writing Africa.

Thinking allowed

For many South Africans, as for the majority of humanity, the basic struggle remains the same: the struggle against material want, the struggle for human dignity, the struggle for the wrongs of the past to be recognised, the struggle for reparations and for representation. At the same time, the ground on which these struggles are fought now seems more complex and ambiguous, and offers fewer signposts and fixed points. The challenge which we set ourselves, and which we set our readers, is to steer a course through these complex and entangled histories, dynamics and genealogies. The essence of critique is to opt for neither a blinkered fundamentalism nor a helpless relativism. Rather, it is to stay close to the particularity of given contexts, and to retain a firm sense of social justice and the political ideal – of the kind so admirably set out in South Africa's Constitution, for example – even as one recognises the kind of real-world constraints which shape lives, direct resources and constrain political ideals. It is to attempt the kind of broadly secular scepticism and humane engagement championed in the work of Edward Said, for example, or in the work of Frantz Fanon, Amilcar Cabral and Njabulo Ndebele.

Thinking about South Africa in this way involves a willingness to situate phenomena in a double set of contexts. Firstly, in the context of a set of specific, local histories, trajectories and genealogies: slavery, colonialism, apartheid, the specific forms that development has taken in the post-1994 period. Secondly, in the context of a set of global trends, developments and dynamics, and in understanding the particular place that South Africa occupies – politically, economically, symbolically – in relation to the West or the North. What Raymond Williams characterised as adding 'that extra edge of consciousness' we would characterise as 'reading through' or 'thinking through' the multiple, sometimes confusing contexts that constitute the present moment in South Africa. Ultimately, it was with this challenge in mind that we approached the idea of *New South African Keywords*, as a guide to some of these thickets and byways.

Regarding the scope of this book and the selection of keywords: at a certain stage we were confronted by the impossibility of being comprehensive in our coverage. In part, the selection of keywords was determined by whether we were able to get just the kinds of chapters that we wanted from our contributors. In part, it was determined by our own interests and predilections. There are some obvious gaps. Where are the chapters on 'state' and 'nation'? Why doesn't 'sexuality' have a chapter on its own? What about 'sport' and 'nationalism'? Ultimately we make no apologies. We hope that, like us, you will take this as the start of a conversation, as a first word rather than a last.

For South Africans, this book offers an understanding of the ways in which we describe ourselves to ourselves in the process of becoming. For observers, it offers a detailed account of the articulation between language and society, in all the particularity of a complex and fascinating social context and historical moment. Thinking allowed.

References
Asad, Talal. 1973. *Anthropology and the Colonial Encounter* (London: Ithaca Press).
Boonzaier, E and Sharp, J (eds.). 1988. *South African Keywords: The Uses and Abuses of Political Concepts* (Cape Town: David Philip).
Derrida, J. 1985. 'Racism's Last Word' in J Henry Louis Gates (ed.), 'Race', Writing and Difference (Chicago: University of Chicago Press), pp. 329–338.
Gillespie, Kelly and Dubbeld, Bernard. 2008. 'The Possibility of a Critical Anthropology after Apartheid: Relevance, Intervention, Politics', Paper presented at the Anthropology Southern Africa annual conference, Pretoria, 26–29 September 2008.
Hammond-Tooke. David 1990. *Imperfect Interpreters: South Africa's Anthropologists, 1920–1990* (Johannesburg: Witwatersrand University Press).
Mbembe, A. 2001. *On the Postcolony* (Berkeley: University of California Press).
Williams, Raymond. 1976. *Keywords: A Vocabulary of Culture and Society* (London: Fontana).

AIDS

Deborah Posel

THE INTERNATIONAL VISIBILITY of post-apartheid South Africa has, unfortunately, had a lot to do with its highly politicised controversy about AIDS. Conflicts about what AIDS is and how to treat it have reached well beyond the country's borders, on to an international stage of argument and confrontation. Among recent incidents, for example, was the storm of protest that erupted in the aftermath of Health Minister Manto Tshabalala-Msimang's interventions at the 2006 International AIDS Conference held from 13 to 19 August in Toronto, during which she advocated various vegetable remedies as alternatives for the antiretroviral therapies recommended by AIDS experts. In the absence of credible scientific evidence for her position, and in the midst of alarming rates of HIV infection in South Africa – currently in the region of five and a half million people – the Minister stirred up strong feelings, ranging from incredulity and bewilderment to vexation, anger and despair.

Stephen Lewis, the UN Special Envoy for AIDS in Africa, strayed from international conference conventions of polite understatement in a strident denunciation of the South African government's stance, as 'more worthy of a lunatic fringe than a concerned and compassionate state' (*The Weekender*, 19–20 August 2006). His frustrations were echoed locally in angry declamations and calls for the Minister's dismissal, from AIDS activists and members of the public through to leaders of the medical and scientific establishment, political analysts and party politicians. The Minister, on the other hand, was undaunted, rejecting Lewis's critique as 'un-African', and holding firm to her scepticism about the conventional science of AIDS ('Whose science?' was her rejoinder to a query about the lack of scientific support for her position).

For a brief while during 2007, many were hopeful of a shift to a more proactive phase in the management of the epidemic and the provision of treatment. While the Minister recuperated from a liver transplant, the then Deputy Minister of Health, Nosizwe Madlala-Routledge, was allocated a leading role in formulating a new government AIDS plan, with the Minister's political nemesis – the Treatment Action Campaign (TAC) – collaborating closely in this initiative. National and international activists and commentators welcomed a seeming change of heart in the government's response to the epidemic. But this was shortlived. In August 2007, Madlala-Routledge was dismissed from her position by President Mbeki, for an alleged breach of government protocol. Nationally and internationally, reaction to her dismissal was dismayed and vehement. The TAC deemed it an indication that 'the President still remains opposed to the science of HIV and to appropriately responding to the [pandemic]' (*Mail & Guardian*, 9 August 2007).

This was only the latest salvo in South Africa's AIDS controversy which has raged since the late 1990s, and which has politicised the epidemic more intensely in this country than anywhere else in the world. South Africa is one of many developing countries overwhelmed by the challenges of managing a large, primarily heterosexual, AIDS epidemic. It is also one of many places where the nature of AIDS is vigorously argued and disputed. But South Africa is unique in having generated heated argument about what AIDS is (and isn't) which emanated from the highest echelons of power – in the Office of the President – catapulting the idea of AIDS and its contested meanings to the very forefront of the political agenda.

In terms of the scientific orthodoxy, AIDS is Acquired Immuno-Deficiency Syndrome, a condition that develops through the destructive effects of the Human Immunodeficiency Virus (HIV). The virus ambushes the immune system, corroding the body to the point of extinction. Although it is as yet incurable, antiretroviral drugs (ARVs) are the only scientifically validated route to relative health.

For the medical profession working in the trenches of the epidemic, the powers of ARVs are near miraculous, summoning an inert, wasting body back to robust and energetic health – even if some patients suffer side effects. So their advocacy of ARVs is passionate and proselytising. This is also the version of AIDS and the appropriate treatment that has motivated huge investments in an NGO sector dedicated to combating the epidemic. Most notable amongst these are organisations such as Soul City and loveLife, which have raised unprecedented amounts of donor monies for a multi-faceted health education drive.

Yet, theirs have not been merely campaigns to educate people about how to prevent and treat AIDS. These became – somewhat unexpectedly – political struggles over the very nature of AIDS. This politics became, likewise, the driving force of the Treatment Action Campaign, formed in 1998, which has since become the sharpest political thorn in the side of the government on the issue of AIDS, and the most assertive and prominent social movement of the post-apartheid era.

This short chapter gives my reading of what the controversy has been about, why it has flared with such intensity, and why this occurred from the late 1990s, in the midst of the efforts to build a 'new' South Africa that transcends the humiliations and breaches of the apartheid past (for more, see Posel 2004, 2005).

The nub of the controversy

The most vociferous arguments, along with the most dramatic political collisions, around AIDS are associated with Thabo Mbeki's Presidency after 1998. But the first eruptions came a few years before. Early signs of a concerted effort to tackle AIDS after the demise of apartheid were promising: a national AIDS plan was produced by the National AIDS Convention of South Africa (NACOSA, established in 1992), and was endorsed by the new democratic government and elevated to the status of a Presidential Lead Project with the promise of appropriate funding. But – as Mandela has since acknowledged, and apologised for – AIDS was anything but a national priority during his term as President, and little progress was made in pursuit of the ambitious national plan.

Instead, the 1994–8 period will be remembered for two scandals in respect of AIDS. The first broke in 1996, when the then Minister of Health, Nkosazana Dlamini-Zuma, flouted state funding rules in offering a lavish sum of donor money for a musical drama, *Sarafina II*, which was to travel the country educating communities about AIDS. The initiative was controversial for both its financial irregularities and its poor return on investment. More prescient of the future trajectory of AIDS politics, however, was the so-called Virodene scandal in 1997, which began the overt politicisation of science and scientific claims to truth in the post-apartheid era. Mounting an unprecedented, and unexpectedly direct, attack on the medical establishment, the Cabinet went out on a limb to back clinical trials of Virodene – a substance that turned out to be nothing more than a toxic industrial solvent – as an AIDS cure. This was in defiance of the authority of the Medicines Control Council (MCC), the independent body which had until then regulated and vetted all clinical trials in the country and which refused to approve the Virodene trial protocol. Alongside public argument that the Cabinet was fanning specious hopes of an African AIDS cure were allegations that the ANC had invested financially in the production of Virodene.

Then Deputy President Mbeki's backing of the Virodene trials was ardent and his critique of the MCC pointed and angry, giving perhaps the earliest signs of what would grow into his more thoroughgoing distaste for the power of the scientific establishment in respect of AIDS. After becoming President, Mbeki's position on AIDS began to resonate increasingly with the views of so-called AIDS denialists or dissidents, including the likes of Peter Duesberg and David Rasnick whose critiques of the scientific orthodoxy had been profiled on various websites alleged to have attracted Mbeki's interest. For almost three years (1999 through to late 2001), Mbeki positioned himself at the helm of a governmental critique of what he deemed a flawed, 'Western' science of AIDS, by querying the reality of the HI virus and attacking international pharmaceutical companies for peddling toxic antiretroviral remedies.

Mbeki made his case in two different ways. One was based on the core dissident critique of the science of AIDS. Dissidents dispute the connection between the HI virus and immunodeficiency, and thus all the diagnostic and treatment reasoning that goes with it. Without explicitly making this case, Mbeki aligned himself with the dissidents through his claim that 'you cannot attribute immune deficiency solely and exclusively to a virus' (*Time*, 16 April 2004).

His other line of argument was to insist that AIDS in Africa was different from AIDS in the West. As he saw it, in Africa AIDS was primarily a heterosexual epidemic that had caused 'millions' of deaths with many more set to come, unlike the largely homosexual incidence of AIDS in the West, with relatively few deaths. Mbeki took this to mean that Western theories and practice were largely irrelevant in the African struggle against the illness. As he put it in a letter to Bill Clinton, Tony Blair, Kofi Annan and others, written on 3 April 2000, AIDS in Africa was a 'uniquely African catastrophe ... It is obvious that whatever lessons we have to and may draw from the West about the grave issue of HIV-AIDS, a simple superimposition of Western experience on African reality would be absurd and illogical' (Mbeki 2000a).

The mainstream version of AIDS and AIDS treatment was thus an expression of the West's scientific imperialism at Africa's expense, with the medical establishment colluding with the pharmaceutical giants who garnered vast profits from the global marketing of ARVs. So Mbeki cast his dissidence in a rhetoric of enlightened resistance to neo-colonial and racist tyranny. Within Africa, he claimed, the AIDS epidemic consisted of a 'syndrome' of symptoms attributable to multiple causes other than a single virus – on the broadest level, AIDS was the result of the ravaging effects of poverty on the body's immune system.

The idea that the scientific orthodoxy on AIDS was contaminated by a neocolonial, racist reading of Africa and blackness was central to Mbeki's stance, and the basis of his rejection of the conventional epidemiology of the illness in South Africa and the continent at large.[1] In July 2000, in an open correspondence in the *Sunday Times* with the then leader of the opposition Democratic Alliance, Tony Leon, Mbeki dismissed what he regarded as 'hysterical estimates of the incidence of HIV in our country and sub-Saharan Africa', coupled with 'many frightening statements ... made with great regularity about ... the threat this poses to our very survival as a country, a continent and as Africans' (*Sunday Times*, 9 July 2000).

Claims about high prevalence rates of AIDS in Africa went hand in hand, for

Mbeki, with assumptions about Africa's sexual promiscuity. As he put it in a speech at the University of Fort Hare in October 2001:

> thus does it happen that others who consider themselves our leaders take to the streets carrying their placards, to demand that because we are germ carriers, and human beings of a lower order that cannot subject its [*sic*] passions to reason, we must perforce adopt strange opinions, to save a depraved and diseased people from perishing from self-inflicted disease … Convinced that we are but natural-born, promiscuous carriers of germs, unique in the world, they proclaim that our continent is doomed to an inevitable mortal end because of our unconquerable devotion to the sin of lust (*Mail & Guardian*, 26 October 2001).

Reaction to Mbeki's stance was strong, nationally and internationally. Many international and national leaders, analysts and observers expressed their incredulity at the controversy, particularly in the face of the deepening crisis of the country's epidemic, worsening death rates, and the seeming indifference of the President to the plight of the infected. Health Minister Tshabalala-Msimang, who would remain a loyal adherent of the President's views, admitted that 'even some of our friends say they don't understand what South Africa is doing' (*San Francisco Examiner*, 11 July 2000).

Extremely outspoken criticism came within the country from the likes of Anglican Archbishop Njongonkulu Ndungane, who compared the government's dereliction of responsibility in the face of the epidemic to the 'crime against humanity' inflicted by apartheid. Support for Mbeki's position was vehement, but limited. By 2002, the controversy was alleged to have brought the ANC closer to internal rupture than any other issue since 1994 (*Business Day*, 28 March 2002). It had provoked open collisions between national and provincial governments and had thrust the post-apartheid government into bruising and humiliating confrontations with the Constitutional Court over the government's obligation to supply 'prevention of mother to child transmission' (PMTCT) treatment to HIV-positive pregnant women.

From late 2000, in the midst of pressure from within the Cabinet, Mbeki retreated from the public debate. The Health Minister then took up the cudgels of the dissident position by way of her critique of the internationally recommended regimen of ARV treatment for AIDS. South Africa's global notoriety in respect of AIDS has since stemmed from the Health Minister's advocacy of olive oil, lemon juice, garlic and beetroot (amongst other vegetables) as an appropriate alternative to the antiretroviral therapies that mainstream science recommends.

Tshabalala-Msimang's dissidence is a more *ad hoc* position than Mbeki's. Although she is medically trained and he isn't, it is he rather than she who donned the mantle of 'learned critique'. Nor did she attempt to stake out anything resembling a systematic argument on the epidemic. Indeed, she has vacillated between a loyal adherence to Mbeki's views and a reiteration of the medical orthodoxy that HIV causes AIDS as the basis of her ministry's policies.[2]

In the midst of this abiding confusion, however, her role has been largely as Mbeki's chorus, particularly on the issue of treatment, repeatedly dismissing ARVs as toxic. More recently, she has tended to embed the treatment controversy in a discourse of democratic choice, insisting that South Africans should be free to choose the treatment regime they prefer. At best, this rhetorical device puts ARVs on a spectrum of treatment options, neither more nor less desirable than her array of vegetables. But, when overlaid with a rejection of AIDS science as Western and partisan, her interventions tacitly undermine the choice of ARVs as un-African.

Explaining the controversy

Why did an intelligent and politically shrewd President, with no expertise or training in matters of health, weigh in so directly and heavily on the question of AIDS, risking all the national and international turbulence provoked by his interventions? Why did this happen in South Africa, one of the few developing countries with the resources to have made a significant dent in the epidemic if it had acted concertedly and unambiguously?[3] What were the temptations of the denialist position in this country, at this historical moment?

These are intriguing questions, which many people have pondered. Some of the suggested answers range from a cynical ploy to free the South African government from carrying the economic burdens of comprehensive ARV treatment – an argument mounted at one point by the Health Minister herself – through to Mbeki's psychology and personal biography. There may be some merit in any one of these views, and a full answer might invoke a range of factors and interests which I won't venture to suggest.

My argument here offers what I see as a necessary – rather than sufficient – condition for Mbeki's positioning and the ensuing AIDS controversy. As I see it, it is impossible to make sense of this controversy without embedding it in the symbolic politics of the 'new' South Africa in transition from the horrors of apartheid. In my view, Mbeki's interventions from high are enormously revealing of the metaphorical significance he attached to the epidemic – as far more than a matter of public health, having wide-ranging political and symbolic repercussions that cut to the very meaning of South Africa's 'liberation' and the prospects of its fledgling nationhood.

Paula Treichler (1999: 1), drawing on the writings of Susan Sontag, has noted that globally the epidemic of AIDS has produced 'an epidemic of significations' – anxieties, debates and controversies over how AIDS is represented and the metaphorical power of these representations. Globally, the politics of AIDS has been, in large part, a politics of knowledge, a politics of representation. Partly a drama about the power of science, the AIDS 'story' has also been a moral saga about dangerous liaisons, unsafe ways of life, and contaminated parts of the world. Arguably, in the case of South Africa, this explosive politics of representation is inseparable from the post-apartheid conjuncture and, in particular, its contiguity of new life and new death.

To make this case, it is necessary to consider the metaphorical density of the AIDS epidemic in post-apartheid South Africa, particularly from the perspective of Mbeki's Presidency, which in turn presupposes a reflection on some of the more prominent symbolic registers of Mbeki's politics and his self-styling as President. Here, I draw on Mbeki's most evocative and revealing speeches, including his address to parliament, 'I am an African', which has become iconic of his positioning as President.

Once President, Mbeki embraced the role of nation-builder, and established the idea of the 'African Renaissance' as his principal rhetorical motif. Images of birth and new life constituted its symbolic core. 'The word "Renaissance"', he explained, 'means rebirth, renewal, springing up anew. Therefore, when we speak of the African Renaissance, we speak of the rebirth and renewal of our continent' (Mbeki 1999a). Thus was the 'new' South African nation, born in 1994, drawn into a larger affirmation of a vigorous life force replenishing the continent at large, adding greater moment and significance to South Africa's rebirth.

In Mbeki's discourse, it was a miraculous rebirth, from a thoroughly 'wretched past' (Mbeki 1997) that had afflicted Africa as a whole. He evoked the humiliations of apartheid amidst a wider landscape of despair – 'the march of African time ... [trodden by] the footprints of misery' (Mbeki 1999b) – that had accompanied Africa's history from colonialism through to the present. Africa's first journey of suffering was to have endured the degradations and brutality of colonial oppression; the next was to have borne the burden of postcolonial regimes that had betrayed 'the promise' of liberation. For example, when colonial Gold Coast won independence as Ghana, Mbeki mused, 'the African giant was awakening. But it came to pass that the march of African time snatched away that promise. Very little seemed to remain along its path except the footprints of despair' (Mbeki 1999b).

In his much-publicised speech 'I am an African', the defining quality that Africans shared was the pain of their past:

> I am an African. I am born of the peoples of the continent of Africa. The pain of the violent conflict that the peoples of Liberia, Somalia, the Sudan, Burundi and Algeria bear, is a pain that I bear. The dismal shame of poverty, suffering, and human degradation of my continent is a blight that we share. The blight on our happiness that derives from this and from our drift to the periphery of the ordering of human affairs leaves us in a persistent shadow of despair. This is a savage road to which nobody should be condemned (Mbeki 1996).

Being African in the time of Africa's Renaissance meant, quintessentially, a refusal to capitulate to this blighted past, a determination to transcend a history of misery and a proud reassertion of the African yearning to prosper. It was to believe that the 'miracle' of renewal and new life 'can come out of Africa, an Africa which in the eyes of the … world is home to an unending spiral of anarchy and chaos, at whose unknown end is a dark pit of an utter, a complete, and unfathomable human disaster' (Mbeki 1997).

Yet, however strong this urge to redemption, the depth of the 'abyss' of the past made the rebirth of the present tenuous and vulnerable. Indeed, as in the text quoted above, Mbeki's evocations of the horrors of the past were typically more forceful and resounding than the injunctions to hope in the future; his yearnings for Africa's transcendence were unsettled by the power with which he evoked the menace of the forces that threatened to undermine it.

> The truth is that we have not travelled very far with regard to the projection of frightening images of savagery that attend the continent of Africa … And so the question must arise about how we – who, in a millennium, only managed to advance from cannibalism to a 'blood-dimmed tide' of savages who still slaughter countless innocents with machetes, and on whom another, as black as I, has turned his back, grateful that his ancestor were slaves – how we hope to emulate the great human achievements of the earlier Renaissance of the Europe of the 15th and 16th centuries? (Mbeki 1998b)

Even when rhetorically mustering confidence in the vitality of Africa's rebirth, the traces of doubt were not fully vanquished, and the declarations of hope themselves became symptoms of a lingering disbelief:

> Whatever the setbacks of the moment, nothing can stop us now! Whatever the difficulties, Africa shall be at peace! However improbable it may sound to the sceptics, Africa will prosper! Whoever we may be, whatever our immediate interest, however much we have been caught by the fashion of cynicism and loss of faith in the capacity of the people, let us err today and say – nothing can stop us now! (Mbeki 1996)

Part of Mbeki's angst derived from the persistence of Western scepticism at the prospect of Africa's regeneration, replete with lingering neocolonial convictions about a continent cursed with disease, disaster and dereliction. But the persistent ambivalence in his discourse – of a hopefulness ever on the verge of negating itself – was a marker of his unease about the subversive forces – threats of destruction and death – *within* Africa, and within the African self.

The Janus Face, the Faustian dilemma, Oscar Wilde's 'Picture of Dorian Gray', the necessary coexistence of good and evil in our cultures, according to which each blessing is its own curse – let the dogs off the leash, there are things in the African bush! – are we not met here to challenge all this troubled imagery, much of which describes our real world! (Mbeki 1998a)

Africa, then, was not safe within itself; the demons were lodged within. And the African Renaissance had to be an effort to vanquish these dualities: 'hopefully our actions will obviate the needs to maintain a pride of guard dogs against those in the world, including *our African selves*, who might be forced to advance against a human advance [*sic*] which for us might represent disempowerment, marginalisation and regression' (Mbeki 1998a; my emphasis).

Africa – 'our African selves' – needed to transform, therefore, from within. Hence Mbeki's insistence that the African Renaissance was a struggle which required commitment and energy from a 'new type of person' born of 'moral regeneration', a person markedly different from 'those in our cities and towns who have lost all hope and all self-worth, who have slid into a twilight world of drug and alcohol abuse, the continuous sexual and physical abuse of women and children, of purposeless wars fought with fists and boots, metal rods, knives and guns, every day resulting in death and grievous bodily harm' (Mbeki 1999c). It was the birth of this 'new type of person' which would finally and irrefutably overthrow the burden of the colonial stereotypes of the African and their tenacious power within 'the African self'.

What, then, of AIDS? AIDS made its presence felt at the moment of South Africa's rebirth. The epidemic was incubated under apartheid but picked up momentum through the 1990s. In 1990, the estimated prevalence of HIV infection was less than 1%; by 1998, it had reached 22.8% – and as much as 32.5% in some parts of KwaZulu-Natal (Marks 2002: 16). By 2000, South Africa – the world's newest paragon of democracy – had the highest number of HIV infections in the world. And rates of death were accelerating among those who ought to have been the principal beneficiaries of the country's liberation, the young and middle-aged. Malegapuru Makgoba, then president of the Medical Research Council, compared the 'high numbers of young men and women who are dying in our country' to the effects of 'a major war' (*Sunday Times*, 9 July 2000). Alongside the birth of their new democratic nation, South Africans were witnessing the proliferation of death among its people.

Mbeki was acutely aware of this conjunction, and explicitly situated debates about AIDS within it. Writing to Clinton and other world leaders, Mbeki said he found it 'interesting' – surely a deliberately ironic word choice – that the most rapid acceleration in the incidence of HIV 'coincided closely' with the first five years after liberation. He spelt out the symbolic and political weight of this 'coincidence' more fully in his opening address to the 2000 International AIDS Conference in Durban, where he juxtaposed the recent birth of 'freedom and democracy' in South Africa – 'new gifts ... only half a dozen years old' – with 'the health catastrophe we face'. He then welcomed the delegates:

> convinced that you would not have come here unless you were to us messengers of hope, deployed against the spectre of the death of millions from the disease ... I am certain that there are many among you who joined the international struggle for the destruction of the apartheid system. You are therefore as much midwives of the new, democratic, non-racial and non-sexist South Africa as are the millions of our people who fought for the emancipation of all humanity from the racist yoke of the apartheid crime against humanity (Mbeki 2000b).

Mbeki was making it clear, then, that when it came to AIDS, the stakes were far higher than simply the issue of the nation's physical health; its ethical well-being, and the integrity of its social and political body, were similarly at risk. In his discourse on the epidemic, the meaning of AIDS was inseparable from the meaning and fate of the country's newfound freedom. AIDS threatened to extinguish the hope that had inspired the liberation struggle and that had animated the birth of the fledgling democracy.

Within Mbeki's metaphorical field, however, different versions of AIDS carried correspondingly different symbolic loads, with different verdicts on the future. In terms of the orthodox science of AIDS, the HI virus was largely sexually transmitted, and in the case of Africa this sexual transmission was also mainly heterosexual. Sex – the seed of new life, new energies, new possibilities – was now the vector of death. So the 'millions' who had died in Africa, *de facto* evidence of the rampancy of sex in Africa, thus became symbols of Africa's death wish – its suicidal inability to escape the destructive demons within. From the standpoint of Mbeki's discourse, then, the symbolic power of the scientific orthodoxy on AIDS extended beyond a reiteration of colonial stereotypes of unbounded black lust; it is also exposed Africa's internal menace – 'the things in the African bush'. The transmission of Africa's fatal and suicidal despair through sex – with a rampancy quantified by the scale of the epidemic – signified the failure of what Mbeki called 'moral regeneration', the birth of a 'new type of person' whose lifestyle and values would instantiate the hopeful aspirations of the African Renaissance.

The dissident position, by contrast, shifted the symbolic politics of AIDS out of this discursive space of sex and death. Mbeki's version of AIDS in Africa did not dispute that it was largely a heterosexual epidemic; indeed he highlighted this as the primary marker of its difference from Western forms of the epidemic. Yet, by positing

AIDS as a cluster of illnesses caused chiefly by poverty, Mbeki's discourse displaced sex from the foreground of discussion (see also Crewe 2000). The problem became centrally a matter of Africa's 'level of development', rather than a racial, cultural or moral one; and the scale of the epidemic became an indictment of Africa's economic decline rather than any judgement on African 'values', 'ways of life' or personhood that might reiterate racist stereotypes of the black African. While AIDS still threatened to wreak havoc in the lives of Africa's people, it could be rendered as a problem external to the 'African self' – a function of the economic and political environment, not a product of African identities and the sexualities associated with them.

Conclusion

I have argued that it is impossible to make sense of the substance and intensity of the AIDS controversy in South Africa without situating it in the symbolic politics of South Africa's transition from apartheid, and the unsettling entanglement of new life and new death within it. The temptation of denialism was arguably its powers to represent AIDS as a function of poverty and neocolonialism, thus displacing the centrality of sex. Not only did this extradite the racist readings of black sexuality that lurk in its Western representations; it also reinstated the prospects of Africa's transcendence by resisting the metaphorical contamination of sex and the symbolic death wish associated with it. The burden of the epidemic could be redefined and repositioned, on the more palatable and manageable African landscape of poverty, as a deficit of 'development'.

Endnotes

1 It's not possible here to review all the controversies surrounding the statistical data on AIDS, including mortality data. The latter have been especially contested, with Mbeki challenging a report released by the MRC in 2001 that claimed that around 40% of deaths of people aged 15–49 were attributable to AIDS.
2 For example, after the release of a report from Mbeki's Presidential AIDS Advisory Panel – comprising a mix of dissident and orthodox members – on 4 April 2001, Tshabalala-Msimang's response was that 'the debates of the panel have not provided grounds for Government to depart from its current approach to the HIV/AIDS problem, which is rooted in the premise that HIV causes AIDS'. See http://www.reclaimthebrain.com/20010404.html
3 According to a UNAIDS Global Aids Epidemic Update Report, whereas South Africa had an HIV infection rate of 1% in 1990, 'a failure to respond timeously allowed it to soar to 30%' by 2005 ... The report states that the most outstanding feature of South Africa's epidemic was the speed at which it evolved' (*The Star*, 22 November 2005, 'Inaction Let HIV Wildfire Rage out of Control').

References

Crewe, M. 2000. 'South Africa: Touched by the Vengeance of AIDS: Responses to the South African Epidemic', *South African Journal of International Affairs*, vol. 7, no. 1, pp. 23–8.

Marks, S. 2002. 'An Epidemic Waiting to Happen', *African Studies*, vol. 61, no. 1, pp. 13–26.

Mbali, M. 2002. 'Mbeki's Denialism and the Ghosts of Apartheid and Colonialism for Post-Apartheid AIDS policy-making', Seminar paper presented to University of KwaZulu-Natal Public Health Journal Club, 3 May 2002.

Mbeki, T. 1996. 'I am an African', 8 May 1996, www.ingwenya.com/I_am_an_African_Thabo_Mbeki_Speech.htm

Mbeki, T. 1997. Address to Corporate Council on Africa's 'Attracting Capital to Africa' Summit, 19–22 April 1997, Virginia, USA, www.dfa.gov.za/docs/speeches/1997/mbek0419.htm

Mbeki, T. 1998a. Statement at the Africa Telecom '98 Forum, Johannesburg, 4 May 1998, www.doc.org.za/docs/speeches.

Mbeki, T. 1998b. 'African Renaissance, South Africa and the World', Speech at the United Nations University, 9 April 1998, www.unu.edu/unpress/mbeki.html.

Mbeki, T. 1999a. Speech at the launch of the African Renaissance Institute, 11 October 1999.

Mbeki, T. 1999b. Statement at the Memorial Service for the late Julius Nyerere, Pretoria, 18 October 1999.

Mbeki, T. 1999c. Address at the Opening of Parliament, Cape Town, 25 June 1999.

Mbeki, T. 2000a Letter to Clinton, Blair, Schroeder, Kofi Annan and other leaders, 3 April 2000, http://free-news.org/tmbeuk01.htm.

Mbeki, T. 2000b. Speech at the Opening Session of the 13th International AIDS Conference, Durban, 9 July 2000, www.virusmyth.net/aids/news/durbspmbeki.htm.

Nattrass, N. 2004. *The Moral Economy of AIDS in South Africa*. (Cambridge: Cambridge University Press).

Posel, D. 2004. 'Lectures de la controverse sur le sida', in Fassin, D (ed.), *Afflictions: L'Afrique du Sud, de l'apartheid au sida* (Paris: Karthala), pp. 47–74.

Posel, D. 2005. 'Sex, Death and the Fate of the Nation: Reflections on the Politicisation of Sexuality in Post-Apartheid South Africa', *Africa*, vol. 75, no. 2, pp. 125–53.

Sontag, Susan. 1990. *Illness as Metaphor: AIDS and Its Metaphors* (New York: Picador).

Treichler, Paula. 1999. *How to Have Theory in an Epidemic* (Durham, NC: Duke University Press).

Van der Vliet, V. 2000. 'AIDS: Losing the "New Struggle"', *Daedalus*, vol. 130, no. 1, pp. 151–84.

CRIME

Jonny Steinberg

IN HIS NOVEL/MEMOIR *Youth*, published in 2002, JM Coetzee writes of an encounter that took place in Cape Town in the late 1950s. One of the protagonists is Coetzee himself, aged 18 or 19. He is walking through the predawn darkness, somewhere in the Southern Suburbs, with his friend Paul. They come across a lone milkman and his horse and buy a pint of milk from him. As the young Coetzee observes the milkman, he is struck by a great fear:

> Deeper than pity, deeper than honourable dealings, deeper even than goodwill, lies an awareness on both sides that people like Paul and himself, with their pianos and their violins, are here on this earth, the earth of South Africa, on the shakiest of pretexts. This very milkman, who a year ago must have been just a boy herding cattle in the deepest Transkei, must know it. In fact, from Africans in general, and even from Coloured people, he feels a curious, amused tenderness emanating: a sense that he must be a simpleton, in need of protection, if he imagines he can get by on the basis of straight looks and honourable dealings when the ground beneath his feet is soaked with blood and the vast backward depth of history rings with shouts of anger (Coetzee 2002a: 17).

Coetzee places these thoughts in the late 1950s, but I am not sure that they belong there. Coetzee himself, as anybody who has read the body of his work will know, is one of those souls burdened with 'a hard-to-articulate sense that they do not belong in the world, that perhaps human beings in general do not belong here' (Coetzee 2002b: 7). And so it is quite possible that an uneventful encounter with a black milkman would have triggered primordial fear in the 18-year-old Coetzee. But I suspect that most white teenaged South Africans of the late 1950s felt themselves sturdily moored to the world, both their place and that of the milkman pretty much written into the nature of things.

As an emblem of white South African consciousness, Coetzee's words are far more apt for the times in which they were written – the immediate post-apartheid period. It would be wrong to talk of white South Africa as a solid bloc of consciousness. But it is probably safe to say that in the mid- and late 1990s, much of white South Africa felt confused and disoriented. On the one hand, there was the beaming, sentimental Mandela and his project of national reconciliation. In exchange for three centuries of humiliation, South Africa's first majority government was to give whites unconditional forgiveness and a place in the sun. No expropriation, no nationalisation, not even a tax increase. We were all to get off scot-free.

Yet something else was happening too, something quite profound, and it concerned the flow of people and things across South Africa's cities and towns. Apartheid had been a remarkably successful project of social isolation. Until the mid-1980s, the movement of black people into white spaces was controlled with admirable bureaucratic efficiency. Yet these bureaucratic controls had long crumbled by the time the ANC came to power in 1994. For the township underworld, whose long pedigree had been invisible to white South Africa, the opening up of urban space heralded something of a revolution. The vastness of the new market was akin to that opened to global capitalism after the fall of the Soviet empire. A criminal culture whose appetite for commodities and for violence was legendary in the townships arrived in the suburbs.

And so, around white dinner tables and at the corner café, a very different story about South Africa's transition began to circulate, and, while the finer details varied, the heart of the tale did not: it was about somebody who had been held up at gunpoint, another who had been shot, another who had been kidnapped in her own car. The anecdotes of guns and blood spread like an airborne disease, becoming something of a contagion. By the end of the millennium, much of white South Africa had died a thousand deaths in their own homes, around their own dinner tables. 'I wonder if there is a more abject community on earth,' Ken Owen remarked of white South Africa in a *Business Day* column a few years ago. 'Their political discourse is dominated by the terrible things they fear may happen to them' (Owen 2002).

It was not long before Mandela's smiling face courted hostility, for it was increasingly understood as a ruse or, at very least, as a hollow gesture. Many whites believed that Mandela's discourse of reconciliation was rendered irrelevant by a far deeper, congenital hostility to the presence of whites at the tip of the continent, and that this hostility found expression in violent crime. In the mid-1990s, the idea that whites were 'here on this South African earth on the shakiest of pretexts' mingled with the idea of crime, such that the two became indistinguishable. It was as if those formidable forces erupting from 'the vast backward depth of history' had simply skirted Mandela's benign new state, settled into the alleyways and crannies of our vast society, and begun to pick off their victims one by one.

And if crime was indeed a toxic expression of vengeance, it was all the more insidious for its shapelessness and its ubiquity. It was not a movement that could be cornered and defeated. It was, rather, a deep seam of unfathomable emotion, with the awesome power to touch every place and everyone at the same time.

* * *

If this was white South Africa's diagnosis of crime, it was spectacularly wrong. It is by no means inconceivable that a populist South African movement will turn its wrath on whites one day, but crime in the late 1990s and early 2000s is not it. A casual comparison of some police station statistics puts things in perspective. Lusikisiki is a district deep in rural Transkei. It consists of two-dozen hillside villages, replete with cows, mud huts and mealie patches, and a town centre with a single main road. On a busy shopping day, the only white face you are likely to see is that of the Médecins Sans Frontières (Doctors without Borders) doctor who treats cases of HIV. In 2003, 109 murders were reported in the Lusikisiki police station precinct, 76 in 2004. Compare this with Parkview police station in the upper-middle-class suburbs of northern Johannesburg, home to perhaps the densest concentration of four-wheel drives and eighteen-carat wedding rings in the country: 2 murders in 2002, 1 in 2003 (SAPS 2005a). None of these 3 victims was white (author's interview 2005).

Indeed, given how large race looms in South African history, it is surprising how little crime has directly to do with racial relations. Whites find themselves vastly under-represented among the victims of violent crime. While 1 in 9 South Africans is white, 32 out of 33 murder victims are not (SAPS 2004: 18).

Why has white South Africa misread crime so sharply? It was also JM Coetzee who, talking of white South Africa, pointed out that 'an inability to imagine a future' is often coupled with paranoia, and that both derive in part from a withdrawal of desire from the world (Coetzee 1996: 198). White South Africa's experience of crime cannot be dissociated from the fact that it no longer finds its identity written into the state and that the official narrative of South Africa's future is no longer its own. The place of crime in its political imagination is in part a symptom of depression, in part of uncertainty.

Yet it would be a grave mistake and, indeed, a betrayal of serious thinking to ridicule or write off white South Africa's understanding of its experience of violence. It is important to separate the various strands that constitute the fear of crime, and to deal with each of them in turn. Levels of middle-class victimisation, both black and white, are high enough for just about the entire middle class to have experienced violent crime at close quarters. It is no exaggeration to say that almost every South African, whether poor or rich, has either had a gun shoved in her face, or has witnessed the trauma of a loved one who has had a gun shoved in her face. These encounters with violence circulate by word of mouth until they become a part of lived experience.

Like every middle class around the world, South Africa's is hardwired into the expectation, indeed the presumption, that one lives one's three score years and ten in comfort and then, with the help of top-rate surgery and decent aftercare, another decade or two longer. The experience of being at the business end of a pistol, multiplied a dozen times over from dinner table to dinner table, is in itself wrenchingly violent. For a milieu in which the idea of mortality has always been hitched exclusively to the elderly and the frail, the constant threat of lethal violence is akin to an earthquake. The profundity of the fear of crime is deep enough to go all the way down, to the existential itself, to the cornerstones of one's relation to the world.

For whites, this new confrontation with mortality is a uniquely post-apartheid experience. Until the very final days of apartheid, it was almost unheard of for a white suburbanite to be held up at gunpoint outside his home. Coetzee speaks of the feeling of 'being on this earth ... on the shakiest of pretexts.' That phrase probably captures the deepest and most resonant moment in the white phenomenology of crime. 'Crime' has nestled inside the most exquisitely intimate and private domains of white experience. It has taken its place among the categories through which people experience the fundamentals of their existence.

* * *

For a country that talks a great deal about violent crime, there is a surprising dearth of information about who is victimised, where and why. The best studies available are for homicide, and even these are by no means unproblematic. The first is an analysis, conducted by the SAPS Crime Information Analysis Centre, of all murder dockets that were closed in 2001. The second is an annual Medical Research Council study of mortuary data collected primarily from South Africa's metropolitan centres.

At first glance, these studies tell an unsurprising story. Around the world, the distribution of violent crime across a society is radically uneven: violence clusters in particular spaces, demographic groups, days of the week and times of the day. South Africa is no different. For instance, the SAPS docket analysis found that of South Africa's 1110-odd police station areas, 33 account for 25% of all murders, and yet contain only 12% of the population (SAPS 2004: 12). Without exception, these stations are situated in inner-city or township settlements in the greater Johannesburg, Cape Town and Durban metropolises. According to the Medical Research Council study, the average victim of a South African murder is a young man: 1 woman is murdered for every 6.5 men murdered; the average age of a South African murder victim is 31 (Matzopoulos 2004: 9).

Murders take place overwhelmingly at weekends, between people who know one another, and in the course of arguments or altercations. According to the SAPS docket analysis, 70% of murders take place on a Friday, Saturday or Sunday, the majority of these at night. In 69% of cases, the murderer and victim know one another by name or by sight. And in 68% of cases, the motive for the murder recorded on the docket is 'misunderstanding or argument'. Finally, to complete the picture, 50% of those murdered are unemployed, while 70% have not finished secondary school (SAPS 2004: 8, 15, 19, 20, 21).

* * *

It is a cliché, but no less true for it, that the abstraction of statistics dulls the colours of the world. Spend a week in the back of a patrol van in a large Johannesburg township – as I did in late 2003 – and you witness something of what these statistics mean for those whose work is shaped by them (see Steinberg 2004; the townships I visited were Toekomsrus and Kagiso, both on Johannesburg's West Rand). Mondays to Thursdays are painstakingly dull. The patrol van marks out its beat, the radio is silent, and the hours dissolve into one another. There is the occasional call: a headmaster complains that a pavement stall is too close to his school; a car's registration details don't match its engine number, and the driver is arrested on suspicion of theft; a group of school boys has vandalised a public phone.

On Friday lunchtime, the sameness is abruptly broken. The police station begins to fill with people, equipment, vehicles and, above all, with adrenaline. The station's holding cells are cleared in preparation for the deluge that will come. A map is placed on the wall marking the jurisdiction's shebeens and taverns. Patrols are planned accordingly.

By 8 pm, the station has mobilised every person and vehicle available, and they fan out into the township. Each patrol's instructions are very simple. When not responding to a call, patrol the streets around a shebeen, fill the back of the van with as many drunk people as it will hold, unload them at the station, charge them with public drunkenness, go back to the streets, and fill the van again. The rationale is brutally simple: the police station's statistics reveal that 85% of violent crime takes place at weekends, that 80% of serious assault and armed robbery cases take place within 500 metres of a shebeen, and that most perpetrators and victims are drunk. It follows that those who spend the night in the holding cells will not be beaten, stabbed or shot out on the streets, and the station's weekend crime stats will look a little more respectable.

In reality, there is little time for the business of loading and unloading the vans with drunks, because there are too many calls over the radio. Three sorts of calls dominate a Friday and Saturday night – domestic violence, assault and robbery on the streets, and disturbance of the peace. By midnight they have reached fever pitch – the patrol van literally responds to one call after another – and by four in the morning they have vanished: the radio is silent, the streets deserted.

The most striking feature of this weeklong cycle is its regiment-like discipline: violent crime is as sure and steady as clockwork. A small section of the world – a large minority of men, most of them under 40 – spend the weekdays idling through the channels of an unwritten truce. The toxins and treachery and bad blood accumulate quietly, to be vomited out in a sudden and violent convulsion on a Friday night.

* * *

None of this is unique to South Africa. The preponderance of young men among the perpetrators and victims of violent crimes, the concentration of crime at weekends and among those who know one another – these attributes are pretty much universal. What makes South Africa unusual is sheer scale. In 1994/5, the per capita murder rate in South Africa was 67 per 100,000 people. It has dropped substantially since then, to 43 per 100,000 in 2003/4 (SAPS 2005b: 19), but that is still breathtakingly high. To put these figures in perspective, the murder rate in the United States in 1991, a notoriously violent moment in the history of a notoriously violent society, was 9.8 per 100,000 (Blumstein 2000: 69).

Why the course of South African history has produced such violence is a deeply sensitive question, one that is wont to trigger anger of the most fraught and opaque sort. Indeed, talk of violence among young black men in South Africa is fast becoming something of a taboo. In an October 2004 edition of his weekly letter, published each Friday on the ANC's website, South African President Thabo Mbeki unleashed his venom on an unnamed 'internationally recognised expert on sexual violence'. The 'expert' in question had been cited in a local newspaper as saying that South Africa's high prevalence of HIV infection and its high incidence of rape were both 'spurred by men's attitudes to women' and that the AIDS epidemic would not end 'until we understand the role of tradition and religion'.

The rage contained in Mbeki's response is surprising: 'In simple language,' he writes, 'she was saying that African traditions, indigenous religions and culture prescribe and institutionalise rape ...' Her view 'defines the African people as barbaric savages' (Mbeki 2004).

Indeed, several years earlier, Mbeki himself had invoked the idea of crime as a chilling spectacle of African degeneration. Addressing parliament in June 1999, Mbeki spoke of 'those in our cities and towns who have lost all hope and all self-worth, who have slid into a twilight world of drug and alcohol abuse, the continuous sexual and physical abuse of women and children, of purposeless wars fought with fists and boots, metal rods, knives and guns, every day resulting in death and grievous bodily harm' (cited in Posel 2003: 23).

From where does this extraordinary and painful sensitivity to the question of black men and violence arise? It has an opaque, albeit suggestive, pre-history. It is there, if inchoately, in the South African liberation movement's standard histories of South Africa, developed in exile between the mid-1960s and the late 1980s. These histories are strangely bifurcated, one is tempted to say schizophrenic. There is a social history on the one hand, and a political history on the other, and they appear to tell the tales of two very different countries.

The standard social histories tell the brutal tale of South Africa's industrialisation: a rural peasantry wrenched from its land and into the frontier towns of early industrial South Africa; a first-generation proletariat living in the gated compounds of the mining industry; an urban working class criminalised by a succession of pass laws; the forced removals of the high apartheid era, creating abandoned communities on the far-flung sand dunes of the Cape Flats and in the hinterland of the interior; the anarchy of mass urbanisation in the last quarter of the century, giving rise to vast shantytowns of the uprooted. In short, modern South African social history is an account of seismic dislocation. Human beings are shunted around the landscape of modern South Africa and forced to live their lives in the most precarious and depraved of settings.

Compare this with the liberation movement's political history of South Africa. A genteel, mission-educated African middle class raises a polite voice of protest in the early years of the twentieth century, culminating in the formation of the ANC in 1912. As the century wears on and the gentlemanly voices of protest continue to fall on deaf ears, so the African intelligentsia hardens. Rationally, and in sober knowledge of the gravity of its decision, it turns to violence. As it does so, it reaches out to the popular classes – the industrial working class, the urban youth, the peasantry – and by the last quarter of the century, most of black South Africa is galvanised behind the liberation movement's moral authority (see, especially, ANC 1980 and ANC 1985).

This simple and noble narrative is striking in the way it cleanses liberation politics of the pathologies of South Africa's social development. The morbidity and violence of social life find no expression here. It is as if the South African masses rose above their wretched circumstances and shored up an essential dignity which transcended time and place.

The reality is obviously far less benign than that. As uncomfortable and dispiriting as this may be, it is hard not to conclude that the systemic violence attendant on the modernisation of South Africa created black communities of weak and tenuous fabric. Anyone attempting a comprehensive theory of South African violence would probably have to begin with the social conventions through which boys become men. One does not have to dig very deep to discover that these conventions have been undermined and broken down, one generation after the next, over the course of the twentieth century.

Indeed, black communities of modern South Africa have been marked by a frailty of social solidarity since the earliest times. It is to be witnessed in the still extant oral histories of the Ninevites and Scottish gangs that terrorised the first generation of black proletarians on the Witwatersrand (Van Onselen 1984); in the excessively violent and remarkably enduring institutions of organised delinquency that marked twentieth-century urban South Africa (Glaser 2000); and even in the 1980s uprisings against apartheid, which, at times, both masked and acted out seismic episodes of generational conflict (Delius 1996).

* * *

It is odd to think of black revolutionaries and white reactionaries colluding in an alliance of forgetfulness, but that is more or less right. During the apartheid era, the respective mainstreams of white and black thought both contrived to blind themselves to the depth and scale of the history of violent crime in South Africa. White thought was blind because the violent symptoms of South Africa's cruel modernisation were literally sealed off in urban and rural ghettos. Black thought was blind because the idea of shallow, frail and mutually suspicious communities did not tally with the idea of the masses as a pure body of political resistance.

The result is that both the old white elite and the new black one were taken aback by the levels of violent crime that have characterised post-apartheid South Africa. That is why, in addition to being so odious, violent crime was also experienced as mysterious, as if it had no history, as if it were a foreign body that alighted on our society in order to corrupt it. It had in fact always been there; the truth is that everyone had chosen to look the other way.

This perhaps explains why both the black and white elites of post-apartheid South Africa have responded to crime with a degree of vengefulness and rage that must be unprecedented in South African history. When the ANC came to power in April 1994, the South African prison population stood at 114,000. A decade later it had climbed to 180,000. It is unlikely that anyone in the early 1990s would have predicted that South Africa's first democratic government would appropriate apartheid's prisons and use them with such zeal. Nor would anyone have guessed why the prisons are bursting at the seams. It is not that more people are being caught or convicted. On the contrary, conviction rates declined during the first six years of democracy. It is, rather, that the democratic parliament has legislated that those who are convicted are sentenced to longer and longer terms of imprisonment (Van Zyl Smit 2004). In other words, the force that is filling the prisons is sheer emotion: fear, anger, but, above all, revenge.

Revenge for what? The simple answer is for disenchantment. The ANC's activists were schooled in a revolutionary tradition; they expected, on coming to office, to unleash a freewheeling programme of vast social change. Instead, they have found that much of the social unhappiness of the past is deeply stubborn, and is to remain in perpetuity. The ANC inherited a country in the grip of an AIDS epidemic, a spectacle that soon overwhelmed it and provoked a curious campaign of denial. The gap between rich and poor has grown since the end of apartheid, a scorching defeat for a former liberation movement whose *raison d'être* remains its capacity to represent all black interests.

Among these ills, the persistence of high levels of violent crime comes as a slap in the face. I have argued here that the bonds that bind black South Africans have always been frail, that throughout the last century people have been as eager to hurt one another as they have been reluctant to trust one another. Apartheid partly masked and partly explained the fragility of social bonds. With apartheid gone, and our propensity for violence not much lower than it has always been, the sores have been stripped naked and exposed. They feel as if they are new. The country at large, but its political elite in particular, experiences the steady persistence of social violence as a painful insult, an intolerable interruption to the sublime story of national redemption it has been telling itself and the world.

'Crime' is thus something of a repository for disappointment and for anger. The 180,000-odd prisoners settling down for the night in South Africa's jails, which have become among the most crowded in the world, are being punished for a good deal more than their own crimes. The debt they are being forced to pay is for a new democracy's inchoate, barely articulated sense of disenchantment.

References

ANC. 1980. 'Strategies and Tactics' [1969] in Turok, Ben (ed.), *Revolutionary Thought in the Twentieth Century* (London: Zed Books).

ANC. 1985. *Minutes of Working Groups at the Consultative National Conference, Kabwe, 1985* (Lusaka: African National Congress).

Author's interview. 2005. Interview with Detective Service Commander, Parkview police station, 3 December 2005.

Blumstein, A. 2000. 'Disaggregating the Violence Trends' in Blumstein, A and Wallman, J (eds.), *The Crime Drop in America* (New York: Cambridge University Press).

Coetzee, JM. 1996. *Giving Offense: Essays on Censorship* (Chicago: Chicago University Press).

Coetzee, JM. 2002a. *Youth* (London: Random House).

Coetzee, JM. 2002b. 'Heir of a Dark History', *New York Review of Books*, 24 October 2002, pp. 7–11.

Delius, P. 1996. *A Lion Amongst the Cattle* (Johannesburg: Ravan).

Glaser, C. 2000. *Bo-Tsotsi: The Youth Gangs of Soweto, 1935–1976* (Oxford: James Currey).

Matzopoulos, P (ed.). 2004. *A Profile of Fatal Injuries in South Africa: 5th Annual Report, 2003* (Johannesburg: Medical Research Council).

Mbeki, T. 2004. 'When is Good News Bad News?', *ANC Today,* vol. 4, no. 39, 1–7 October, at www.anc.org.za.

Owen, K. 2002. 'Implacable Contest over Land', *Business Day,* 21 October 2002.

Posel, D. 2003. '"Getting the Nation Talking About Sex": Reflections on the Politics of Sexuality and "Nation-Building" in Post-Apartheid South Africa', Paper presented to the Sex and Secrecy Conference, Wits Institute for Social and Economic Research (Wiser), Johannesburg.

SAPS. 2004. *Murder Analysis RSA* (Pretoria: SAPS Crime Information and Analysis Centre).

SAPS. 2005a. 'Annual Crimes Statistics' at www.saps.gov.za.

SAPS. 2005b. *SAPS Annual Report: 2003/2004* (Pretoria: SAPS).

Steinberg, J. 2004. *Sector Policing on the West Rand: Three Case Studies* (Pretoria: Institute for Security Studies).

Van Onselen, C. 1984. *The Small Matter of a Horse* (Johannesburg: Ravan).

Van Zyl Smit, D. 2004. 'Swimming Against the Tide: Controlling the Size of the Prison Population in the New South Africa' in Dixon, B and Van der Spuy, E (eds.), *Justice Gained? Crime and Crime Control in South Africa's Transition* (Cape Town: UCT Press), pp. 227–58.

CULTURE

Harry Garuba and Sam Raditlhalo

In the name of culture

THE RECENT RESURGENCE OF CULTURE – both as an authorising platform for the performance and practice of everyday life and as an explanatory category in academic discourses – has been one of the truly remarkable developments of the contemporary moment. Culture has become a ubiquitous category invoked in both everyday speech and intellectual analyses. When a young woman or man donning a particular dress or sporting a specific hairstyle tells you that they are doing this because it is part of their culture and they are proud of it, then we know that we are witnessing the use of culture as authority for a lifestyle choice. When social relations between groups and patterns of behaviour previously explained in the language of economics, employing the grammar of class, are suddenly accounted for by recourse to culture and difference, then we know that culture is being invoked as a medium of intellectual analysis. Culture is suddenly present everywhere – from the smallest event of everyday life to the most rarefied levels of academic analysis.

With the collapse of the Soviet Union and the rise of neoliberalism, it would appear that the conventional paradigms which provided the frameworks of intellectual analysis of society and history have given way and, in their place, there is a new emphasis on the importance of culture. When, for example, someone tries to draw upon culture as an explanation for the difference in the level of economic development between South Korea and Ghana today, countries which were at roughly similar levels when Ghana became politically independent in the 1950s, then we know that culture is being used in new ways (Huntington 2000).

It is fair to say that there has been a discernible shift from the grand economic or materialist explanations to a greater recognition of the importance of the cultural dimension. In the name of culture, there have opened up new domains of social life and activism, political struggle and economic competition over resources, as well as new avenues of academic inquiry. In the academic disciplines, culture as an object of intellectual analysis used to be the special preserve of anthropologists who studied 'primitive' societies. But in the last two decades or so, virtually every other discipline in the humanities and social sciences has laid its own claims to this previously exclusive turf. The multidisciplinary field of cultural studies that developed from this extended the study of culture to modern, urban societies and to the popular culture previously ignored by the academic apostles of 'high culture'. But beyond the themes and issues foregrounded in the field of cultural studies, questions of culture have in general become pertinent to many more disciplines than we would traditionally associate with it.

It is, of course, simplistic to see the rise of culture only as a consequence of the rise of neoliberalism and to attribute it mainly to the recession or collapse of old paradigms. There are certainly many more factors responsible for it than this. Among these, we can immediately identify three that are highly significant for the purposes of this chapter. First, there is the recognised failure of the Enlightenment project of modernity. This project, we may recall, was premised on the idea of a harmonious community of affiliation based on a homogeneous citizenry with equal rights, in political and juridical terms, living within a polity defined by social equality.

But, as the historical experience of African-Americans and women, to take just two examples, showed, this was never in reality an objective ever realised, nor, for that matter, was it actively pursued. This historical failure of the dream of homogeneity, horizontal affiliation and juridical citizenship with respect to blacks and women demonstrates that claims in the name of sameness and a common humanity did not amount to much in practice when applied to minorities and other marginalised groups, whether they were marginalised on the basis of race, religion, cultural practices, gender or sexual orientation.

To these groups, it became increasingly evident that claims for access and rights stood a better chance of recognition if they were framed in the language of culture and difference. 'Disillusionment with the legislative and judicial practices of liberal democracies and their models of neutral justice and formal equality' led to 'attempt[s] to change societal discrimination [becoming] focused on "culture" at the level of discourse and representation' (Cowan et al. 2001: 2).

A second factor was the history of colonialism in which racial and cultural differences were deployed as bases for social and political discrimination and oppression. The rhetoric of the 'civilising mission' which colonialism adopted was premised on this idea of difference as a categorical distinction that made discrimination valid. This difference, often constructed in racial or cultural terms, focused on a morphology of physical features or a detailed inventory of cultural practices. Taken singly or in combination, these defined some groups as somewhat lower down on the scale of human evolution and were thus somewhat less than fully human.

The third factor followed from this construction of difference on the ground of cultural evolution. Oppressed on the basis of culture, subjected people, in turn, converted culture into a domain of political resistance. In this way, culture became a site of contestation and struggle against oppression, domination, and marginalisation. In short, culture came to be used as a shorthand for many of the claims – political, social and economic – that the oppressed would make for equality and access to resources. And with the advent of globalisation, this has led, inevitably, to calls for the recognition and revaluation of culture – constructed as the ultimate site of difference – within contemporary imaginings of liberal democracy and multiculturalism. Through this tangled history, the Enlightenment ideas of homogeneity and equality were turned on their head as the demand for equality now came to be made on the basis of difference.

It can hardly be disputed, therefore, that culture has taken centre-stage in the analysis of the construction of identities and modes of self-identification, in many ways overshadowing the significance once accorded to class consciousness. From being seen as marginal to the constitution of modern subjects and identities – the passive object within the rationalisation of all spheres of modern life – culture has become central to thinking about forms of subjectivity and sociality, social life and agency, knowledge and knowledge systems, and the very nature of our being-in-the-world.

Where does one then begin to untangle culture's implications – through this circuitous history – in all these discourses? We are tempted to follow the beaten track and ask, as many others have done: What is this thing called 'culture' in which so much is invested in so many domains of life and thought? But we will resist this temptation and ask instead: How has the concept of culture been produced, together with the many usages and meanings that now attach to it? A good way of approaching this question is to begin broadly with a look at the ways in which culture has been described and defined in general, and then explore the ways in which cultural theorists and social scientists have approached the question of culture in colonised and postcolonial societies. Thereafter, we proceed to examine the ways in which culture has been appropriated and transformed within the new discourses of globalisation. Proceeding in this manner, we believe, will lead us to a better understanding of what culture means and why it has become so important in contemporary social and political life.

Defining culture: patterning the weeds

Raymond Williams noted that culture is one of the two or three most complicated words in the English language and has come to acquire a number of different meanings and usages. These have been usefully summarised by Robert Bocock (1992: 234) as follows:

1. Culture = cultivating the land, crops, animals.
2. Culture = the cultivation of the mind; the arts; civilisation.
3. Culture = a general process of social development; culture as a universal process (the Enlightenment conception of culture).
4. Culture = the meanings, values, ways of life (cultures) shared by particular nations, groups, classes, periods (following Herder).
5. Culture = the practices which produce meaning; signifying practices.

We would like to flesh out this summary as briefly as possible to put it into contemporary perspective. It is important to do this so that we can identify which of these available meanings those who use the term 'culture' are drawing on in their usage. We should note also that it is possible to draw upon these either singly or in various combinations simultaneously.

The first meaning obviously derives from the etymological roots in the Latin word from which 'culture' derives. First used in the fifteenth century to refer to the tending of crops and animals, it can still be seen in such modern words as 'agriculture' and 'horticulture' or when scientists speak of a 'germ culture'. The idea of tending and cultivating present in the root word is nowhere close to disappearing in modern times; rather it seems to have acquired more specialised meanings.

Indeed, it would appear that the second meaning of culture as civilisation is simply an extension of the first from the physical into the domain of the abstract, the cultivation of minds. If minds, like crops, can be cultivated, what were seen as the marks of this cultivation? From the sixteenth century, when this usage first appeared, till the present, this idea of culture as the cultivation of minds has been closely associated with the arts and philosophy. When we describe a well-bred gentleman who understands and enjoys literature, classical music, painting and sculpture as a 'cultured' man, we are drawing upon a meaning of culture that is very different from what we mean, for instance, when we speak of the 'culture' of the San. Here we begin to discern a hierarchy of significance, culture as a way of evaluating people on the basis of the possession of certain qualities. Ideas of 'high culture', 'folk culture' and, in our day, 'popular culture' all flow from this usage as a mark of distinction between the 'cultivated' or 'civilised' and the 'uncivilised'.

The third idea of culture as a general process of human and social development, conceived of as a unilinear historical process in which some nations or people were further up the scale than others, is one that is usually associated with the European Enlightenment. Not surprisingly, highest up on the ladder of culture and civilisation was Europe and all other people were placed lower down, depending on prevailing conceptions of the ways in which cultural and civilisational value were to be determined. In general, the closer a culture or group was to European criteria of civilisation, the higher up it could be found on the scale. This process of ranking was one of the justifications for the colonisation of other peoples and places, and much of the rhetoric of the 'civilising mission' was predicated on this conception of culture.

The German philosopher JG Herder was one of the first to question this idea of culture and civilisation, arguing that every group of people or nation has its own distinctive way of life, its shared system of beliefs and values, and thus its own 'culture'. Instead of speaking of 'culture' in the singular, he argued it was best to recognise the presence of 'cultures' in the plural. Debunking the universalised history of the world that placed European civilisation at the apex, he claimed that the idea of a universal history uniformly applicable to all corners of the globe was an insult to the 'majesty of Nature'. Raymond Williams argues that Herder's ideas were decisive in promoting an alternative idea of culture from the Enlightenment-sanctioned one then prevailing. This fourth definition was to become central to the discipline of anthropology and is often now referred to as the (old) anthropological definition of culture. So influential has this idea become that many claims made by minorities and indigenous communities are predicated on this idea of culture. The entire discourse of multiculturalism draws on this notion of culture as the unique, distinctive way of life of a particular group that marks it apart from other groups.

The fifth definition, which has become increasingly important in academic circles, owes something to the fourth but is more solidly anchored in newer conceptions of meaning-making processes within society.

> It differs in emphasis from the fourth definition, however, by concentrating more on the symbolic dimension, and on what culture *does* rather than what culture *is*. It sees culture as a social practice rather than a thing (the arts) or a state of being (civilisation). This way of thinking about culture is grounded in the study of *language*, a practice which is seen as fundamental to the production of meaning … According to this definition, then, 'culture' is the *set of practices by which meanings are produced and exchanged within a group* (Williams 1976: 233).

We should note the emphasis placed on the process of production and exchange in this definition, in contrast with conceptions of culture which basically see it as something inherited, passed down over time from one generation to the other. While the fourth definition presents a monolithic, ahistorical notion of culture that often denies or erases present agency, the fifth does not: in fact, the fifth allows us to recognise the process of contestation that is at the heart of signifying practices and processes rather than simply seeing culture as a homogeneous set of beliefs and practices consensually shared by members of a group.

These ways of looking at culture have become fairly standard in the literature on culture. However, there have been specific developments in the definition of culture that can be traced to the history of colonialism. The ways in which culture has been conceived and theorised in colonial and postcolonial contexts are somewhat different from the 'canonical' narrative that we have presented above. Let us now examine the uses (and abuses?) of culture in these contexts.

Culture in colonial and postcolonial contexts

Earlier in this chapter, we noted that one of the reasons that culture has become such a powerful category of identity and social and political mobilisation in recent times is the failure of the Enlightenment project of equality and its dream of homogeneity and juridical citizenship. If we recall that – along with the project of a common humanity – the old belief in a cultural 'melting pot' has evaporated even in places where it was at least formally pursued, we may then ask what happened in places where this shared humanity was not affirmed but actively negated. And, more importantly, what happens when 'culture' is recognised in the fourth, 'anthropological', sense of the word but placed alongside 'culture' in the hierarchical, evaluative sense described in the third definition? The result, as we see from the history of colonialism, was institutionalised discrimination and oppression.

The idea of the 'civilising mission' that was generally deployed as the rationale for colonisation rested on the notion that there were peoples whose cultures were fixed at the lower rung of the ladder of human progress and who needed to be 'civilised' and moved up this ladder. The widespread policy of 'indirect rule' which was implemented by the imperial powers advocated the establishment of separate institutions for different groups in accordance with the level of their placement on this ladder. Mahmood Mamdani (1996: 8) describes the nature of the state that emerged from this process as 'bifurcated'.

> The African colonial experience came to be crystallised in the nature of the state forged through that encounter. Organised differently in rural areas from urban ones, that state was Janus-faced, bifurcated. It contained a duality: two forms of power under a single hegemonic authority. Urban power spoke the language of civil society and civil rights, rural power of community and culture. Civil power claimed to protect rights, customary power pledged to enforce tradition. The former was organised on the principle of differentiation to check the concentration of power, the latter around the principle of fusion to ensure unitary authority (18).

Institutionally, therefore, a state-enforced policy of separation was implemented that created an 'outer domain' of civil society and rights from which the colonised were excluded and an 'inner domain' of culture and tradition into which they were inserted (see Chatterjee 1993). Defined officially as subjects of culture, not yet ready for civil society, the colonised began to see 'culture' as the domain over which they could claim sovereignty and thus convert into a site of resistance. As Mamdani (1996: 24) argues, 'Every movement of resistance was shaped by the very structure of power against which it rebelled.' The colonised turned culture into an instrument of political resistance by affirming their exclusive proprietorship of this domain and asserting its fundamental value beyond the denigrations of colonialism. Culture was what you could truly own and where you could truly be yourself beyond the dispossession and alienation of colonialism. Herein lay the origins of the modern deployment of 'culture' as a platform of political resistance.

Historically, in South Africa, while race was used as the overarching rationale for discrimination, culture was employed more specifically in the apartheid years as the rationale for dividing the country into various 'homelands' or Bantustans where Africans could (so it was claimed) enjoy political rights and give expression to their own culture and language. This strategy ensured that culture and language would also be seen by dominated groups as instruments of resistance. For black South Africans, from as early as the Rev. Tiyo Soga through to Steve Biko and the Black Consciousness Movement of the 1970s, an interest in African culture – either in the mild form of cultural preservation or the more radical form of cultural self-definition – was seen as one of the ways of reclaiming and reaffirming an African identity. Between the two moments in time represented by the figures of Soga and Biko, we can place a host of other figures and their literary and cultural output. Cultural resistance has been just as closely part of the history of Afrikaner nationalism as well. Because the growth of Afrikaner nationalism is seen as a response to subjugation by the British, an almost instinctive recourse to culture and language as instruments of resistance and identity persists in much of post-apartheid discourse on the place of the Afrikaner in contemporary South African society.

Since within this framework culture was 'read' in the somewhat essentialist terms of Raymond Williams's fourth definition as the shared beliefs and bonds that mark the identity of a nation, postcolonial nationalist leaders and thinkers have returned again and again to the category of culture as a marker of national identity and as a tool for popular mobilisation. From Leopold Senghor's philosophy of *Négritude*, which prioritised intuition, emotion, music, dance and rhythm as common denominators of a shared African culture and civilisation, to Jomo Kenyatta's *Facing Mount Kenya*, an auto-ethnography of Gikuyu cultural practices and beliefs, nationalist politicians of all shades found it necessary to locate themselves in the domain of culture either in the broad, pan-Africanist sense or in terms of a local ethnicity. Two major nationalist thinkers who advanced the use of culture as an instrument of resistance were Frantz Fanon and Amilcar Cabral. In their writing, they added new dimensions to conceptions of culture and colonisation, which are worth noting.

In the essay 'On National Culture', Fanon critiqued the idea of a pan-African or pan-Negro culture, such as Senghor proposed, seeing it only as a phase in the struggle against colonial domination. For Fanon, the proper arena for the cultural struggle against colonialism was the nation. He argued that it is ultimately in the domain of culture that 'the legitimacy of the claims of the nation' can be affirmed because 'Colonialism is not satisfied merely with holding a people in its grip and emptying the native's brain of all form and content. By a kind of perverted logic, it turns to the past of the oppressed people, and distorts, disfigures and destroys it. This work of devaluing pre-colonial history takes on a dialectical significance today' (2001: 167, 169).

What we want to emphasise in this often-quoted passage is the 'dialectical significance' which arises from the colonialist devaluation that Fanon speaks about. What he is saying here is that by devaluing the past, the colonialist draws the true nationalist's attention to the past as the site from which cultural affirmation should begin. The nationalist should therefore focus on retrieving or recuperating a cultural past and revaluing it and affirming its worth and dignity. As the novelist Chinua Achebe put it, the goal was to teach Africans 'that their past – with all its imperfections – was not one long night of savagery from which the first Europeans acting on God's behalf delivered them' (1989: 45).

But Fanon was also quick to point out that this focus on the past as the site of cultural restoration was at the same time the result of the 'native' intellectual's realisation of the failure of the assimilationist claims of European culture as well as his or her alienation from the culture of his or her own people in the present. Perhaps Fanon's most fundamental contribution to the debate on colonialism and culture was the clear distinction he drew between culture as located in the past (as in Raymond Williams's fourth definition) and culture as a practice of the present (as in the fifth definition). He saw this distinction as the difference between 'custom' and 'culture'. In a stringent critique of the 'native' intellectual's hankering for the glories of the past and ancient African civilisations, he drew out this distinction between past and present, saying that 'the intellectual runs the risk of being out of date'.

> He wishes to attach himself to the people; but instead he only catches hold of their outer garments. And these outer garments are merely the reflection of a hidden life, *teeming and perpetually in motion … Culture has never the translucidity of custom; it abhors all simplification. In its essence it is opposed to custom, for custom is always the deterioration of*

culture. The desire to attach oneself to tradition or bring abandoned traditions to life again does not only mean going against the current of history but also opposing one's own people (2001: 180–1; emphasis added).

For Fanon, 'culture' was a practice of the present rather than a thing of the past. He clarified this further in terms of using culture as an instrument of anti-colonial resistance: 'It is not enough to try to get back to the people in that past out of which they have already emerged; rather we must join them in that fluctuating moment which they are just giving a shape to ... it is to this zone of occult instability where the people dwell that we must come' (2001: 182–3). It is clear, in sum, that culture as site of resistance to colonial domination was central to Fanon's thought though he was also very careful to delineate the kind of 'culture' that he was talking about.

Amilcar Cabral also saw colonialism and nationalist resistance as highly invested in culture. In his essay 'National Liberation and Culture', he claimed that there was no instance in recorded history where a colonial power had succeeded in completely imposing itself culturally on the colonised. He later extended this point by arguing that 'The greater the differences between the culture of the dominated people and the culture of the oppressor, the more possible such a victory [of cultural resistance] is. History proves that it is much less difficult to dominate and continue dominating a people whose culture is similar or analogous to that of the conqueror' (1973: 48). For Cabral, like Fanon before him, cultural resistance was therefore imperative in situations of domination. For both theorists, anti-colonial nationalism was thus as much a political struggle as it was a cultural one, and though most nationalist leaders may have mobilised Williams's fourth definition of culture, Fanon and Cabral saw the need to move to the fifth, that of a practice of the present.

In South Africa, culture has always been regarded as a significant tool of struggle and resistance and, more recently, as a means of constructing new identities. In 1987, for example, an historic conference was held in Amsterdam with the theme 'Culture in Another South Africa' (CASA). It followed two other conferences that had dealt with the question of culture at a time of increasing economic, educational and cultural sanctions against South Africa. The earlier conferences were 'Culture and Resistance' organised by Medu Cultural Ensemble in Gaborone in July 1982, and the 'Voice of Resistance: Dutch and South African Artists Against Apartheid' in Amsterdam in December 1982. While the earlier conferences were explicitly concerned with culture as an instrument of resistance in the sense in which Fanon, Cabral and indeed Steve Biko had envisioned it, the 1987 conference was more concerned with culture as an instrument for forging identities in a new South Africa.

Participants invited to CASA came from within South Africa and from the exile community, in an effort to bring together all the various strains of culture in an oppressive society. A conference of this nature would seem improbable in any normal society, but precisely because of the abnormality of South Africa and the role that culture had played in the struggle to overthrow apartheid, it was important that those who had been involved in that struggle should articulate a vision of the new society. The fields covered at the conference included prose, poetry, fine art, photography, journalism, music, theatre and video. In his keynote address, Pallo Jordan (1992) argued that culture in South Africa was the product of the melding of people from three continents: Africa, Asia and Europe. Thus, to seek to unscramble the 'historical omelette' was unsound because the emergent democratic culture, though distinctly South African, would not be animated by shallow chauvinism. It would acknowledge its debt to other cultural traditions and continue to pride itself not only on its ability to absorb and learn from others but also on its capacity to teach others, infused with an internationalist spirit and a humanist perspective.

In the present, post-1994 age of reconciliation in South Africa, there are concerted efforts to ignore the past, even though the 'historical omelette' spoken of by Pallo Jordan continues to bind South Africa together. It is impossible not to be reminded of the past if the award-winning play *Ghoema* by David Kramer and Taliep Petersen is anything to go by. This musical returns South Africa to its very roots in the Dutch Cape and makes it clear that the colony was built on the backs of slaves from Zanzibar, India, Malaysia and Madagascar. In the rendition of *ghoemaliedjies* lies the very hybridisation of South African culture that nearly four hundred years of oppression and manipulation could not eradicate. And the resilience of a hybrid culture is manifest too in internationally acclaimed plays like *Umoja*, with the artistry of the gumboot dances harking back to the days of Johannesburg as a small mining town, and Lebo M's *The Lion King*, which recasts the narrative of good and evil in an African setting. Culture in South Africa continues to be vibrant, elastic and multifarious, illustrating Raymond Williams's dictum that culture is really about everyday life.

Culture and globalisation

Perhaps the most significant new feature that globalisation has added to these uses of culture has been to turn culture itself into an object of consumption. Before the advent of contemporary globalisation, it was already clear to social theorists that culture had become subject to the process of objectification and commodification to which all things in capitalist society invariably succumb. All the same, it was globalisation that finally blew off the veil that had concealed this metonymic reduction of culture to marketable objects and signs. It is true that in the classical age of empire in the nineteenth century, objects from distant lands were collected and displayed as signs and representations of particular cultures. But these were signs of European mastery over the world, expressions of the domestication of threatening Others by the imperial power and a celebration of that power. They had not yet become objects of individual consumption on a general scale in the full-blown manner of today when it is possible to buy a piece of Ghanaian *kente* cloth from a street in New York or to have dreadlocks braided in one's hair in salons from London to Paris.

The commodification and consumption of African culture, or, more appropriately, the objectified, metonymic signs of this culture, are evident in dress and hairstyles, music and dance forms, sculpture and art, all over the world. Indeed, one can say that it is the overt or perceptual 'cultural labelling' of goods that makes them marketable in the global market of cultural commodities – from a piece of Ghanaian cloth to the aesthetically accomplished novels of Chinua Achebe, to take two examples.

Globalisation has made it possible to combine the essentialist rhetorics of culture with the stylistics of multiculturalism and identity in ways that package the nationalist desires of old (with their emphasis on nationalism and resistance) and reduce them to marketable commodities available for consumption. On the literary plane the work of Zakes Mda comes to mind, as does the music of kwaito artists at the level of popular culture. There is certainly a whiff of irony and paradox here, evident in the collapse of grand political resistance into stylistic appropriation. But we need not overstate the case because in essence this reversal is no different from the one we began with when we traced the circular route through which the Enlightenment dream of equality, initially premised on a common, culture-neutral humanity, came to be staged on the ground of cultural difference.

To sum up, what do we do with a term as protean as 'culture', whose meanings tend to go in several directions at the same time, a word that resists reduction to a neat, singular definition? Though the term 'culture' tends to present itself as existing outside the temporalities of history as ontology and essence, what we should always watch out for whenever the term is evoked is the historical context in which the specific usage is embedded. For, ultimately, it is the specificity of its historical production and usage that gives culture its meanings.

References

Achebe, Chinua. 1989. 'The Novelist as Teacher' in *Hopes and Impediments: Selected Essays* (New York: Doubleday), pp. 40–6.

Bocock, Robert. 1992. 'The Cultural Formations of Modern Society' in Hall, S and Gieben, B (eds.), *Formations of Modernity* (London: Polity Press).

Cabral, Amilcar. 1973. 'National Liberation and Culture' in Africa Information Service (ed.), *Return to the Source: Selected Speeches by Amilcar Cabral* (New York: Monthly Review Press with Africa Information Service)

Chatterjee, Partha. 1993. *The Nation and Its Fragments* (Princeton: Princeton University Press).

Cowan, Jane K, Dembour, Marie-Benedicte and Wilson, Richard A (eds.). 2001. 'Introduction',

Culture and Rights: Anthropological Perspectives (Cambridge: Cambridge University Press).

Fanon, Frantz. 2001 [1963]. 'On National Culture' in *The Wretched of the Earth.* (New York: Penguin Books).

Huntington, Samuel. 2000. 'Cultures Count' in Harrison, Lawrence E and Huntington, Samuel P (eds.), *Culture Matters: How Values Shape Human Progress* (New York: Basic Books), pp. xiii–xvi.

Jordan, Zweledinga Pallo. 1992. 'Keynote Address on Behalf of the National Executive Committee of the ANC' in Campschreur, William and Divendal, Joost (eds.), *Culture in Another South Africa* (London: Zed Books).

Mamdani, M. 1996. *Citizen and Subject: Contemporary Africa and the Legacy of Late Colonialism* (Princeton: Princeton University Press).

Williams, Raymond. 1976. *Keywords: A Vocabulary of Culture and Society* (London: Fontana).

Democracy and Citizenship

Bettina von Lieres and Steven Robins

On 29 October 2007, the *Cape Times* published a letter from Elma Carolissen, a sufferer from osteoporosis, who noted that 'many of us suffer from osteoporosis as a result of the poor diets our families were forced to take because of poverty during the apartheid years'. She called upon doctors 'to help us fight this scourge', and for pharmaceutical companies to be pressured to reduce their prices. She also insisted that the media ought to highlight the plight of osteoporosis sufferers, who she urged should link up with the International Campaign on Osteoporosis. This letter was indicative of new forms of 'health citizenship' that emerged after 1994, having been absent during the apartheid era. With the establishment in 1998 of a vibrant AIDS activist movement, the Treatment Action Campaign (TAC), and the emergence of other health social movements, it appeared as if health matters had become highly politicised. This chapter focuses on new discourses and practices of citizenship that have emerged as a result of post-apartheid struggles to redefine society and state. It focuses specifically on the role of AIDS activism in facilitating the development of new forms of health citizenship. These developments, it will be argued, also helped significantly to extend the scope of other kinds of citizenship claims and 'rights talk' after apartheid.

The multi-party, non-racial elections in 1994 ushered in a democratic constitution and a wide range of new democratic institutions. Since then, the term 'citizenship' has slowly emerged as an important cornerstone of 'democracy' discourses in post-apartheid South Africa. Above all, it has come to represent a new political imaginary rooted in the political principles of liberal democracy, a rights-based politics and new possibilities for democratic participation. Associated with the wider project of democracy, the term 'citizenship' is multifaceted and has undergone many shifts. It has come to signify both an affirmation of the democratisation project and also a critique of it. On the one hand, it suggests new expressions of democratic self-identity and society; on the other hand, it signals the limits of state-driven attempts to define democracy and state–society relations. Taking as its starting point the importance of situating the multiple meanings of 'citizenship' in context, this chapter traces key themes in the development of 'citizenship' discourses and practices in South Africa after apartheid.

'Citizenship' is viewed by most key political actors as a product of post-apartheid society's struggle against social and economic exclusion. There are, however, real differences in the ways in which various political actors use 'citizenship' discourses to define the boundaries between civil society and the state, and to broaden definitions of politics in order to recognise new political subjects, themes, spaces and institutions. In this chapter, we suggest that the successes and shortcomings of the term in accurately describing contemporary political life are a result of widespread normative approaches to understanding citizenship, which tend to obscure the contextual dimensions of political life in South Africa post-1994.

In what follows, we first discuss the shifting conceptual frameworks for the term 'citizenship', especially in the global South. We then sketch the political context within which the term 'citizenship' has emerged in South Africa since 1994, laying out the disagreements and contradictions that define current debates on democracy and citizenship. We show how the term 'citizenship' is embedded in discourses usually associated with 'national unity', 'rights' and 'participatory governance'. We then discuss how shifts in the changing and conflictual terrain between 'civil society' and 'the state' are linked to a more explicit citizenship discourse that has emerged in recent years. We draw on a case study of the Treatment Action Campaign to illustrate the emergence of these new forms of citizenship practices. The case also highlights some of the inherent tensions in the ideas and practices of citizenship currently used by various civil society actors in South Africa.

Citizenship and its multiple meanings

Mainstream perspectives on citizenship in both the North and South are often framed with reference to a critique of liberal conceptions of citizenship. Most liberal notions of citizenship emphasise the legal rights that establish the relationship between citizens and the state, and accord a central role to the state in protecting and fulfilling citizenship rights. Liberal notions of citizenship have been criticised for being 'state-centric'. For critics of the liberal paradigm, citizenship must go beyond an inactive acceptance of state-determined social and political duties and responsibilities. Rejecting the idea that citizens are primarily subjects of the sovereign state, these critics emphasise the everyday practices of citizenship that bind and connect people to each other and to their chosen and ascriptive communities through multiple and diverse relations and practices (Kabeer 2005; Isin and Wood 1999; Mamdani 1996).

In many countries of the South, ideas and practices around citizenship extend beyond the liberal conception of the citizen as an individual bearer of rights and include a wide range of ideas and practices with more substantive content. In many parts of Africa, for example, rights-based citizenship discourses are often viewed with scepticism by those who were excluded from formal citizenship under authoritarian colonial regimes. For those previously excluded, a range of discourses focusing on substantive claims to political and economic equality have come to symbolise democratic citizenship. And in many contexts, citizenship is an inherently 'messy' practice that may involve participation in a range of political institutions and relationships. In the daily scramble for livelihood and security, poor people tend to adopt several strategies and draw on multiple political identities, discourses and social relationships to navigate daily life. For them, citizenship is defined by highly localised processes of identification and political mobilisation and not only by the claims of the rights-bearing citizen vis-à-vis the state. And even when citizens engage with the state, it is often as clients of state patrons and paternalistic state regimes.

In the South, discourses about citizenship are also discourses about the 'unresponsive state' and its relation with 'the people'. What is often absent from the citizenship literature of the North is an account of states that are absent, ineffective or distant. Although there is a growing literature on 'failed states' in Africa (Bayart 1993; Bayart, Ellis and Hibou 1999; Mbembe 1992), the implications of such states for notions of citizenship are seldom explored. For example, what happens when health-care provision and other key social services are provided by transnational donor agencies, non-governmental organisations, or humanitarian and relief agencies? How does this alter our understanding of what it means to be a citizen? What about 'traditional' and non-state institutions such as chiefly courts, clans, militias, warlords, and occult and religious movements that continue to form important parts of the social and political landscape in many countries? In some contexts, these may become viable alternatives to the absent state.

From the perspective of liberal citizenship, what might be regarded as 'the solution' in such cases would be a 'good dose' of 'good governance' to strengthen state institutions and accountability. Yet, such interventions might be completely unrealistic when viewed from the perspective of people living with failed states. How long will such 'citizens' have to wait for these 'state-strengthening programmes' to take root in places like Sudan, Iraq and Zimbabwe? Even in relatively strong and stable states, accessing government programmes can be extremely frustrating. Moreover, such state-driven programmes often end up undermining agency by turning citizens into passive recipients of state interventions.

Against this background there has emerged a concept of citizenship as 'the right to have rights', 'the right to participate', or 'citizenship from below' (Gaventa 2002; Dagnino 2005). This conception speaks to a set of common challenges in the South: the democratisation of civil society–state relations, the gaps between legally guaranteed rights and actually lived experiences of citizenship, and the persistence of social and economic structural conditions in the face of democratic political reforms. In this approach, citizenship is not bestowed by the state or by a set of legal norms, but is enacted in a set of diverse practices and spaces, and involves multiple identities and struggles around concrete issues. This conception of citizenship is seen to constitute a more 'robust' version than the liberal one with its emphasis on the primacy of the autonomous individual and the state as the primary provider of rights. It includes not 'only political and civil rights, but also social rights, and in some cases the right to participate in claiming rights, and to participate in creating new rights' (Gaventa 2002). Citizenship as 'the right to have rights' indicates 'the emergence of new political subjects, actively defining what they consider to be their rights and struggling for their recognition' (Dagnino 2005: 5). We now turn to some of the key themes which animate debates on 'citizenship' in contemporary South Africa.

The emergence of 'citizenship': debates on 'national unity', 'inclusive citizenship' and 'participation'

Public uses of the term 'citizenship' in post-apartheid South Africa have been embedded in the idea of 'rights'. Since 1994, reference to the term 'rights' has provided common ground – and a connecting principle – for a diverse array of political actors who found in the language of rights a way of expressing their claims, and helping them to find a place in the new democratic society. In the early 1990s, at the heart of emerging debates on democracy and citizenship was an emphasis on political rights, especially the right to vote. This quickly expanded into demands for social and economic rights. It also included claims based on cultural, linguistic and land rights for minority groups like the San and Afrikaners.

The term 'citizenship' was also implicit in the emerging discourse on 'national unity'. In the months following the ANC victory in the 1994 elections, images of 'non-racialism' and 'national unity' and the phrase 'the rainbow nation' were routinely recycled in television advertisements, talk shows and soap operas. Vigorous debates took place about the meaning of an overarching 'African' identity. Tensions and differences over the meaning of 'national unity' and the country's new national identity reflected widespread preoccupations with diversity, political inclusion, as well as the need to deal with the dual legacies of racism and structural inequalities.

A crucial aspect of the early political context from which the term 'citizenship' evolved was the particular configuration of both the state and civil society, and their mutual relationship in the years immediately after the end of apartheid. Early on, tensions started to develop between political leaders, on the one hand, who saw little difference between state and society (in their view the new democratic state was already the legitimate and representative voice of 'the masses', i.e. the broader society) and, on the other, civil society leaders who asserted the distinctions and boundaries between 'the state' and 'civil society'. At the same time, social movements increasingly began to exercise their autonomy vis-à-vis the state. In state-driven discourses on democracy, a conceptual separation between 'civil society' and 'the state' was made in public discussions, but not in practice.

The conceptual conflation of state and civil society was, however, not only the product of distinct ideological choices on the part of the ANC-led state and its political discourses on the 'National Democratic Revolution' (NDR). It also reflected the marked absence of local institutions and spaces mediating the relation between state and civil society after apartheid. The new political order had in fact inherited a society with few institutional and structural opportunities for citizens to 'oversee' the state. In the initial post-apartheid phase, state officials and government ministers were primarily concerned with de-racialising institutions and installing new models of governance and public programmes of service delivery. In the minds of many in government, there seemed to exist an implicit convergence of 'state' and 'civil society', given that, for many, 'citizenship' primarily entailed ensuring people's rights to the provision of basic services by the state.

The largely taken-for-granted deployment of the term 'citizenship' in the early years after apartheid morphed into more explicit uses as the country entered new phases. The early focus on diversity and inclusive citizenship through which the term 'citizenship' evolved soon shifted to new debates on local government reforms and 'participatory governance', with an emphasis on community participation and public involvement in local decision-making. In the process of redefining local government as an 'independent' sphere with legislative and executive powers, new definitions of 'citizenship' emerged that placed stress on public participation in decision-making. The intention was to facilitate citizens' capacity to make demands and insist upon accountability from the state. New local governance discourses were premised on the distinction between a citizen 'in right' and a citizen 'in practice', and the success of development was seen to be dependent on the extent to which citizens exercised their rights in practice (Chipkin 2005). This was accompanied by a shift in viewing the rights of citizens not simply as those of 'basic needs', but in 'furnishing the conditions for individuals and households to sustain themselves socially and economically' (Chipkin 2005).

In the late 1990s, emerging discourses of participatory governance began to root themselves in ideas about state accountability, state responsiveness and 'citizen participation'. 'Citizen participation' is increasingly seen by analysts and activists alike as a requirement, a condition, as well as a guarantee of citizenship. In practice, however, new local citizen institutions such as ward committees, aimed at increasing citizen participation, have been given little real power over decision-making. Although discourses of 'participatory governance' seek to promote a more empowered citizenry capable of overseeing the state, they also tend to provoke continuing tensions between state and civil society, especially when they involve the idea of an autonomous citizenry with institutions over and beyond those provided by the state and ruling party.

Redefining citizenship: social movements and 'the right to have rights'

During the past decade, the notion of 'citizenship' has increasingly come to prominence with the emergence of social movements and the rise of popular protests against the lack of service delivery. Campaigns such as the Anti-Eviction Campaign in Cape Town and the Soweto Electricity Crisis Committee in Johannesburg have mobilised poor township residents to assert their constitutional rights and resist eviction from their homes and disconnection from essential services. In the field of HIV/AIDS activism, there have been significant successes in forging new spaces for citizens to engage across the society–state divide. In the process, new strategies of popular mobilisation have developed that make use of multiple sites of engagement, locally, nationally and even globally. Social movements like the Treatment Action Campaign (TAC) have helped create formal and informal intermediary spaces in which activist organisations and their marginalised constituencies engage, both collaboratively and critically, with the local, provincial and national institutions of the state. The case of TAC highlights the fact that in many countries of the South, citizens' political lives and identities are not necessarily framed by the bifurcated model of civil society and state. The TAC, on the contrary, provides an example of organisational practices that cut across institutional and non-institutional spaces, and are capable of generating multiple relations with different institutions and actors within the state. In this way the TAC has enabled ordinary citizens to build their political capabilities for democratic engagement. Its interventions have allowed its members to emerge from the margins of the political system and to initiate new struggles for a more active 'citizenship' rooted in everyday life. As a result the TAC has expanded the very notion of 'citizenship'. Whereas the anti-apartheid struggle was fought largely to secure political rights, the TAC in its activism around the AIDS pandemic has politicised health and transformed it into a question of citizenship and rights.

The TAC was established on 10 December 1998 when a group of about 15 people protested on the steps of St George's Cathedral in Cape Town to demand medical treatment for people living with the virus that causes AIDS. By the end of the day, the protesters had collected over a thousand signatures calling on the government to develop a treatment plan for all people living with HIV. TAC's membership has grown dramatically in the ten years since it was established. Its rank-and-file members consist mainly of young urban Africans, who are mostly female and unemployed, with some secondary schooling. The TAC has also managed to attract health professionals, journalists, academics and university students as well as garnering support from a large number of civil society organisations.

The visible face of the organisation is Zackie Achmat, a 40-something, former anti-apartheid and gay activist. Until recently, Achmat, who is himself HIV-positive, had made it known that he refused to take antiretroviral drugs (ARVs) until these were available in the public health sector. When TAC was founded, it was generally assumed that anti-AIDS drugs were beyond the reach of developing countries, thereby condemning 90% of the world's HIV-positive population to a painful and inevitable death. In 2004, following concerted pressure from AIDS activists and other groups, and a steep drop in the price of antiretrovirals, the South African government finally agreed to 'roll out' a national ARV programme.

While TAC's main objective has been to lobby and pressure the South African government to provide AIDS treatment, it has over the years begun to address a much wider range of issues. These include tackling the pricing structures of the global pharmaceutical industry in the media, the courts, and the streets; fighting discrimination against HIV-positive people in schools, hospitals and the workplace; challenging 'AIDS dissident' scientists; and lobbying for better conditions for health workers.

Soon after its establishment, TAC, in collaboration with the South African government, became embroiled in a lengthy legal battle with international pharmaceutical companies over AIDS drug patents and the importation of cheap generics to treat HIV-positive poor people in developing countries. Largely as a result of highly visible global and national media campaigns by TAC and its allies, the pharmaceutical industry backed down and allowed developing countries to manufacture ARV generics. In December 2001, shortly after this court victory, TAC's legal representatives were back in court arguing that the South African government had a constitutionally bound obligation to promote access to health care, and that this necessarily involved the provision of antiretroviral treatment.[1]

Part of TAC's success in lobbying government to provide AIDS treatment to its citizens has been its highly effective mobilisation of human rights and citizenship discourses in the international arena as well as locally and nationally. TAC activists nevertheless stress that grassroots mobilisation has been the real key to their success. This promotion of health citizenship was carried out through AIDS awareness and treatment literacy campaigns in schools, factories, community centres, churches and *shebeens* (informal taverns), and through door-to-door visits in the townships. These strategic engagements at the local level involved mobilising and educating poor and working-class communities around HIV issues as well as using the courts to challenge the marketing of scientifically untested AIDS 'cures' in the townships.

Nationally, campaigns were undertaken to protect the autonomy of scientific institutions such as the Medical Research Council (MRC) and Medicines Control Council (MCC) from government interference. During the course of these campaigns, TAC has managed to draw in an extraordinarily broad and diverse constituency within the townships, the public health sector, trade unions, universities, media and many other sectors of South African society. These activist networks and citizenship practices, which straddled global, national and local spaces, involved people from diverse race, class, ethnic, national, occupational and educational backgrounds. Yet the majority of TAC volunteer activists were poor and unemployed African women, many of them HIV-positive mothers desperate to gain access to life-saving drugs for themselves and their children.

While the thrust of TAC's challenges to the South African government focused on citizens' rights to health care, the campaigns also involved broader issues relating to questions of scientific authority and expertise. TAC raised troubling questions about science and citizenship, and drew attention to the ongoing debate about the scientific 'truth' of AIDS that raged between TAC, the trade unions and health professionals on the one side, and President Mbeki and his inner circle on the other (see Robins 2004, 2005).

At the same time the TAC and Médecins Sans Frontières (MSF) also attempted to develop new conceptions of health citizenship and scientific literacy amongst its members and the wider citizenry through the establishment of treatment support groups and AIDS awareness and treatment literacy campaigns. In support of this campaign they disseminated reports, scientific studies, website documents, newsletters and media briefs which refuted government and AIDS dissident claims that ARVs were dangerously toxic, ineffective, costly and incapable of implementation owing to infrastructural and logistical problems such as inadequate management structures and shortages of trained staff. These initiatives gave support to doctors, hospital superintendents and medical researchers who, by virtue of their research reports or provision of ARV treatment, found themselves on the wrong side of the government and subject to high-level political interference and intimidation.

These examples of health citizenship reflect at a local level the dramatic spread worldwide of 'global health initiatives' promoted by international donors, NGOs, health agencies and social movements such as TAC. These initiatives have contributed to the proliferation of community-based AIDS organisations that draw on practices of 'self-help' and what Vihn-Kim Nguyen refers to as ethical projects of self-fashioning and 'care of the self' (Nguyen 2005). For Nguyen, these projects can also produce new forms of therapeutic citizenship involving political claims and demands based on 'responsibilised' citizenship (see Robins 2006; Rose 2007; Rose and Novas 2005).

In order to gain access to life-enhancing ARVs, the 'targets' of these HIV prevention and treatment programmes are required to develop new ways of being 'responsible' in their sexual lives, diets, lifestyles, and adherence to treatment regimes and medical check-ups. Ideas like these about 'responsibilised' or 'biological' citizenship reflect the prevailing imperatives of liberal rationalities of government in advanced liberal democracies in the North (Rose and Novas 2005; Petryna 2002). In the global South, they often imply forms of exclusion or 'social triage' in that NGOs and medical practitioners, often funded by global donors, have to decide who lives and who dies. For example, those considered 'irresponsible' in their sexual behaviour and lifestyles can be excluded from accessing ARV treatment.

In South Africa, TAC activists and MSF health workers have been extremely successful in mediating these global discourses on health citizenship. The Christopher Moraka Defiance Campaign was a good illustration of TAC's form of 'citizenship from below'. It began in July 2000, after HIV-positive TAC volunteer Christopher Moraka died, suffering from severe thrush. The TAC claimed that the drug fluconazole could have eased his pain and prolonged his life, but it was not available on the public health system because it was too expensive. In October 2000, in response to Moraka's death, TAC's Zackie Achmat visited Thailand where he bought 5000 capsules of a cheap generic form of fluconazole. When TAC announced Achmat's mission in a press conference, the international public outcry against the pharmaceutical giant Pfizer intensified as it became clear how inflated the prices of name-brand medications were. No charges were brought against Achmat, and the drugs were successfully prescribed to South African patients. By March 2001, Pfizer made its drugs available free of charge to state clinics.

This David and Goliath narrative of TAC's successful challenge to the global pharmaceutical giants captured the imagination of the international community and catapulted TAC into the global arena. Preparation for the court case had also consolidated TAC's ties with international NGOs such as Oxfam, Médecins Sans Frontières, the European Coalition of Positive People, Health Gap and Ralph Nader's Consumer Technology Project in the US. This success, and the many others that followed, provided a glimpse of what health citizenship had become as a powerful, rights-based politics that operated simultaneously at local, national and international levels. It was indeed a form of global citizenship 'from below'.

Conclusion

Structural poverty and marginalisation are clearly key barriers to citizen participation in post-apartheid South Africa. In addition, the state is holding on to state-centred definitions of citizenship which limit the space for redefinitions of citizenship 'from below'. New social movements and groups of protesting citizens are, however, changing the spaces where engagement does take place. This raises a series of questions about forms of participation among marginalised groups in contexts where there is a marked absence of institutions for citizen participation. Any approach to citizen participation among marginalised peoples must confront the deeper problem of how people who are excluded come to develop a sense of their own participation as worthwhile and as effective in a context where there are complex dynamics of power and participation. In post-apartheid South Africa, new democratic arenas are often transplanted onto institutional landscapes in which historical patterns of political engagement can potentially weaken new forms of citizen participation. Examples of these historical patterns include clientelism and neo-traditional forms of patriarchal power.

Disparities between the official democratic discourses on political rights and citizenship and the political and economic realities on the ground often have the effect of alienating marginalised groups from the public sphere, as they are forced into informal and hidden social and economic practices by the state's unwillingness to recognise these very real conditions. This can result in a wider politics of disengagement from the state and a situation whereby the ordinary person becomes more and more alienated from public institutions because they seem increasingly remote and unresponsive to their needs. We need to understand how specific political and power dynamics affect the process of democratisation and democratic 'citizenship', and to consider the multiple ways in which power is negotiated across the divide between the state and civil society. The TAC case study provides one example of the potentially empowering outcomes of such forms of citizen engagement.

Endnote
1 The South African Constitution is unique in providing for water and housing (along with health care and a clean environment) as basic rights in the Bill of Rights.

References
Bayart, JP. 1993. *The State in Africa: The Politics of the Belly* (London: Longman).
Bayart, JP, Ellis, S and Hibou, B. 1999. *The Criminalization of the State in Africa* (Oxford: James Currey).
Chipkin, I. 2005. '"Functional" and "Dysfunctional" Communities: The Making of Ethical Citizens' in Robins, S (ed.), *Limits to Liberation: Citizenship and Governance after Apartheid* (Oxford: James Currey).
Dagnino, E. 2005. 'Meanings of Citizenship in Latin America', IDS Working Paper (Brighton: Institute of Development Studies, University of Sussex).
Gaventa, J. 2002. 'Introduction: Exploring Citizenship, Participation and Accountability', *IDS Bulletin*, vol. 33, no. 2 (Brighton: Institute of Development Studies, University of Sussex).
Isin, EF and Wood, P. 1999. *Citizenship and Identity* (London: Sage).

Kabeer, N. 2005. 'Introduction: The Search for Inclusive Citizenship: Meanings and Expressions in an Interconnected World' in Kabeer, N (ed.), *Inclusive Citizenship* (London: Zed Books).

Mamdani, M. 1996. *Citizen and Subject: Contemporary Africa and the Legacy of Late Colonialism* (Princeton: Princeton University Press).

Mbembe, A. 1992. 'The Banality of Power and the Aesthetics of Vulgarity in the Postcolony', *Public Culture*, vol. 4, no. 2, pp. 1–30.

Nguyen, Vinh Kim. 2005. 'Antiretroviral Globalism: Biopolitics and Therapeutic Citizenship' in Ong, A and Collier, S (eds.), *Global Assemblages: Technology, Politics, and Ethics as Anthropological Problems* (Oxford: Blackwell).

Petryna, Adriana. 2002. *Life Exposed: Biological Citizens after Chernobyl* (Princeton: Princeton University Press).

Robins, Steven. 2004. '"Long Live Zackie, Long Live": AIDS Activism, Science and Citizenship after Apartheid', *Journal of Southern African Studies*, vol. 30, no. 3, pp. 651–72.

Robins, Steven (ed.). 2005. *Limits to Liberation after Apartheid: Citizenship, Governance and Culture* (Oxford: James Currey).

Robins, Steven. 2006. 'From Rights to "Ritual": AIDS Activism and Treatment Testimonies in South Africa', *American Anthropologist*, vol. 108, no. 2 (June 2006), pp. 312–23.

Rose, Nikolas. 2007. *The Politics of Life Itself* (Oxford: Blackwell).

Rose, Nikolas and Novas, Carlos. 2005. 'Biological Citizenship' in Ong, Aihwa and Collier, Stephen J (eds.), *Global Assemblages: Technology, Politics, and Ethics as Anthropological Problems* (Oxford: Blackwell).

DEVELOPMENT

Kees van der Waal

IN CONTEMPORARY SOUTH AFRICA, 'development' evokes images of projects aimed at improving living conditions, such as dams, housing and electrification. It is in particular the rural and urban poor who are viewed as the proper beneficiaries of development interventions. Given the daunting economic inequalities in South Africa, there is wide scope for development talk and action, but despite the ubiquity of the term, the meaning and practice of development remain contested. This chapter looks at the new understandings that have grown up around the term, examines the successes and failures of state-driven development in South Africa since 1994, and considers the processes involved in actual interventions on the ground. The contested nature of development interventions is apparent in many concrete situations where the relations of power often appear mystified in planning and decision-making. It is, therefore, important to prioritise local experiences and perceptions of development. The modern notion of development, however, has a history of nearly sixty years, which tracks its slowly transforming meanings.

The notion of development: evolving meanings
The idea of development as economic improvement came about in the wake of the Second World War. Development was then understood to be primarily the provision of infrastructure and modern technology to poor countries in need of modernisation so as to break out of the supposed inertia of traditional culture. The idea of development as modernisation was reinforced by the writings of the economist WW Rostow, who argued that all countries pass through similar stages of economic development: from low levels of economic activity in traditional society to high rates of productivity and mass consumption in modern society.

Proponents of modernisation looked to the economic and technological advances of the North as the model for global development from which benefits would 'trickle down' to the poor. On the basis of this understanding, poor postcolonial states were politically manipulated by the capitalist 'first world' and the socialist 'second world' during the Cold War through the provision of development assistance. A number of national (or bilateral) organisations, such as the United Kingdom's Department for International Development, and international (or multilateral) organisations, such as the World Bank, were created to channel huge amounts of development aid to the developing world.

However, a strong critique of the notion of development as modernisation was mounted by the neo-Marxist dependency school in Latin America in the 1970s. Introducing a political dimension into the argument, André Gunder Frank pointed out that development had to be seen in conjunction with 'underdevelopment' – the condition of poverty and exploitation that former colonial countries experienced at the hands of the industrialised nations in the North. Even when specific ex-colonies were said to be 'developed', relations between North and South remained exploitative. As Frank pointed out, the South was increasingly disadvantaged and made dependent, largely through greater flows of capital to the North (as outflowing repayments for loans from the International Monetary Fund and World Bank) than to the South (in the form of incoming loans and development aid).

The solution that Frank and others proposed was 'delinking' from the exploitative system of systematic underdevelopment associated with the illusion of economic growth. Samir Amin, for example, argued the case for 'autocentric economies' in Africa. In this line of thinking, even development projects of a welfare nature were thought to make no difference to underlying inequalities, as they did not challenge the prevailing structures and relationships of power (Escobar 1995; Gardner and Lewis 1996: 7, 18; Olivier de Sardan 2005: 47).

More recently, 'post-development' scholars and activists have been strongly influenced by the critical ideas of the dependency theorists and the poststructuralist theories of Foucault on the need to analyse systems of control as discourses with hidden power relations. They reject the notion of development as desirable and rather see it as a 'destructive and self-serving discourse propagated by bureaucrats and aid professionals that permanently entraps the poor in a vicious circle of passivity and misery' (Edelman and Haugerud 2004: 86). In this view, empowerment became a form of subjection and participation in development only served to conceal existing power structures.

Therefore, some scholars and activists opted for the idea of an 'alternative development', which would go beyond mainstream ideas of development. This sought to strengthen local initiatives for development independent of brutal modernisation interventions by states (such as the US through its international development agency

USAID) and big business associated with capitalist economic development (Escobar 1995; Sachs 1992). This brand of post-development thinking posed a strong democratic and ethical challenge to promote innovative, alternative approaches such as 'fair trade' and 'participatory budgeting' in local government (Edelman and Haugerud 2004: 103–4). It also placed strong emphasis on participation in development planning by the people concerned as well as the creation of sustainable forms of organisation, based on the idea of 'development from below', including the use of resources, social organisation and energies available in local contexts and communities.

The assumption that the 'community' is a coherent and conflict-free social unit is, however, very problematic, since contests about approaches and resources occur in every social setting (Thornton and Ramphele 1988). Indeed, when local knowledge is idealised in a populist and normative way and prioritised above everything else, our understanding of the situation in front of us can become distorted. This romanticisation can be seen for example in the words of the 'prophet' of participatory rural appraisal (PRA), Robert Chambers: 'Rural populations are generally long-suffering, hard working, ingenious and very resistant' (quoted in Olivier de Sardan 2005: 117). PRA methods used by outside development facilitators aim at facilitating local planning on the basis of local knowledge. However, participatory methods in development can easily fail to overcome optimistic rhetoric, and exclude marginalised social categories from participating meaningfully in key decisions. Merely emphasising 'community' or 'public' participation often fails to take class, gender and age differences into account. Such ritualised use of participation becomes a form of abuse, whereby only strong local players benefit from project resources (Gardner and Lewis 1996: 111–14).

In contemporary understandings of development influenced by post-modern thinking, the linear and progressive master-narratives of both modernisation and Marxism have been rejected. Less emphasis is now placed on monolithic theories and more focus is given to deconstructing development as discourse and revealing the diversity of approaches and reactions within it. There is now a focus on the complexity of local conditions and local reactions to intervention. At the same time, a more inclusive meaning of development has become popular, namely the understanding of development as improved human well-being, which takes a stand against the previous emphasis on economic growth, through new conceptions of 'human development', 'social development' and 'sustainable development'. No longer is development seen primarily as measurable in terms of GDP and other economic indicators. Instead, levels of education, life expectancy, political participation and access to resources are now combined with income levels to provide 'Human Development Indicators', which are used to rank countries and to prioritise development programmes.

The current emphasis on 'sustainable development' prioritises several dimensions of well-being that were previously neglected. Foremost is the ecological vulnerability of the planet, especially to the over-exploitation of limited natural resources. Industrial development in the 'developed world' is having a negative impact on the planet and its natural resources, leading to a search for sustainable resource utilisation. Another dimension of this new understanding of development is the concern to promote the social relationships (institutional development) and competencies of those who are supposedly 'empowered' by development. As an example of this, we can note the increasing insistence on the accountability and progressive democratisation of state institutions in order to prevent a lack of transparency and responsiveness to the needs of the population.

In view of all these new understandings, scholars of development no longer see development as a moral imperative or an ideal condition, but rather as a social phenomenon emerging out of complex relationships among individuals, institutions, historical contexts and micro-level dynamics. Development is also a market of models to be pursued, and an arena where agents and structures exercise power (Olivier de Sardan 2005: 71).

Although some of the critiques of development by the dependency school and the post-developmentalists have been ideologically rigid and overly generalising about supposedly monolithic aid organisations and other members of the 'development industry', their emphasis on the need to deconstruct relations of development, on the strong political nature of development, and the importance for contextualisation in terms of the political economy provides a useful contribution for understanding the issues at stake.

What is more, modernisation theory, dependency theory and post-development ideas all share an emphasis on the central role of capitalism and the state in development. Where they differ is in determining how the relationship between the state and the 'people' should be organised. Populist understandings of the state and of development in socialist and social democratic nations would emphasise the broad responsibilities of the 'developmental state' towards meeting the needs of the population. A neoliberal approach, on the other hand, would limit the role of the state to facilitating developmental entrepreneurship. A neoliberal state would put effort into 'rightsizing' its bureaucracy, often to the detriment of a wide range of social services. It is the contest between these two poles that has been part of the public debate about development in South Africa since 1994.

Expectations of South African modernity

The democratic transformation of 1994 was expected to bring huge improvements to the living conditions of the impoverished majority of South Africans. The new government came into power on the basis of a broadly supported national development plan, the Reconstruction and Development Programme, or RDP (ANC 1994), which was meant to address the effects of past injustices. Some of the socialist ideals of the liberation movements appeared in the RDP plan, especially with regard to land redistribution and the nationalisation of water and minerals. The RDP was based on the Freedom Charter of 1955, and both documents were informed by the 'two stage' theory of revolutionary transformation: national liberation followed by socialism. Some even saw the new government as a 'developmental state' that was responsible for providing fully for the needs of the poor and marginalised. As with most grand development programmes, the RDP did not materialise as intended, although it still functions in the minds of many government supporters as a roadmap to modernisation.

One reason for the demise of the RDP was weakness of implementation. But perhaps the most important impulse for the unpopular decision to disband the RDP programme only two years after the democratic transition came from the impact of globalisation on the economy and the state. The new government felt increasing international pressure to control state spending, and believed that development could not be implemented without a strong economy based upon neoliberal economic principles. The abandonment of the RDP marked an important move away from the idea of state-driven development to a concept that was more in line with neoliberal ideas and practices. The new macroeconomic approach was the Growth, Employment and Redistribution (GEAR) strategy, introduced in 1996, which led to restrictions on government spending in its social development programmes.

As a result of the recent performance of the South African economy and the huge developmental needs that confront the state, there are indications that the ANC is again shifting its approach, to a more interventionist one. Increasingly, the Presidency is playing a centralising and management role in the field of development by setting service targets and monitoring progress made in development (Lutchman 2006: 3). However, the pressures of the world economic system and the problems of capacity may prevent the government from realising the 'developmental state' it envisages (Southall 2006a: xvii, xxxvii). The Bill of Rights in the Constitution of 1996 makes provision for the protection of socio-economic rights, such as access to housing, food, water, social security and education. However, the constraints that the state faces in this regard have become more obvious. When these rights were tested in the Constitutional Court in the Grootboom case, the state was found to be responsible for the progressive realisation of rights within the limits of available resources (Govender 2006: 98, 114).

At the end of the first decade of South Africa's new democracy, much public attention was focused on how the new government had performed in realising the ideals of the Freedom Charter and the RDP. In 2005 President Mbeki argued that much had been achieved in terms of the goals set in 1994. Social grants were being widely distributed, over 10 million people had gained access to drinking water, and over 2 million housing subsidies had been granted. While it is clear that progress has been made on the macroeconomic front and in addressing the basic needs of the poor rural and urban population, the realisation of the ideals has been more difficult than originally imagined and huge backlogs remain. The growth in urban household numbers had aggravated the backlogs in service delivery (Hemson and O'Donovan 2006: 17); unemployment (measured as a percentage of employable adults) was at a high 26% in 2003; and 45–55% of the population was categorised as poor (Daniel et al. 2005: xxii).

The discrepancies between plans and eventual outcomes can be seen most vividly in the housing sector, the leading project of the RDP. A major goal for development in the first five years of the new government was the delivery of one million new houses. This target was reached only after nine years through the provision of free housing grants to the unemployed and subsidies to those with low incomes. In every city and town new 'RDP housing schemes' sprang up with the provision of basic accommodation in rows of unimaginative 'matchbox houses'. For the recipients who had formerly lived in the unpleasant conditions of rural areas and informal settlements, the acquisition of a house as a first capital investment represented a huge improvement. Nevertheless, for many people the process also had a negative side, with many stories circulating of corruption and the manipulation of waiting lists to benefit politicians or their cronies. Enormous backlogs remain, estimated at 2.1 million houses in 2004 and projected to be 2.4 million in 2008 (Hemson and O'Donovan 2006: 24–5), even though the funding for housing often goes unspent by the implementing authorities.

Another major development initiative promoted by the government has been its intervention in the economy to facilitate the creation of a black middle class. Before 1994 very few Africans had access to lucrative business opportunities in the formal economy. A programme of Black Economic Empowerment, or BEE, was launched to open up the boardrooms of corporate capital, tendering and business to men and women of colour. Legal frameworks were put in place that required companies and organisations to reflect the composition of the population in their workforce and management and to stimulate black entrepreneurship. In a relatively short time a new economic and social elite ('the BEE-llionaires') has been created.

While the emergence of this new class challenged old racist stereotypes and did effect some transfer of economic wealth and decision-making power to the African community, the downside was the growth of economic inequality among black South Africans. Furthermore, the impact on the economy and on employment was relatively low as the new black owners of companies had huge empowerment-deal debts to service (Southall 2006b). In 2005 the ANC in fact conceded in a policy document that inequality in South Africa had actually worsened in the post-apartheid era and that the challenges of high unemployment and poverty remained (Southall 2006a: xxi; Terreblanche 2002). Many people in the townships and rural areas, where the needs were the highest, began to complain about the lack of services due to corruption and capacity problems. Protests by angry crowds about perceived injustices in access to resources have become a regular sight on TV news reports in recent years. Sometimes the clashes with the security forces have been violent. Cases of forced removals and the use of rubber bullets occur from time to time, reminiscent of news images from the old South Africa.

Provision of basic infrastructure ('development' and 'service delivery' in the eyes of the masses) is a responsibility of local government, a sphere of government where there had been a huge overhaul of governance structures in the decade after 1994. Although municipalities are responsible for managing development democratically, this has proved difficult. In the rural areas, conflict about the respective roles of traditional leaders and democratic local government authorities in development initiatives has retarded the provision of services. In theory at least, participation by the local citizenry in decision-making is organised through ward committees and public participation processes such as the formulation of Integrated Development Plans for every municipality. All the same, the role of the public in development planning and decision-making is often marginal, as these processes are usually dominated by experts from government and by highly paid consultants. In fact, non-governmental organisations (NGOs) often play a larger role in the planning processes than the poor. 'Civil society' is mostly populated by NGOs funded by the same international donors as in the pre-1994 period. Now, though NGOs have a smaller role to play in the field of development and the government has taken on many of their functions, they are still much better organised and resourced than the smaller community-based organisations (CBOs) such as civic associations in poor areas.

Having looked at the historical evolution of the concept of development and the ambiguous meaning of the notion in the new South Africa, we shall now consider the process of development on the ground in more detail by looking at specific local situations and the impacts of development projects. A core issue in this regard is the relationship between those with expert planning power and local people.

Development intervention as projects in local contexts

A development intervention usually consists of a discourse and a set of practices initiated by outsiders in a specific setting. The format tends to aim at manageable, temporary projects each consisting of controlled steps in a project cycle. The discourse of development planning and management is strongly based on perceptions held by expert outsiders who act from the top downwards. This often includes the view that the tradition and culture of recipients are problematic (e.g. that local perceptions of time and lack of a sense of individual responsibility are at the root of the failure of projects). The 'development industry' uses a standardised set of terms, including 'scoping', 'empowerment' and 'participation' and employs formal techniques such as 'log-frame analysis' (tables with one-way mono-causal project relationships) as well as more people-oriented techniques such as participatory rural appraisal.

Despite the good intentions of most development projects, people on the ground perceive them and react to them in their own terms and according to local understandings based on practical 'common sense' and local experience. Standardised approaches to development, which become 'travelling models' for policy and action, often hide an insufficient understanding of local contexts. The models are often based on false stereotypes (e.g. assuming the existence of consensual solidarity, shared goals and homogeneity in a 'community'), which lead to problematic new forms of cooperation and decision-making in a project (Olivier de Sardan 2005: 73–4). In fact, most development projects fail because of a lack of institutional sustainability that comes about when planned outcomes are not valued similarly by planners and intended beneficiaries, or resources are insufficient to sustain an initiative.

Another challenge is community involvement. Claims that beneficiary participation will be built into a project are mostly rhetorical and very difficult to achieve because of the social differentiation in any community along the lines of gender, age and income. Even when development projects are successful in terms of technical aims, they can have very mixed impacts. Projects may require that people move to a new location where their livelihoods could be more vulnerable and where a sense of local community may be lost. This has happened to many communities that were moved because of nature conservation or the building of dams.

All this raises the question of how development projects actually impact on people. In an influential ethnographic study on global development organisations in Lesotho, James Ferguson (1990) showed how the World Bank's Country Report contained many inaccuracies about the role of Lesotho's migrant workers and economic relationships with South Africa because of the need to represent the country as a stagnant, traditional, isolated economy that required intervention. The discourse of development in the Report (in the case study, an agricultural project in a relatively isolated mountain valley) ignored the social conditions of the project, and instead focused solely on technical aspects. Even though the development project failed in its own aims, it had important unintended effects. As Ferguson pointed out, the agricultural development work of international NGOs in Lesotho unintentionally led to increased bureaucratic and military power of the government over areas that were associated with its political opposition.

In order to understand these consequences in their full complexity, it is necessary to look at development as a social construct and a process of social interfaces in a specific context. This means that the discourses of development planning and implementation need to be critically deconstructed in terms of both their multiple meanings and the underlying relationships between role-players. Whenever local people accept an innovation or scheme, it becomes embedded in local social and cognitive patterns and reinterpreted into something much more hybrid than originally intended (Olivier de Sardan 2005: 104–6). To understand 'development', the intended and unintended effects of development interventions have to be uncovered.

This kind of critical approach has been promoted by the anthropology of development, which in turn has been influenced by the work of Michel Foucault. The focus is on a critical understanding of development interventions as both discourse and action. It foregrounds the analysis of unequal power relationships between government organisations or NGOs and people in the local context and investigates the multiple understandings involved in development interventions on both sides. The critical analysis of a development project involves asking uncomfortable questions about who benefits from an intervention, what the networks and events in the course of a project mean for all the 'stakeholders', and how the project's impacts can be understood in terms of the broader political-economic context. In documenting and interpreting a development intervention as a complex process on various levels of analysis, anthropologists like Ferguson (1990) and Mosse (Mosse et al. 1998) have found that development is not the smooth implementation of beneficial change as is sometimes projected by the 'development-speak' of planners and politicians.

Some of the more generalising critical analyses exhibit an ideological need to deconstruct all development as merely a top-down form of capitalist exploitation (e.g. Escobar 1995). But not all development interventions should be seen as purely manipulative. Interventions vary enormously in their structural relationships, their impacts and the manner in which people understand and react to them. The impact of the state, and of development more generally, can be easily overestimated, hiding the complex ways in which local beneficiaries react, whether through selective acceptance or hybridised integration. These ways can take various forms: 'cultural revitalisation, overt and covert expressions of resistance, protest, evasion, feigned compliance, circumvention, foot dragging, compromise, accommodation, selective appropriation and the embrace of the signs, commodities and practices of consumer capitalism and the modern state, as well as voluntary and enthusiastic participation in development projects' (Robins 2003: 283).

One example of the diversity in reactions to development intervention is the Integrated Development Plans (IDPs) that local governments in South Africa are required to create for their areas of jurisdiction. These need to be based, according to the legal requirements, on strong inputs from local communities in a formal process of public participation. In the case of an urban environment like Stellenbosch, there was sufficient planning capacity available and many skilled members of the public who could contribute to and question the IDP. In poor, rural areas, such as the lowveld of Limpopo Province, the IDP process was, on the other hand, much more consultant-driven and conflict-ridden and less participatory (Van der Waal 2001). Within this single region, local reactions of various 'stakeholders' differed substantially, with traditional leaders resisting their loss of jurisdiction over local development, councillors competing for infrastructure development projects in their wards, and various social categories (women, youth and local communities) vying for their share of the 'development cake'.

Conclusion

Development is a highly contested notion. Political leaders, government officials and NGO personnel all use ideas about 'progress' to convince local people to accept planned interventions as an improvement of their living conditions. Local perceptions may be very diverse about the supposed benefits of what is presented as development, as gender and other divisions can result in differences of access to resources and impacts of change. Development is therefore a field of contestation that needs to be analysed in terms of the power relations underlying the technical and economic changes that are introduced. Globally, and in South Africa too, the dominant approach followed at present still seems to be the 'trickle-down' idea of incremental progress based on neoliberal economic growth. This approach requires constant questioning of the effects of development interventions on the recipients and the 'fit' of the ideas and practices of development with the democratic and human rights of the Constitution. Fortunately, the approach to development in South Africa is highly contested. With the state becoming a stronger player in the recent past, there is now a useful counterbalance to the power of external development agencies.

Inherent in the idea of development, whether that advanced by neoliberal economists (development as an achievable ideal) or the post-development alternatives (development as domination), is the belief in the possibility of achieving human progress, even if via very different models or interventions. For people who lack basic services, development as modernisation remains a powerful attraction. Students of development should focus perhaps not so much on 'development' intervention and projects as assumed solutions, but rather on the broader issues of poverty and inequality and on the complex ways these are addressed by the state and NGOs in their attempts to have a positive impact on the needs of the poor (Edelman and Haugerud 2005: 50).

References
ANC. 1994. *The Reconstruction and Development Programme* (Johannesburg: Umanyano).
Daniel, J, Southall, R and Lutchman, J. 2005. 'Introduction: President Mbeki's Second Term:

Opening the Golden Door?' in Daniel, J, Southall, R and Lutchman, J (eds.), *State of the Nation: South Africa 2004–2005* (Cape Town: HSRC).

Edelman, M and Haugerud, A. 2004. 'Development' in Nugent, D and Vincent, J (eds.), *A Companion to the Anthropology of Politics* (Oxford: Blackwell).

Edelman, M and Haugerud, A. 2005. 'Introduction: The Anthropology of Development and Globalization' in Edelman, M and Haugerud, A (eds.), *The Anthropology of Development and Globalization: From Classical Political Economy to Contemporary Neoliberalism* (Oxford: Blackwell).

Escobar, A. 1995. *Encountering Development: The Making and Unmaking of the Third World* (Princeton: Princeton University Press).

Ferguson, J. 1990. *The Anti-Politics Machine: 'Development', Depoliticization, and Bureaucratic Power in Lesotho* (Cambridge: Cambridge University Press).

Gardner, K and Lewis, D. 1996. *Anthropology, Development and the Post-Modern Challenge* (London: Pluto).

Govender, K. 2006. 'Assessing the Constitutional Protection of Human Rights in South Africa during the First Decade of Democracy' in Buhlungu, S, Daniel, J, Southall, R and Lutchman, J (eds.), *State of the Nation: South Africa 2005–2006* (Cape Town: HSRC).

Hemson, D and O'Donovan, M. 2006. 'Putting Numbers to the Scorecard: Presidential Targets and the State of Delivery' in Buhlungu, S, Daniel, J, Southall, R and Lutchman, J (eds.), *State of the Nation: South Africa 2005–2006* (Cape Town: HSRC).

Lutchman, J. 2006. 'Politics: Introduction' in Buhlungu, S, Daniel, J, Southall, R and Lutchman, J (eds.), *State of the Nation: South Africa 2005–2006* (Cape Town: HSRC).

Mosse, D, Farrington, J and Rew, A (eds.). 1998. *Development as Process: Concepts and Methods for Working with Complexity* (London: Routledge).

Olivier de Sardan, J-P. 2005. *Anthropology and Development: Understanding Contemporary Social Change* (London: Zed).

Robins, S. 2003. 'Whose Modernity? Indigenous Modernities and Land Claims after Apartheid', *Development and Change*, vol. 34, no. 2, pp. 265–85.

Sachs, W (ed.). 1992. *The Development Dictionary: A Guide to Knowledge as Power* (Johannesburg: Witwatersrand University Press).

Southall, R. 2006a. 'Introduction: Can South Africa Be a Developmental State?' in Buhlungu, S, Daniel, J, Southall, R and Lutchman, J (eds.), *State of the Nation: South Africa 2005–2006* (Cape Town: HSRC).

Southall, R. 2006b. 'Black Empowerment and Present Limits to a More Democratic Capitalism in South Africa' in Buhlungu, S, Daniel, J, Southall, R and Lutchman, J. (eds.), *State of the Nation: South Africa 2005–2006* (Cape Town: HSRC).

Terreblanche, S. 2002. *A History of Inequality in South Africa 1652–2002* (Pietermaritzburg: University of Natal Press).

Thornton, R and Ramphele, M. 1988. 'The Quest for Community' in Boonzaier, E and Sharp, J (eds.), *South African Keywords: The Uses and Abuses of Political Concepts* (Cape Town: David Philip).

Van der Waal, CS. 2001. 'Anthropological Perspectives on Rural Institutional Development in the Northern Province', *Africanus*, vol. 31, no. 1, pp. 48–74.

Empowerment

Edgar Pieterse

Empowerment is a self-evident good that no one in his or her right mind could be against. It is a moral no-brainer. Yet, it is almost impossible to find people who can actually define what they mean by empowerment, except perhaps for the technical prescripts associated with economic empowerment of women and black people. To make this task manageable, the essay begins by considering the broad field of development policy and practice, using government pronouncements as the starting point. The ANC's Reconstruction and Development Programme (RDP) placed empowerment at the centre of the government's priorities and programmes. I will first review this understanding of empowerment and then explore how it was translated into a very particular architecture of policies and programmes to achieve various social, political and economic outcomes.

However, many scholars and activists are profoundly critical of the architecture, and especially the effects, of the government's approach to empowerment. Drawing on international debates, they suggest that empowerment as defined and implemented by state institutions serves to reproduce the structural disempowerment of the poor in South Africa but in a way that makes the poor feel they are indeed part of the national project of reconstruction and development. According to these critics, the primary reason for the state's behaviour has been its adoption of neoliberal economic and social policies despite its Left-sounding rhetoric. I review both sides of the debate and explore a way past this conceptual stand-off in the last section of the essay.

State-driven empowerment

Our people, with their aspirations and collective determination, are our most important resource. The RDP is focused on our people's most immediate needs, and it relies, in turn, on their energies to drive the process of meeting these needs. Regardless of race or sex, or whether they are rural or urban, rich or poor, the people of South Africa must together shape their own future. *Development is not about the delivery of goods to a passive citizenry. It is about active involvement and growing empowerment.* In taking this approach we are building on the many forums, peace structures and negotiations that our people are involved in throughout the land … The central objective of the RDP is to improve the quality of life of all South Africans, and in particular the most poor and marginalized sections of our communities. This objective should be realized through *a process of empowerment* which gives the poor control over their lives and increases their ability to mobilize sufficient development resources, including from the democratic government where necessary. The RDP reflects a commitment to grassroots, bottom-up development which is owned and driven by communities and their representative organizations (ANC 1994: 5 & 15, emphases added).

This policy statement starts off by placing people – in particular, poor black people – at the centre of development initiatives. Here, 'our people' are simultaneously the focus, beneficiary and driver of the development process. The more the people participate in their own development processes, the more they will be empowered. In other words, in the absence of citizen participation, empowerment cannot occur.

After the publication of the RDP document, the government proceeded to create a vast institutional framework into which the poor would have to insert themselves to access development resources. Tellingly, this model of participation was presented as proof that the ANC was indeed committed to bottom-up development 'owned and driven by communities and their representative organizations'. This approach should be seen against the backdrop of longstanding criticisms of development efforts as being agency- or state-driven and hence 'top-down' instead of 'bottom-up', as the RDP would have it (Clarke 1989). From the perspective of bottom-up development empowerment arises from active participation in development processes.

The quotation also reveals a number of further assumptions. Firstly, the people are invoked in very homogeneous terms, apart from the identification of 'poor' and 'marginalised' sections of communities. Secondly, the development project is seen as essentially about addressing 'immediate needs', echoing the return of the basic needs discourses of the 1970s, which made a comeback with the 1990 World Development Report on poverty alleviation (Friedmann 1992). Most South Africans wanted not only the right to vote and an end to racial discrimination, but, finally, an opportunity to be citizens with rights to a dignified life free from hunger and poverty. Thirdly, the RDP assumed participation would take place in organisations that were continuous with the bodies that made up the Mass Democratic Movement before 1994. This assumption is significant because the government presumed that one could simply redirect the grassroots network of civil society organisations under the aegis of the ANC towards a new, collective purpose: reconstruction and development. Consequently, when the RDP ministry disbursed funds for development projects, it required civil society organisations to be registered, to be focused on poverty alleviation and participant in local development forums. This initial practice set the tone for a very narrow and instrumentalist approach to participation.

Given the important role of participation in facilitating empowerment, we need to consider the various avenues and sites of participation that the government established after 1994. These can further be categorised as service delivery to address household needs, political participation and economic empowerment.

Participation in the delivery of basic services

In terms of the RDP, the government expected that citizens (especially the poor) would involve themselves in various kinds of local, interest-based civil society organisations such as civics, religious bodies, cultural associations, poverty relief organisations and various service-delivery-oriented forums. Most sectoral services in the domain of national and provincial administrations are subject to the overview or input of various types of community participation to make the service more attuned to local needs. For example, the Health Department interfaces with community-based Primary Health Care Committees, which are meant to influence and monitor the practices of primary health-care clinics; the Education Department affords substantial decision-making powers and influence to school governing bodies; police stations support and depend on community policing forums. There are other, similar community-based service delivery forums in the domains of water management, environmental planning, sport and cultural development, and so on.

Though there has been very little scholarly assessment of these bodies, what is clear is that participation is largely restricted to the operational aspects of these services and tends to avoid engagement with the underlying policies and interests at play in the service. Essentially this form of community participation happens on the terms set by the various government departments and is usually highly localised, whereas most of the important trade-offs and choices occur at higher levels of decision-making. For instance, most government departments execute policy priorities in terms of White Papers and legislation which determine the parameters for service delivery at a local level. Consequently, community-level participatory structures tend to operate within a predetermined policy framework and are expected to focus exclusively on the terms and quality of service delivery at the local level. The ideological underpinnings of a particular service are not meant to be within their purview.

Furthermore, crucial decisions about financial allocation within various programmes in a sectoral department (e.g. higher education vs early childhood development) are made largely within government and, most importantly, in the Budget Council run by the National Treasury. Consequently, community organisations have to operate within a predetermined financial envelope that makes debates about cross-subsidisation almost impossible. As a result, participatory mechanisms can in fact obscure where the real power lies and in this sense amount to a form of co-option.

In support of these participatory forums, the government has also made provision for development-oriented civil society organisations (CSOs) for whose functioning various government departments and agencies provide direct funding if their objectives coincide with government programmes. CSOs which become service-delivery partners of the government are in theory able to gain financial support for their activities through them (Pieterse and Van Donk 2004). The track record of this particular policy thrust is abysmal. Not only have inefficiency and corruption plagued many of the state's funding bodies such as the National Development Agency but, more disconcertingly, these bodies take an almost welfarist approach to their role and, as a result, restrict their support to project-based CSOs that avoid advocacy and oppositional politics.

Participation in local governance
Since the local government elections in 2000, when the present system of municipal government came into being, much of the government's agenda to address the basic needs of the poor has been driven by local government. Through the Integrated Development Planning (IDP) process local communities are enabled to participate in determining strategic and budgetary priorities for development in their own municipalities. The intention has been to create deliberative forums for planning and assessment so as to ensure that municipalities are driven by priorities that have been determined by elected representatives as well as by communities and various organised interest groups. But in practice the story is very different. As the wave of protests against the lack of service delivery by municipalities over the past few years suggests, basic needs are not being met fast enough; and where they are addressed, often the 'beneficiaries' do not have the requisite incomes to pay the ongoing service charges to use the service or infrastructure.

One should be cautious about taking the formal discourses of empowerment and participatory democracy at face value. According to Faranak Miraftab, these potentially transformative notions have been turned into depoliticising 'tools of the trade for governments [and] establishments such as the World Bank' (2004: 239). To understand how this has taken place, Miraftab has analysed the initiative of the Cape Town municipality to outsource waste removal to local contractors in the township of Khayelitsha, which was intended as an act of community empowerment. Instead of bringing benefit to many, however, the scheme in fact enriched only a very few entrepreneurs, who paid their workers well below the minimum wage.

Miraftab notes that the drivers of the scheme saw this initiative as a great example of black empowerment because it would give work to the unemployed and also bolster the number of entrepreneurs in Khayelitsha. For Miraftab (2004: 249) this demonstrates how 'empowerment is clearly reduced to its economic dimensions and to something that is acquired and consumed individually'. Insidiously, the rhetoric of empowerment is used to divert attention from the fact that it is not 'out of refuse' but out of the underpaid labour of the local workers that the entrepreneurs make a profit.

This is precisely what neoliberal reform across the world is currently about. Neoliberal reform has involved economic liberalisation along with public sector reforms so as to open up the field of service delivery to market forces and dynamics. As a consequence of these reforms, state budgets for social wage expenditures are reduced and private sector actors are brought into the realm of public services through privatisation. The result has been that public services have been thoroughly commoditised and all those who make use of a service must pay the full market value for that service irrespective of their economic position. In societies with already high levels of inequality and exclusion, this essentially means that those who cannot afford to pay are cut off from public support. To soften this hard and unforgiving core of the neoliberal agenda, it is necessary, ideologically, to make the problem of exclusion an individual one as opposed to a collective or societal one. Following this line of critique, Miraftab suggests that her case studies reveal how 'Participation and empowerment are treated as independent of the structures of oppression, and simply processes by which programs foster individuals' sense of worth and esteem. This individualization inherently depoliticizes the notion of empowerment, often reducing it to individual economic gain and access to resources, and leaving the status quo unchallenged' (2004: 242).

This is precisely the case with the South African government's discourses about participation and empowerment. Miraftab (2004: 253) argues that we must consequently look beyond the rhetoric and start 'paying attention to the post-apartheid government's efforts to *tame* community participation and *control* the claims of citizens on the state'. This seam of analysis appears in a growing body of literature that explores community-level protests against municipal authorities across the country (e.g. Bond 2005; McDonald and Pape 2002; Miraftab and Wills 2005). But as I argue below, despite the growing appeal of this perspective, it is partial and therefore inadequate.

Broad-based black economic empowerment

It took the government an inordinately long time to formulate a comprehensive and credible policy approach to economic empowerment of the black majority in South

Africa (Meintjies 2004). I do not have the space to explore the reasons for this but will simply summarise the notion of economic empowerment in the Broad-Based Black Economic Empowerment (BBBEE) policy. Firstly, one has to appreciate the distinction the government draws between the so-called first and second economy.

> One of the major consequences of the change in the structure of the economy is that 'two economies' persist in one country. The first is an advanced, sophisticated economy, based on skilled labour, which is becoming more globally competitive. The second is a mainly informal, marginalised, unskilled economy, populated by the unemployed and those unemployable in the formal sector. Despite the impressive gains made in the first economy, the benefits of growth have yet to reach the second economy, and with the enormity of the challenges arising from the social transition, the second economy risks falling further behind if there is no decisive government intervention (Presidency 2003: 97).

The golden egg that must be protected is the globally integrated first economy. For the government the overriding political imperative is to ensure that the economically excluded in South Africa can migrate from the second to the first economy as quickly as possible, without undermining the first economy's viability and growth. Various measures have been proposed to support people in the second economy, such as

- strengthening small, medium and micro-enterprises through more effective supply-side programmes (i.e. training opportunities, financial support and preferential access to state contracts), with a bias towards women;
- monitoring the enterprise development aspects of the BBBEE codes;
- expanding the public works programme in order to reach more unemployed people;
- tackling youth unemployment through targeted programmes (GCIS 2006).

This strategy is premised on the idea that interventions in the second economy must be leveraged off the first economy.

The first economy is also a critical site for advancing the economic empowerment of previously disadvantaged black South Africans. The primary policy intervention to facilitate such empowerment is the BBBEE strategy. At the heart of this is an approach that moves away from the original focus on ownership and management, to include issues like skills development, preferential procurement and enterprise development. The most significant innovation of this framework, because of its potential impact on the whole economy, is the provision that all state bodies must procure goods and services from companies on the basis of a BEE scorecard. If companies want to offer goods and services to the state, they in turn have to apply the scorecard further down in the value chain to all the companies they transact with. Consequently, one can anticipate massive compliance with the new BEE framework, which should accelerate levels of black ownership and black enterprises in the medium term. This suggests that the BBBEE strategy will be significant and potentially far-reaching in its effects despite the slow start made in the first decade of democracy.

Nonetheless, the government's strategy has been criticised from a number of quarters. Some critics attack the idea of the conceptual framework of a first and second economy because of the implied structural break between the two (Devey et al. 2006). They argue that there are close interdependencies between the formal and informal economies in South Africa manifested, for example, in informal clothing manufacturing destined for formal retail stores, or the purchasing of goods in the informal economy from formal businesses. However, as long as empowerment is based on a fundamental disconnection between two economies, substantive policies focused on the informal sector are unlikely to emerge.

Two other criticisms of government strategy can be mentioned. If one considers the scale of the unemployment problem, its concentration amongst the youth and the challenge of competitiveness into the future, it is difficult to understand how the crisis of unemployment will be addressed within a generation. (Unemployment is meant to be halved by 2015 in line with the Millennium Development Goals.) Furthermore, there is nothing in the government's agenda thus far that can address the growth of income inequality – which obviously militates against economic empowerment – stemming from the structural shift of the economy into more skill-intensive sectors. In short, for the foreseeable future massive levels of poverty will remain a fact of life in South Africa, especially since poverty is closely related to a lack of income (Parnell 2005).

A number of Left scholars argue that the primary reason for the inequality blind spot in the government's economic policy is the unviable policy architecture that seeks to combine socially inclusive policies with a neoliberal economic project (Bond 2005; Miraftab 2004; Miraftab and Wills 2005). At the heart of this critique is the argument that the South African government has taken a fundamentally neoliberal turn since the adoption of the GEAR strategy but manages to defuse criticism by employing progressive-sounding ideas like empowerment, social cohesion and participation.

Two responses flow from this position. Firstly, those of the crude instrumentalist persuasion tend to see the ANC government as irrevocably tainted by neoliberal ideologies, and by now so materially invested in its preservation through crony BEE ventures that an alternative political project to the left of the ANC is the only route to social transformation. This criticism is complemented by an analysis that promotes or highlights the often militant resistance of poor communities who are fighting back against these oppressive features of the state. There is an unmistakable moral certitude to this genre of analysis and critique. Other critics, typically in the Foucauldian mould, rely on the hope that if current episodes of resistance can be connected through an alternative discursive field of power and underpinned by concrete action, the neoliberal hegemony will crack and create opportunities for more empowering discourses and practices to emerge.

All the same, we need to bear in mind that the South African transition was a politically negotiated compromise that established very clear parameters for the terms of the rebuilding of the state and the services it provides to society at large (Marais 2001). At the same time the country has also become more, not less, open to influences and ideas that flow relentlessly across the globe today. Many of these forces are underpinned by the undeniable and considerable power of those who benefit from the capitalist system. Yet, we also know that the capitalist system in itself is not uncontested and there are various competing models or patterns of capitalism, some more inclusive and compassionate than others. Moreover, we need to be clear about how different kinds of social transformation can be expected to unfold simultaneously within the capitalist system. More often than not, conditions will not be ideal and very localised acts of advancement will unfold or become possible without necessarily changing the full logic of the system.

If we are to reposition empowerment so as to retain the seeds of transformative change, it is essential to appreciate the symbiotic connection between individual and collective modes of empowerment. The rights-based discourses on citizenship that stress the indivisibility of individual and collective human rights form a useful starting point but they must lead on from there and incorporate an emphasis on restoring 'the political' at the heart of the conceptual approach to empowerment as participation. This means a focus on projects of social redistribution through equitable service-delivery regimes, economic inclusion through truly broad-based economic development, and more effective support for co-operative and informal businesses that buttress the livelihoods of the poor. Figuring out what a transformative agenda might be at the structural, technological, institutional and cultural levels in these two domains – access to services and economic resources – is a formidable task in itself. For one thing, it requires grounded research into viable alternatives and working through emergent experiments on the ground, some of which may be genuinely transformative, but most probably not. But it also requires strategic map-making so that it becomes possible to plot political opportunities for (small and large) transformative incursions across various terrains of political imagination and practice (see e.g. Pieterse 2006).

Conclusion

In this chapter I have attempted to show that the concept of empowerment was central to the imaginary of the liberation movement and the first democratic state at the dawn of South African's political freedom. At the outset, empowerment was linked in the RDP to a people-centred development philosophy focused primarily on addressing the basic needs of the black majority. In operationalising this approach, the ANC-led state linked participatory systems to the provision of various social services such as education, health care and water provision, with local government as the privileged institutional actor. At the intersection of community-level participation and the extension of basic social services to those previously denied them, the state effectively drove social and political empowerment at the same time. Towards the end of 1990s the state complemented this thrust with a more focused set of strategies to advance economic empowerment so as to overcome the chasm between the so-called first and second economies – the root cause of the systematic economic exclusion of the majority despite moderate and increasingly robust rates of economic growth.

Many scholars on the Left have criticised these formal governmental strategies to enhance political, social and economic empowerment, pointing out the stark contradictions that accompany them when they are pursued within a neoliberal fiscal framework. But as I have argued, a more rounded conceptualisation of empowerment requires us to move beyond an obsession with neoliberalism in order to imagine and implement concrete alternatives that can only arise from critique and experimentation.

Acknowledgement

I want to thank the editors and Vanessa Watson for their incisive comments that forced me to think more clearly about the ideas expressed here; but I obviously remain solely liable for the content.

References

ANC. 1995. *Reconstruction and Development Programme* (Johannesburg: ANC).

Bond, P. 2005. 'Globalisation /Commodification or Deglobalisation /Decommodification in Urban South Africa', *Policy Studies*, vol. 26, nos. 3–4, pp. 337–58.

Clarke, J. 1989. *Democracy and Development* (London: Earthscan).

Devey, R, Skinner, C and Valodia, I. 2006. 'The State of the Informal Economy' in Buhlungu, S, Daniel, J, Southall, R and Lutchman, J (eds.), *State of the Nation: South Africa 2005–2006* (Pretoria: HSRC Press).

Friedmann, J. 1992. *Empowerment: The Politics of Alternative Development* (Oxford: Blackwell Publishers).

GCIS (Government Communications and Information Service). 2006. *The South Africa Yearbook 2005/2006* (Pretoria: GCIS).

Marais, H. 2001. *South Africa: Limits to Change. The Political Economy of Transition*, 2nd edn (London and Cape Town: Zed and UCT Press).

McDonald, D and Pape, J (eds.). 2002. *Cost Recovery and the Crisis of Service Delivery in South Africa* (London: Zed Books).

Meintjies, F. 2004. 'Black Economic Empowerment: Elite Enrichment or Real Transformation', *Isandla Development Communiqué*, vol. 1, nos. 9 & 10 (accessed from: www.isandla.org. za/newsletter/news9.htm on 8 July 2006).

Miraftab, F. 2004. 'Making Neo-liberal Governance: The Disempowering Work of Empowerment', *International Planning Studies*, vol. 9, no. 4, pp. 239–59.

Miraftab, F and Wills, S. 2005. 'Insurgency and Spaces of Active Citizenship: The Story of Western Cape Anti-Eviction Campaign in South Africa', *Journal of Planning Education and Research*, vol. 25, no. 2, pp. 200–17.

Parnell, S. 2005. 'Constructing a Developmental Nation: The Challenge of Including the Poor in the Post-Apartheid City', *Transformation*, no. 58, pp. 20–44.

Pieterse, E. 2006 'Building with Ruins and Dreams: Exploratory Thoughts on Realising Integrated Urban Development through Crises', *Urban Studies*, vol. 43, no. 2, pp. 285–304.

Pieterse, E and Van Donk, M. 2004. 'Developmental Local Government: Squaring the Circle between Policy Intent and Outcomes' in Van Donk, M, Swilling, M, Pieterse, E and Parnell, S (eds.), *Consolidating Developmental Local Government: Lessons from the South African Experience* (Cape Town: UCT Press).

Presidency, The. 2003. 'The Ten Year Review' (Pretoria: GCIS).

ETHNICITY

John L Comaroff and Jean Comaroff

Ethnicity defies easy definition. Max Weber once remarked that 'if we define our terms exactly, "the" ethnic group ... is unsuitable for rigorous analysis' (1968: 395). As this suggests, ethnicity is an elusive concept; this in direct proportion to the degree to which its meaning, its frames of reference, its sociological substance are taken for granted – in everyday life, in contemporary perceptions of politics, in scholarly discourse. Its salience also shifted significantly during the 'long twentieth century'. It has become commonplace to note (i) that, with the rise of neoliberalism, assertions of identity have replaced most other kinds of collective action in pursuit of power, interest, rights and recognition; (ii) that they have become the vehicle through which human subjectivity is increasingly experienced and negotiated; and (iii) that within the domain of identity, ethnic consciousness, being vested in a fusion of blood and culture, is archetypically taken to be the most basic, most 'primordial'. Whether or not any of this is actually so, it has forced ethnicity into the centre of several intersecting disciplinary debates. Which is ironic: the very fact that it is invoked and experienced in so many diverse ways, and with such contrasting social, symbolic, material, moral and political implications, has led some scholars to argue that the category covers too wide a range of things to be reduced to an object of theory in itself – let alone to an analytic construct. But this is to begin at the end. Let us return to basics.

The concept of ethnicity has a deeper history in sociology than in anthropology; this largely under the influence of Weberian theory, for which cultural identity inheres in 'status groups' – above all, the 'ethnic group' – in contrast to distinctions based on class, party and other modes of association (Gerth and Mills 1946: 180–95). Taken to be a measurable phenomenon in the positivist social sciences, ethnic identity is typically treated as an independent variable with the autonomous capacity to shape social processes and life-chances. In this tradition, ethnicity itself has been explained by recourse to two epistemes: primordialism, according to which it is founded on the irreducible facts, real or fictive, of shared biology, ancestral origins, and innate disposition (Cohen 1974: xii); and instrumentalism, which sees it as a social construction wrought in reaction to threats against the self-determination, integrity or interests of persons who imagine themselves to have a common, culturally rooted destiny (Wallerstein 1972) – even where their traditions are invented (Hobsbawm and Ranger 1983).

The debate between these epistemes persists, mutedly, although many US sociologists, concerned with efforts to build nationhood amidst cultural heterodoxy (Conzen and Gerber 1992: 4), have long argued that ethnic identity arises 'from the solidarity created by a common socioeconomic position among people who ... see themselves as sharing ancestry and historical experience' (Bankston and Henry 2000: 382, after Glazer and Moynihan 1970, 1975). Bankston and Henry add that 'the emotive, primordial character of ethnicity', which they take as given, remains a 'useful basis for political organisation' – also for the pursuit of material interests, sometimes by violent means. In this compromise, Allahar (1994) suggests, ethnicity is reduced to 'the social construction', for utilitarian ends, 'of primordial attachment'.

Ethnicity, as precept and problem, interpellated itself into the intellectual archaeology of anthropology quite recently; as late as 1969, Frederik Barth (1969: 9) could observe that it was 'of great, but neglected, importance' to the discipline. Anthropologists, classically, had studied peoples who were presumed to share common cultures – and who were thought to take their cultural identities as axiomatic; culture, to deploy an old cliché, was like the water in which fish swim, invisible and unmarked. Identity, in short, only came into question in historical situations in which difference took on social, material and political relevance: in 'complex civilisations' (Moerman 1967), in colonial encounters (Ekeh 1975, 1983), and, especially, in urban agglomerations (Epstein 1958; Cohen 1974) and industrial centres (Mitchell 1956) – under conditions that anthropology, in the absence of a working theory of history, tended to gloss as 'social change'. As Cohen (1974: ix) put it: 'the tribes, villages, bands, and isolated communities, ... until recently our traditional subject-matter, are everywhere today becoming integral parts of new state structures and are thus being transformed into ethnic groupings'.

When, at last, anthropologists began to interrogate ethnicity, they tended to stress its historical, socially constructed properties. Barth's *Ethnic Group and Boundaries* (1969) is perhaps paradigmatic, remaining influential, though its analytic language is somewhat dated. Barth argues that the cultural content of ethnic consciousness may be a product, rather than the constitutive basis, of 'ethnic group organisation' (11); that there is no one-to-one relationship between ethnicity-as-experienced and the 'objective' facts of difference (14); that it is the boundary distinguishing a population from others that defines it as a group, not its inherent 'cultural stuff', the corollary being that ethnicity is less a thing than a relationship rooted in a dialectic of identification and contrast (15); that identities can and do change, sometimes dramatically; and that the problem, for anthropology, is to establish the conditions of their emergence and development. Barth himself goes on to consider ecological, economic, demographic and political 'factors' in answer to this last question. Others concerned with the social dynamics of ethnicity, like the Manchester School in urban Africa, also made much of its capacity to provide cognitive maps and social resources for Africans in unfamiliar, heterogeneous environments (e.g. Mitchell 1966).

To the degree that it is possible to draw broad generalisations from anthropological studies of ethnicity since the 1960s, three suggest themselves.

First, there has been an enduring, steadily growing effort to counter primordialist understandings of ethnicity with ever more nuanced constructionist ones; at the same time, it is now widely acknowledged that ethnic identity is often perceived, subjectively, to be primordial in origin. Increasingly, too, that identity is experienced, at once, in two different registers: as a product of genetics, where it serves as a stand-in for earlier notions of 'race', *and* as a matter of choice, made manifest, most notably, in patterns of consumption (Bankston and Henry 2000: 383–5).

Second, the conditions that give rise to ethnogenesis – they often have to do with the sedimentation of relations of inequality, clothed in cultural difference (Halter 2000: 12f) – are not necessarily the same as those that sustain ethnic consciousness (Comaroff 1987: 313). But once ethnic identities take root, they are typically held to account for both the past and the present predicament of those who bear them, thus coming to appear as an autonomous principle of social determination (313). As the life-blood of ethno-national movements of various kinds, these attachments have fuelled mass political action in modern times, including identitarian violence, warfare, even ethnocide.

Third, ethnicity is always relational, its cultural and affective content depending on the politics, economics, ethics and aesthetics of difference in which it comes to be embedded; what is more, it is usually experienced both positively and negatively, as an assertion of collective right, value and entitlement, and as a claim of loss, victimhood, desires denied. This has two corollaries: that, being a historical construction, ethnic identity is (i) a perpetual process of becoming, never fully realised, always demanding to fulfil itself, either peacefully or brutally; and (ii) at once one thing and many, similar in its form yet infinitely variable in its substance, its expressive strength, its semiotic elaborations.

In recent times, however, a fresh chapter has opened in the unfolding history of ethnicity. Elsewhere we refer to it as 'Ethnicity, Inc.' (n.d.). Partly as an effect of the increasing heterodoxy of nation-states, partly a consequence of the global turn in politics away from struggle between classes and ideologies toward contestation in the name of ID-ology[1] – the pursuit of recognition, right, interest and empowerment under the sign of identity – more and more ethnic groups are coming to act like corporations: as enterprises in which genetic ascription confers shares and by which culture may be produced, possessed, purveyed as 'naturally copyrighted' property.

As this implies, Ethnicity, Inc. consists in a counterpoint of two processes: the incorporation of identity, whereby a body corporate is created for the mutual economic benefit, however it may be derived, of all of those who share in it; and the commodification of culture, the assertion of sovereign ownership over, and the entitlement to profit from, vernacular knowledge, practices, rights or expressive forms (cf. Brown 1998, 2003). These are not necessarily cynical, alienating processes. In many places they are said to reinforce, even deepen, the affective attachment of ethnic populations to the cultural property they put into circulation (Dávila 2001: 2; Xie 2003).

Ethnicity, Inc. is proceeding in many parts of the world, albeit in different ways, to different degrees, along different dimensions. In some contexts, as among Alaskan Native peoples, incorporation has occurred as a result of state law (Brown n.d.); in others, as among casino-owning American Indians, it is the outcome of a convoluted politico-legal history (Castile 1996: 745; Cattelino 2004); among the Bafokeng of South Africa, perhaps the richest 'tribe' in Africa, it arose from owning land, bought under individual title in the nineteenth century, beneath which there happen to be rich veins of platinum; among the Pueblo Indians of Sandoval county, New Mexico, it was the branding of blue corn, a ritually important grain that became a popular gourmet food in the USA, and led to the establishment of an enterprise composed of five indigenous groupings; among the San of southern Africa, pejoratively known as 'Bushmen', it was the knowledge of *hoodia* cactus, since patented as a fat-fighting food supplement and franchised by a global pharmaceutical company, thus implicating the hunter-gatherers in a multi-billion dollar industry. In all these cases, and many others, ethnic populations have moved quickly down the road to becoming corporations, their leaders more like CEOs than 'traditional' chiefs – and their cultural property ever more commodified, even when it has had to be invented *ab initio*.

Thus it is that culture infuses the market and the market infuses cultural identity. Nor is this confined to ethnicity. It is occurring, as well, among nation-states, which are also branding and patenting their 'traditional' property more and more. None of this is entirely new: culture, despite received anthropological conceits, has always been, in some sense, a commodity; the nation and the ethnic group, always immanently corporate. What the history of the present is witnessing is the hyper-extension of those tendencies. Let us offer two examples of Ethnicity, Inc. Together they make plain some of its less obvious dimensions.

A tale of two ethnicities: of platinum, plants and the making of peoples

The first of the two stories takes us to the Land of the San, at the edges of the Kalahari Desert. It involves the *hoodia* cactus, which the 'Bushmen' call *!khoba*. By all accounts, they have imbibed cuttings of this plant since time immemorial. In the past, when hunting in the inhospitable reaches of the desert, they relied on it to stay their appetites and thirst; it is used for the same purposes these days, not in order to hunt, but to stave off the effects of poverty. San suffered severely from the social predations of colonialism and postcoloniality: severely stigmatised, victims of various forms of violence, removed from their ancestral lands by governments, prey to illness and alcohol, their numbers had diminished greatly and most of their communities had disappeared over the previous century; much of their remaining population, in fact, had dispersed into the immiserated segments of the South African 'coloured' population.

The best summary of the early chapters of the *hoodia* story comes from a South African journalist, Gavin Evans (2003: 12–16); he captures well the hundreds of accounts of what exactly happened *before* the international media frenzy began, a frenzy that saw CBS's 60 Minutes attest to the efficacy of the plant and speak in awe of its promise for the fat-fighting industry (21 November 2004) – and persuaded the BBC to send one of its correspondents 'deep inside the Kalahari desert', home of 'one of the world's oldest and most primitive tribes', to sample this 'extremely ugly cactus' that 'kills the appetite, attacks obesity ... [and] has no known side effects' (BBC News, 30 May 2003). According to Evans, the South African Council for Scientific and Industrial Research (CSIR) became interested in the medicinal properties of the cactus in 1963; this, it seems, was stimulated by the research of a Dutch ethnobiologist first published in 1937 and by reports of its use by San deployed as trackers by the South African army. The CSIR tested the appetite suppressant capacities of the plant, corroborated them, identified their bioactive component, and, in 1997, took out a patent on it under the label P57.

It is not clear why the process took almost 35 years, but the CSIR licensed P57 to Phytopharm, a British pharmaceutical company – which, after expensive and extensive clinical trials, licensed it on to Pfizer for $21 million; ironic perhaps, since *!khoba* is said to have, as a side effect, some of the same properties as Viagra. It is at this point that the story becomes especially interesting for our purposes.

The San first heard about the patent when Phytopharm announced P57 to the media. Or, more precisely, it was Roger Chennells,[2] a savvy human rights lawyer, who read a quote from the head of Phytopharm, Richard Dixey, to the effect that the San, the people from whom the knowledge of the effects of *hoodia* had derived, were extinct. At the time, Chennells was representing the ≠Khomani San in a land claim (see Robins 2003: 12–14; Isaacson 2002), in the course of which there emerged an NGO, the South African San Institute (SASI), itself mandated by the Working Group of Indigenous Minorities in Southern Africa (WIMSA), one of numerous such organisations that surfaced in the country with the end of apartheid, with neoliberalisation and with the new multicultural assertiveness occasioned by the postcolonial politics of identity.

The array of institutions and organisations that grew up around San identity at this time is quite bewildering.[3] But suffice it to say that Chennells realised very quickly that the 'Bushmen' were victims of biopiracy, that the eventual commercial value of the *hoodia* patent could run into many millions of dollars – its value in the US market alone has been estimated at $3 billion a year (Evans 2003: 16) – and that this represented an opportunity to assert a collective identity under the San Council, a new body established to give political shape to, and claim sovereignty for, their ethnic aspirations (Evans 2003: 14).

Richard Dixey may have been disingenuous in asserting the extinction of the San; the material advantages to Phytopharm were obvious enough. When the San Council, again represented by Chennells, protested to the CSIR, it acknowledged the error of its ways, Dixey confessed his 'embarrassment' at his statements and, in time, a 'memorandum of understanding' was signed by all interested parties. Since then, for reasons that need not concern us here, Pfizer has pulled out as licensee, and Phytopharm has franchised the patent to Unilever. Since then, too, the San Trust, set up to manage the incoming funds, has received its first royalties, has begun to tackle the problems of distribution among the San of South Africa, Namibia and Botswana, and has initiated legal action against illicit producers, of which it is aware of 26. Since then the San, as an ethno-corporation, appears to have been taking ever more articulate shape.

In point of fact, Richard Dixey had not been altogether wrong. The San may not have been extinct, *sensu stricto*, but their *socio*cide – or, more properly *ethno*-cide – had gone quite a long way. Having been violently cast out of the social ecology which had long framed their shared existence, 'they' did not evince much of a coherent collective identity; beyond scattered fragments of remaining population, their dispersal into the grey racial space of South African 'colouredness' made it impossible to do so. But the assertion of intellectual property – coupled, significantly, with the land claim that occurred in tandem with it – had the effect of sedimenting a San 'identity'. And giving it ever 'thicker', ever more dense substance; a symptom of this, interestingly, being a sudden increase in conflict arising out of people accusing each other of 'not being San' (South African San Institute 2001–2).

Thus it is that there has been a language revival, reversing a process which saw fewer and fewer remaining speakers, that genealogies are being collected, and youth are being trained in the task, in order to create a population register; that SASI is concerning itself with 'the development of San culture, the management of cultural resources, and the encouragement of cultural practices', especially on the part of people who had long left them behind; that a 'cultural resources auditing and management project' has been set up; that programmes have been designed for 'San-controlled income generation projects that use cultural and intellectual resources in a sustainable manner'; that opportunities have been sought for San to 'exploit their cultural and indigenous knowledge systems to build a better future'; that a legal programme has been set in motion to 'create an appropriate rights base' for the San, thereby to protect their interests. And that, as the director of a project called ≠Khomani Sisen ('We Work') put it, the 'newly empowered San' are being encouraged 'to channel their cultural heritage into useful modern-day crafts that provide them with dignity and capital' (*Sunday Independent*, 8 September 2002).

This has had some unexpected uptake: for example, Sanscape One, a project in which some of London's top dance producers were invited to take 'the healing songs of the Bushman' and remix them to yield 'an album which ... highlights the plight of the San' in, one might add, a somewhat Sanitised version (*Cape Times*, 24 April 2002). When we asked Roger Chennells whether a new ethnic identity had been produced by the process of incorporation here, he answered in the affirmative. He is correct. The presumption that 'the' San actually *had* a collective identity – or, more properly, an ethno-sociology – prior to the colonial dispersal of a complex *population* (note, not a 'society' or a 'culture') of hunter-gatherer groups referred to collectively as the 'Bushmen' is itself highly contentious: who or what 'they' were, or were not, remains the subject of bitter scholarly debate. But none of that matters any more. Today they are fast becoming not just an assertive ethnic corporation, but a transnational one: as we said, 'the' San, and the San Council that makes manifest their sovereignty, straddle three of the countries of southern Africa.

The other story involves the Bafokeng: the people made wealthy by platinum, the people whose recent kings have repeatedly been spoken of as CEOs, the people who are actually referred to by the mining industry and the South African media as Bafokeng, Inc. The history of their incorporation has its prolegomenon long before the dawn of the Age of Platinum. It begins with land; specifically, with the fact that one of the present ruler's nineteenth-century forebears, Mokgatle, came to realise that, to protect their territory from settler predation, his people ought to purchase their land (Cook n.d.[a]: 5-6). Again, the details need not detain us: Mokgatle sent regiments of young men to the diamond fields in the late 1860s and 1870s as labourers, had them deposit a portion of their wages in a special fund, and used the cash for its designated purpose. Fearing dispossession if the Bafokeng bought the land in their own name, however, the chief elicited the help of a German missionary who acquired it in his; later, to avert problems of title after his death, the real estate was transferred to the colonial government in trust for the 'tribe'.

The subsequent colonial history of South Africa did not make it easy to hold on to this land, but by establishing the Bafokeng 'as a private, corporate land owner', these acts of purchase enabled their chiefs to defend their territory from various efforts to expropriate it and the rights to minerals found beneath it (Cook n.d.[a]: 6 and *passim*), especially after the discovery of platinum here in 1924 and its leasing to Impala Platinum (Implats), a large mining company, in the 1960s (Cook n.d.[a], n.d.[b]). The greatest challenge, in this respect, came when the puppet homeland government of Bophuthatswana, set up by the apartheid state, exiled the Bafokeng chief and negotiated mining contracts directly with Impala; this sparked a protracted series of legal actions against Bophuthatswana, which ended with the demise of apartheid in 1994, and against the mining company, which yielded a victory for the Bafokeng in 1999 – and, with it, a radical rearrangement of their share of the takings from the production of platinum. All of which made the 'tribe' so adept at litigating their interests that, as one journalist put it, 'their traditional weapon [became] the law, not the *knobkerrie* [club]' (*Mining Weekly*, 17–23 November 2000).

The growth of Bafokeng, Inc., its emergence as an 'ethnic corporation' (Cook n.d.[b]) in the wake of the recognition and renegotiation of its rights to the proceeds of platinum mining on its real estate, is nothing short of breathtaking. This nation of 300,000 shareholders – membership is defined primarily by patrilineality – has substantial stakes in, is paid royalties by, or otherwise benefits from, a complex network of companies; their interest in Impala alone yielded R80 million (about $8 million at the time) in the financial year 2001/2. Among their many holdings in a portfolio that seems to grow by the month are two large mining operations, in each of which they have a 50% share valued at R2 billion (about $322.5 million in April 2005), one with Anglo American Platinum and the other with Rustenburg Platinum; a pair of profitable partnerships – Phoka Petroleum and Geared Lubricants (Pty) Ltd – with Mobil Oil SA, a subsidiary of Exxon; a major construction company acquired, along with a number of large-scale building projects, in 1996 and later liquidated; 20% of Astrapak, South Africa's second largest packaging business; and almost 35% of the company formerly known as SA Chrome, now renamed Merafe Resources (*merafe* is the Setswana word for 'nations'). The Bafokeng even own one of the country's premier football teams.

Recently, in December 2005, it was announced that 'Africa's richest tribe just got richer'. Impala Platinum had chosen the Royal Bafokeng Nation to be its 'empowerment partner' under the national policy of Black Economic Empowerment (BEE), a R3.4 billion cash deal that gave the Bafokeng 49% of Impala Refinery Services (*Cape Times*, Business Report, 15 December 2005). But there is more to Bafokeng, Inc. than a large, fast-growing inventory of interests. It is also organisationally complex. The government of the nation is vested in the Royal Bafokeng Administration

(RBA), an elaborate bureaucracy, one of whose departments is charged specifically with community development. Its financial engine is Royal Bafokeng Holdings (RBH), which oversees an ever more global portfolio. RBH is centred in Johannesburg, reports to a bi-annual public meeting (*kgotha kgothe*) back in Bafokeng, is staffed by professional money-managers and has, as its company chairman, King Leruo. RBH has four subsidiaries – Royal Bafokeng Industrial Holdings, Royal Bafokeng Resources, Royal Bafokeng Management Services and Royal Bafokeng Finance – each of which looks after the companies, investments and interests relevant to its domain. At one point in time, Royal Bafokeng Resources was said to be on the verge of becoming a listed *public* company (*Business Day*, 30 August 2002). Were it to do so, 'the Bafokeng' would become the ultimate ethno-prise: one in whose finances, and futures, it would actually be possible to purchase shares.

What is missing in all this? On the surface, it would seem, the cultural element of Bafokeng cultural identity. King Leruo and the financial operatives of Bafokeng, Inc. are hard-headed business people primarily concerned with the material conditions of a sustainable future as laid out in Vision 2020, an ambitious plan to develop Bafokeng into a 'self-sufficient', fully employed, globally oriented nation by the second decade of the new century (Gray 2003: 13–14).

Of late, however, there has been much more culture talk. Since being installed in an elaborate ceremony – a ritual saturated with the trappings of a tradition partly historical, partly invented, powerfully vernacular – the young king has spoken of seeking solutions to the problems of the future in 'African values', celebrating the ways and means of 'traditional governance', and arguing that, 'in moving forward', his people must 'reaffirm' their culture (see Gray 2003: 14); in particular, those elements of it that may carry them into the global age of 'Afro-modernity'. In short, Bafokeng, Inc., the manifest commodification of Bafokeng identity, appears to be reaching toward a sense of a cultural self in order to complete itself.

Running the San and the Bafokeng together, the dynamics at the heart of Ethnicity, Inc. reveal themselves clearly. Membership in both nations has come to be defined genealogically, with some contestation either evident or imminent; in both, commercial enterprise has been instrumental either in crystallising or in reproducing the putative sociological entity in which cultural identity is presumed to inhere; in both, venture capital from outside has been crucial; both have asserted their new-found sovereignty against the state and have based their ethnic incorporation on land claims, past or present. And both have fought their battles directly by means of lawfare. What is more, they have fought them as class actions at the interstices of tort, intellectual property and human rights law, and, in the process, naturalised the trope of identity around which their 'rights' adhere.

This is particularly striking in the case of the San. It could be argued that knowledge of the properties of the *hoodia* was produced not by '*the* San' at all – who may or may not have existed at the time – but by hunters of the Kalahari Desert, a class once defined, if we may be so old-fashioned, by their relationship to a mode of production. The projection of a vernacular right to intellectual property onto 'the San', a putatively 'primordial' collectivity, has the effect of *ex*tinguishing a class of producers as it *dis*tinguishes and materialises a cultural identity – not incidentally, as it does so, giving ontological primacy to the idea of identity itself. Thus does ideology become ID-ology and hide itself in a neoliberal sense of the natural, the inevitable, the given.

Most of all, though, the stories of the San and the Bafokeng, precisely because they are such extreme instances of the process – and it *is* a process of becoming rather than a finished phenomenon, a total social fact in the historical making – demonstrate that Ethnicity, Inc. rests on a dialectic between the incorporation of identity, of its commodification by taking on visible capital value, and the commodification of culture. Whether the process starts with the incorporation of identity, as it did with the Bafokeng, or with the commodification of cultural property, as in the San instance, it evinces a drive to complete itself in the other. Thus it is that a dispersed group of 'Bushmen' have become 'the San', replete with a sense of its own ethno-sociology, its own sovereign governance, and its own range of institutions to make this real.

Thus it is that Bafokeng, Inc. is (re)turning to its vernacular ways and means in the name of an African cultural modernity that it seeks to inhabit as it reaches towards its Vision 2020, the vision of a sustainable economic future. Nor is either surprising. After all, Ethnicity, Inc., to the degree that it naturalises collective right, material entitlement and sovereignty, requires both the incorporation of identity and a cultural substance of some sort to realise, recognise, complete itself. Which is why it tends to begin in land, then to make claims to sovereignty, to secure its cultural property, and then to invest in some sort of future. The future of ethnicity does seem to lie in ethno-futures.

Endnotes

1 At least to our knowledge, this term was first used by Rapule Tabane and Ferial Haffajee in an article entitled 'Ideology Is Dead, Long Live ID-ology', *Mail & Guardian*, 27 June – 3 July 2003, p. 6; see also Comaroff and Comaroff (2003).

2 John Comaroff interviewed Roger Chennells in Stellenbosch (South Africa), on 24 February 2005; we are grateful to him for sharing with us the information recorded here.

3 As will be clear from the SASI *Annual Review*, April 2001–March 2002. We have drawn extensively on this review for our summary account here; see www.san.org.za/sasi/ann_rep_2002.htm.

References

Allahar, Anton. 1994. 'More than an Oxymoron: Ethnicity and the Social Construction of Primordial Attachment', *Canadian Ethnic Studies*, no. 26, pp. 18–34.

Bankston, Carl L III and Henry, Jacques. 2000. 'Spectacles of Ethnicity: Festivals and the Commodification of Ethnic Culture among Louisiana Cajuns', *Sociological Spectrum*, no. 20, pp. 377–407.

Barth, Frederik. 1969. 'Introduction' in Barth, F (ed.), *Ethnic Groups and Boundaries: The Social Organization of Culture Difference* (Boston: Little, Brown).

Brown, Caroline. n.d. *Native, Inc.: A Geography of Alaskan Native Politics*, draft PhD diss., Department of Anthropology, University of Chicago.

Brown, Michael F. 1998. 'Can Culture Be Copyrighted', *Current Anthropology*, vol. 19, no. 2, pp. 193–222.

Brown, Michael F. 2003. *Who Owns Native Culture?* (Cambridge, MA: Harvard University Press).

Castile, George Pierre. 1996. 'The Commodification of Indian Identity', *American Anthropologist*, vol. 98, no. 4, pp. 743–9.

Cattelino, Jessica R. 2004. 'Casino Roots: The Cultural Production of Twentieth-Century Seminole Economic Development' in Hosmer, B and O'Neill, C (eds.), *Native Pathways: Economic Development and American Indian Culture in the Twentieth Century* (Boulder: University of Colorado Press).

Cohen, Abner. 1974. 'Introduction: The Lesson of Ethnicity' in Cohen, A (ed.), *Urban Ethnicity* (London: Tavistock).

Comaroff, Jean and Comaroff, John L. 2003. 'Reflections on Liberalism, Policulturalism, and ID-ology: Citizenship and Difference in South Africa', *Social Identities*, vol. 9, no. 4, pp. 445–74.

Comaroff, John L. 1987. 'Of Totemism and Ethnicity: Consciousness, Practice, and the Signs of Inequality', *Ethnos*, no. 52, pp. 301–23.

Comaroff, John L. and Comaroff, Jean. n.d. *Ethnicity, Incorporated*, Book MS.

Conzen, Kathleen N and Gerber, David A. 1992. 'The Invention of Ethnicity: A Perspective from the U.S.A.', *Journal of American Ethnic History*, no. 12, pp. 3–42.

Cook, Susan E. n.d.[a]. 'Caught in the Act: Implications of Communal Land Reform in South Africa', Paper presented at the Annual Meeting of the African Studies Association, New Orleans, November 2004.

Cook, Susan E. n.d.[b]. *Language, Ethnicity, and Nation in the New South Africa*. In preparation.

Dávila, Arlene 2001. *Latinos Inc.: The Marketing and Making of a People* (Berkeley: University of California Press).

Ekeh, Peter P. 1975. 'Colonialism and the Two Publics in Africa: A Theoretical Statement', *Comparative Studies in Society and History*, no. 17, pp. 91–112.

Ekeh, Peter P. 1983. *Colonialism and Social Structure: An Inaugural Lecture* (Ibadan, Nigeria: University of Ibadan Press).

Epstein, AL. 1958. *Politics in an Urban African Community* (Manchester: Manchester University Press).

Evans, Gavin. 2003. '"Extinct" San Reap Rewards' in De Waal, S and Makhanya, M (eds.), *Mail & Guardian Bedside Book 2003* (Johannesburg: Jacana).

Gerth, HH and Mills, C Wright (eds.). 1946. *From Max Weber: Essays in Sociology* (New York: Oxford University Press).

Glazer, Nathan and Moynihan, Daniel P. 1970. *Beyond the Melting Pot: The Negroes, Puerto Ricans, Jews, Italians and Irish of New York City* (Cambridge, MA: MIT Press).

Glazer, Nathan and Moynihan, Daniel P. 1975. *Ethnicity: Theory and Experience* (Cambridge: Harvard University Press).

Gray, Paula. 2003. 'People of the Dew', *Leadership*, August, pp. 10–16.

Halter, Marilyn. 2000. *Shopping for Identity: The Marketing of Ethnicity* (New York: Schocken).

Hobsbawm, Eric J and Ranger, Terence O. 1983. *The Invention of Tradition* (Cambridge: Cambridge University Press).

Isaacson, Rupert. 2002. *Healing Land: A Kalahari Journey* (London: Fourth Estate).

Mitchell, J Clyde. 1956. *The Kalela Dance* (Manchester: Manchester University Press).

Mitchell, J Clyde. 1966. 'Theoretical Orientations in African Urban Studies' in Banton, M (ed.), *The Social Anthropology of Complex Societies* (London: Tavistock).

Moerman, Michael. 1967. 'Being Lue: Uses and Abuses of Ethnic Identification' in Helm, J (ed.), *Essays on the Problem of Tribe* (American Ethnological Society: Proceedings of the Annual Meeting, 1967).

Robins, Steven. 2003. 'Whose Modernity? Indigenous Modernities and Land Claims after Apartheid', *Development and Change*, vol. 34, no. 2, pp. 1–21.

Royal Bafokeng Holdings. 2007. *Royal Bafokeng Holdings Annual Review 2006* (Johannesburg: Royal Bafokeng Holdings).

South African San Institute. 2001–2. *SASI Annual Review*, April 2001–March 2002 (www.san.org.za/sasi/ann_rep_2002.htm).

Wallerstein, Immanuel. 1972. 'Social Conflict in Post-Independence Black Africa: The Concepts of Race and Status Group Reconsidered' in Campbell, E (ed.), *Racial Tensions in National Identity* (Nashville: Vanderbilt University Press).

Weber, Max. 1968. *Economy and Society: An Outline of Interpretive Sociology*, ed. by Roth, G and Wittich, C (New York: Bedminster Press).

Xie, Philip Felfan. 2003. The Bamboo-beating Dance in Hainan, China: Authenticity and Commodification', *Journal of Sustainable Development*, vol. 11, no. 1, pp. 5–16.

FAITH

Jean Comaroff and John L Comaroff

THE SACRED, IT SEEMS, is becoming ever more prominent in profane places. 'Jesus is the answer,' declares a crude sign besides the highway to Sun City, northwest of Johannesburg. Then there was the image of the Virgin Mary that revealed itself to a group of road-workers in Chicago in 2005, which likewise proclaimed the presence of ineffable divinity in the byways of life: the Virgin appeared on an expressway underpass, drawing crowds and disrupting traffic. Despite efforts made to obliterate her, she kept shining through (BBC News 2005). Such things have become ubiquitous in everyday America, nothing being too humble to bear the spirit; hence born-again bumper-stickers, hamburgers wrapped in homilies, Jesus golf balls, Jerusalem diets. And not only in the US. In South Africa, accoutrements of the great traditions – yarmulkas and hijabs, mega churches and street-sweepers in 'Jesus Saves' overalls – erode received distinctions between the sacred and the secular. The paraphernalia of home-grown faith are also abundantly evident. Since 1994, African spirituality is assertively evident in the urban scape: bands of Zionists move more freely to baptismal waters, initiation 'huts' spring up along freeways, sacrificial animals are sold in street markets and slaughtered on suburban lawns. And flyers advertising the services of traditional healers are distributed in shopping malls.

A new religious realism

None of these things is new, but their presence is increasing, and ever less regulated. In South Africa, it is tempting to ascribe these signs to the transition to a postcolonial society. They *do* speak resonantly of local history. Yet they also bear the imprint of global conditions, having parallels with other places that have undergone dramatic regime change (Central Europe, for instance). In fact, in many contexts, the radical embrace of faith has accompanied political-economic liberalisation. Along with the growing commitment to market rationalisation, we are witnessing a strong, apparently contrary strain: a new religious realism – whether it be Pentecostal or Latin, Jewish, Muslim or Hindu – pervading modern life, often where it has long been marginal. US efforts to reverse abortion rights, and insert creationism into school syllabuses, are paralleled by the rise of *Shariah* in many parts of Africa, the Middle East and Asia. In a recent ten-nation survey of Pentecostal and charismatic Christians, the *Pew Forum on Religion and Public Life* found that adherents of such 'renewalist' faiths made up 'at least half the population of Brazil, Guatemala and Kenya, and about one-third that of South Africa and Chile' (Associated Press 2006). These populations, it adds, are prone to bringing their commitments into public debate, with real consequences for government policy. Theologico-politics, a concern of seventeenth-century rationalists like Spinoza, is again a lively reality. Returned, too, is early nineteenth-century Christian political-economy, now infused with the spirit of neoliberal capitalism.

Of course, faith has never been separate from commerce. 'Jesus taught in the temple and the marketplace,' notes evangelical Pastor Rick Warren; nineteenth-century Italian wine merchants sought papal endorsements (Cave 2005); and Victorian Methodist missionaries deployed commodities to propel the Word at home and abroad (Comaroff and Comaroff 1997). Nor are we seeing a simple growth in religious observance: recent US surveys report that the numbers of those who profess no faith are also on the rise (*American Atheist* 2001). We may well be in the midst of a religious revival – Robert Fogel (2000) calls it the Fourth Great Awakening – but 'revitalisations' have recurred repeatedly over the centuries. African Independent Churches, for instance, have a long charismatic history, born of the dynamic interplay of vernacular spirituality and colonial evangelism. Nor is it even that faith has 'gone public' in unprecedented ways, reconfiguring existing ideas of the sacred and the secular with the rise of ever more state-like, religious organisations. For, despite its worldly pretensions, modernity never really *was* disenchanted. The liberal democratic state itself, Schmitt (1985) and Balibar (1991) have insisted, has always been treated as sacral.

But a particular ontology has become dominant in many places: a mode of being-in-the-world that, however varied its content, relies less on post-Enlightenment reason than on revealed truths and absolute imperatives. This ontology rejects basic axioms of liberal humanism, among them (i) that truth, meaning, morality and sovereignty are shaped by human agents or historical conditions; and (ii) that people come to know the world by means of empirically grounded reflection, debate, theory-work. The new absolutism is not limited to born-again Pentecostalists: Benedict XVI has been described as 'a 14th century pope with a 21st century communications network' (Monbiot 2005). Media are key to the message, as we shall see. A deep suspicion of philosophical argument, sociological inference or anthropological relativism is shared by all foundationalists, from political neoconservatives to market fundamentalists. This has had palpable effects on understandings of the sacred, human agency, and the way things happen in the world.

Revelation, for example, has become an explicit basis for action, personal and public. The steady rise of Pentecostalism in Africa, Central Europe and Asia, the large-scale conversion to Evangelicalism in Latin America, and revitalisations within Islam, Hinduism and Judaism have all been marked by a desire to return to fundamentals and, in the face of uncertainty, to re-ground faith in foundational texts. According to the new Pope, 'We are moving towards a dictatorship of relativism, which has as its highest goal one's own ego and one's own desires' (Monbiot 2005). Without absolutism, humankind is on a slippery slope to moral chaos, 'back' to a Hobbesian state of nature.

The turn to absolutism is not concerned merely to reverse the dangerous drift of meaning and value in a world in which 'all things are relative'. It aims, also, to erode some of the foundational features of modernity; among them the distinction between the sacred, the realm of privatised, elective association, and the domain of 'neutral', secular civil society. Revitalised movements strive to unify these spheres, turning all of secular existence into the means of divine purpose. As Ted Haggard, former president of the National Association of Evangelicals, put it: 'God-in-everything, and anything-can-be-holy' (Newton 2006). This is why religious organisations have reclaimed functions of state that many governments have relinquished. To be sure, the recent expansion of faith-based social services has challenged the separation of powers that underlay the ideals, if not always the practices, of most twentieth-century liberal democracies. The life of the spirit extends ever more tangibly beyond the space of the sanctuary, the time of worship and the 'private' sphere, thus to herald a significant reorganisation of modernist social order as a whole.

Organised religion has patently made a place for itself in the world of politics, the market and the secular media. Even more, it takes on their work. This evinces a shift from the division of institutional labour captured in signal modernist accounts, like those of Durkheim (1947) and Weber (1930). It also diverges from the rationalised religiosity of orthodox Protestantism, which treated faiths that blurred the distinction between sacred and secular, church and state, as 'enchanted'– or, as in colonial South Africa, where indigenised Christianity stressed pragmatic healing, inspired leadership and holistic care, as 'syncretic', even as a 'bridge ... back to heathenism' (Sundkler 1961).

Large American mega churches deliberately blur received distinctions, to encompass the diverse domains of secular life, from business and schooling to athletics and day care. They have been called 'surrogate governments' (Mahler 2005). A similar impetus toward Christian holism is evident in many parts of the world, where vibrant

Pentecostal institutions often contrast with eroding organisations of other kinds, be they mainstream churches or labour unions. Take the New Life Church in Mafikeng, South Africa, an offshoot of the organisation of the same name founded in Colorado Springs in 1984. New Life typifies a brand of upbeat, technically savvy faith that aspires to fill the moral void left, allegedly, by the withering of civic norms in the postcolony. The congregation, part of a global network, mixes a lively charismatic realism with frank materiality, a theology comfortable with this worldly desire. It offers a range of services, from marriage guidance to financial counselling, casting pastoral care in a service-oriented key. 'It might sound heretical,' says the pastor, 'but we strive to make worship exciting, affecting. Our competition, after all, is the video arcade, the movie house and the casino.' In New Life's sparkling sanctuary, a sophisticated sound stage replaces the altar. A large screen part karaoke, part PowerPoint flashes the lyrics, monitored by a technician at the rear. Membership spans a wide spectrum of race, age and class, all drawn by the pulsating vitality, the readiness to acknowledge worldly appetites.

While Pentecostalism has developed luxuriantly in the US, it is even more vibrant in the global South, where it resonates with forms of spiritual pragmatism never really captured by Protestant orthodoxy. The 'New Christian Revolution' (Jenkins 2002: 3) is centred in Latin America, Africa and Asia; together, it comprises an escalating majority of the estimated 2.6 billion Christians world-wide. These movements are now major competitors to Catholicism, which is itself becoming more charismatic. Here, too, it is not merely that faith-based initiatives are expanding, assuming a wide array of civic features – especially where state sovereignty has been compromised. At issue, too, is the growing impact of religious revelation on ordinary understandings of self, identity and history.

Mass media are critical components of this process, not just because they amplify the scale, speed and directness of address, but because they have become integral to the way that revelation stages itself. Of course, mass media have been used to spread the Word since the advent of the printing press. Evangelists in Africa and elsewhere were quick to use novel means of communication, from magic lanterns to movies. At the same time, the reach of popular religious broadcasting on the continent today seems unprecedented. Transnational Evangelical and Muslim groups have taken advantage of deregulated state media to build enterprises that impact powerfully on the circulation of images and the creation of subjects and publics. Not only do religious media conduct a growing proportion of business on the continent – from paid religious programming to Pentecostal video-cassettes, gospel CDs, and tapes bearing the *baraka* of sheikhs (Soares 2004). Religious vernaculars are also colonising popular culture. In the huge West African video industry – exemplified by Nigeria's Nollywood – movies range from crime dramas to witchcraft horror. But most tend to project a 'Pentecostalite' worldview in which the surreal meets the supernatural (Meyer 2004). Local ritual is being significantly affected by these electronic genres. In South Africa's rural North West Province, healers offer internet and TV divinations, and Pentecostal preachers urge followers to 'download Jesus' into their lives. In 2005, a Brazilian preacher told his audience of hundreds in the gleaming new Universal Church of the Kingdom of God in central Cape Town: 'When the film credits roll at the end of your life, they will not acknowledge the South African government; they will thank us at the Universal Church.'

This exuberance defies easy explanation. While there seems to be an elective affinity between Pentecostalism and the unruly vitality of neoliberal economics, not all evangelicals extol 'free market faith'. What is more, while pragmatic preaching might have intensified in recent decades, its core features go back a long way: to the 'positive thinking' associated with Christian Science in late-nineteenth-century America, or to the 'name it and claim it' Rhema doctrine, first propounded by Kenneth Hagin of the Assemblies of God in Texas in the 1930s. The Rhema Bible Church in South Africa, founded by the flamboyant Ray McCauley, claims a following of 20,000, counting black elites among its largely white, middle-class congregation. Sometimes, too literal a belief in the practical power of faith turns against the actual workings of market enterprise. This was the case with Miracle 2000, a South African pyramid scheme whose born-again founder promised a 220% return on investments in 42 days. When he was put on trial, hundreds of outraged believers marched on the High Court in Pretoria, demanding the release of their 'Messiah'. Their placards warned: 'Do My Prophet No Harm' (Bokaba 2000).

What then *does* make sense of the exuberant growth of 'new' religiosity in recent times; of its continuities with, and breaks from, the past? There is much to suggest that the character of contemporary faith is indeed integral to the advent of neoliberalism; that the latter is less of an historical rupture with the past than an intensification of some of the core features of industrial capitalism. And this, in turn, has transformed the institutional scaffolding of liberal democracies, and the cultural terms through which it is apprehended and lived. While these shifts vary in their local manifestations, they also display broad similarities that call for explanation. How might the reformed social landscape speak back – with latter-day insight – to Weber's classic conception of the kinship between the Protestant Ethic and the Spirit of Capitalism?

The same again, but not quite: the neo world order
What has come to be glossed as 'neoliberalism' has been characterised in a variety of ways, few of which capture the mix of continuity and rupture, intensification and transformation. At issue it entails an epochal shift in relations among capital, labour, consumption and place. For one thing, the generation of wealth is more reliant than

ever before on abstract means: on the transaction of quasi-monetary instruments across space and time in the electronic economy; on the market in futures; on the extraction of wealth from intellectual property. For another, primary production has been reorganised as the quest for cheap, tractable labour has eroded existing bases of industrial manufacture, has globalised the division of labour, and has significantly liberated corporate enterprise from state regulation. The connection between sites of manufacture and consumption has become increasingly opaque and distanced, undermining the very idea of a national economy, in which interest groups recognise each other as interdependent components of a commonweal.

In the upshot, the spheres of politics and economy do not map easily on one another – as has become apparent to South Africans, struggling to comprehend the meaning of liberation under conditions of liberalisation, when porous borders, privatisation and global financial pressures drastically undermine the workforce and threaten promises of enfranchisement. These experiences disrupt efforts to re-imagine the nation as a unified entity, complicating understandings of belonging, citizenship, attachment. They also erode commonsense assumptions about the relation between signs and meanings, the real and the counterfeit, the sources of misfortune and evil.

It is such forces that structure the terrain on which revitalised religion takes shape. These movements, we stress, are not simple, autonomic responses to 'neoliberalism'. They are also vanguards for a vision which endorses earthly desire and entrepreneurial enterprise. Nor are they uniquely 'global': the Roman Catholic Church has been global for two thousand years. But, over the centuries, the nature of 'globalism' has changed. Whereas the Christian commonwealth forged by colonial evangelists followed the map of a Eurocentric, international order, postcolonial spirituality evinces different translocal trajectories – electronic, economic, emotive – that link newly salient centres and peripheries. Examples here are the south–south ministries of the Universal Church and what is thought to be the largest single congregation in the world, Paul [David] Yonggi Cho's Pentecostal church in Seoul. Old diasporas also take on new life. This is especially evident in the traffic in faith across the black Atlantic, with Nigerian churches flourishing in major American cities, and 'postmodern' African-American evangelists, like TD Jakes, drawing vast audiences in cities like Nairobi (Lee 2005). Startling new sacral economies are apparent. North American and European Catholic churches now send Mass intentions, or requests for prayers to remember the dead, to clergy in Kerala by e-mail. Here they are performed at a fifth of the cost in the West, in a process of devout outsourcing (Rai 2004), providing more evidence that the worldliest of vehicles can be made to serve the divine.

Three dimensions of the relationship between new religious movements and neoliberalism, broadly defined, are especially striking. The first is sociological: the tendency of the fastest-growing faiths to take the form of theocracies, embracing a wide array of once secular activities and regulatory functions in the quest to reclaim the world. The second is ontological: the impetus to counter relativism and the loss of meaning by fixing signs and establishing absolute truths. The third is cultural: transactions with the sacred, particularly in prosperity gospels, often seek, in striking ways, to harness the creativity of market forces. While these features are identifiable in many revitalised faiths across the planet, our main focus here is Pentecostalism in southern Africa, and the link between its particularities and the larger world conditions.

Making us whole again

Across the ages, religious utopianism has repeatedly sought to return to holiness through wholeness (Douglas 1966). The prophetic movements that rallied black South Africans in the wake of colonial conquest are a clear instance of this impetus (Peires 1989); so too the Zionist churches, which have long offered cogent visions and unifying codes of conduct (Comaroff 1985). Contemporary mega movements carry this project into the late modern era. They seek to build Christendom anew by healing breaches deepened by economic and political deregulation, forces that unsettle imagined communities and received perceptions of locality and class. A recent study suggests, for example, that even though they do not reject their national identity, the 'vast majority' of South Africans think of themselves primarily as members of 'an ethnic, cultural, language, religious or some other group', and 'attach their personal fate' to those groups (Gibson 2004: 2; cf. Chidester et al. 2003).

The evangelical organisations that have arisen, resembling ethno-national movements and 'surrogate governments' (Mahler 2005), are all of a piece with these general historical developments. In South Africa, revitalised religious communities – Muslim, Christian, Jewish, nativist – are waxing at the expense of older, mainstream denominations. They are less concerned to pressure government than to create their own forms of sovereignty, countering popular insecurity with their own regimes of order, power, enrichment.

Newly holistic movements, we stress, are part of the neoliberal turn, both *reactively* and *intrinsically*. In their readiness to offer welfare services that states no longer provide, Pentecostals often develop robust organisations for tending the sick and destitute. This is hardly a novel feature of religion. But with the downsizing of government, provision of care has become ever more prominent. Religious networks span continents, sustaining far-flung migrants with intimacy and communion in the absence of other kinds of cultural capital, as did African churches in colonial times (Welbourn and Ogot 1966). Of course, the upsurge in revivalist faith must also be related to widening disparities of wealth, exacerbated by mass unemployment in many places. In South Africa, while Rhema preachers target the would-be wealthy, the Universal Church and its ilk focus on the more marginal – among whom they are gaining ground in relation to the Zionist denominations, which have long tended the excluded.

At issue in much revitalisation is an ontology of how the world works. Mass conversions confirm that evangelical theology and worship fit less and less with secular social and political theory – or with its telos of modernisation and development. As Malaysian Methodist theologian Hwa Yung notes (1995: 2): 'There is even less reason today for non-Western Christians ... to allow their theologies to be domesticated by Enlightenment thinking, something which Western Christians themselves find increasingly dissatisfying.' For many, the impact of metaphysical forces is more palpable in their lives than intangibles like 'society', 'economy', 'history', whose structures of plausibility seem seriously eroded.

A stone we can touch: or, St Paul of Texas

Revitalisation rests as much in problems of meaning as in the effects of structural deprivation. A notable feature of recently reborn faiths is the centrality of revelation. How, if at all, might this be connected to changes in economy, society and the state? In distinguishing *neo*liberalism from the classic liberalism that preceded it, Foucault stressed transformations in the relationship between state and economy (Lemke 2001: 200). Whereas, previously, the former directed and monitored the latter, the neoliberal turn makes 'the market itself the organizing and regulative principle underlying the state'. Enhancing profitability and promoting entrepreneurial citizens have become both the ends and the measure of good statecraft. As in new religious movements, this mode of governance breaks down the separations between moral, economic and political institutions – and to unseat the relative autonomy of these distinct spheres. Neoliberal administrations have eroded rationalities and moralities beyond the market, especially in the US, eliminating the independent bases from which a critique of *laissez-faire* can be mounted. A similar observation has been made of prosperity gospels: 'Is there nothing about our free-market economy', Greg Newton asks, 'that God's Reign questions?' (Newton 2006). In collapsing the distinction between church and world, Pentecostals risk losing the critical tension between faith and context which makes it possible for each to hold the other accountable – as when churchmen in South Africa declared apartheid a heresy, or when the Dutch Reformed Church was accused of distorting Calvinist theology to underpin an ideology of segregation.

Pentecostals tend to be wary of anything coming between God and the market. They support governments that protect the liberty of commerce and religion, rather than social reform and redistribution. While apparently far removed from Weber's Puritans, they share the belief that profit is proof of compliance with divine design.

'I take all I have as a gift from God,' says apocalyptic author the Rev. Tim LaHaye. 'I don't see that God puts any priority on poverty' (Boston 2002). Echoes here of Luther (Weber 1930: 160); and of St Paul's indifference to worldly inequality.

More than one observer has seen the spirit of St Paul in the theologico-political culture of our times. For Badiou (2003), the significance of Paul's 'anti-philosophy' was its rootedness in revelation – the witnessing of a foundational event, an end that is also a beginning – *not* in knowledge of, or argument about, the world. Under these conditions, human agency rests on conviction, a truth that compels by the sheer force of its miraculous ineffability, by the power to act decisively as a vehicle of divine grace.

The certainty of revelation serves to restore original meaning and law. The quest for foundational truth is in tension – in all faiths – with the fact that humans can only know divinity through a glass darkly. But this strain has been heightened in modern times, when the 'retreat of the Gods' forced humans to become their own measure. The existential angst of life in a world without fixed referents has been exacerbated even further in 'postmodern' times, as signs and currencies seem to be in free-fall, as borders appear more labile, and nations have increasing trouble separating their own from invasive aliens. From Russia to Rwanda, people see arcane forces at work: witches, mafiosi, terrorists, what Kenyan Pentecostals call 'Satan the deceiver' (Blunt 2004). In South Africa, an Occult Related Crimes Unit was founded within the Police Service in 1992 by a born-again police investigator, striving to link conviction with convictions, to render satanic crime tractable within the terms of criminal justice (Comaroff and Comaroff 1999). Here, divine intrusion interrupts time, recalibrating distorted signs and meanings on the Ground Zero of truth. The revitalised share with Walter Benjamin (1978) the sense that only messianic intervention can redeem law and language from the perversions of a God-forsaken history.

Privatising the millennium

Millennial visions can take many forms, but in so-called neoPentecostal churches, rebirth into 'original truth' promises to unlock a power that will equip the faithful to achieve this-worldly redemption. These movements promise swift payback to those who embrace Christ, denounce Satan and 'make their faith practical' by 'sacrificing' all they can to the movement. Here the immediacy of magic meets neoliberal enterprise, contrasting markedly with mainstream Protestantism, which has long been ambivalent about worldly appetites. In 'fee-for-service' Taiwanese roadside churches (Weller 2000), as in other denominations of this kind, a choice of ritual services is advertised for passers-by. The Universal Church near the taxi-rank in central Mafikeng announces daily specials, from cures for depression and witchcraft to remedies for unemployment. It has scores of regular members, but much of its business is also with itinerant clients, who are drawn by particular offerings. A collage of advertisements for BMWs and lottery winnings adorns the altar of the Mafikeng church beneath the heading 'Delight Yourself in the Lord and He Will Give You the Desires of Your Heart (Psalms 37: 4).' The walls bear testimonies to the impact of divine intervention on material well-being: 'I have a job and am making down-payments on a Beamer 325. Thanks be to Jesus!' In such congregations, the ideal of patient toil and paradise postponed has been superseded by the promise of more immediate returns on investment. These longings for rapid accumulation of wealth may be mercenary, but they are often also tied to a more complicated longing for empowerment and grace.

For the ability to deliver in the here-and-now, a potent form of space-time compression, is evidence of God's covenant with the faithful – just as riches in the hands of the faithless make tangible Satan's equally global threat. Apocalyptic visions proffer a private millennium, personalised rather than communal rebirth. Eternal questions of suffering, meaning and hope are addressed, here, in an idiom at once old and new. If Wesley's sermons on the precious stewardship of money echoed the labour theory of value, the language of godly enterprise in neoPentecostal liturgy mimics the logic of finance capital.

This quality plays on the millennialism inherent in capitalism, a millennialism that has been enhanced with the rebirth of *laissez-faire* in its fundamentalist form. To the degree that this is a moment of significant social rearrangement, of ideological shift, of revival, it fuses the premodern and the postmodern, possibility and impossibility – precisely the juxtaposition associated with cargo cults and revitalising movements in other times and places. This redemptive promise is found in a range of vernacular versions, appealing across a wide social spectrum: to libertarians impatient with the strictures of an older faith; to those who seek the spirit in spiritless times; to those left out of the promise of prosperity. While the neoliberal turn held out the prospect that everyone would be free to accumulate and speculate, to consume and indulge, the majority remain without visible enrichment. For those who call themselves the 'poors' in post-apartheid South Africa (Desai 2002), the citadels of power and privilege seem as impregnable as ever.

Conclusion

In the *Protestant Ethic*, Max Weber (1930: 175) italicises a passage from John Wesley: '*We must exhort all Christians to gain all they can, and to save all they can; that is, in effect, to grow rich.*' Weber saw the Protestant Ethic as sanctifying the maximising ethos of early industrial society and nurturing its habits. Are we not witnessing a later chapter in the same long story of the kinship between evangelicalism and capitalism, in South Africa as elsewhere?

Yes, and no. The historical relationship of Protestantism to capitalism is more nuanced than Weber allowed. For one thing, his teleological prediction that modernity would be accompanied by a growing secularism proved wrong. Protestantism, not to mention Catholicism and Judaism, contributed substantially to the ideological mix that congealed in industrial capitalism in its various versions in the West. And it was transformed by it in turn: by its new media of exchange, by commodification, and by the liberal political and legal institutions that arose to regulate its modes of production, material and moral. To be sure, the dialectic of religion and economy was never severed. 'Disenchantment' was nowhere the simple byproduct of capitalist modernity. Just as colonial evangelists like David Livingstone saw commerce, Christianity and civilisation as conditions of each other's possibility, just as the Universal Church identifies godly aspiration with consumer desire, so capitalism and conviction have always played out a complicated counterpoint.

But many features of contemporary Pentecostalism, like those of other revitalised faiths, *are* new. This is not to say that they are mere reflections of the workings of the 'free' market. On the contrary, they are reciprocally involved, in intricate ways, with economic forces sharpening in our times: the expanding scale and abstraction of transactions across the globe, the tension between the mobility of capital and the fixities of the nation-state, the growing inequities in wealth and power characteristic of the 'new world order', the erosion of many of the institutional forms of liberal democratic society. The received antinomies of modern bureaucratic states – sacred and profane, public and private, state and society – are being sundered by fresh forms of theodicy; forms essayed by religious authorities who seek to counter the insecurities of the age, and to intervene where humanists – like those in South Africa who have championed truth, reconciliation and human rights – run up against the neoliberal malaise. The Spirit of Revelation is among us once more, ministering to those whose lives seem at odds with secular rationalism, those especially who have seen little yield from promises of postcolonial liberation and development. Its genius is to address the dis-ease, displacement and desire of our times, to make terror, violence, crime and pandemic seem like signs of apocalypse. Humanist critics, both within the religious fold and beyond, would be foolish to underestimate this spirited enterprise.

References

American Atheist. 2001. 'Survey Indicates More Americans "Without Faith"', *American Atheist*, 22 November 2001; www.athiests.org/flas.line/athiest4.htm.

Associated Press. 2006. 'Pentecostal Christians Widening Influence, Says Poll Friday', 6 October 2006; www.foxnews.com/story/0,2933,218230,00.html.

Badiou, Alain. 2003. *Saint Paul: The Foundations of Universalism* (Stanford: Stanford University Press).

BBC News. 2005. '"Virgin Mary" on US Motorway Wall', World edition, 21 April 2005; http://news.bbc.co.uk/2/hi/americas/4468275.stm.

Benjamin, Walter. 1978. 'Critique of Violence' in *Reflections: Essays, Aphorisms, Autobiographical Writings* (New York: Schocken Books).

Blunt, Robert. 2004. 'Satan Is an Imitator: Kenya's Recent Cosmology of Corruption' in Brad Weiss (ed.), *Producing African Futures: Ritual and Reproduction in a Neoliberal Age* (Leiden and Boston: Brill).

Bokaba, Selby. 2000. 'Hero's Welcome for Miracle 2000 Mastermind', *The Star*, 31 July 2000; www.iol.co.za /general/newsprint.php3? art_id=ct20000731204009474M624397.

Boston, Rob. 2002. 'If Best-Selling End-Times Author Tim LaHaye Has His Way, Church-State Separation Will Be ... Left Behind', Americans United for Separation of Church and State; www.au.org/site/News2?page=NewsArticle&id=5601&news_iv_ctrl=0&abbr=cs.

Cave, Damien. 2005. 'How Breweth Java with Jesus', *New York Times*, 23 October 2005, Week in Review, p. 4.

Chidester, D, Dexter, P and James, W (eds.). 2003. *What Holds Us Together: Social Cohesion in South Africa* (Cape Town: HSRC Press).

Comaroff, Jean. 1985. *Body of Power, Spirit of Resistance: The Culture and History of South African People* (Chicago: University of Chicago Press).

Comaroff, Jean and Comaroff, John L. 1999. 'Occult Economies and the Violence of Abstraction: Notes from the South African Postcolony', *American Ethnologist*, vol. 26, no. 3, pp. 279–30.

Comaroff, John L and Comaroff, Jean. 1997. *Of Revelation and Revolution: The Dialectics of Modernity on a South African Frontier*, vol. 2 (Chicago: University of Chicago Press).

Desai, Ashwin. 2002. *We Are the Poors: Community Struggle in Post-Apartheid South Africa* (New York: Monthly Review Press).

Douglas, Mary. 1966. *Purity and Danger: An Analysis of Concepts of Pollution and Taboo* (Washington, DC: Frederick Praeger).

Durkheim, Emil. 1947 [1893]. *The Division of Labor in Society*, transl. by George Simpson (Glencoe, IL: The Free Press).

Fogel, Robert. 2000. *The Fourth Great Awakening and the Future of Egalitarianism* (Chicago: University of Chicago Press).

Gibson, James L. 2004. *Overcoming Apartheid: Can Truth Reconcile a Divided Nation?* (New York: Russell Sage).

Hwa Yung. 1995. 'Critical Issues Facing Theological Education in Asia', *Transformation*, vol. 12, no. 4, pp. 1–6.

Jenkins, Paul. 2002. *The Next Christendom: The Coming of Global Christianity* (Oxford: Oxford University Press).

Lee, Shayne. 2005. *T.D. Jakes: America's New Preacher* (New York: New York University Press).

Lemke, Thomas. 2001. 'The Birth of Bio-Politics: Michel Foucault's Lecture at the Collège de France on Neo-Liberal Governmentality', *Economy and Society*, vol. 30, no. 2, pp. 190–207.

Mahler, Jonathan. 2005. 'The Soul of the New Exburb', *New York Times Magazine*, 27 March 2005, pp. 30–57.

Meyer, Birgit. 2004. '"Praise the Lord": Popular Cinema and Pentecostalite Style in Ghana's New Public Sphere', *American Ethnologist*, vol. 31, no. 1, pp. 92–110.

Monbiot, George. 2005. 'My Heroes Are Driven by God, but I'm Glad My Society Isn't', *The Guardian*, 11 October 2005, p. 31.

Newton, Greg. 2006. 'Free Market Christianity', *Travelers: Theological Conversation for the Journey;* http://travelersjournal.blogspot.com/2006/03/free-market-christianity.html. http://shop1.mailordercentral.com/newlifechurch/prodinfo.asp?number=0785265147.

Peires, Jeff. 1989. *The Dead Will Arise: Nongqawuse and the Great Xhosa Cattle-Killing Movement of 1856–7* (Johannesburg: Ravan Press).

Rai, Saritha. 2004. 'Short on Priests, U.S. Catholics Outsource Prayers to Indian Clergy', 13 June 2004, *NYTimes.com*; https://webmail.uchicago.edu/horde/imp/message.php?Horde =fe3019d7f77d60499f03398c.

Schmitt, Carl. 1985. *Political Theology: Four Chapters on the Concept of Sovereignty*, transl. by George Schwab (Cambridge, MA: The MIT Press).

Soares, Benjamin. 2004. 'Muslim Saints in the Age of Neoliberalism' in Brad Weiss (ed.), *Producing African Futures: Ritual and Reproduction in a Neoliberal Age* (Leiden: Brill).

Sundkler, Bengt GM. 1961. *Bantu Prophets in South Africa* (London: Oxford University Press for the International African Institute).

Weber, Max. 1930. *The Protestant Ethic and the Spirit of Capitalism* (London: Unwin University Books).

Welbourn, Frederick and Ogot, Bethwell. 1966. *A Place to Feel at Home* (London: Oxford University Press).

Weller, Robert P. 2000. 'Religion, Capitalism and the End of the Nation-State in Taiwan' in Jean and John Comaroff (ed.), *Millennial Capitalism and the Culture of Neo-liberalism*. Special edition of *Public Culture*, vol. 12, no. 2, pp. 477–98.

GENDER

Helen Moffett

WHY DOES GENDER MATTER so much? For starters, because it so profoundly determines what sort of lives children will lead as adults. A few years ago, a friend with a small child visited an elite pre-school in Cape Town. The staff gave her a guided tour of the various play areas: the art corner, the exercise corner, and the fantasy corner – where that day, the four-year-olds were playing 'Mommies and Daddies'. The teacher proudly explained, 'Here the Daddies are all in meetings and the Mommies are all on diet.' (My friend withdrew her son's application and fled.)

While the term 'gender' is one of the most critical for navigating life in the twenty-first century, it is also one of the fuzziest. Gender is one of the most complex and most misunderstood terms in use today – and yet our basic survival, as families, as communities, as nations, even as a planet, is absolutely dependent on how we approach gender issues in this century.

Together with race, no other concept is so integral to our private and public lives, to our most intimate moments and our grandest gestures. Yet one of the difficulties with using the term is that it overlaps and is therefore confused with several other important concepts and keywords, including women, feminism and sexuality. These categories are not necessarily all neat subsets of each other – women, for example, are not necessarily feminists, and people interested in gender are not necessarily women.

To demonstrate this complexity, consider these snapshots of the post-apartheid landscape:

1) Click! In 1999, South Africa has the most enviable rate of female political representation in the world. At the same time, it has the worst rates of violence, particularly sexual violence, against women anywhere in the world not at war. Repeat both sets of statistics for 2000, 2001, 2002, 2003, 2004, 2005, 2006, 2007 and counting.

2) Click! In 2001, I attend a dinner party at which a university professor asks me what it is that I do. On hearing that I'm a research fellow at the University of Cape Town's African Gender Institute, he says in alarm, 'Oh Lord, you're not one of these feminists, are you?'

3) Click! In 2006, South Africa celebrates the 50th anniversary of the famous Women's March to the Union Buildings to protest the extension of the hated pass laws to black women. At the festivities, Joyce Mujuru, deputy president of ZANU-PF, who has presided over the brutal repression of women in Zimbabwe, and is notorious for her denunciations of feminism, is an invited and honoured guest of the South African government. Some prominent local gender activists are so disgusted by her presence that they leave the event.

These three random examples demonstrate how any discussion of gender is blurred by apparent contradictions. Snapshot 1 shows that putting women in government isn't a quick fix for gender inequality, let alone gender-based violence. Snapshot 2 demonstrates the common assumption that anyone working in gender studies is a card-carrying feminist (not always true). It also reveals a persistent stereotype of feminists as a dangerous and angry species, touting a rigid and man-hating ideology. And Snapshot 3 proves that a pair of ovaries can be confused with a concern for women's rights, even in the face of glaring evidence to the contrary. Unfortunately, not every female politician is concerned about gender inequity.

Clearly, even very clever people are confused about gender, feminism, sexuality and women, never mind where men fit into the picture. And ordinary folk are bewildered, frightened, hurt, and even endangered by the misconceptions spinning around. I take a brief look at the concepts of feminism, patriarchy, sexuality and identity below before making some comments on how gender constructions are feeding the whirlwind of extreme sexual violence in South Africa.

Gender and sex

First of all, a working definition of gender: *socially constructed rather than biologically determined notions of 'femininity' and 'masculinity'.*

Sex differences are determined by DNA. Along with characteristics such as green eyes or an allergy to strawberries, DNA determines whether an egg that has just been fertilised by a sperm will develop into a male or female foetus. Those with two X chromosomes will develop vaginas, breasts and ovaries; those with a Y chromosome will develop penises and testicles. These and other organs release hormones at puberty that will determine the amount and distribution of muscle tissue on the body, where body hair grows, and the pitch of the voice. Apart from very rare cases, these biological sex differences are clear, easily identifiable, and can be altered only by radical surgical intervention and lifelong hormone therapy.

Gender socialisation is an entirely different ball game. It begins the minute the biological sex of a child is known (several feminist scholars have pointed out that adults do not know what tone and words to use in speaking to a baby or small child until they know its sex), and continues to be deeply and minutely socially constructed hourly and daily for the rest of that child's life. And so baby girls are dressed in pink and boys in blue, girls are given dolls and boys cricket bats or toy guns to play with, young women plan the perfect wedding dress, and young men plan the perfect career. A woman who is successful at work may be described as pushy and aggressive, perhaps even a 'ballbreaker' or a 'bitch', but a man who uses identical tactics is likely to be praised for his dynamic, no-nonsense leadership.

What drives this process of gender socialisation? The complex social, cultural and legal processes that translate biological sex into gender differentiation arise from patriarchal distributions of power. Patriarchal systems are generally based on the premise that reproductive function determines not only personal and social characteristics, but *one's role and therefore one's value as a human being as well.* Crudely, the logic is that their biological sex makes men natural leaders, braver, stronger, more logical, more intelligent, more rational, and *therefore more deserving of the goodies in life.*

Does this mean that men are evil oppressors, their feet planted on the necks of suffering women? It does not. Hierarchical patriarchal social structures that work to keep power in the hands of some members (and out of the hands of others) are the problem; and it is in the interest of any hierarchically organised system to silence or punish anyone who destabilises the system by demanding equality, justice, freedom and transparency. Of course, those whose privilege is threatened are most likely to act against those demanding equality and justice, but it's fairly common for right-minded people to rebel against unjust systems regardless of their colour, caste, creed or gender. Just as some whites battled against apartheid, and some blacks collaborated with it, some men vigorously oppose patriarchy, and some women endorse and enjoy the limited benefits it offers them.

Gender socialisation, as should be clear by now, affects both men and women. Every single human being has a fundamental component of their identity – their masculinity or femininity – constructed for them by exceptionally powerful social, cultural, religious, ethnic and even legal forces. While most will agree that it is not acceptable for these forces to violate human rights (as they do every day in the form of 'honour' killings, the forced burning of widows, dowry murders, the trafficking of women and children, and homophobia-driven hate crimes), what is less clear is the extent to which it is acceptable for these forces to override personal choice. My mother came third in her year when she graduated with a BA degree, and longed to study further; but it was considered 'wasteful' at the time to allow a woman to exercise her mind in postgraduate study. And she was one of the lucky ones – under repressive regimes all around the globe, there are millions of women whose access to even basic education is hampered and, in some cases, forbidden. And what about the boys who want to play with dolls, or the men who would love to stay at home raising their children? In a few liberal societies, such choices may no longer be absolutely forbidden – but almost nowhere are they widely accepted or supported.

Feminism and Black Consciousness

What role does feminism play in helping us to critique patriarchal social structures and to understand how gender operates? Feminist ideologies have been consistently mocked and misunderstood since they first made an appearance in the nineteenth century in North America and Europe. They nevertheless gave us the first substantial theoretical tools for analysing what had largely been considered the normal vagaries or hardships of life or 'a woman's lot'.

In many anglophone African academic institutions, historical outlines of feminism begin with an account of the development of liberal feminism, followed by a canter around the outposts of radical and Marxist feminism, a survey of black feminism, and a nod at the impact of postmodern and postcolonial thought on feminist ideologies, before winding up with an account of African feminisms (now plural). However, my understanding of feminism was forged in a different crucible. In 1984, I read a banned copy of Steve Biko's *I Write What I Like* (1978), and was transfixed by the notion that true liberation began with deep self-knowledge and self-love. Black Consciousness was the first truly flexible ideology I had encountered, with principles that were essential to any group suffering the 'mind-forged manacles' of long-term oppression. It had never before occurred to me that I did not need to strive to succeed in a man's world, on a man's terms. Or to be more accurate, I did not need to meet patriarchal standards for success *because those standards themselves were invalid*.

Instead, I could begin to imagine a dramatically different world – one that did not rest on categories of 'us' and 'them'. For several years, I read radical feminist theory voraciously through the lens of Black Consciousness. The notion of separation or withdrawal from racist and sexist social structures for a time, in order to explore what it meant to be black or female outside a culture that consistently created one as Other, held strong appeal. Not only was Biko's untimely death at the hands of apartheid security police a tragic loss, but as a nascent nation, we are still paying the price for the stifling of the BC movement. Years in the classroom seeing my students struggling to grasp their own worth, striving to meet external criteria for success without interrogating those criteria and their validity, have only increased my conviction that Black Consciousness is a vital way-station for post-apartheid South Africans.

Feminism(s), for me, continue to evolve. I have found the contributions of postcolonial scholars particularly helpful in polishing my tools of feminist analysis. I find theoretical models of power that translate across disciplines handy as a feminist, especially the field of subaltern studies, which investigates the subtle power and agency manifested by those at the margins of class, race, gender, community or caste exclusion. And in terms of creating an alternative world, I am an increasingly engaged eco-feminist. All this is by way of saying that the fundamental premises of feminism – that women are entitled to full human rights everywhere, and that patriarchal social structures need to be deconstructed along with their allied vertical hierarchies of class and race – are political principles that remain responsive to changing contexts.

Sexuality and courtship rituals

So how does sexuality fit into the picture? It forms a sometimes perilous bridge between the concepts of biological sex and gender. Unlike most other mammals, human beings are able to enjoy sex outside the biological reproductive process. Because we experience sexual attraction outside and beyond our reproductive functions, a significant minority of human beings in all cultures have always experienced sexual and romantic attraction for others of the same biological sex.

The rage, terror and revulsion with which this has been regarded in many cultures is known as homophobia, and stems, among other things, from the disruption such 'transgressive' desire and pair-bonding presents to patriarchal systems. For this reason, sexuality is a realm that is frantically constructed, scripted, ritualised and culturally over-determined, at the same time that we are assured that these rituals are, once again, 'natural' or culturally or religiously ordained.

When I took up a fellowship at an American university some years ago, of all the trappings of foreign culture around me, it was the courtship or 'dating' rituals I found most alien. I kept reading signals wrong, sometimes disastrously so, simply because as an outsider I had little understanding of the carefully prescribed scripts and rigid rules involved.

There is nothing romantic about the genesis of 'the Date'. It is a specifically American courtship ritual that evolved during the post-World War Two boom in that country to cater to the burgeoning motor and fast-food industries, all fuelled (literally) by dirt-cheap oil. In a country where cars are inexpensive and teenagers can get driver's licences at 16, heterosocial interactions could be taken out of the home or immediate community environs, and into the mushrooming malls and entertainment centres. And of course, money had to be spent. So what was once a social interaction with the potential to become romantic or sexual became primarily an economic transaction – one that was highly gendered, with alarming levels of risk on both sides. Males did the asking and the fetching and the paying, which meant opening themselves to the risk first of rejection (and even ridicule) and then financial exploitation. But the risks that girls were obliged to assume were far greater; they were suddenly under pressure to reciprocate (through charm, appearance, 'niceness' and sexual favours) for the cash laid out on them at the same time that informal structures of family and community chaperonage were removed.

I continue to tease my American colleagues, inverting the stereotype of Western anthropologists arriving in Africa to observe 'exotic' and 'primitive' behaviours; I point out to them that as an African observing Americans, I find their fundamental courtship ritual, in which two comparative strangers embark on risky, rigidly scripted and potentially humiliating sexual/romantic auditions, nothing less than bizarre. 'You do this willingly? And more than once?' I ask, wide-eyed. Colleagues from the Caribbean agree; for them, 'dates' that involve only twosomes, as well as access to transport and the expenditure of significant amounts of money, are planned within relationships that are already established as 'exclusive', and are generally reserved for special occasions.

One of the sadder changes to the social face of post-apartheid South Africa has been our wholesale and uncritical embrace of North American courtship rituals as a major platform for selling consumer goods. Dating, US-style, is good for the economy, die-hard capitalists might argue; but the impact on gender relations in South Africa has been pernicious. A panoply of branded goods, from clothing and accessories to electronic goods, from food and drink to entertainment, now attaches to the ritual and performance of dating (and sexuality), with expenditure and expectations flowing along strictly gendered lines. This has led to increasingly narrow and rigid constructions of masculinity in particular. Young women and men, but especially the latter, are no longer defined by what they believe or do, but by what they purchase and consume. The increasingly overt gendering and packaging of sexuality that drive this process also present women as objects for consumption. So a 'brother' is respected for the car he drives, the clothes he wears, and the 'yanga-yangas' clinging adoringly to his arm.

Gender and identity

By now it should be clear that the performance of gender (and sexuality) is often a channel that enables access to and performance of other forms of identity, notably race and class. As Judith Butler has pointed out, 'it becomes impossible to separate out "gender" from the political and cultural intersections in which it is invariably produced and maintained' (1990: 3). For many, gender identity is a vital means of establishing and performing their group membership; think, for instance, of the claim 'I am a good Muslim/Jewish/Xhosa woman'. This also works in the other direction – when Mbulelo Goniwe was bustled out of parliament on 'sex pest' charges, much was made of the fact that he allegedly reprimanded a co-worker who had rejected his advances with the words, 'I thought you were a real Xhosa girl.'

Moreover, the worst excesses of patriarchal behaviour are often defended as the vigorous and authentic espousal of a particular identity, whether cultural, religious or ethnic. This was clearly seen in Jacob Zuma's much-vaunted claim to be '100% Zulu-boy' in response to rape charges that revealed him as an unrepentant chauvinist who had acted (at best) with reckless impropriety and irresponsibility. Unbelievably, this slogan had such currency that it was printed on T-shirts and worn by Zuma's supporters. Academic and gender analyst Terri Barnes responded astringently: 'I also think that the verdict and acquittal reinforce a fundamental South African (not ethnic) tradition on social and personal power: a man can do whatever he wants. I think … that's a large part of what the crowds outside court were toyi-toyiing in celebration of' (2006, e-mail communication).

Such cultural camouflage is a common trend, seen around the globe in response to uncomfortable gender practices that are clearly rights abuses, such as female genital cutting. This practice is now 'legally' outlawed in most of the countries in which it is common; but given that most families in these communities will have no truck with marriage negotiations involving a woman who has not experienced such mutilation, legislation banning the practice is almost irrelevant.

Many women would be bereft at the thought of claiming some vague and abstract notion of freedom or equality if it cost them their patriarchally endorsed status in the community as a wife or 'good woman'. Rights cannot replace the wages a husband brings home at the end of the week – and ideology is no substitute for the standing her marital status accords a woman even after her husband deserts her and their children. Still more women identify themselves *primarily* as members of a culture, religion, political party or even a family, rather than as women, not to say oppressed women – which is one of the reasons we saw elderly village women chanting in support of Jacob Zuma at his trial.

Gender and gender-based violence in South Africa

Although middle-class, educated women certainly have more opportunities than they did fifty years ago, gender roles are more inflexible, more publicly performed, and more violently policed than ever before. But what of our post-apartheid landscape?

The bad news – and it is indeed very bad news – is that post-apartheid South Africa remains a country at war with itself. Only this time, it is nothing less than gender civil war. Just one week of glancing at newspaper headlines reveals that sexual violence in particular is out of control, with higher levels of rape of women and children than anywhere else in the globe not at war or embroiled in open civil conflict. Survey after survey produces the same grim findings: at least one in three South African women can expect to be raped in her lifetime; and one in four will be beaten by her domestic partner (see Moffett 2006 for a review of this literature).

Yet narratives about rape continue to be rewritten as stories about race, rather than gender. From the President downwards, everyone assumes that any effort to discuss rape is a short jump to condemning the barbarism of black men. In a society battling to shake off the legacy of institutionalised racism, it still seems a bridge too far to acknowledge that gender is at the heart of this acute social problem. Instead, one hears repeatedly that apartheid and its ills (such as the migrant labour system) 'emasculated' black men, left them 'impotent' and experiencing a 'crisis of masculinity'. Though these remarks are troublingly embedded in unquestioned patriarchal discourses, they contain a grain of truth. But these explanations explicitly exclude white men, thus implying – however unwittingly – that they do not rape.

There can be no doubt, however, that something is terribly wrong, and writer Sindiwe Magona is no longer prepared to let black men off the hook. In her novel *Green Freedom of a Cockatoo* (in press), she has a feisty character harangue the inhabitants of a street in Gugulethu:

Very deliberately, Cordelia focused her attention back on the men.

'By the way,' she said, 'I wish I didn't hate my black brothers. I *wish* I had no reason to hate my black brothers. I *wish* there was a rumour out there, a hint, even a soupçon of a rumour – that by cover of night, white men creep into our black townships and rape our little girls, rape our infant daughters.' Her eyes combed the room. 'But that is NOT what I'm hearing.'

Now she turned to the women, pointedly ignoring the men: 'What I'm hearing, my beloved sisters, what I'm hearing is that fathers are raping their own daughters; stepfathers, their stepdaughters; uncles, their nieces. Neighbour raping neighbour's daughters. And these are black men.

'Our children are at risk – HIGH risk – of rape and often murder. Not from the Special Branch or the *Broederbond* – no! From men these little girls know. Men who should be their protectors – their shield to keep them safe from harm.' [....]

'But not all black men are rapists. *Uyadelela, nje*!' yelled Gabula.

'Not all black men are rapists, you say?' said Cordelia, narrowing her eyes: 'Well, of course not! But enough of them are – so the cap fits!' She glowered at everybody, then delivered her final shot:

'Besides, where is this army of outraged black men out to stop the evil ones? Where?'

These difficult questions cry out for answers. Feminist scholars and local analysts have identified many factors feeding the tendency by South African men of every stripe to attack and ravage women and children within their own communities.

Pumla Dineo Gqala (2006) has noted that by touting equality for women at the same time as refusing to critique patriarchy, the liberation movement made a tactical and ideological error for which South African women are now paying dearly. In my own writing, I have pointed to the inevitable clash between South Africa's heritage of overlapping patriarchies (colonial, apartheid, Calvinist, missionary, traditional African) and the post-democratic, rights-based Constitution (which guarantees political equality for all groups, including women). This clash has widened the split between the public and private spheres, creating a devil's bargain in which women are accepted as equal in the former as long as they remain subordinate in the latter, with sexual violence enforcing this shift from equality in public realms back to submission within domestic and intimate spaces (Moffett 2006).

Our truly terrifying statistics on rape, child abuse and HIV infection in South Africa throw into sharp focus the growing rigidity of men's and women's prescribed gender roles, particularly within marriage and the family. This insistence on clinging to narrowly defined and enforced gender roles during a period of political transition and therefore social instability is perhaps understandable, but it is literally killing us.

The night of Zuma's acquittal on rape charges, the following was posted to the Gender/Women's Studies in Africa listserve, a closed email list that allows activists and scholars focusing on women and gender in Africa to share ideas, materials, findings and news, and to devise both regional and pan-African strategies. It also sees its fair share of extreme pain, as this shows:

> Zuma is NOT GUILTY! I WANT TO SCREAM CRY AND DIE TODAY!
> What voice do I have if the one I have is so weak?!!!!!!!
> Where is justice? Where are women judges? Why [are] such cases not given to a panel of judges?
> Does it mean to be raped once gives a person a right to be raped again and again and again?
> I feel so agitated I feel cold and I am shivering, my stomach is empty! empty! Empty! Who am I? [....]
> I am so angry with myself my own helplessness to protect me and my sisters!
> Do I have power? Where is it? How is it?
> I am cold and shivering!!!!!! Stupid and useless, helpless and wasted!!!!!!!!!
> What logic is logic? Whose logic? What must I wear to be a good woman?
> I am nothing!!!!!

These words, which I have reproduced unedited, were written by a young academic who subsequently gave me permission to use them in my writings on the impact of the Zuma trial. Most practitioners would immediately recognise these as the words of yet another traumatised survivor of violence, most probably sexual or intimate. I cite them here so that readers can see what even just a *climate* of intimate violence does to women. An event such as the Zuma judgment can trigger this kind of acute post-traumatic stress: the shivering, the sense of agitation and emptiness, of helplessness and worthlessness, are textbook symptoms. South Africans who experienced torture during the struggle against apartheid are haunted by similar symptoms; surely we have enough walking wounded in this country already.

In South Africa, some men believe that by resorting to sexual violence, they are participating in a socially approved project to keep women within certain boundaries and categories, as well as a state of continuous but necessary fear. Men who do the work of enforcing this reign of gender terror do not necessarily like what they do, or even want to do it; it makes many of them acutely miserable, or involves a degree of denial or numbing greatly enhanced by alcohol or drugs, which in turn pump up the volume of every kind of violence. Nevertheless, performances of violent and punitive rituals of control over women and their bodies have become standard markers of identity for some young South African men.

Moreover, the complex blend of peer and societal pressures men experience regarding the need to 'police' feminine subversion exists against a backdrop that tells them that rape is a 'safe' crime to commit (and perhaps not a real crime after all);[1] there are unlikely to be legal consequences; and that any shame attached to the act will adhere to the victim, not themselves. In short, many men rape not because they want to or are 'tempted', but *because society tells them they can (and in some cases, should) do so with impunity.*

The escalation of particularly brutal rapes, including the spate of baby rapes in recent years, has nevertheless shamed the nation into asking, 'What is wrong with our men?' This is where I believe that the field of masculinity studies, an offshoot of gender studies, has much to contribute. The study of masculinity involves the scrutiny of the construction of maleness rather than the assumption that maleness is a default and normative standard of humanity. It thus offers hope by investigating how masculinities are taught, learned, performed and unlearned. If I believed that men were biologically and inherently programmed to rape – that, as a variety of patriarchies would have me believe, this is *natural* behaviour for the male of the species – I would emigrate to another planet. Scholars and researchers of masculinity offer other options; while there is no doubt that men are in trouble, they offer diagnosis, aetiology and ultimately (we hope) solutions.

Nevertheless, we cannot address the factors that continue to fuel patriarchal brutality, or join hands with men in combating the scourge of sexual violence, until we have debunked the distracting and dangerous myths arising from our past that continue to hijack the debate on rape. I have already pointed out that many of these focus on race in ways that harden racial barriers, demean black men, silence black women, and let white men off the hook, as well as creating a climate of discomfort and distrust that stifles debate and makes any investigation of the gendered causes of rape seem racially intrusive (Moffett 2002).

Conclusion

Gender directs our most intimate moments. It is present whenever we decide we need to behave, act or perform as a 'man' or a 'woman', with all that is implied at these moments of choice. Gender reminds us that the private is deeply political. Gender is at the heart of the transaction that transpires when, eyes glazed with desire, two naked people are approaching that point of no return – the decision to use a condom or not. Gender is at the heart of the tension that arises when one partner wants to, and the other doesn't. Gender determines whether that condom is used. If the person who loses the condom argument changes their mind and says, 'No! Then we're not having sex!', gender determines whether a rape will then take place. Finally, it is gender that will determine whether someone gets infected with HIV that night. So it is no exaggeration to say that gender is a matter of life and death.

But gender, and how we perform it and draw identity from it, can and should be a source of deep satisfaction and pleasure. It is critical that gender categories remain fluid and flexible, as should our attitudes to gender and sexuality. If we return to the story at the beginning of this piece, it should be clear that the aim of gender analysis is not to create a world in which little girls aspire to be in meetings and little boys on diets. Rather, to return to the vision of Steve Biko and others like him, we need to envisage different ways of being in the world, to reject the insanity of societies where options are divided up and then assigned to different genders or races. Rather we should aspire to flexibility and possibility, and deep recognition that the work of deconstructing any hierarchical system of privilege is lifelong, and not only utterly necessary, but deeply rewarding.

Endnote

1 In Lloyd Vogelman's study (1990) of South African rapists who had evaded the criminal justice system (and who thus had no legal fear of admitting to or even boasting about their crimes), some of them expressed indignation that an act as normative as rape should be criminalised.

References

Biko, Steve. 1978. *I Write What I Like*, ed. A Stubbs (New York: Harper).

Butler, Judith. 1990. *Gender Trouble: Feminism and the Subversion of Identity* (New York: Routledge).

Gqala, Pumla Dineo. 2006. Ruth First Memorial Lecture, University of the Witwatersrand, Johannesburg, November 2006.

Magona, Sindiwe. In press. *Green Freedom of a Cockatoo.*

Moffett, Helen. 2002. 'Entering the Labyrinth: Coming to Grips with Gender Warzones, Using South Africa as a Case Study' in *Partners in Change: Working with Men to End Gender-Based Violence* (Santo Domingo: United Nations INSTRAW).

Moffett, Helen. 2006. '"These Women, They Force Us to Rape Them": Race, Rape and Citizenship in Post-apartheid South Africa', *Journal of Southern African Studies*, vol. 31, no. 3.

South African Women's Health Project. 1996. *The South African Women's Health Book* (Cape Town: Oxford University Press).

Vogelman, Lloyd. 1990. *The Sexual Face of Violence* (Johannesburg: Ravan).

HERITAGE

Nick Shepherd

RECENTLY ON DISPLAY at the cash desk of Exclusive Books, the local upmarket booksellers, was a slim book with the title *South African Heritage: A Guide to Our Land, Our People, History and Culture* (Mitchley 2005). On the cover are photographs of Nelson Mandela, Thabo Mbeki, FW de Klerk, a traditional healer, two women dressed in beads and embroidered cloths, a protea flower and a San rock painting. The contents of the book are divided into five parts: a section on 'Our Nine Provinces', a section on 'Our People and Our Eleven Official Languages', a biography of Nelson Mandela, a section headed 'Our Earliest Origins Revealed' (with subsections on 'The Karoo Rocks', 'The Last 100,000 Years', 'Sterkfontein Caves' and 'The Kingdom of Mapungubwe'), and a short chronological history of South Africa. This begins in 28,000 BC, the surmised date of the oldest San rock painting in southern Africa, and ends in 2004, with the entry 'South Africa wins bid to host 2010 Soccer World Cup'.

Perhaps the most interesting part of the book from a conceptual and discursive point of view is the second part dealing with 'Our People and Our Eleven Official Languages'. Here we might expect to meet the cast of 'the Rainbow Nation', a favourite phrase in the book. There are sections on each of South Africa's official languages ('IsiXhosa', 'IsiZulu', 'Afrikaans', 'English' and so on), as well as sections on 'The Coloured People', 'Asians' and 'The San'. One is aware of being confronted with a phenomenon which manifests itself, in part, through acts of classification and categorisation. What is the nature of the category 'heritage' which holds together in a single frame Nelson Mandela, the Karoo Rocks, a King Protea, San rock paintings and a classification of persons loosely derived from an apartheid schema? And what can it tell us about the nature of post-apartheid society or, more concretely, about the forms of public culture and historical imagination that inform a putative 'new South Africanness'?

Defining heritage

Providing an adequate definition of the notion of heritage (literally 'that which is inherited') turns out to be no easy matter. Heritage occupies a paradoxical, perhaps even a uniquely paradoxical, conceptual space. At the same time, its paradoxical nature provides a key to understanding its social effects. The notion of heritage offers a language through which to discuss contested issues of culture, identity and citizenship in the postcolony, even as it determines and delimits this discussion in particular ways. The oddness of the list of contents of the little book, its 'official' nature, and its mix of the aspirational and the mundane ('Nelson Mandela', 'The Karoo Rocks') alert us to one of the paradoxical aspects of the notion of heritage: while it exists fundamentally as a corporate entity, as a set of values and objects held in common, it is always experienced from an individual standpoint. The notion of heritage hovers uneasily in the space between the individual consciousness and the collective, between the idiosyncratic and what is held in common.

In fact, the notion of heritage has posed particular challenges, both within the academy and in everyday life, where it is used in several different and only partially compatible senses. To talk about heritage involves, first of all, finding which language of heritage is in play, the different densities and hardnesses attributed to the notion of heritage. Do we mean treasures, monuments and gems of cultural lore to be recovered, saved, handed down to future generations? Or is a more playful, less reverential sense of the term in play, the approach of heritage theme parks and township tours, heritage as understood by the GrandWest Casino and Cape Town's V&A Waterfront? Or are the latter not *true* heritage? Do we reserve the term for the weighty, the consequential, the culturally rooted?

I have already suggested that the notion of heritage hovers uneasily between individual and collective conceptions of history. It also sits uneasily between past and present. Heritage is *of* the past *in* the present, but the exact nature of this relationship seems unclear. Is it a surfacing or imaging of the past in the present? Or is it more in the nature of a projection, from the standpoint of the present, of an idealised past? In addition to this indeterminacy around past and present, the notion of heritage is also divided between the material and the intangible. In one familiar aspect, it refers to buildings, monuments, landscapes and artefacts; but it can also refer to values and ideas held in common, bodies of memory, even personality traits. The National Heritage Resources Act specifically refers to a category of 'living heritage', which includes such phenomena as cultural tradition, oral history, performance, ritual, popular memory and 'indigenous knowledge systems'.

Conceptually speaking, heritage appears as a point of both identity and difference. For example, the preamble to the National Heritage Resources Act claims extraordinary powers for the notion of heritage: '[Our heritage] helps us to define our cultural identity and therefore lies at the heart of our spiritual well-being and has the power to build our nation. It has the potential to affirm our diverse cultures ... it contributes to redressing past inequalities. It educates, it deepens our understanding of society ... It facilitates healing and material and symbolic restitution.' We recognise echoes of the anti-colonial discourse of, for example, Biko and Fanon ('the restoration of an African past restores us to our full humanity'), and the archaeological discourse of the Truth and Reconciliation Commission ('uncovering the truth of the past sets us free'). Once again we encounter the double nature of the notion of heritage, its potential to bring about a kind of benign social magic and the perception of danger, its dual valencies of inclusivity and exclusivity, the tension, which lies at its heart, between the forces of memory and forgetting.

In practical and managerial terms, the notion of heritage appears equally paradoxical. In the self-mythology of heritage, it arises from 'below', spontaneous and decentralised. In practice, it more often comes from 'above', through official projects of memorialisation and celebration. The claim to be available and accessible to all is fundamental to the nature of heritage in post-apartheid South Africa. In fact, it tends to be managed and controlled by highly bureaucratised and, I would add, largely unaccountable structures and agencies.

For example, the accidental discovery in 2003 of an early colonial burial ground near Prestwich Street, Cape Town, became the occasion for a passionately fought campaign that set archaeologists, professional heritage managers and pro-development city officials against a group of clerics, social activists and academics from the historically black University of the Western Cape. Drawing on tactics from the anti-apartheid struggles of the late 1980s, and mobilising the symbolic space of St George's Cathedral, the Hands Off Prestwich Street campaign sought to bring about a more sympathetic and inclusive discussion around the fate and disposition of the dead (Murray et al. 2007; Shepherd 2007).

King Proteas, Nelson Mandela, GrandWest Casino, a disturbed resting place of the urban poor, the aspirational language of the National Heritage Resources Act; in each of my examples, past and present intertwine in interesting ways. Rather than being perplexing, and distracting from its core nature, we recognise this simultaneity of past and present, of deeply felt emotion and strategic calculation, of high and low, of lightness and moral seriousness, as being part and parcel of the notion of heritage, its very stuff and the key to its social operation.

Managing heritage

There is close to a century of heritage legislation in South Africa, the terms and nature of which act as a barometer of South African social and political history. One of the earliest pieces of legislation was the Bushman Relics Protection Act of 1911, passed shortly after the Act of Union. It protected rock paintings and petroglyphs, as well as the anthropological contents of graves, caves, rock shelters, middens and shell mounds. A subtext to the Act, as historians Martin Legassick and Ciraj Rassool (1999) have pointed out, was an attempt to halt the trafficking of human remains identified as Bushman. Local institutions and museums in Europe were eager to acquire type specimens of what, in terms of the racist discourse of the day, was understood to be a primitive form of humanity.

The National and Historical Monuments Act of 1923 extended legislative protection to monuments and built structures, as well as to 'areas of land having distinctive or beautiful scenery, areas with a distinctive, beautiful or interesting content of flora and fauna, and objects (whether natural or constructed by human agency) of aesthetic, historical or scientific value ... [including] waterfalls, caves, Bushman paintings, avenues of trees and old buildings'. It also established the first statutory body responsible for heritage management, the Commission for the Preservation of Natural and Historical Monuments of the Union, or the Historical Monuments Commission as it became known. The Commission was made responsible for compiling a register of the monuments of the Union of South Africa, and could pass by-laws to protect them. It became involved in the repair and restoration of a number of historical buildings and sites, including the Groot Constantia homestead in Cape Town (which was damaged by fire in 1925), the first house built in Grahamstown, and the Old Raadsaal in Bloemfontein.

Eleven years later, the Historical Monuments Commission was given increased powers in terms of the Natural and Historical Monuments, Relics and Antiquities Act of 1934. The same year saw the founding of the Bureau of Archaeology, under the directorship of Peter van Riet Lowe, a civil engineer turned archaeologist. The director of the Bureau also served as secretary to the Commission, an arrangement which gave archaeologists a particular prominence in the conceptualisation and management of heritage. In the period between the passing of the Bushman Relics Act and the late 1940s, conceptions of heritage in South Africa and arrangements around heritage management operated in particular ways, connected to settler histories, British Empire and the role of the sciences (Shepherd 2002, 2003).

A number of archaeological discoveries in the 1920s, including Raymond Dart's naming of the *Australopithecus africanus* fossil in 1924, combined with the role played by General (later Prime Minister) Jan Smuts as a promoter of archaeological endeavour in the Union to give the discipline of archaeology a particular prominence as a science. In a process that Saul Dubow (1996) has described as the 'South Africanisation' of the sciences, this took the form of a localisation of archaeological terminology, and the writing of the story of archaeological discovery and uniqueness into the emergent script of national settler identity. In the incipient globalism of Empire, this was understood to connect South Africa in particular ways to developments elsewhere on the continent (to archaeological discoveries in East Africa, for example), as well as to position it in particular ways in relation to the metropole.

In a related set of developments in botany, the naming of the Cape floral kingdom and the development of the National Botanical Gardens at Kirstenbosch were understood to stake a claim for the significance of this branch of the sciences, as well as to establish its uniqueness in relation to the parent discipline in the metropole (Van Sittert 2003). Both archaeology and botany, in turn, played a central role in a conception of heritage as being bound to notions of scientific progress, as having an instructional role, as being tied to national institutions, and as being linked to the aspirations of the emergent settler state in the context of the British Empire.

Two events combined to transform this conception of heritage in South Africa. The first was the whites-only election of 1948 that DF Malan's National Party won on an apartheid platform. The second was the death of Smuts in 1950. Increasingly, through the coming decades, conceptions of heritage in South Africa came to be framed in terms of a more narrowly conceived white Afrikaner cultural history (Shepherd 2002, 2003). Events in the 1930s established the background for these developments, in particular the re-enactments of the Great Trek in 1938 that culminated in the laying of the foundation stone of the Voortrekker Monument (Moodie 1975; Thompson 1985). One of the first major public events of this transformed conception of heritage was the Van Riebeeck Tercentenary Celebrations of 1952, a set of events which elevated Jan and Maria van Riebeeck to the pantheon of Afrikaner folk heroes (Witz 2003).

Notions of landscape are closely tied to conceptions of heritage. In the earlier period, notions of heritage were linked to the imagined geography of the new national space constituted by the Act of Union, now also conceptualised as a field of scientific endeavour. In the later period, this switched to the sacred landscapes of Afrikaner political mythology, whose routes were marked by the passage of the ox-wagons and the course of Trekker history.

Rapid economic growth throughout the 1960s combined with increased political repression to create a climate in which heritage became subsumed as part of the cultural apparatus of the modernising apartheid state (Hall 1984, 1990; Shepherd 2003). The increased pace of construction and economic development had its corollary in a growing public awareness by white South Africans of issues of heritage conservation and saw the establishment of several influential conservation organisations including the Simon van der Stel Foundation, the Vernacular Architecture Society of South Africa, and the Historical Homes of South Africa Limited. Partly as a result of the efforts of these organisations, new legislation in the form of the National Monuments Act was promulgated and adopted in 1969. Under the Act, the Historical Monuments Commission was replaced by a statutory body, the National Monuments Council, which now fell under the Minister of National Education. The Act formalised a transition that had been under way for some time: the switch to a predominantly architectural notion of heritage focused on the built environment. Successive conceptions of heritage in South Africa had thus seen it pass from the domain of archaeologists and prehistorians, to the domain of Afrikaner folk historians, and thence to the domain of architects and town planners.

The late 1960s and early 1970s were also a period of forced removals and the destruction of inner-city precincts like District Six, so that notions of urban conservation operated within a highly selective purview (Jeppie and Soudien 1990). On the one hand, this consisted of a nostalgic reading of settler history and the material record of its various events and institutions – conquest, racial slavery, border wars, and wars of dispossession – and on the other hand by a pragmatic assessment of the desirability of apartheid rule. At the same time, a characteristic feature of heritage management in the late-apartheid period was its resistance to African nationalist currents, perhaps most articulately realised in the Black Consciousness Movement. This saw the exacerbation of a profound disconnection between popular or mass notions of heritage and official or state-sanctioned notions of heritage reproduced in various heritage institutions.

Two developments served to transform this conception of heritage and to give shape to the characteristic landscape of heritage management of the present moment. The first was the adoption of heritage management discourse from predominantly North American sources in the late 1980s. The second was a formal transformation process that began after the demise of apartheid. In short order, this saw the formation and report of the Arts and Culture Task Group (ACTAG), the formulation of a White Paper on Arts, Culture and Heritage, and the adoption of the two main current pieces of heritage legislation, the National Heritage Resources Act (NHRA) of 1999 and the National Heritage Council Act of 1999. In terms of the NHRA, a new structure, the South African Heritage Resources Agency (SAHRA), replaced the National Monuments Council, and significant aspects of heritage management were devolved to regional structures. The Act places an emphasis on public participation in heritage management, with heritage conceptualised as part of a broader process of socio-economic development.

More generally, heritage has been reconceptualised around notions of redress, and the explicit recognition of previously marginalised narratives and categories of heritage (like intangible and living heritage). Aspects of this programme include an ongoing public process of renaming of sites, towns, cities, streets and public amenities, and the introduction of a series of Legacy Projects. These include the Chief Albert Luthuli Legacy Project, the Samora Machel Project, the Nelson Mandela Museum, the Constitution Hill Project, and the Khoisan Project. At the same time, a decision was made not to expunge the memorials of Afrikaner nationalist history, but rather to retain them as a record of apartheid, and to set them in dialogue with newer, more critically inclusive sites, memorials and histories. Perhaps the most powerful realisation of this approach has been the Freedom Park Project on Salvokop outside Pretoria, opposite the largely unreconstructed Voortrekker Monument.

Critiques of heritage management discourse have focused on its tendency towards managerialism, and on its narrow, rigid and technicist definitions of heritage value and notions of public consultation and participation (Shepherd 2007). Rather than opening up the field of heritage management to the kind of radically inclusive and broadly accountable approaches suggested by liberationist discourses and contemporary groups like the Hands Off Prestwich Street Committee, the effect of current heritage management discourse has been to contain and manage such energies. In this sense, the advent of this discourse at the moment of political transition in South Africa is no accident but is part of a broader process of managing the process of political transition itself, and setting what the anthropologist Steven Robins (2006) has described as the 'limits of liberation'. At the same time, some of the most interesting developments have taken place around more *ad hoc* forums and citizens' groups concerned to develop more radically accountable forms of public heritage discourse framed around notions of public memory and historical redress. A leading example of such an approach is that of the District Six Foundation, the parent body of a community social history museum that works with 'the experiences of forced removal and with memory and cultural expression as resources for solidarity and restitution' (Rassool 2006).

Heritage in the academy

What have been the dominant modes of theorising or thinking about the notion of heritage? In the first place there is the familiar conception of heritage as fixed and culturally rooted, denoting deep archives of memory and practice. In this conception, heritage involves essential or core identities and modes of being, requiring preservation and commemoration. Its enemies are not only the habits of forgetting and the erosions of time, but also social processes of homogenisation and hybridisation, and the disruptions involved with migration and the breaking of ties to territory. This notion of heritage is connected to nationalist projects, as well as to other essentialised forms of identification like some ethnic and religious identities. Heritage appears as nostalgia of a particular sort, a desire not for the familiar landscapes of home, but for a former greatness, for an imagined secure identity in the past, for a lost self. Contemporary conceptions of so-called Indigenous Knowledge Systems (IKS) display some of this conception of heritage in so far as they refer to an idea of knowledge as rooted, local and timeless.

At the same time, a marked feature of academic conceptions of heritage has been the reaction against such a notion of heritage in the past two decades. In contrast to a conception of heritage as stable and culturally rooted, recent academic approaches have been concerned to show its constructed, changeable and contingent nature. In this conception, heritage is always in motion (rather than fixed), tied to the present (rather than to an imagined past), and coursed through by the currents of commercial exploitation and popular culture (rather than belonging to high culture). If heritage is the place where a sense of the past meets the present, then what emerges is tacky and tawdry, history as kitsch and cliché. Heritage becomes a merely sentimental attachment to the past, without the rigour and steel that come from comprehending history in its full complexity, or facing up to the horrors of the past. What about subaltern histories? Women's histories? Histories of work and labour? The engaged academic historian might find herself putting up information boards at Cape Town's Waterfront describing the working conditions of black dockworkers, or the struggle for rights in Cape Town's fishing industry, a salutary douche of cold water for the holidaymakers licking their ice-creams (Worden 1996, 1997).

An early statement of this disenchanted view of heritage was Roger Hewison's *The Heritage Industry* (1987). A further line of approach has focused on cultural and heritage tourism as contemporary growth industries, beginning with Nelson Graburn's formative work on the anthropology of tourism (1983), and continuing in the work of Edward Bruner and Barbara Kirschenblatt-Gimblett (2005). In a South African context Leslie Witz, Martin Hall, Gary Minkley, Ciraj Rassool and others have written about heritage tourism in the context of globalisation, (hyper-) modernity and the construction of post-apartheid national identities (Hall and Bombardella 2005; Rassool and Witz 1993, 1996; Witz 2006; Witz et al. 2000).

Heritage in the postcolony

As an opening move in setting forth a conception of heritage in the postcolony, I want to suggest that a lived relation to heritage lies between the two poles outlined above. In the notion of heritage, we recognise the rootedness *and* constructedness of identities, cultural ties which feel deep but which are open to transformation. The paradoxical conceptual space occupied by the notion of heritage turns out to be just that, only apparently contradictory. The relation between the binaries which mark out the notion of heritage is more a case of both-and rather than either-or. Heritage appears as a concept in two keys, as a simultaneity of deep cultural values and playfulness, irony and profundity.

A further observation concerns the salience and ubiquity of the language of heritage in post-apartheid society (Rassool 2000). From President Mbeki's speeches, peppered with references to a deep history of indigenous cultural achievement at sites like Mapungubwe and Timbuktu, to the opening of the Origins Centre at the University of the Witwatersrand which brings together as heritage the disciplinary histories of palaeontology and rock art research with the current Genographic Project,[1] to discussions around the role of traditional leaders and traditional practices in public life, to initiatives around institutional transformation in South African universities, the language of heritage provides a vehicle for addressing complex issues of culture and identity, as well as more difficult and troubling questions of origins and authenticity.

In fact, I want to suggest that heritage discourse operates as one of the principal sites – perhaps *the* principal site – for negotiating issues of culture, identity and citizenship in the postcolony. This position goes well beyond the notion that heritage authorises a 'narrative of the nation', or that it addresses certain cultural nationalisms, in that it sees questions of heritage as standing at the point of negotiation of key social rights and entitlements.

The work of Jean and John Comaroff (2006) provides one context for understanding this position. In an important argument, they note that Mahmood Mamdani's (1996) characterisation of the bifurcated colonial state might equally be taken to characterise notions of citizenship in the postcolonial state, which itself becomes bifurcated between two parallel and only partially compatible modes. On the one hand, persons appear as citizens of the modern, secular state, in which their status is defined by rights and entitlements framed as individual rights and guaranteed by the apparatus of the courts and the constitution. On the other hand, the majority of such citizens simultaneously appear as subjects of what the Comaroffs term the 'Kingdom of Tradition', where their existence is defined by cultural rights and obligations. Furthermore, there are multiple instances in which the assertion of rights is incompatible across these two spheres, as, for example, in practices of patriarchy cast as cultural practices of male ascendancy.

I want to suggest that in quite specific ways, heritage discourse becomes a way of mediating and nuancing these alternative modes of citizenship in the postcolony. The very ambiguity of the notion of heritage, its ability to hold together in the same frame an apparently contradictory set of contents, allows it to be pressed into service to address (or to appear to address) a real contradiction: secular citizenship versus the claims of entrenched cultural identities. One way of reading the new South African heritage legislation is as a strategic mobilisation of rights discourse in the context of issues of cultural property and cultural practices. The result is a series of heroic-sounding formulations which do little to address the real conflicts that emerge. Culturally speaking, heritage provides a way of 'speaking culturally' in a context in which histories, identities and bodies of experience are fractured, ambivalent, in competition.

This strategic use of heritage discourse is not confined to the postcolony. In a justly celebrated essay, Arjun Appadurai (1993) notes that national states resort to the language of heritage in an attempt to resolve the disjunctures of the global cultural economy. Indeed, one of the ironies of the global postmodern has been the increasing salience and ubiquity of the language of heritage more generally, whether through the opening of new museums and heritage routes, emergent practices of heritage tourism, or the popular use of genomic techniques to trace genealogies and individual histories.

This presents us with a final and powerful paradox: an apparently embedded concern with origins, rootedness, tradition and authenticity which, as it were, shadows the global postmodern. How are we to make sense of this apparently contradictory phenomenon? As with so much connected with the notion of heritage, I want to suggest that this is only apparently contradictory. The contemporary interest in heritage may be less a concern with the 'really real', than with the spectacle of authenticity. There is a sense in which the tourists taking part in an earnestly presented heritage trail, and the boatloads of visitors to Robben Island, are aware of the constructedness of the experience, its elisions and blind spots, even as they enjoy the frisson of authenticity, the kind of doubleness which comes from taking part in a staged performance which is haunted by the 'really real'. Heritage, a notion that begins by suggesting the kinds of essential qualities that we associate with the thought of modernity, turns out to be in some ways a quintessentially postmodern concept.

The 'heritage effect'

In fact, rather than thinking of heritage as a set of objects, it may be more useful to think of it as a set of effects. In an important essay, Barbara Kirschenblatt-Gimblett describes what she calls the 'museum effect', i.e. the manner in which 'ordinary things become special when placed in museum settings' (1991: 410). In the museum, the particular staging of the object, the use of light, the display cases and pedestals work together in 'rendering the quotidian spectacular' (413). In a similar fashion, what we might call the 'heritage effect' lies in edging us towards essentialised notions of culture and identity. Heritage weighs down on the side of its own reification. It places notions of culture and identity beyond critique, associating them with the sacred, the ineffable, the given. Heritage just *is*, self-evident, entire, enclosed within its own logic.

This extends to its ability to absorb new contents, to make them appear fixed, culturally rooted, to bathe them in the light of historicity. Here we are in the territory of the invented tradition, the simulacrum, of staged authenticity. Culturally speaking, this makes the notion of heritage a source of great interest. It joins a small number of other concepts – ideas about race, gender and the nation, for example – through which society and the individual subject make themselves. The notion of heritage is a site of active cultural construction – fabricating present pasts, finding accommodation between different factional interests and competing conceptions of culture and identity – even as it sweeps aside the traces of such labour, adds its own particular hush.

It is this, finally, that makes it a source of interest and potential in the postcolony. Not as a guide to a fossilised past, but as a sphere of practice in public life which presents a rich set of opportunities for confirming and contesting settled identities, and versions of the self and the nation (Shepherd 2005). As such, heritage refers us to a tangled web of present dreams and aspirations, as much as to the detail of past events and bodies of memory. The paradoxical nature of the notion of heritage, its mixture of the sacred and the profane, its quality of being fixed and on the move, opens up a critical space in the public sphere in which to imagine new modes of being, new forms of identity, new conjunctions of place and person. For all its mystifications, what the preamble to the National Heritage Resources Act recognises is that it is here that the nation remakes itself, that the new ceremonies of inclusion and exclusion are invented and enacted, that the sins of the past are symbolically expiated. How do we turn the burden into a birthright? How do we harness the energies of the heritage effect towards affirming ends? Can we imagine new modes of the self that include the possibility of being invested simultaneously in tradition and modernity, of having roots and wings, a homeboy at home in the world? And what kinds of freedoms would this require?

Endnote

1 A collaborative research project between *National Geographic* Magazine and the IBM Corporation which aims to collect 100,000 DNA samples from what it terms indigenous peoples around the world, to 'help people better understand their ancient history'. It is being opposed by the Indigenous Peoples Council on Biocolonialism, among other organisations.

References

Appadurai, A. 1993. 'Disjunction and Difference in the Global Cultural Economy' in During, S (ed.), *The Cultural Studies Reader* (London: Routledge).

Bruner, EM and Kirschenblatt-Gimblett, B. 2005. *Culture on Tour: Ethnographies of Travel* (Chicago: University of Chicago Press).

Comaroff, J and Comaroff, JL. 2006. 'Reflections on Liberalism, Policulturalism and ID-ology: Citizenship and Difference in South Africa' in Robins, S (ed.), *Limits to Liberation after Apartheid; Citizenship, Governance and Culture* (Oxford: James Currey), pp. 33–56.

Dubow, S. 1996. 'Human Origins, Race Typology and the Other Raymond Dart', *African Studies*, no. 55, pp. 1–30.

Graburn, NHH. 1983. 'The Anthropology of Tourism', *Annals of Tourism Research*, no. 10, pp. 1–11.

Hall, M. 1984. 'The Burden of Tribalism: The Social Context of Southern African Iron Age Studies', *American Antiquity*, no. 49, pp. 455–67.

Hall, M. 1990. '"Hidden History": Iron Age Archaeology in Southern Africa' in Robertshaw, P (ed.), *A History of African Archaeology* (London: James Currey).

Hall, M and Bombardella, P. 2005. 'Las Vegas in Africa', *Journal of Social Archaeology*, vol. 5, no. 1, pp. 5–25.

Hewison, R. 1987. *The Heritage Industry* (London: Methuen).

Jeppie, MS and Soudien, C. 1990. *The Struggle for District Six: Past and Present* (Cape Town: Buchu Books).

Kirschenblatt-Gimblett, B. 1991. 'Objects of Ethnography', in Karp, I and Lavine, SD (eds.), *The Poetics and Politics of Museum Display* (Washington, DC: Smithsonian Institute), pp. 386–443.

Legassick, M and Rassool, C. 1999. *Skeletons in the Cupboard: Museums and the Incipient Trade in Human Remains, 1907–1917* (Bellville, Cape Town: University of the Western Cape).

Mamdani, M. 1996. *Citizen and Subject: Contemporary Africa and the Legacy of Late Colonialism* (Cape Town: David Philip).

Mitchley, C. 2005. *South African Heritage* (Cape Town: Mill Street Publications).

Moodie, TD. 1975. *The Rise of Afrikanerdom: Power, Apartheid, and the Afrikaner Civil Religion* (Berkeley: University of California Press).

Murray, N, Shepherd, N and Hall, M. 2007. *Desire Lines: Space, Memory and Identity in the Post-apartheid City* (Oxford: Routledge).

Rassool, C. 2000. 'The Rise of Heritage and Reconstruction of History in South Africa', *Kronos*, no. 26, pp. 1–21.

Rassool, C. 2006. 'Community Museums, Memory Politics and Social Transformation: Histories, Possibilities and Limits' in Karp, I, Kratz, C, Szwaja, L and Ybarra-Frautso, T (eds.), *Museum Frictions: Public Cultures/Global Transformations* (Durham, NC: Duke University Press), pp. 286–321.

Rassool, C and Witz, L. 1993. 'The 1952 Jan van Riebeeck Tercentenary Festival: Constructing and Contesting Public National History in South Africa', *Journal of African History*, no. 34, pp. 447–68.

Rassool, C and Witz, L. 1996. 'South Africa: A World in One Country: Moments in International Tourist Encounters with Wildlife, the Primitive and the Modern', *Cahiers d'Etudes Africaines*, no. 143, pp. 335–71.

Robins, S (ed.). 2006. *Limits to Liberation after Apartheid: Citizenship, Governance and Culture* (Oxford: James Currey).

Shepherd, N. 2002. 'Disciplining Archaeology: The Invention of South African Prehistory, 1923–1953', *Kronos*, vol. 28, pp. 127–45.

Shepherd, N. 2003. 'State of the Discipline: Science, Culture and Identity in South African Archaeology', *Journal of Southern African Studies*, no. 29, pp. 823–44.

Shepherd, N. 2005. 'Roots and Wings: Heritage Studies in the Humanities' in Marcus, T and Hofmanner, A (eds.), *Shifting Boundaries of Knowledge: A View on Social Sciences, Law and Humanities in Africa* (Pietermaritzburg: University of KwaZulu-Natal Press).

Shepherd, N. 2007. 'Archaeology Dreaming: Postapartheid Urban Imaginaries and the Bones of the Prestwich Street Dead', *Journal of Social Archaeology*, no. 7, pp. 3–28.

Thompson, L. 1985. *The Political Mythology of Apartheid* (New Haven: Yale University Press).

Van Sittert, L. 2003. 'From "Mere Weeds" and "Bosjes" to a Cape Floral Kingdom: The Re-imagining of Indigenous Flora at the Cape, c.1890–1939', *Kronos*, no. 28, pp. 102–26.

Witz, L. 2003. *Apartheid's Festival: Contesting South Africa's National Pasts* (Bloomington: Indiana University Press).

Witz, L. 2006. 'Museums on Cape Town's Township Tours' in Shepherd, N, Hall, M and Murray, N (eds.), *Desire Lines: Space, Memory and Identity in the Post-apartheid City* (London: Routledge).

Witz, L, Rassool, C and Minkley, G. 2000. 'Tourist Memories of Africa', Paper presented at the Conference on Memory and History, University of Cape Town, 9–11 August 2000.

Worden, N. 1996. 'Contested Heritage at the Cape Town Waterfront', *International Journal of Heritage Studies*, no. 2, pp. 59–75.

Worden, N. 1997. Contesting Heritage in a South African City: Cape Town' in Shaw, B and Jones, R (eds.), *Contesting Urban Heritage* (Ashgate: Aldershot), pp. 31–61.

Indigenous Knowledge

Part I by Kai Horsthemke

'African solutions to African problems' has become a widely used slogan in the years since the transition to democracy in South Africa. In so far as HIV/AIDS is (also) an African problem, it is little wonder that several 'solutions' have been suggested, ranging from a diet of African potatoes and garlic to the *amaqhikiza* system (a type of mentorship programme among older and younger girls 'to ensure sexual abstinence' until the latter are 'ready to take full control of their affairs') and *ukuhlolwa kwezintombi* or 'virginity testing' in girls (that 'seeks to achieve the goal of purity in the context of the spread of HIV/AIDS'; Ntuli 2002: 61–2). More often than not, suggestions such as these are referred to as examples of 'indigenous knowledge', as are conflict resolution, traditional healing in general, and also soothsaying, acquaintance with the *tokoloshe* and *mantindane*, rainmaking and the like.

What, then, is 'indigenous knowledge'? Oddly, this question is usually treated as secondary to the question 'What is the emphasis on indigenous knowledge meant to achieve?' In response to the latter, there are several related ideas that appear again and again (see Semali and Kincheloe 1999; Higgs et al. 2004; Odora Hoppers 2002, 2005): reclamation of cultural or traditional heritage; decolonisation of mind and thought; recognition and acknowledgement of self-determining development; protection against further colonisation (and its modern heir, globalisation), exploitation, appropriation or commercialisation; legitimisation or validation of indigenous practices and worldviews; and condemnation of, or at least caution against, the subjugation of nature, and of the general oppressiveness of non-indigenous rationality, science and technology (Semali and Kincheloe 1999: 27–9, 43).

'Indigenous knowledge' is generally taken to refer to alternative, informal forms of knowledge, including ethnomusicology, ethnomathematics, and indigenous science. Indigenous science is usually taken to cover indigenous astronomy, indigenous physics, 'ethnomedicine', 'ethnobotany', 'ethnozoology', as well as 'ethnopsychiatry'. According to Odora Hoppers:

> Categories of these traditional knowledges include agricultural, meteorological, ecological, governance, social welfare, peace building and conflict resolution, medicinal and pharmaceutical, legal and jurisprudential, music, architecture, sculpture, textile manufacture, metallurgy and food technology. There is cultural context surrounding the practice of these knowledges, including songs, rituals, dances and fashion; it also includes technologies that range from garment weaving and design, medicinal knowledge …, food preservation and conservation, and agricultural practices … to fisheries, metallurgy and astronomy (2005: 3).

Regarding the purported definition of 'indigenous knowledge', it is generally understood to cover local, traditional, aboriginal or 'oriental' or (in our case) African beliefs, practices, customs and worldviews. Odora Hoppers writes:

> the notion of indigenous knowledge systems (IKS) has been defined as the sum total of the knowledges and skills which people in a particular geographic area possess, and which enables them to get the most out of their environment … Traditional knowledge is … the totality of all knowledges and practices, whether explicit or implicit, used in the management of socio-economic, spiritual and ecological facets of life. In that sense, many aspects of it can be contrasted with 'cosmopolitan knowledge' that is culturally anchored in Western cosmology, scientific discoveries, economic preferences, and philosophies (2005: 2).

Before I go on to interrogate the notion of indigenous knowledge, I want to state that I am in principle in complete agreement with what underpins many indigenous knowledge projects. Firstly, occidental knowledge, science, technology and 'rationality' have led to, or have had as a significant goal, the subjugation of nature, and so far have been devastatingly efficient. The pursuit of nuclear energy, wholesale deforestation and destruction of flora and fauna, factory farming of nonhuman animals for human consumption, vivisection and genetic engineering are deplorable and, indeed, of questionable 'rationality'. Secondly, the devaluation of indigenous people's practices, skills and insights has, to a large extent, been arrogant and of similarly questionable rationality, not to mention morality. Thirdly, present attempts by wealthy industrial and high-tech nations to (re)colonise or appropriate for commercial gain these practices, skills and insights are exploitative and indicative of contempt for humankind, and for nature generally.

Having said this, however, I consider blanket appeals to the concept of indigenous knowledge, and its 'legitimisation' or 'validation', as a remedy or countermeasure, to be completely misguided. 'Indigenous knowledge' involves at best an incomplete, partial or, at worst, a questionable understanding or conception of knowledge. It might, fairly non-controversially, refer to indigenous acquaintance- or familiarity-type knowledge and to indigenous practical or procedural knowledge. If, on the other hand, it is intended to convey 'knowledge' in the factual, theoretical or declarative sense, then one might doubt either whether it is essentially 'indigenous' (because the knowledge in question would hold not only locally but transculturally) or whether it is a matter of 'knowledge' (as in the case of belief in witchcraft or in ancestors' agency, or that sex with a virgin prevents or cures HIV/AIDS). Thus, what is called 'indigenous knowledge' in this sense is interpreted more plausibly either as knowledge proper (that is, not essentially 'indigenous') or as mere (indigenous) belief or beliefs – in the absence of truth and perhaps even justification. As a tool in anti-discrimination and anti-repression discourse, in the struggle for decolonisation of the mind (the seat of cognition and knowledge-that), then, 'indigenous knowledge' is largely inappropriate.

If something is referred to as 'indigenous knowledge' in the sense of factual or declarative knowledge, it must meet the requisite criteria: belief, truth and adequate justification. If it does, it is similar to and, indeed, equal to 'non-indigenous' knowledge in a particular area or field. Thus, the traditional healer's knowledge would be as significant, epistemologically, as that of a general medical practitioner and the knowledge of a naturopath or homoeopath. The insights into climate change, animal behaviour and plant life cycles of the San, Inuit or Native Americans would be no less important than those of occidental analysts, climatologists and biologists. In fact, they could arguably learn from each other. It is important to bear in mind that there is no question here of different truths (different beliefs perhaps, different methods of justification almost certainly), no question of (radically) different knowledges. Truth and reality are essentially not in the eye of the beholder.

A San elder's insight into the appetite- and thirst-suppressant properties of the *!khoba* cactus, or *Hoodia gordonii*, constitutes an insight that may not be shared by many – indeed, not even by the younger San – but it has translocal value and application. There is a staggering amount of common ground between cultures, not only in terms of factual knowledge but also in terms of values. A rapprochement between so-called 'indigenous' and 'non-indigenous' insights is not only possible but also desirable – on educational, ethical and political grounds.

I consider this conception of declarative knowledge to be not only plausible but also indispensable for clearing up some of the confusions in debates around indigenous knowledge. The philosophical account of the nature of knowledge should be used as a yardstick. The onus then would be on anyone who is opposed to my analysis to propose an alternative and more feasible definition, one that is sufficiently unambiguous and comprehensive to address the issues and problems raised here.

Finally, in order to illustrate the force of the proffered account, I want to suggest a thought experiment. The Truth and Reconciliation Commission (TRC) was set up after the first democratic elections in South Africa in order to bring to light the injustices and moral wrongs committed under apartheid – and indeed to 'heal the divisions of the past' and contribute towards establishing 'a society based on democratic values, social justice and fundamental rights' (see Horsthemke 2004). One of the principal contributions of the TRC was to turn *knowledge* – in other words, what so many people already knew – into public *acknowledgement*, allowing the nation to acknowledge atrocity for what it is. Asked to name the most significant achievements of the TRC in a national survey, the vast majority of South Africans, irrespective of race, referred to the disclosure of the *truth* about the past (Villa-Vicencio 2003: 15).

Let us pause to think about the present use of the terms 'knowledge' and 'truth'. Is the former something that is essentially uncertain, unstable, an individual or social construct, something that necessarily expresses power relations? Is the latter a matter of discussion or debate, synonymous with 'consensus'? I want to suggest that the use of the terms 'knowledge' and 'truth' in the particular enterprise referred to here cannot be relativist, that knowledge and truth are not relative to a particular culture or social context. If it did not involve an understanding of truth as transcultural or universal (and as objectively anchoring knowledge), as reflecting what actually happened, i.e. facts about South Africa's past, setting up a commission like this would be pointless.

Part II by Lesley JF Green

Kai Horsthemke's argument on 'indigenous knowledge' takes a universalist position on knowledge: that 'knowledge and truth are not relative to a particular culture or social context' (see above). While we have significant differences, his argument is correct in four respects. Defining what is 'indigenous' about indigenous knowledge (IK) is indeed complex; distinguishing between the sciences and other knowledge traditions is not as straightforward as it might seem; cultural relativism is not a helpful approach to resolving that division; and the discourse on 'indigenous knowledge' is heavily influenced by social and political power. However, these threads of the argument can – and should, I believe – be spun differently, and woven together in a pattern that is not determined only by the two poles of relativism and universalism.

That noted, our differences take form around several issues. In this chapter I discuss these by means of a series of lines of inquiry around knowledge diversity and power.

Rethinking the descriptor 'indigenous knowledge'

The first thread with which I would weave a different pattern is the notion of 'the indigenous'. Several decades of scholarship have demonstrated that 'culture' and 'nation' are *not* synonymous, and modernist ideas about culture that suggest it has existed without internal differences of opinion, innovation or contact with new ideas throughout human history are demonstrably false. For this reason, the idea that 'a knowledge' can be wholly 'indigenous' to 'a people' whose traditions go back into the dawn of human history without any contact with others, is not a complete picture. The history of the idea of indigenous knowledge has, however, taken form in struggles against political domination: struggles which have been characterised by marginalised people's appropriation of the conceptual tools of modernism. In other words, the mobilisation of the idea of 'indigenous knowledge' is itself a vehicle of modernity, and a political instrument in the era of globalisation. Thus, there is a rich irony in that the concept of 'indigenous knowledge' is itself a hybrid creation which emerges in counterpoint to globalisation, and draws from a romantic Western notion of culture as static and bounded (see Thornton 1988). There is an equally rich irony to the reality that at the very moment in which the marginalised have begun to use the terms of modernism to claim political space in the global order, the conceptual apparatus it uses has been rejected in the 'centres' of international scholarship (Coplan 1994: 245).

Defending the use of the concept of 'indigenous knowledge' against those who would discard it, cartographer and anthropologist Mac Chapin (2004) argues that because the term is of such strategic importance in tasks such as the demarcation of lands and in the defence of environmental knowledge, it should not be abandoned despite its conceptual weaknesses. In other words, its strategic usefulness outweighs concerns about its conceptual use. But anthropologist Arne Kalland argues the opposite. The term, he says, does a disservice to knowledges of people who for historical reasons find themselves with a weak claim to 'indigeneity' (2003: 320ff). In other words, Kalland is concerned about the political and historical contexts in which certain claims to indigenous knowledge are authorised and others denied, and calls for the recognition of the social dynamics attending the very definition of IK in specific contexts. In South Africa, for example, 'coloured' fishing communities are not generally considered to be bearers of 'indigenous knowledge' even though fragments of knowledge of marine life and how to harvest it may have been passed across many generations. Should what they know be excluded from a national database of indigenous knowledge because it is not considered 'indigenous'?

In response to dilemmas such as these, the term 'traditional ecological knowledge', or TEK, has come to replace 'indigenous knowledge' in many quarters (see Nadasdy 2004: 114ff). It is not a significant improvement. While TEK does not imply the same claims about culture and nationhood, the term 'traditional' is equally problematic for people who have a great deal of knowledge of a place but a weak claim to the notion of 'traditionality' (Spiegel and Boonzaier 1988). For these reasons, I prefer to use terms such as 'knowledge practices' or 'knowledge traditions' (note the plural, which includes the sciences) or just simply to talk of 'knowledge diversity'. In so far as 'culture' is involved, culture is better understood as skills learned in relation to an environment (Ingold 2000): an approach that is not dependent on the selection of a particular line in one's genealogy to confer identity, and allows for lifelong learning, wherever one is (see Ingold 2000: 132ff). In particular contexts, the phrase 'indigenous knowledge' may be strategically appropriate. But, as will become clear, it should be used with care for an additional reason: the term IK perpetuates its artificial distinction from 'science'.

Rethinking the dualism 'indigenous knowledge and the sciences'
Perhaps the most damaging consequence of the use of the term 'indigenous knowledge' is that it sets IK in opposition to 'scientific knowledge': a distinction made all the more unwelcome in that it slips into race-based notions of social evolution from primitive to civilised.

Political scientist Arun Agrawal argues that 'attempts to draw a strict line between scientific and indigenous knowledge on the basis of method, epistemology, context-dependence, or content ... are ultimately untenable' (2002: 293; 1995). For example, it has been argued by Robin Horton (1993) that science is 'open' to question its own claims while traditional knowledge is 'closed' to the possibility that its truths are questionable. The argument is deeply flawed: learning, innovation and change could not have occurred at all if societies were 'cold' or 'closed'.[1] In my experience of fieldwork in the northern Amazon, some people there are as enthusiastic to learn different ways of solving specific problems as any scientific innovator, and others are as resistant to change as some of the crustier professors I've encountered on campus. It is not possible to characterise entire societies with single descriptors; much less is it possible to characterise all 'indigenous knowledge' as uniform. Even the natural sciences are strung between the reductionists and the complexity theorists, each advocating different methods and approaches.

On the point of its context-dependence – or the idea that IK is relevant only to a specific context – Agrawal points out that the sociology of scientific knowledge demonstrates the extent to which scientific truths are context-dependent (1995: 426). In obstetric medicine, for example, the calculation of risk factors in a pregnancy depends on how specific elements are statistically weighted. Where one group of obstetricians weighs a factor such as maternal age differently from another, the interpretation of the same foetal measurements can differ enormously. This kind of reasoning forms the basis for life or death decisions.

Recognising the uncertainties that attend scientific knowledge, sociologists Andrew Pickering (1992) and Bruno Latour (1993, 2004) have argued for recognition of the ways in which communities of practice shape concepts, meanings and results. Endless studies of the social and political construction of knowledge do not, however, enable one to establish what is knowledge and what is not. This is crucial for democracies, where decisions need to be taken on the basis of the best available knowledge. There is a need, then, for a sociology of knowledge which is, in the words of Susan Haack, 'neither uncritically deferential to the natural sciences nor uncritically cynical about them, and which, rather than competing for control of the territory, cooperates with epistemology to understand the scientific enterprise' (2003: 201). The next two sections deal with each in turn: a sociology of knowledge whether 'indigenous' or scientific, and questions of epistemology.

Society, power and the valorisation of knowledge traditions

While the social study of scientific knowledge demonstrates the relationship between power, practices of knowledge production, and social consensus about truth in scientific settings, there is an equivalent need to explore those dynamics in relation to claims to indigenous knowledges. In a study based in present-day India, Nandini Sundar (2002) drew attention to the involvement of the state in the authorisation of 'indigenous knowledge'. In 2001, in an attempt to establish Hindu 'indigenous knowledge' within the university system, a former government of India promoted the founding of departments of Vedic astrology within faculties of science. The project was immensely controversial, not least because it sought to explore the forecasting of the future. On the basis of this case study, Sundar argues that in the context of ethnic nationalisms, the valorisation of knowledge depends especially heavily on who is in power.

In South Africa, claims about indigenous knowledge need to be carefully explored. In recent publications on the subject, several writers have tended to set up a worldview comprising Africa versus the West, in which the terms of the debate are characterised as nature versus culture, real versus artificial environments, spiritual integrity versus alienation, enchantment versus rationality, and ecological sentience versus technoscientific detachment. The intriguing part of this worldview is that it draws as much from Thabo Mbeki's argument that 'the material conditions in our society ... have divided our country into two nations, the one black and the other white' (1998) as it does from a theory in which culture is bounded in space and time, and ideally sealed off from the pollution of outsiders. When constructed in this way, it forms a very similar view of culture to that propounded by the *volkekundiges*, the Afrikaner nationalist anthropologists whose work drew inspiration from 1930s Germany and whose theorisation of culture undergirded apartheid. The major difference, of course, is that in the revised version, the values associated with either category are transposed: the West becomes 'bad' because it is 'alienated', and Africa is 'good' because it is not.

These observations call for a careful and critical scholarship that explores the conditions of power under which knowledge is produced, whether under the title of 'science' or 'the indigenous'. Such a scholarship needs to assess ways in which research agendas are defined, to question the reasons for which knowledge production is funded, and to assess carefully the epistemological grounds on which knowledge is claimed. This kind of approach would be as valuable in disputes over climate science in Washington DC, as they would be in regard to debates over the place of Vedic astrology in Delhi or the role of sangomas in responding to HIV in Khayelitsha, Cape Town (see Wreford 2005).

Questions of epistemology

Although careful and critical scholarship on the social conditions in which knowledge is valorised as truth may enable one to deconstruct myth-making, it cannot provide a comprehensive answer to the question of how to distinguish knowledge from belief. To explore this issue further, there is a need to engage with questions of epistemology.

The history of that branch of philosophy known as 'epistemology' has been strung between the foundationalists, such as René Descartes, who emphasise universal laws for the production of knowledge, and the coherentists (or consensualists), such as Ludwig Wittgenstein, Richard Rorty and Thomas Kuhn, who argue that knowledge is a product of social consensus (Elgin 1996). More recently, the debate between foundationalism and coherentism has been rethought in the work of philosophers like Nelson Goodman (1978) and Catherine Elgin (2004). 'The picture I am proposing', writes Elgin (1996: 100), 'is more complicated than the one [foundationalists] espouse; the success of our cognitive endeavours is no longer assured. But it does, I think, introduce a via media between the abandoned absolutes of Cartesian epistemology and the potentially arbitrary games Wittgensteinians would have us play.'

Elgin argues for an evaluation of models of knowledge on a very simple principle: their efficacy in producing understanding that is appropriate to context (2004: 121). She points out that science uses devices, such as models, metaphors and thought experiments, to advance understanding, but that these don't purport to be true. An easy example: immunology uses metaphors of 'invasion' and 'attack' which are not considered 'true' in the strict sense of the term, but they advance scientific understanding

– although these same metaphors often undo the possibility of furthering that goal, as Susan Sontag illustrated in *Illness and Metaphor*.

Arguing for a way of regarding scientific laws and models that moves away from the assumption of literal truth, Elgin points out that in the sciences, precision, accuracy and falsehood are a matter of context. Newtonian physics, for example, is true enough for specific purposes, rather than universally true. In accepting models, she writes, we must accept that they are not mirrors of nature, for 'not every theory is a conjunction of sentences, all of which are supposed to be true. Rather, a theory may be composed of both factual and fictional sentences, and the fictional sentences may play any of several different roles' (2004: 128). In sum, her studies argue that scientific laws are not 'true' in the strict sense of the term, but 'true enough'. In other words, in providing explanatory models, the laws of physics routinely draw on a mid-point between 'knowledge' and 'belief', which is 'acceptance'.

I would argue that this approach to the question of epistemology in the sciences applies equally to different knowledge traditions. In Palikur astronomy, for example, the annual movements of specific constellations are related to seasonal rains in a way that describes those constellations as the boats of shamans who bring the rains. The constellations, in other words, are given material form, and cause is attributed to them. If one were to reject as unscientific any explanatory model of the world that does not operate within a strict realism, one could not accept this narrative as knowledge. Yet there is certainly a correlation between the appearance of specific constellations in the hour before dawn and specific seasons. One could even go further to argue that the orbit of the earth around the sun brings those constellations into view and at the same time causes the meteorological effects that bring the rains. Is this narrative that attributes causal agency to inanimate objects really so different from the immunologist's metaphors of attack and defence, which attribute agency to cellular processes as if soldiers in a war? In other words, science does not operate within a framework of strict realism in using its own models. Why then judge a different knowledge as false where it uses narrative models?

If 'true enough' is valid for the purposes of communicating understanding in the laws of physics, I want to suggest that the model of the relationship between the stars and the rains is adequate to the task of communicating understanding of the complex movements of stars in relation to the seasons. It is 'true enough' in its context. One might believe in the shamanic guiding of the star boats, or one might accept these sentences of the model as metaphorical. Either way, they do not need to be eliminated in order for the model of the sky to be valid. Such models can be taught in school curriculums; they can also (to use a previous example) be included in the corpus of knowledge promoted by the state in the task of extending citizenship to people who explain the ecosystem with reference to the rains that come at the same time as certain stars.

Such an approach does not reduce the entire world to one form of rationality. It offers the *via media* or middle road of 'acceptance' between the poles of knowledge and belief (see Cohen 1995). Nonetheless, the issue of belief is a critical one in considering different knowledge traditions.

Secularism and knowledge: issues in metaphysics

During the Enlightenment, the sceptics wrested control of the authorisation of knowledge from the fideists (the believers, or the faithful) in the Church. The distinction between belief and knowledge enabled the origins of science as we know it, and is at the core of the division between the sciences and indigenous knowledge. There is no easy resolution of a debate that has been polarised for centuries. However, several lines of approach are useful in the effort to move beyond polemic.

A first line of approach involves recognising that the polemic itself has a social consequence: that the structures of indigenous or local knowledge systems are too hastily discarded because they include a belief component, without due consideration of the value of different representations of complex realities. As discussed above, science routinely uses the creative arts, and not literal truths, to explain complex realities (Elgin 2004). Consistency would require that critics of IK should neither assume that (a) all 'sentences' of a proposition are held to be equally true, nor that (b) a model or a metaphor should always be evaluated within a paradigm of strict realism, but rather that they should be judged on their ability to advance understanding. The degree to which explanatory models are believed real to holders of indigenous knowledge almost certainly varies, both over time and by individual and group, as does any belief anywhere else. The issue underscores the value of distinguishing between knowledge, belief and acceptance (see Cohen 1995).

A second line of approach that is useful is that of the distinguished cosmologist and mathematician George Ellis (2006), who argues against a narrow scientism which claims that the entire world can be explained with reference only to physics. Using the example of the human brain, Ellis demonstrates that physics and chemistry alone cannot explain human consciousness.

Thirdly, the belief that science can and does explain everything is part of what anthropologist Talal Asad calls 'the triumphalist history of the secular' (2003: 25) – i.e. the idea that the history of civilisation is characterised by evolution from superstition and theology to science and secularism. The argument is a font of prejudice held between the sciences and 'indigenous knowledge'. Yet on historical evidence alone, this 'secularisation thesis' is a disputed one (Berger 1999). Moreover, as Asad argues, secularism itself constitutes a set of beliefs about the world, and there is not one but many forms of secularism that give form to scholarship. Recent work in anthropology on secularism argues for a careful consideration of the historical conditions under which secularism has become the dominant paradigm for research on culture (see Cannell 2005; de Pina-Cabral 2001). Within much writing on culture, social scientists claim reality only for the observable, and have sought to explain away the spiritual experiences of their research participants by a turn to constructionism and phenomenology, or the experience of perception (see Ball 2002). Yet without secularism, many scholars argue, what spaces are available for governance, or for scholarship, that privilege no particular religion? Is pluralism possible? In responding to this question in a reflection on secularism in anthropology, João de Pina-Cabral argues:

> So it happens with secularism as happens with human rights: anthropologists do not really have strong enough theoretical reasons to argue for the necessity of these norms, but if they do not come to be adopted as a kind of global ground-rule, then the free pursuit of the rational analysis of human social and cultural life, as should ideally define our discipline, will be seriously hindered (2001: 332).

However, secularism guarantees respect and tolerance neither in international politics nor in anthropology. Secularism – in so far as it is predicated on a refusal of the supernatural – is likewise not a guarantee of ethical practice: in training in the shamanic arts in the course of his research, Stoller was horrified to find that his curse on a man might have had an ill effect (Stoller and Olkes 1989). Moreover, pluralism, if it is to be consistent with its own principles, cannot be based on one belief system, whether agnostic or otherwise. Tolerance and ethics do not necessarily flow from any particular belief about the world. I want to suggest that the secularist position has gained dominance in modernity because it is assumed that the relationship between self and other is not possible across differences and, for that reason, it has become the researcher's duty to efface the self, i.e. to mask any beliefs to which he or she may hold that might contrast with those of the researched. On the contrary, an ethical post-modern and postcolonial anthropology requires a commitment neither to a dogma of secularism nor to the practice of professional distance. In their place, what is needed is a rethinking of what it means to be a Self among Others, a way of engaging with difference that does not require the effacement of belief or histories of belief (Green 2005).

Concluding comments

In this chapter, I have sought to highlight what I believe are four interrelated questions about knowledge that are relevant in contemporary critical scholarship: issues of prejudice (or the ways in which 'self' and 'other' manifest in the science versus indigenous knowledge debate); questions of power and knowledge, whether scientific or 'indigenous'; epistemology; and metaphysics. The scale of these issues may seem overwhelming. Yet even from a brief examination, it is clear that they have emerged within the sciences and humanities as much as they proceed from the challenges posed by proponents of the IK movement. They are not raised here in some naive hope of changing the history of Western scholarship to accommodate IK. Rather, they proceed from a position of immense respect for the accomplishments of scholarship, and from an equivalent respect for the wisdom and insights that are abundant in many knowledge traditions currently excluded from scholarship. Like the sciences, such knowledge traditions, I would argue, are strong enough to countenance careful, fair-minded inquiry that evaluates knowledge in relation to its explanatory context.

My argument, then, is not a relativist one, but it takes a different view from that proposed by Kai Horsthemke. There is not, I believe, one universal knowledge to which science is privy and to which all other knowledge traditions must defer. Rather, all knowledge, including Newtonian physics and Palikur astronomy, is produced with relevance to specific contexts and questions, and it is within these contexts of use that knowledge, along with its cognitive devices such as models, laws, narratives and metaphors, must be evaluated. What is crucial is that scholars pursuing research on the interface between science and IK explore the grounds for distinguishing between 'being right' and 'satisfying conditions of rightness' (Elgin 1996: 98). Such an approach eliminates a situation in which superstition is taught as science, and avoids the converse problem in which, in the quest to avoid error, science overlooks the importance of 'sensitivity, relevance, informativeness, and cognitive efficacy' (Elgin 1996: 59). By engaging carefully with practices of producing and justifying knowledge across all fields, scholars may begin to offer a more welcoming home to a wider range of knowledge practices, and, what is more, will benefit from doing so.

Endnote

1 The history of scholarship on culture and rationality is long. With more space, a detailed discussion here would include the works of EB Tylor, who argued that logic is contextual; Emile Durkheim, who compared 'Westen' thought with 'primitive' thought; Lévy-Bruhl, who argued that each type of society has its own mentality; and EE Evans-Pritchard, who suggested that scientific and non-scientific mentalities coexist in every culture and that religious beliefs are rational in their context.

References

Agrawal, A. 1995. 'Dismantling the Divide between Indigenous and Scientific Knowledge', *Development and Change*, vol. 26, pp. 413–39.

Agrawal, A. 2002. 'Indigenous Knowledge and the Politics of Classification', *International Social Science Journal*, vol. 173, pp. 287–97.

Asad, Talal. 2003. *Formations of the Secular: Christianity, Islam, Modernity* (Stanford, CA: Stanford University Press).

Ball, MW. 2002. '"People Speaking Silently to Themselves": An Examination of Keith Basso's Philosophical Speculations on "Sense of Place" in Apache Cultures', *American Indian Quarterly,* vol. 26, no. 3, pp. 460–78.

Berger, Peter L (ed.). 1999. *The Desecularization of the World: Resurgent Religion and World Politics* (Grand Rapids: William B Eerdmans).

Cannell, Fenella. 2005. 'The Christianity of Anthropology', *Journal of the Royal Anthropological Institute,* vol. 11, pp. 335–56.

Chapin, Mac. 2004. 'A Challenge to Conservationists', *Worldwatch Magazine,* December.

Cohen, LJ. 1995. *An Essay on Belief and Acceptance* (Oxford: Clarendon Press).

Coplan, David. 1994. *In the Time of Cannibals* (Chicago: Chicago University Press).

De Pina-Cabral, João. 2001. 'Three Points on Secularism and Anthropology', *Social Anthropology,* vol. 9, no. 3, pp. 329–33.

Elgin, CZ. 1996. *Considered Judgment* (Princeton: Princeton University Press).

Elgin, CZ. 2004. 'True Enough' in Sosa, E and Villaneuva, E (eds.), *Epistemology* (Boston: Blackwell).

Ellis, George. 2006. 'Academic Life and Holistic Viewpoints', Unpublished notes from a talk, University of Cape Town.

Goodman, Nelson. 1978. *Ways of Worldmaking* (Indiana: Hackett).

Green, LJF. 2005. '"Ba pi ai?": Rethinking the Relationship between Secularism and Professionalism in Anthropological Fieldwork', *Anthropology Southern Africa,* vol. 28, no. 3&4, pp. 91–8.

Haack, Susan. 2003. *Defending Science – Within Reason: Between Scientism and Cynicism* (New York: Prometheus Books).

Higgs, P, Lillejord, S, Mkabela, Q, Waghid, Y and Le Grange, L (eds.). 2004. 'Indigenous African Knowledge Systems and Higher Education', *South African Journal of Higher Education,* vol. 18, no. 3, pp. 40–5.

Horsthemke, K. 2004. '"Indigenous Knowledge", Truth and Reconciliation in South African Higher Education', *South African Journal of Higher Education,* vol. 18, no. 3, pp. 65–81.

Horton, Robin. 1993. *Patterns of Thought in Africa and the West* (Cambridge: Cambridge University Press).

Ingold, Tim. 2000. *The Perception of the Environment: Essays in Livelihood, Dwelling and Skill* (London: Routledge).

Kalland, A. 2003. 'Indigenous Knowledge: Prospects and Limitations' in Ellen, R, Parkes, P and Alan Bicker, A (eds.), *Indigenous Environmental Knowledge and Its Transformations* (Amsterdam: Harwood Academic Publishers).

Latour, Bruno. 1993. *We Have Never Been Modern* (Cambridge, MA: Harvard University Press).

Latour, Bruno. 2004. *Politics of Nature* (Cambridge, MA: Harvard University Press).

Mbeki, Thabo. 1998. 'Reconciliation and Nation Building', Statement at the Opening of the Debate in the National Assembly, Cape Town, 29 May 1998'; http://www.dfa.gov. za/docs/speeches/1998/mbek0529.htm, accessed 5 November 2005.

Nadasdy, Paul. 2004. *Hunters and Bureaucrats* (Vancouver: University of British Columbia Press).

Ntuli, PP. 2002. 'Indigenous Knowledge Systems and the African Renaissance: Laying a Foundation for the Creation of Counter-hegemonic Discourses' in Odora Hoppers, C (ed.), *Indigenous Knowledge and the Integration of Knowledge Systems: Towards a Philosophy of Articulation* (Cape Town: New Africa Books).

Odora Hoppers, C. 2002. 'Indigenous Knowledge and the Integration of Knowledge Systems: Towards a Conceptual and Methodological Framework' in Odora Hoppers, C (ed.), *Indigenous Knowledge and the Integration of Knowledge Systems: Towards a Philosophy of Articulation* (Cape Town: New Africa Books).

Odora Hoppers, CA. 2005. *Culture, Indigenous Knowledge and Development: The Role of the University*, Occasional paper no. 5 (Johannesburg: Centre for Education Policy Development), pp. 1–50.

Pickering, A. 1992. *Science as Practice and Culture* (Chicago: Chicago University Press).

Semali, LM and Kincheloe, JL (eds.). 1999. *What is Indigenous Knowledge? Voices from the Academy* (New York: Falmer Press).

Sontag, Susan. 2001. *Illness as Metaphor: Aids and Its Metaphors* (London: Picador).

Spiegel, Andrew and Boonzaier, Emile. 1988. 'Promoting Tradition: Images of the South African Past' in Boonzaier, E and Sharp, J (eds.), *South African Keywords: The Uses and Abuses of Political Concepts* (Cape Town: David Philip).

Stoller, Paul and Olkes, Cheryl. 1989. *In Sorcery's Shadow: A Memoir of Apprenticeship among the Songhay of Niger* (Chicago: Chicago University Press).

Sundar, Nandini. 2002. '"Indigenise, Nationalise and Spiritualise": An Agenda for Education?', *International Social Science Journal*, vol. 173, pp. 373–83.

Thornton, Robert. 1988. 'Culture: A Contemporary Definition' in Boonzaier, E and Sharp, J (eds.), *South African Keywords: The Uses and Abuses of Political Concepts* (Cape Town: David Philip).

Villa-Vicencio, C. 2003. 'No Way Around the Past', *Sowetan*, 23 June 2003, p. 15.

Wreford, J. 2005. 'Missing Each Other: Problems and Potential for Collaborative Efforts between Biomedicine and Traditional Healers in South Africa in the Time of AIDS', *Social Dynamics*, vol. 31, no. 2, pp. 55–89.

LAND

Thembela Kepe, Ruth Hall and Ben Cousins

'We, the marginalised people of South Africa, who are landless and land hungry, declare our needs for all the world to know. We are the people who have borne the brunt of apartheid, of forced removals from our homes, of poverty in the rural areas, of oppression on the farms and of starvation in the Bantustans ... We will not sit back and watch as the wealth builds up in the cities, while on the edges of the cities, in the small towns and in the countryside, we continue to suffer and starve.' – Land Charter adopted at Community Land Conference, 1994

'My land is not just my land – it's my life.' – A white commercial farmer reported in *Farmer's Weekly*, 2005

THE OCCUPATION AND THEN CONFISCATION of over 80% of white-owned farmland in Zimbabwe between February 2000 and 2005, accompanied by catastrophic economic decline, sent shock waves across southern Africa. In South Africa, where most agricultural land was, and still is, in white hands despite an ambitious government land-reform programme, the occupations in Zimbabwe sparked sharply divergent responses.

An opinion survey in 2001 revealed that most black South Africans (68%) approved of the farm occupations in Zimbabwe, agreeing with the statement 'Land must be returned to blacks in South Africa, no matter what the consequences are for the current owners and for political stability in the country' (Gibson 2001). Almost no white respondents agreed. In June 2000, the secretary-general of the African National Congress (ANC), Kgalema Motlanthe, endorsed the occupations, describing them as 'protest action' against the failure of land reform (*Mail & Guardian* 2000). More recently, the Landless People's Movement (LPM) have hailed President Robert

Mugabe as a hero and invited him to address their members, while South African cabinet ministers have repeatedly said that important lessons on how to speed up land reform can be learned from Zimbabwe.

Most media reports on Zimbabwean farm occupations have, however, portrayed them as a violent attack on private property rights, benefiting mainly the black elite tied to the ruling ZANU-PF party, and as the prime cause of both the collapse of commercial agriculture and the larger economic crisis in Zimbabwe. Human rights abuses (of black farm workers as well as white farmers) were widely reported and informed the view, widely held in South Africa, that Zimbabwe demonstrates most clearly how *not* to engage in land reform.

Despite contrasts in gut-level responses, a broad consensus has emerged: the key lesson from Zimbabwe is the need for more rapid progress in land reform in South Africa – otherwise land occupations could erupt here too (*Mail & Guardian* 2005). Many white commercial farmers have now embraced land reform as 'necessary for their own survival' (*Farmer's Weekly*, 26 May 2000). On the other hand, few people in South Africa appear to believe that land reform will contribute much to economic growth and development, or poverty reduction. There is widespread scepticism about the potential of agriculture to reduce poverty for large numbers of people. So the political imperative that land be redistributed rests on contested foundations, with deep divisions between those believing that it is essential for broad-based growth and development in the rural areas and those believing it will come at a cost to the country's economy.

This presents a paradox of sorts for policy-makers: what kind of land reform programme should be designed, on what scale and for which beneficiaries? Beyond policy lies a deeper set of questions about the multiple, diverging and sometimes contested meanings of 'land' in contemporary South Africa. These help explain the disconnection between the political and economic dimensions of land reform.

Political party manifestos demonstrate the discursive agreement across most of the political spectrum on the importance of land reform, the urgency of the process, and the need to ensure that the transfer of land rights translates into improved livelihoods and reduced poverty in the rural areas. For example, ahead of the 2004 general election, the ANC claimed it would 'reduce poverty by half through economic development, comprehensive social security, land reform and improved household and community assets. [In the next five years, we will] complete the land restitution programme and speed up land reform, with 30% of agricultural land redistributed by 2014, combined with comprehensive assistance to emergent farmers' (ANC 2004).

At the same time, the opposition Democratic Alliance (DA) used similar language to oppose the target-driven focus of land reform, and criticised the failure of land reform to support growth in the agricultural sector: 'The DA will ensure that rural land reform is not about simply filling numerical quotas: our land reform programme will be carried out with the very clear objectives of making life better for the beneficiaries of land reform and increasing the prosperity of South Africa as a whole' (DA 2004).

In this chapter we explore the multiple meanings of 'land', including its use as a potent signifier of collective identity and belonging, and its practical significance within diverse livelihood strategies. We argue that land carries a powerful symbolic charge for many black South Africans not only because of their recent memories of racialised dispossession of their land, but also because inequalities in land ownership 'stand for' and evoke the broader inequalities that post-apartheid policies have yet to undo.

Land is an important symbol for white South Africans, too. Commercial farmers, and some urban Afrikaners, see land and identity as deeply intertwined. For middle-class city-dwellers, rural landscapes are often associated with simpler and more ecologically integrated ways of life, and are valued for leisure activities. For other whites, 'land ownership' also symbolises the system of private property rights that underpins their wealth and security in an era when they no longer wield political power.

'Land' thus carries a heavy weight of historical meaning. We must understand past struggles over land if we are to make sense of the present. This chapter first explores the processes through which many South Africans were dispossessed of land. Secondly, our attention turns to the importance of land as a source of livelihood for some of the poorest South Africans. Thirdly, noting that land is important symbolically as well as materially, we discuss the ways in which land informs identity, and how different groups and political traditions invoke the imagery of 'land' to forge solidarity. In particular, we note the significance of land in the course of the struggle for national liberation. Fourthly, we consider how access to and control of land form a source of power within as well as between groups, and how control over land has been used to define and defend 'tradition'. Intimately linked to this is how land rights structure the social relations between men and women. Finally, we reflect on the new meanings of land in democratic South Africa, the role of land reform as a post-apartheid project to remedy past wrongs, and the special status accorded to 'land'.

Land dispossession

Much of South Africa's early history was a story of conquest and dispossession. As a result, indigenous people lost ownership of their land to white settlers and their independence to the colonial states that were established in the subcontinent. This story involved three main processes: colonial expansion; the discovery of minerals and subsequent industrialisation; and the policies of segregation and apartheid in the twentieth century (Davenport and Saunders 2000).

The arrival of Dutch settlers at the Cape in 1652 marked the beginning of colonial expansion in South Africa. Though the intention was to establish a halfway station for the Dutch East India Company to its Indian Ocean empire, within a few years farming land around Cape Town was allotted to European settlers. By the early 1700s, colonists had ventured into the surrounding areas and settled on farms, in the process dispossessing the indigenous Khoisan inhabitants of their land and incorporating them into the colonial economy as slaves or servants.

Expansion to the east was met with determined resistance by the Nguni people but after the British took over control of the Cape in 1806, this resistance was crushed by the British army in a series of frontier wars that lasted for almost a century. The British army was also responsible for bringing to an end the independence of the Zulu kingdom and subsuming it within the British colony of Natal. Expansion to the north across the Orange River was spearheaded by Dutch colonists from the Cape in what has become known as the Great Trek. With the establishment of the Boer republics of the Transvaal and Orange Free State, the conquest and dispossession of local African people continued apace. Finally, with the establishment of the Union of South Africa in 1910, white control over the country was confirmed.

With the discovery of diamonds in Kimberley in 1867 and gold on the Witwatersrand in 1886 and the subsequent industrialisation of the country, the colonial states turned to the conquered African people as a potential source of labour on the mines (Bundy 1988). In an attempt to force blacks to become wage labourers, laws were passed that restricted land ownership by blacks, and imposed taxes that could only be paid by cash. In this respect, the first significant law was the Cape's Glen Grey Act of 1894, which introduced a one-man-one-lot system and individual quitrent lots of about four morgen (about three hectares) and imposed a labour tax on able-bodied black men who had not worked outside their home district for at least three months in the previous year. The intention was to create a landless class dependent on wage labour.

After Union was established in 1910, parliament soon began to pass a series of laws that formalised and extended the system of segregation that had been haphazardly and differentially developed and applied in the previous colonies and states. Of key importance was the Natives Land Act of 1913, which prohibited Africans from owning or occupying land outside the reserves and locations, and reserved just 7% of the national territory for exclusive black occupation. This was increased to 13% by the Native Trust and Land Act of 1936, which also deprived the last remaining African voters in the Cape of their franchise. After 1948, the Nationalist government introduced its policy of apartheid. Under Hendrik Verwoerd, the African reserves, themselves the rump of the formerly independent African chiefdoms, became the building blocks of the so-called Bantu homelands, which in terms of the policy of separate development were given 'independent' status – though their independence was never recognised by any other country than South Africa. As the homelands of the various ethnic groups (Xhosa, Zulu, Tswana, Venda and so on) into which the African population was divided, they also became the dumping grounds for their ethnic nationals, especially those without work, from the cities and towns of South Africa, which were designated as belonging to whites only. Similar ethnic cleansing took places in the towns and cities, where people were strictly segregated by race according to the Group Areas Act of 1950. An estimated 3.5 million people were forcibly removed during the period 1960 to 1983 in and from the cities and from farms (Platzky and Walker 1985).

Given this history, land dispossession must be understood as a complex and textured historical process, rather than as a specific moment in time. It has shaped the lives of generations of Africans and sparked numerous local and national struggles, not least the struggle for liberation. Because rights to land form a basis for citizenship, dispossession has been equated with disenfranchisement. Liberation movements like the ANC and PAC recognised the inherent land rights of indigenous people (conceived of as 'first-comers') and invoked a narrative which foregrounded and criminalised colonial conquest, arguing that national liberation required that dispossession be undone. It is this position that forms the basis of the land restitution policy of the post-apartheid government, which we shall consider later.

Land and livelihoods

In rural areas, land is important for agriculture, grazing, residence, and the collection of natural resources. Although subsistence agriculture plays a limited role in meeting the livelihood needs of rural people compared to other sources such as formal employment and government grants, rural land and the natural resources on it do serve as a safety net for the poor (Kepe and Cousins 2002; Shackleton and Shackleton 2004). Evidence collected by researchers indicates that rural landscapes often contain numerous benefits to poor people, including natural resources, which are not fully acknowledged by policy-makers (Cousins 1999; Kepe 2002; Shackleton 2005). Almost all these studies conclude by emphasising that rights to land need to be strengthened if these benefits are to be enhanced.

In areas such as Pondoland in the Eastern Cape, where there is a long history of struggle for land, rural people have been aware that regaining their rights gives them bargaining power, and is the basis for their economic emancipation. This is illustrated in statements by residents of the coastal village of Lambasi – whose land was forcibly taken to make way for a government-controlled tea plantation, as well as being demarcated through betterment planning – who said, 'Jobs and land rights do not clash. The two are both important. We can get our land rights back and let people with money develop the land' (Kepe 2005: 276). Here the villagers were indicating that they saw their control of land as giving them a voice at the negotiating table with those who wanted to invest on the land.

The value of rural landscapes to livelihoods also highlights the heterogeneous nature of the rural communities, as well as the heterogeneous nature of the goals these communities have for use of the landscape. In other words, not only do local people have different visions for rural landscapes from outsiders, but rural people themselves often have conflicting views about what land means and how it should be used. In her study of conflict over water and cattle in Botswana, Pauline Peters (1984) shows how struggles over resources are often underpinned by struggles over meaning. Thus, resistance to dispossession and demand for the restoration of land involve the aspiration not only for land as a physical asset, but for political, economic and often also spiritual autonomy and healing. A key ingredient underpinning the different meanings that various individuals or groups attach to land has to do with their identity. We therefore move on to the issue of land and identity.

Land and identity

'Land' has two broad meanings: the landscape valued for its natural resources (cultivation, living space and natural beauty) and the territory with which a particular people identify (Jary and Jary 1995). There are many facets to these two broad meanings. Depending on history, geography and culture, what 'land' means to different people is socially embedded, and is subject to different interpretations, contestation and negotiation (Peters 1984; Goheen 1993). The day-to-day meaning of land in South Africa is as complex as the country's history and people.

In South Africa, as elsewhere, there appears to be a special meaning assigned to land based primarily on who holds rights to it, how it was acquired, and how it is currently used. South Africa's history of conquest and dispossession, which we have already discussed, informs most of the different understandings of land that South Africans have. Over time the significance of land as a source of identity may also change. As a result of urbanisation, a growing proportion of South Africans no longer rely directly on the land. This has led some analysts to argue that land has become less important, as a source of identity and as an instrument for 'development'. 'Rural land reform is not the answer to mass rural poverty ... we must stop overloading "land reform" by expecting it to deal with all the evils of apartheid and rural neglect ... We must discard rural romanticism' (Bernstein 2005).

However, many people in South Africa's increasingly urbanised society retain strong links to the land where they were born and where their ancestors lived. In Xhosa, people speak of their rural home as their *umnombo*, meaning their 'roots'. Literally, *umnombo* is the wick of a lamp, which transfers the liquid from the paraffin below to the flame above, fuelling it with energy. Xhosa people also refer to a person's *inkaba* (umbilical cord), which is buried after birth, to denote the place where his or her physical and emotional identity is based and signify a lifelong attachment with that place. Many people who have left their 'roots' to go to the big cities often mention their place of attachment. Even after years of living elsewhere, many Xhosa people choose to return to their *umnombo* or *inkaba* either to retire or to be buried. Thus both *umnombo* and *inkaba* are metaphors that signify a source of life that is closely tied to the area of one's birth.

Throughout the years of the struggle against apartheid, there was a consistent discourse among blacks of the 'loss of land as a form and symbol of conquest' (Kepe 2004: 688). Many 'freedom songs' were instrumental in spreading this view. One of the most popular captured the meaning of land in the struggle against oppression of blacks by whites in this way:

Thina sizwe esimnyama (We the black nation)
Sikhalela izwe lethu (We cry for our land/territory/nation)
Elathathwa ngamabhulu (Which was taken by whites)
Mabawuyeke umhlaba wethu (They must let go of our land)
Mabawuyeke umhlaba wethu (They must let go of our land)

Among the liberation movements there were different visions of who should control the land after whites had relinquished political control. The ANC, in one of the clauses of its Freedom Charter, envisaged a situation where 'The land shall be shared among those who work it!', including all races (ANC 1955). On the other hand, the slogan of the Pan Africanist Congress (PAC) was *Izwe lethu* ('The land is ours'). According to the PAC, blacks in South Africa would never be free unless they regained control of the land. Given the current slow pace of land reform, people who subscribe to both these views have reason to be dissatisfied. This is particularly so when one considers the fact that many people equate land hunger with poverty (Ncapayi 2005).

Even as land reform is being pursued by a democratic government, rural people have reminded us of their continuing marginality by mobilising under the banner of the 'landless'. What does it mean to identify oneself as 'landless'? Land activists have underscored the historical relationship between land dispossession and political conquest, and questioned what 'freedom' can mean for those who lack basic means of survival, and whose land has not been returned (Moyo and Yeros 2005). This thinking was evident, for instance, when the Landless People's Movement (LPM) was launched in 2001, under the slogan 'Landlessness = Racism'. By locating the issue of land within a framework of racism, LPM activists hoped to drive home the point that the economic conditions in which they and their followers live amount to a perpetuation of racism and of apartheid. This was reiterated in the LPM's later campaign to call on rural voters to boycott national elections in 2004, under the slogan 'No Land, No Vote'.

To understand the significance of land in South Africa, one also needs to remember the ways in which people's relations with land form the basis of their membership of communities, ethnic groups and nations. Land is not only a productive resource and an economic asset; it also denotes a political entity. Both the liberation movement and Afrikaner nationalist discourses have invoked the idealised imagery of 'the land'. Land has been a potent signifier of nationhood in nationalist discourses. The apartheid-era national anthem, *Die Stem van Suid-Afrika* ('The Call of South Africa'), epitomised the equation of land with the sectarian and nationalist identity of Afrikaners. It evoked the suffering and courage involved in the conquest of land, and emphasised the importance of retaining control of the land as essential to preserving the heritage of the past and ensuring continuity of Afrikaner power into the future.

Land is a central motif in various political traditions. This points to the rural roots of many South African identities. For example, *boer*, literally meaning 'farmer', has long been used as a common descriptor for white Afrikaans-speaking South Africans, often in a derogatory context – such as police being called *boers* or *boere*, and the slogan popularised by former ANC Youth League leader Peter Mokaba: 'Kill the *boer*, kill the farmer'. Even so, *boer* is a term being reclaimed by a new generation of Afrikaners as a unifying concept that links them to a shared rural past.

'Land' is thus a powerful signifier of a range of collective identifications, which often bump up against one another in the rough and tumble of identity politics in post-apartheid South Africa.

Power, tradition and gender

Not only is land a basis for identity, but it also shapes power relations – within households, in communities, and in society at large. Social relations in South Africa, and thus also relations in respect of land, have been structured along lines of gender, generation and other hierarchies as well as along those of race (Claassens 2001). In rural communities control of land is a source of power for men. Marriage customs in most rural South African cultures are 'patrilocal' (on marriage, women are expected to move to the village or residence of their husband's family). Because access to land is mediated through unequal social relations with men, and often through marriage, women's rights to the land they live on and cultivate remain insecure (Meer 1997; Walker 1994). Single women and widows are often particularly vulnerable.

While the control of land was the basis of much of the power of European settlers in South Africa, traditional African authorities have also tried to use control of land to consolidate their power in rural areas, both during and after apartheid (Cousins and Claassens 2004). This control is a distortion of precolonial systems of traditional governance, in which most land administration was dealt with at lower levels of social organisation, such as the ward or the neighbourhood, not at the level of the chieftaincy (Chanock 1991; Cousins 2007). Since 1994 traditional authorities have lobbied government to recognise their custodianship of land in communal areas. Patekile Holomisa (2004: 114), a Thembu chief and president of the Congress of Traditional Leaders of South Africa (Contralesa), has stated:

> I am responsible for the historical land of amaHegebe resident in Thembuland … The institution of traditional leadership is inextricably intertwined with the land … Our advice to Government is that legal title to communal land be in the name of the relevant traditional authority. Failing to do so would further erode the role of traditional leaders in the life of our people, and would serve to cut the ties among the land, the people, and their ancestors who bequeathed the land to us.

Traditional authorities thus see land as a key to the retention of their power in rural areas. But they face mounting challenges from those espousing the democratic principles of the post-apartheid dispensation (Ntsebeza 2005). This struggle was evident in bitter controversies surrounding the passage of the Communal Land Rights Act through parliament in 2003 and 2004 (Cousins and Claassens 2004). The Act allows the transfer of title to communal land from the state to 'communities', which must register their rules before they can be recognised as 'juristic personalities'. Individual members are to be issued with a deed of communal land right that must be held jointly by all spouses, though female members of land-holding households who are not spouses are not provided for. The Act allows modified tribal authority structures, now known as 'traditional councils', to administer the land and represent the 'community' as owner. At least one-third of the membership of a land administration committee must be female.

The provision that where traditional councils exist, they will act as land administration committees was greeted with jubilation by the traditional leader lobby, but with dismay by community groups and NGOs, which saw this as undermining fundamental democratic rights. Criticism focused mainly on the fact that the Act does not provide adequately for democratic and accountable institutions for land administration. Some observers have suggested that the last-minute inclusion of this provision in the draft law was the result of a back-room political deal in the run-up to the national election. The Act is currently subject to a Constitutional Court challenge by four rural communities. Implementation is yet to begin, but if and when this commences, it is likely to generate further controversies, for example over the boundaries of 'communities' and the content of 'community rules'.

Reflections on land in the democratic era

Land occupies a central place in the post-apartheid dispensation. Although apartheid involved the loss of other assets and opportunities besides land, the new South African government has privileged the restitution of land over restitution or compensation for the devastating impact of other aspects of apartheid, like Bantu education.

Through forced removals and other processes of exclusion, however, black South Africans lost more than land. They lost livelihoods, homes, personal possessions, livestock, implements, infrastructure, social networks, and entire livelihoods and ways of life. While other forms of redress are acknowledged in law and in popular discourse, restoring land to the dispossessed has been given the status of a concrete, rights-based initiative to confer specific rights on specific people so as to redress past injustice. In both state and popular discourses the experience of dispossession and subjugation has been reduced to 'land'. By reducing the devastation of dispossession to 'land', the post-apartheid state has identified a concrete manner in which society can attempt to undo some part of what was unjust.

In its attempt to recognise rights and reconstitute fractured communities, land restitution can be understood as 'restored citizenship' (James et al. 2005). But the unified struggle to 'return to our land' has frequently given way to competition over this resource. Class conflicts have sometimes emerged between the restored owners of private property and their former tenants who also experienced dispossession, as in the case of the former 'black spots' of Cremin (Walker 2004) and Roosboom (Sato 2006) in KwaZulu-Natal, or where farm workers have been displaced by the transfer of commercial farms to claimant communities, as in the case of the ≠Khomani San in the Northern Cape (Bradstock 2006; Ellis 2006).

Recent experience with restitution shows how political processes can fail to address the multiple meanings of land. In Pondoland, villagers of Mkambati have fought a 70-year-old battle with government and with neighbouring villagers to regain control of a coastal strip of land amounting to 17,400 hectares (see Kepe 1997). Following the 'return' of this land (which remains a protected area) through a restitution process in 2004, the conflict has not subsided. At the heart of the problem is the fact that the restitution agreement worked out by government sees the original and rightful claimants of Mkambati as sharing land rights with six other villages which happen to fall under the same chief (Kepe 2004). The R60 million that the government has injected in the area as part of the settlement clearly did not mollify the locals. Something bigger than money was at stake: the respect and power that goes with ownership of land. As the settlement yielded unclear tenure rights for both Mkambati residents and the other villages, the certificate of ownership handed to all seven villages by the Minister of Land Affairs meant very little.

Despite an ambitious national programme consisting of land restitution, as well as wider land redistribution and reforms to the tenure rights of non-owners, land reform has been roundly criticised – across the political spectrum – both for being too slow and for failing to improve the livelihoods of people receiving land (ICG 2004). As a result, it has made only minimal inroads into South Africa's deeply unequal social relations. In the absence of adequate support to new landowners, the current thrust of land reform policy is to secure 'strategic partnerships' and joint ventures with private-sector investors (an 'agri-business' version of land reform). This approach is unlikely to bring real and lasting benefits to more than a select few people. New approaches are thus needed to address the impasse in land reform.

In the context of current land reform initiatives, land has become equated with agricultural land, and disconnected from land in the urban centres. In practice, the democratic era has privileged private property rights as the goal of land reform, obscuring the ways in which the rights of the people – farm workers, people in communal areas, and residents of informal settlements – who live on land owned by others continue to be marginalised (see for instance Wegerif et al. 2005). Ntsebeza (2007) has argued that the constitutional protection of private property, though not absolute, legitimates both past dispossession and the current ownership of property acquired through colonial conquest and apartheid – and is an intrinsic limitation on any programme of reform and redress. Instead, the existing property regime has been protected through the process of political transition, and so the only transformation that can be brought about is by transferring individual properties from one private owner to another.

The dominance of the private ownership model in the democratic era, and in the land reform programme itself, is indicative of the ways in which land has been commodified. Throughout the land reform programme, the equation of land with private property is evident. It has privileged the transfer of private title to individuals, households or larger groups, over initiatives to provide access to (rather than ownership of) land, such as the municipal commonage programme. This suggests that land reform that does not result in the transfer of ownership from white property owners, or the state, to black people is not considered to be 'real' land reform. The transferral of private title to individuals, households or larger groups has meant that these groups, often organised into legal entities such as communal property associations (CPAs), have received ownership of whole properties, which they own jointly. This has left the internal allocation and administration of rights within the group to internal processes, which have been frequently beset by conflict and contestation. So the democratic era has not seen the disappearance of the complex politics of land, but rather its reformulation in changing circumstances.

Conclusions

This chapter has highlighted the charged emotions around the land issue in South Africa today. These are rooted in a deeper set of questions about the multiple, divergent and sometimes contested meanings of land in contemporary South Africa. It is unlikely that these will be resolved in the near future, given the structural origins of many of these contestations, namely the persistence of rural poverty; high levels of unemployment in the formal economy; continuing ties between urban and rural areas; increasing class inequality; and the continued salience of land as a symbol of generalised racial dispossession. It seems that these deeply entrenched issues cannot be resolved by the post-apartheid state's commitment to market-based development, the protection of private property rights which this implies, and support for large-scale commercial farming.

Despite this, the many problems that beset government's land reform programme at present will not lead to its abandonment. It will, however, remain a source of tension. The long-term sustainability of the current cautious approach is doubtful, since it leaves unresolved the land question that has bedevilled South African society for centuries. Given the wide range of interests, views and meanings attached to land, the rethinking of land policy must involve inclusive, deliberative processes that address its multi-faceted character and generate both new policies and the resources required to implement them. Land remains a major challenge for post-apartheid democracy.

References

ANC (African National Congress). 1955. *Freedom Charter*, adoped at the Congress of the People, Kliptown, 26 June 1955.

ANC (African National Congress). 2004. http://www.anc.org.za/elections/2004/index.html

Bernstein, A. 2005. 'Time to Ground the Debate', *Business Day*, 27 May 2005.

Bradstock, A. 2006. 'Land Restitution and Livelihoods: the ≠Khomani San', Paper presented at the Conference on Land, Memory, Reconstruction and Justice: Perspectives on Land Restitution in South Africa, 11–13 September 2006, Houw Hoek Inn, Grabouw.

Bundy, Colin. 1988. *The Rise and Fall of the South African Peasantry*, 2nd edition (Cape Town: David Philip).

Chanock, Martin. 1991. 'Paradigms, Policies and Property: A Review of the Customary Law of Land Tenure' in Mann, Kristin and Roberts, Richard (eds.), *Law in Colonial Africa* (Portsmouth, NH: Heinemann Educational Books), pp. 61–84.

Claassens, Aninka. 2001. '"It Is Not Easy to Challenge a Chief": Lessons from Rakgwadi', Research report no. 9 (Bellville: Programme for Land and Agrarian Studies, University of the Western Cape).

Community Land Conference. 1994. *Land Charter*, Unpublished charter adopted at the Community Land Conference, Bloemfontein, 12 February 1994.

Cousins, B. 1999. 'Invisible Capital: The Contribution of Communal Rangelands to Rural Livelihoods in South Africa', *Development Southern Africa*, vol. 16, no. 2, pp. 299–318.

Cousins, B. 2007. 'More than Socially Embedded: The Distinctive Character of "Communal

Tenure" Regimes in South Africa and Its Implications for Land Policy', *Journal of Agrarian Change*, vol. 7, no. 3, pp. 281–315.

Cousins, B and Claassens, A. 2004. 'Communal Land Rights, Democracy and Traditional Leaders in Post-apartheid South Africa' in Saruchera M (ed.), *Securing Land and Resource Rights in Africa: Pan-African Perspectives* (Cape Town: Programme for Land and Agrarian Studies, University of the Western Cape).

Davenport, TRH and Saunders, C. 2000. *South Africa: A Modern History*, 5th edition (New York: St. Martin's Press).

DA. 2004. http://www.da.org.za/DA/Site/Eng/campaigns/2004/misc/manifesto.pdf.

Ellis, W. 2006. 'The ≠Khomani San Land Claim Against the Kalahari Gemsbok National Park: Requiring and Acquiring Authenticity', Paper presented at the Conference on Land, Memory, Reconstruction and Justice: Perspectives on Land Restitution in South Africa, 11–13 September 2006, Houw Hoek Inn, Grabouw.

Farmer's Weekly. 2005. 'Levubu: The Litmus Test for Land Reform', 4 March 2005.

Gibson, James L. 2001. *The Land Question in South Africa: Clouds on the Horizon* (Cape Town: Institute for Justice and Reconciliation).

Goheen, M. 1993. 'Chiefs, Sub-chiefs and Local Control: Negotiations over Land, Struggles over Meaning', *Africa*, vol. 63, no. 3, pp. 389–414.

Holomisa, P. 2004. 'Securing Rights on Communal Land' in Roth, M, Sibanda, S, Nxasana, V and Yates, T (eds.), *Finding Solutions, Securing Rights* (Durban: Butterworths).

ICG (International Crisis Group). 2004. *Blood and Soil: Land, Politics and Conflict Prevention in Zimbabwe and South Africa* (Brussels: International Crisis Group Press).

James, D, Ngonini, AX and Nkadimeng, GM. 2005. '(Re)constituting Class? Owners, Tenants and the Politics of Land Reform in Mpumalanga', *Journal of Southern African Studies*, vol. 31, no. 4, pp. 825–44.

Jary, D and Jary, J. 1995. *Collins Dictionary of Sociology*, 2nd edition (Glasgow: Harper Collins).

Kepe, T. 1997. 'Environmental Entitlements in Mkambati: Livelihoods, Social Institutions and Environmental Change on the Wild Coast of the Eastern Cape', Research report no. 1 (Bellville: Programme for Land and Agrarian Studies, University of the Western Cape).

Kepe, T. 2002. 'Grassland Vegetation and Rural Livelihoods: A Case Study of Resource Value and Social Dynamics on the Wild Coast, South Africa', PhD, University of the Western Cape.

Kepe, T. 2004. 'Land Restitution and Biodiversity Conservation in South Africa: The Case of Mkambati, Eastern Cape Province', *Canadian Journal of African Studies*, vol. 38, no. 3, pp. 688–704.

Kepe, T. 2005. 'The Magwa Tea Venture in South Africa: Politics, Land and Economics', *Social Dynamics*, vol. 31, no. 1, pp. 261–79.

Kepe, T and Cousins, B. 2002. 'Radical Land Reform Is Key to Sustainable Rural Development in South Africa', Policy brief no. 3 (Bellville: Programme for Land and Agrarian Studies, University of the Western Cape).

Mail & Guardian. 2000. 'ANC Secretary-General Motlanthe Endorses Zanu-PF Land-Grab Policy', 2 June 2000.

Mail & Guardian. 2005. 'Land Reform: SA Should "Learn from Zimbabwe"', 10 August 2005.

Meer, S (ed.) 1997. *Women, Land and Authority* (Oxford: Oxfam).

Moyo, S and Yeros, P (eds.). 2005. *Reclaiming the Land: The Resurgence of Rural Movements in Africa, Asia and Latin America* (London: Zed Press).

Ncapayi, F. 2005. 'Land Need in South Africa: Who Needs Land for What?', MPhil thesis, Programme for Land and Agrarian Studies, University of the Western Cape.

Ntsebeza, L. 2005. *Democracy Compromised: Chiefs and the Politics of Land in South Africa* (Leiden: Brill Academic).

Ntsebeza, L. 2007. 'Slow Delivery in South Africa's Land Reform Programme: The Property Clause Revisited' in Ntsebeza, L and Hall, R (eds.), *The Land Question in South Africa: The Challenge of Transformation and Redistribution* (Cape Town: HSRC Press).

PAC (Pan Africanist Congress). 2007. The Pan-Africanist Congress of Azania. Website: www.panafricanperspective.com/pac/ (accessed 28 June 2007).

Peters, PE. 1984. 'Struggles over Water, Struggles over Meaning: Cattle, Water and the State in Botswana', *Africa*, vol. 54, no. 3, pp. 29–49.

Platzky, L and Walker, C. 1985. *The Surplus People: Forced Removals in South Africa* (Johannesburg: Ravan).

Sato, C. 2006. 'Land Restitution and Community Politics: A Case of Roosboom in KwaZulu-Natal, South Africa', Paper presented at the Conference on Land, Memory, Reconstruction and Justice: Perspectives on Land Restitution in South Africa, 11–13 September 2006, Houw Hoek Inn, Grabouw.

Shackleton, CM and Shackleton, SE. 2004. 'The Importance of Non-timber Forest Products in Rural Livelihood Security and as Safety Nets: A Review of Evidence from South Africa', *South African Journal of Science,* vol. 100, nos. 11 and 12, pp. 658–64.

Shackleton, SE. 2005. 'The Significance of the Trade in Natural Resource Products for Livelihoods and Poverty Alleviation in South Africa', PhD thesis, Rhodes University.

Walker, C. 1994. 'Women, "Tradition", and Reconstruction', *Review of African Political Economy*, no. 61, pp. 347–58.

Walker, C. 2004. '"We Are Consoled": Reconstructing Cremin', *South African Historical Journal*, no. 51, pp. 199–223.

Wegerif, M, Russell, B and Grundling, I. 2005. *Still Searching for Security: The Reality of Farm Dweller Evictions in South Africa* (Polokwane: Nkuzi Development Association and Johannesburg: Social Surveys).

Market and Economy

Thomas Koelble

FEW CONCEPTS PROVOKE as much political debate as 'the economy', whether it is determined by 'the market' or not. The term 'economy' is often used to describe the space in which commodities are produced and consumed. This interpretation concentrates on the productive capacities and sectors of that economy (e.g. mining, agriculture, manufacture and services). The analytical emphasis is often placed on whether these sectors produce efficiently or not and whether they are internationally competitive or not. What tends to be forgotten in this restrictive definition is that there are several aspects to the contemporary global economy, especially the international financial markets, in which it is not commodities that are traded but derivatives, futures and options (essentially risks) instead.

The term 'market' is often used to describe the space in which commodities and goods are bought and sold. Here the analytical emphasis is placed on the actions of producers and consumers, on the institutions, rules and regulations guiding that behaviour, and on the mechanisms of supply and demand. To ascertain the performance of national economies and markets, analysts focus on the performance and composition of the local stock markets. Again, this restrictive notion of the market neglects the fact that there are markets in which commodities play a subordinate role. The largest global market today, by far, is that for derivatives in which large investment and hedge funds operate and speculate on everything from exchange rates to political country risks. This market alone is many times larger in dollar terms than the wealth concentrated in all national stock markets globally combined.

The terms 'market' and 'economy' have both a technical meaning, in the sense that economists subject them to scientific analysis and prediction, and a political meaning. Before we turn to these technical and political discourses in South Africa, it is useful to think of the ways in which economic philosophers interpret the relationship between economy, market and society, and examine the different views on what the proper relationship between these entities ought to be.

Economic theories: liberals, Keynesians, corporatists and Marxists

Liberal and the more contemporary neoliberal economists argue that the state should interfere as little as possible in market mechanisms (essentially the law of supply and demand). Markets, according to this point of view, are self-regulating institutions and will, if left to their own devices, find the most efficient ways of satisfying demand. Interference by the state in the market, through the artificial creation of demand or regulation, always has the effect of inefficiency and higher costs and ought to be avoided. If the state refrains from interfering, the economy is likely to be a very efficient producer of goods and services.

Moreover, liberals argue that the state ought to play a minimal role as both employer and provider of welfare to its citizens, because public enterprises tend to squeeze out private investment (which is held to be more efficient and productive than the state sector) and encourage dependence on welfare hand-outs. In other words, if the state leaves the economy to the private sector and market forces, an efficient economy will emerge. This form of liberal economic thought has been labelled 'laissez-faire'.

In contrast, Keynesian economists argue that there is a role for state interference, particularly when the economy finds itself in a major downswing. Both liberal and Keynesian economists agree that the economy is driven by the business cycle in which the economy is subject to expansion (the upswing of the business cycle in which products are invented, production takes off, jobs are created, and prosperity increases) and recession (the downside of the business cycle in which demand for products is saturated, factories close, and jobs are lost). Keynesian economists agree, too, with liberal economists that the state should avoid interfering in the working of the marketplace as the business cycle is a normal occurrence leading to both expansion and contraction.

However, Keynesian economists suggest that sometimes recessions cannot be overcome by the 'natural' mechanisms of the market, and in such times the state has to intervene in order to avoid an economic meltdown (depression). With controlled state spending (demand stimulation), the economy should be stimulated and supply will follow. Moreover, Keynesians believe that state institutions can be used to overcome the tendency in capitalism towards inequality between the social classes by mechanisms of redistribution (taxation, regulation of certain sectors and activities, and social policy). While Keynesians may disagree among themselves as to the extent of the welfare state or levels of regulation, the consensus is that the modern state needs to function as a mechanism to avoid or reduce social and economic inequality. Such interference in the economy functions as a stimulator to the economy through the demand for goods and services by those otherwise unable to afford basic goods and services.

Marxist economists believe that the capitalist economy ought to be regulated by the state because it has an inherent tendency towards an unequal distribution of wealth, and those holding capital are always in an advantageous position in relation to those selling their labour power. Capitalist economies are, by their very nature, based on exploitation and the extraction of labour power, and produce unequal social and economic relations between social classes. In order to achieve equality, the state has to be deployed to redistribute wealth from rich to poor.

A variation on the view that the state ought to guide the economy is expressed by the corporatist school of economics. Here the emphasis is placed on the nationalist project in which the state is seen as the key mechanism to create, build and stimulate a successful national economy through protection of its domestic industries in order to establish a powerful nation-state (Gourevitch 1986).

The battle between these various points of view (there are several others but we have stayed with the most important schools of economic thought) has been decisively won in the US and some parts of Europe by the liberal point of view, which dominates economic thinking. With the collapse of communism, Marxism has lost its global influence whereas Keynesian economics is still prevalent in many parts of Europe and the developing world. In recent years, with the globalisation of the world economy, the neoliberal point of view has been the dominant paradigm in such institutions as the World Bank and the International Monetary Fund. These global institutions advise governments of lending nations to adopt neoliberal economic policies and require that countries hoping to borrow from either institution adopt their economic policy prescriptions.

The rise and fall of apartheid and the South African economy

During the apartheid era, National Party politicians used to argue that the South African state and regime stood as a lonely beacon of market-driven, and by implication liberal, economies and as a bulwark against the state-directed and -controlled economies of much of the rest of Africa, inspired by either the communist Soviet Union or China (O'Meara 1996). This association with market economies and the West was only partially correct as the economy contained large-scale public enterprises that functioned to provide public service employment primarily for the Afrikaner community. In that sense, the South African economy was not a liberal economy but one that had more in common with heavily regulated communist or nationalist economies such as Russia or Germany, and with the corporatist model rather than the liberal one.

At the same time, South Africa's racial policies so heavily manipulated the labour and other markets that the association with the capitalist economies of the West was more a political and rhetorical gesture than a reflection of the true nature of the apartheid state, economy and society. The structure of the South African economy earned it the label of 'racial capitalism' since it functioned to benefit whites at the expense of the non-white communities (Wolpe 1988). While South Africa was a world leader in the export of minerals and agricultural produce, this system of labour exploitation was an economic success for its corporate sector and the white community (Minter 1986). During the apartheid years the political-economic debate moved between the socialism of much of the anti-apartheid movement (the African National Congress (ANC), the South African Communist Party (SACP) and large parts of the trade union movement), the liberalism of the white English-speaking opposition (supported by parts of the corporate sector), and the state corporatist model of the National Party.

The systematic exploitation of the black workforce, coupled with inferior education and training, proved to be the undoing of the economy and regime once its mainstays, mining and agriculture, lost their pre-eminent status as foreign income earners by the mid-1970s (Price 1991). From the point of view of the up-and-coming manufacturing, banking and service industries, and the high-technology-oriented 'new economy' generally, the apartheid regime became an impediment to growth. Based on technical skills and know-how, such an economy had little room for the abundant, low-skill labour produced by apartheid.

Moreover, the increasing isolation of the country meant that several important, export-oriented sectors came under increasing pressure from their customers and clients to 'do something' about the racial policies of the pariah state. Those sectors and firms looking to access international markets, particularly the financial markets, found themselves isolated and, not surprisingly, became the vanguard of the business community's efforts to bring about the democratic transition in the mid- to late 1980s (Terreblanche 2002). By the mid-1980s, it had become abundantly clear to the large South African corporations that if they did not join the international marketplace, they would not be able to compete effectively in the future. This realisation is at the very foundation of the new South African dispensation and explains the support the new government received from these corporations in the transition period between 1986 and 1994.

It is one of the ironies of the transition that all three competing economic conceptions have found a home in the ANC government. A socialist and corporatist wing and opposition exist but liberal ideology has become entrenched as the economic strategy of the government and its key financial ministries. At the same time, socialist and some corporatist elements compete with their liberal counterparts over policy, patronage and power. The struggle between these ideological groupings has become more pronounced in the so-called battle for succession, the search for President Mbeki's successor.

The new South Africa: dismantling racial capitalism and its legacies through the RDP

With the advent of the new democratic dispensation in 1994, the meaning of the terms 'free market' and 'economy' took on several new dimensions. While the early political rhetoric and ideology of the ANC indicated a commitment to some form of state socialism or, at least, Keynesian social democracy, the actions of the ANC government can be described as broadly in line with the internationally dominant neoliberal paradigm, sometimes also referred to as the Washington Consensus (Marais 2001).

The trajectory from a supposedly interventionist to a free market approach was rapid and can be linked to the fortunes of the South African currency on the international financial markets as well as to the policy options most favoured by the large corporations. The early Mandela administration enjoyed a honeymoon on the international markets for about 18 months or so after the 1994 elections, but soon found itself exposed to the vagaries of the international financial markets. The story of the South African economy and market is in large part driven by the responses of the international and domestic markets and perceptions of the new government's behaviour in relation to the regulation of the economy (Koelble 2004; Koelble and LiPuma 2006).

At first, the ANC adopted the Reconstruction and Development Programme (RDP) as its main economic policy platform. The goal of this approach was to address the legacies of the apartheid regime through a targeted set of social and economic policies that would deal with the exceptionally high levels of inequality between black and white, rich and poor, skilled and unskilled. South Africa was (and still is) the most unequal society on the face of the planet next to Brazil and Guatemala in terms of wealth distribution and the ANC proposed to do something about this. During the electoral campaign preceding the first fully democratic elections in April 1994, the ANC suggested that its RDP would create millions of jobs and houses, and form the basis of a flourishing economy that would be able to tackle poverty, inequality and misery.

Moreover, a concerted policy approach would eradicate discrimination on the labour market and would redistribute the wealth of the nation in far more equitable ways through the use of state spending to assist the previously disadvantaged. It is therefore not surprising that the ANC has stressed the importance of 'service delivery' in its political rhetoric and has found itself in an uncomfortable situation when its promises of delivery fail to materialise.

In the middle of 1996, the government redesigned its economic approach, announcing that while the RDP was still the main economic platform, a new strategy – the Growth, Employment and Redistribution (GEAR) programme – would now set the scene for government policy. The adoption of GEAR coincided with the first major devaluation of the South African currency in 1996 when the currency lost 25% of its value in a few weeks. GEAR aimed at reducing inflation and the budget deficit, and liberalising the economy through a commitment to privatisation of the state sector and loosening of exchange control.

The issue of exchange controls was particularly controversial as the new government had retained its predecessor's regulations that made it difficult to transfer capital outside South Africa. The larger corporations pushed for the abolition of these controls arguing that they were ineffective, inefficient, anachronistic, and an obstacle to attracting foreign capital to the country. They were also keen to divest from the South African stock exchange and enter the larger, more lucrative European and US stock and consumer markets. Several of the large corporations – De Beers, Anglo American, SA Breweries and Old Mutual, to name a few – divested as soon as they could, with negative spin-off effects on the South African currency. Nonetheless, the decision by the ANC government to loosen exchange controls in 1996 was largely driven by the desire to stabilise the value of the currency.

Essentially, GEAR turned out to be an austerity programme in which government spending levels were curtailed, and inflation and the budget deficit were drastically reduced. At the same time, interest rates were held considerably higher than the inflation rate in order to attract investment in the local currency and to the local economy. In effect, this policy led to a squeeze on economic activity, mostly reflected in the spiralling number of unemployed and the closure of businesses. The austerity policy of the government held until the budget of 2002, when the fortunes of the South African rand took a positive turn and economic activity showed real signs of an economic take-off. Trevor Manuel, the Minister of Finance, declared that the years of hardship would now be followed by years of harvest, indicating that he himself saw the years between 1996 and 2002 as years of austerity.

Although spending in education, health care and social programmes (particularly the child and pension grants) have been increased substantially since 2002, the question remains whether this can ameliorate the depth of poverty as the rate of unemployment increases. There are several studies that indicate that while state spending has increased, it has not kept pace with the needs of the general population, and the demand for social grants outstrips supply (Daniel et al. 2005). Similarly, the ANC's commitment to land reform, one of the hottest and most politically symbolic issues, must be questioned when less than 0.1% of the annual budget is devoted to that issue.

More than ten years after the first elections, observers are sharply divided over the success or failure of the government in addressing issues of unemployment, poverty and the distribution of wealth. Defenders of the government argue that the ANC has succeeded in creating the economic conditions that will allow for the South African economy to 'take off' by introducing a macro-economic approach that reduced inflation from its historically high levels of 15% or more in 1994 down to less than 4% in 2005. The government has also reduced its budget deficit to less than 2% of GDP, which, by any standard, is an exceptional achievement. It has been able to push down interest rates to less than 10% in the last two years (at the time of writing in June 2007, the repo rate was at 9.5% while the interest rate charged by the Reserve Bank had just increased to 13%) and thereby reduced the cost of borrowing. The government has, moreover, created over a million jobs; has provided several million houses; connected millions of households to water and electricity; and ensured that education, social services and the welfare system have been extended to the entire population instead of serving a small minority (ANC 2004). While unemployment remains stubbornly high – at over 26% of the active working population – the government has succeeded in putting the economy on 'the right track'. It is therefore no wonder that one hears President Mbeki and several of his ministers, particularly the Minister of Finance, claim that the 'economic fundamentals' are in place.

In sum, the term 'market' took on a much more liberal connotation under the ANC government from 1996 onwards. The market was to be utilised to address many of the socio-economic problems confronting the nation and the economy was to be liberalised so as to make it competitive in the global economy. As a result, ANC economic strategy moved away from its initial Keynesian approach to one compatible with the neoliberal view espoused by international financial institutions and global organisations such as the World Bank and the IMF.

The post-apartheid economy as a house with two floors and no stairs in-between: from race to class and back

While still Deputy President, Thabo Mbeki made several speeches pointing out that South Africa consisted of 'two nations', one black and poor, the other white and affluent. He characterised this situation as unsustainable and in need of redress. After 1999, the rhetoric of the President shifted. In several addresses, he made the point that the South African economy is divided sharply between a largely formal economy in which participants (mostly white but including an increasing number of black, Indian and coloured South Africans) are doing well and a largely informal one (mostly populated by black South Africans) in which the great majority of citizens find themselves with little chance of achieving prosperity.

The President has, on several occasions, reminded the local business community that 'business has never had it so good' and that those in the first economy are doing exceptionally well as a result of the opening up and liberalisation of the economy after 1994. The President has pleaded with the business sector to take into account the large informal economy and open up pathways between first and second economies to help alleviate the tensions between the 'haves' and the 'have-nots'. His rhetoric represents a stick and carrot approach– if the business community transforms itself voluntarily and assists in diminishing poverty and inequality levels, then the government will not be forced to adopt more drastic measures in terms of taxation and redistribution policies. If, however, the business community fails to do so, then the ensuing conditions may not only be negative for business, but will reinforce the need for the government to intervene. In other words, the state will be forced to abandon the current laissez-faire approach and become far more interventionist.

There is one economic policy arena in which the government has been explicitly interventionist and that is the issue of black economic empowerment, or BEE. Largely through the use of government procurement, and also through legislation requiring transformation in management and ownership structures, the government has attempted to encourage companies and firms to embrace 'transformation'. This approach is designed to open up firms and corporations to those previously disadvantaged and to force white-owned businesses to take on black owners, managers and employees. BEE is aimed at changing the ownership and workforce composition of business to become much more representative of the composition of the nation (Southall 2005).

Currently, the proportion of white- as opposed to black-owned capital is still highly skewed in favour of whites. Similarly, in terms of the composition of company boards and management structures, black directors and managers are a rarity. Advocates of BEE claim that the ANC is well on its way to achieving its goals as levels of inequality between white and black have decreased substantially and, while the composition of corporate boardrooms may still be predominantly white and male, it is slowly becoming more mixed in terms of race and gender. Critics, on the other hand, argue that the BEE approach has indeed created a small, extremely affluent black elite as well as a broader black middle class, but has done nothing to alleviate the living conditions of the poor or even ordinary black workers.

To summarise, the political rhetoric of the ANC government has moved from a view of the market and the economy as being biased towards a racial group – whites – to a more nuanced stance in which those in the 'first' economy benefit, though at the expense of those in the informal economy. While the ANC appears to agree with liberal economists that the economy is largely a technical and not a political terrain, it has used its economic policy approach to pressure domestic capital to address the issue of racial injustice. The main attempt to deal with the imbalances inherited from the apartheid past has been through a policy of black empowerment, though this has left many with the impression that a relatively small elite of black, coloured and Indian individuals benefit rather than the broad majority of citizens. In other words, the discourse of 'affirmative action' and 'black empowerment', which borrows heavily from the US debate, has replaced earlier notions of radical transformation.

Is the ANC's economic strategy 'neoliberal' or not?

Critics of the government claim that the ANC has lost its way. According to these critics, very often members of the ruling party, the government has sold its soul to domestic and international capital and that it has adopted the maxim 'Ask not what capital can do for your country but what your country can do for capital' (Saul 2002). One of the most vocal critics, Patrick Bond (2005), argues that the situation of the poor under the ANC government has not only not improved but has, in fact, deteriorated since the coming of democracy. He points out that while there may be some truth in the contention that services like electricity and water have been extended to those in dire need of it, the policy of making impoverished people pay for them means that those least able to afford such services are the first to be disconnected when they fall in arrears with payment. There has been resistance to the rates policy of the government ranging from widespread theft of electricity through illegal connections, to the formation of non-governmental organisations, such as the Soweto Electricity Crisis Committee (SECC), whose sole purpose is to campaign for free electricity for the poor.

In short, these critics – President Mbeki has referred to them as 'the ultra-left' – claim that the ANC's economic strategy has enriched the affluent while impoverishing the poor, and that the supposed 'trickle-down' effect of liberal economic policy has not eventuated. Just as the poor got poorer in countries like the US and Britain as a result of neoliberalism under Reagan and Thatcher, they are getting poorer in places like South Africa that have imitated the neoliberal economic paradigm. Faced as well with the effects of the HIV/AIDS pandemic, the lot of the poor has deteriorated since the 'liberation' of 1994. Organisations such as the Landless People's Movement (LPM) or the SECC believe that the ANC has abandoned any commitment to socialism and the 'two-stage theory of national liberation' in which freedom would be followed by socialism.

Defenders of the strategy argue that the ANC was faced with the unpleasant task of 'rightsizing' a bloated state apparatus, unwieldy public enterprises and an over-regulated siege economy, and that it has done so remarkably well (Hirsch 2005). From an international perspective, the situation confronting the ANC was not unlike that of other left-of-centre political movements that came to power after prolonged dictatorships and authoritarian regimes. Such regimes had built up a large state apparatus by means of which they could dispense patronage, create employment and maintain sufficient political support. After the regimes collapsed, the new democratic dispensations that succeeded them were faced with the task of establishing a much more efficient basis for the economy, one that required a smaller state, less taxation, deregulation of all sorts of markets, and the privatisation of state assets.

In South Africa, bringing down inflation and the deficit, liberalising the financial markets, and guaranteeing the independence of the Reserve Bank were all steps towards international recognition and acceptance to attract foreign investment. No emerging market economy, unless it produces a great deal of oil, can afford to disregard the dictates of the international financial markets in its economic policy choices. The assumption here is that once the economy is set on the path to prosperity, resources will accrue to the government to help fund policies designed to alleviate poverty, social inequity and unemployment. To attempt to do so before correcting the faults of the past would be to invite economic instability with all its negative side-effects.

The 'entrepreneur'

One of the remarkable aspects of the adoption of neoliberal economic policy has been the emergence of the term 'entrepreneur' in the South African political and cultural lexicon. This term was hardly ever used during the apartheid regime, except to indicate a businessperson of exceptional qualities. The term did not fit particularly well with the corporatist model of the South African economy, even though there were impressive business leaders who stood above the rest in terms of wealth and power such as Harry Oppenheimer or Anton Rupert. On the political Left, the word was tainted and was used as a term of derision for particularly rapacious capitalists.

In the new South Africa, the term has taken on a variety of new meanings, and describes a wide range of individuals and their activities. There is talk of the 'township entrepreneur', plucky individuals who have lifted themselves up by their own bootstraps, achieved a modicum of wealth, and therefore should be seen as role models for the rest of society. These individuals have taken responsibility for their own success and have, with drive and determination, overcome the odds stacked against them. Then there are the 'social entrepreneurs' who have used part of their business success to help others less fortunate either through corporate responsibility programmes or through some form of charitable organisation designed to help those in need.

Of greatest importance are the successful 'black entrepreneurs', who through their own considerable effort have achieved great wealth and success. Very often, these individuals have risen from the ranks of the ANC and have used their position to climb to positions of great wealth and power in a short period of time. Defenders of these developments argue that the emergence of this group (also known as 'black diamonds') is part and parcel of a much broader growth of a considerable black middle class which is currently fuelling the consumer frenzy in the South African economy. Critics, on the other hand, claim that these individuals represent the tendency of the capitalist system to entice former opponents into its ranks and silence the most vocal and articulate of its critics. One fascinating aspect is that the term has taken on a largely positive connotation right across the South African political spectrum, and mirrors the consensus, at least among the major political parties, in respect of the neoliberal economic policy direction.

Did 'globalisation' make them do it?

Amongst critics, there are those who argue that globalisation forced ANC policy-makers into the approach they eventually took. Others suggest that this is a mere ruse, evidence of either a lack of conviction in bringing about a true transformation of the South African economy or a sell-out to the interests of the corporate sector in return for a luxurious lifestyle – or both. However, there is something to be said for a more sophisticated analysis of global conditions. Both defenders and critics of the government's actions need to realise that the context within which emergent market democracies are now forced to design their policies is highly circumscribed by market movements that are both difficult to predict and hard to stop. The devaluation of the rand in 2001, and the political controversy it caused, should serve as a reminder of the complex interplay between global and local economic interests and the web of restraint they impose on any government that wishes to regulate its economy.

The story here is that despite low inflation, low budget deficits and high interest rates, the rand suffered in 2001 an enormous devaluation, which seems to have been triggered by the complex interplay between local and international firms speculating against the currency. The government even created a commission of inquiry into the depreciation in order to find out who might have been responsible. Although fingers were pointed at Deutsche Bank in particular for speculating against the currency, it appears that all the large financial institutions in South Africa (and those with substantial rand holdings globally) were speculating against the rand, driving it to lower and lower levels. Many of these companies had engaged in an activity called 'asset swapping', which the Reserve Bank considered to be on the borderline of the illegal and in need of regulation.

When the Bank signalled its regulatory intentions, these financial institutions began to sell off the currency in order to clear their books. While the details of the story are murky and extremely complex, the result of the sell-off was that inflation and interest rates rose, and the 'economic fundamentals' achieved by GEAR austerity were placed in jeopardy by international and domestic currency speculators.

What this story illuminates is that the government is not free to design its economic polices as it wishes but does so with a keen sense of the reactions of both domestic and international financial markets to its social, economic and regulatory policies. And this observation raises all sorts of questions about the democratic nature of the world economy, the democratic nature of the local economy, and the impact of global markets on local and supposedly democratic decisions. There are global structural constraints on emerging market democracies such as South Africa. And while the ANC attempts to move the economic debate into a more technical and less political realm, talk of 'the market' and the 'economy' is saturated with political symbolism and ideological rhetoric. Global constraints and local demands on the government to provide 'a better life for all' (one of the ANC's earliest campaign slogans) are clearly at odds with one another, and require government to maintain a precarious balance between satisfying the demands of global and local business and a large swath of citizens trapped in poverty. Making the market and the economy work for all is the challenge the ANC has set itself. The jury is still out as to whether it has succeeded in doing so.

References

ANC. 2004. *Ten Year Review*, http://www.anc.org.za.

Bond, Patrick. 2005. *Elite Transition* (Pietermaritzburg: University of Natal Press).

Daniel, J, Southall, R and Lutchman, J (eds.). 2005. *State of the Nation 2004–2005* (Cape Town: HSRC).

Gourevitch, Peter. 1986. *Politics in Hard Times* (Ithaca: Cornell University Press).

Hirsch, A. 2005. *Season of Hope: Economic Reform under Mandela and Mbeki* (Pietermaritzburg: University of KwaZulu-Natal Press).

Koelble, Thomas. 2004. 'Economic Policy in the Post-colony: South Africa between Keynesian Remedies and Neo-liberal Pain', *New Political Economy*, vol. 9, no. 1, pp. 57–78.

Koelble, Thomas and LiPuma, Edward. 2006. 'The Effects of Circulatory Capitalism on Democratization: Observations from South Africa and Brazil', *Democratization*, vol. 13, no. 5, pp. 605–31.

Marais, Hein. 2001. *South Africa: Limits to Change* (Cape Town: University of Cape Town Press).

Minter, Alan. 1986. *King Solomon's Mines Revisited* (New York: Basic Books).

O'Meara, Dan. 1996. *Forty Lost Years: The Apartheid State and the Politics of the National Party, 1948–1994* (Randburg: Ravan).

Price, Robert M. 1991. *The Apartheid State in Crisis* (Oxford: Oxford University Press).

Saul, John S. 2002. 'Cry for the Beloved Country' in Jacobs, S and Calland, R (eds.), *Thabo Mbeki's World* (Pietermaritzburg: University of KwaZulu-Natal Press), pp. 27–52.

Southall, Roger. 2005. 'Black Empowerment and Corporate Capital' in Daniel, J, Southall, R and Lutchman, J (eds.), *State of the Nation: South Africa 2004–2005* (Cape Town: HSRC).

Terreblanche, Sampie. 2002. *A History of Inequality in South Africa* (Pietermaritzburg: University of Natal Press).

Wolpe, Harold. 1988. *Race, Class and the Apartheid State* (London: James Currey).

RACE

Zimitri Erasmus

Why does 'race' remain central in post-apartheid everyday life and consciousness?[1] Is a future beyond race simply a fantasy, or is it a real possibility? Answers to these questions lie in asking others first. How did the idea of race emerge? How do these ideas shape the ways in which most South Africans use the term 'race' today? What would it take to unmake race or, at least, to make it less central? Here I highlight some key moments in the history of the concept of race in order to show how these have shaped its current uses.

Race, modern science and apartheid

Before the European Enlightenment, humans conceived of the natural world and its impact on their lives as the work of God or the gods. It was accepted that individuals, although equal before God, were unequal socially and legally. To be a slave or a member of the lower orders was a legal or often religious status rather than a natural, biologically defined one. This changed with the onset of modernity[2] when science took on the task of defining and ordering the natural world.

Nineteenth-century biology was instrumental in defining 'man' as a species of the animal kingdom and thus part of nature. At the same time, the discipline of geology introduced, in place of biblical time, the idea of time as evolutionary and linear. This temporal order shaped both the evolutionary biology and the physical anthropology of that century (McGrane 1989). In the context of evolutionary thinking, natural scientists became concerned to find the 'missing link' between humans and animals.

Transposed on to socio-cultural aspects of human life, ideas of natural evolution shaped conceptions of human development as progressing in evolutionary fashion from primitive to civilised and so helped explain human differences both over time (e.g. the Celtic warrior vs the modern Briton) and contemporaneously (e.g. the 'Bushman' vs the Victorian gentleman). Drawing on this matrix of evolutionary thought, life sciences in the nineteenth century were anchored by theories of origins, descent and kinship. The modern idea of race emerged from these scientific discourses of lineage, origins and evolution, 'making it, like nature, about roots and origins' (Haraway 1996: 321–2). Within this paradigm, race, understood as a biological fact, became intricately connected to hierarchically structured models of humanity and culture.

Southern Africa's place in the making of this race science in the early nineteenth century was that of a 'human laboratory'. Indigenous Khoisan peoples became 'specimens' – living and dead – used by mainstream scientists to prove the controversial 'missing link' between apes and humans, and the existence of primitive human 'types' (Dubow 1995). This is exemplified in the now well-documented story of Saartje Baartman (Abrahams 1997; Gilman 1985; Gould 1985; Magubane 2001; Strother 1999). Building on the work of the eighteenth-century taxonomist Linnaeus, the French anatomist Georges Cuvier, who dissected Baartman's body, used her to advance the idea of race as a natural 'type' or 'kind'. This idea implied that visible as well as invisible differences among groups of people reflected typological differences (themselves placed in a hierarchy) that were not only natural and unchangeable but also unbridgeable.

Paradoxically, the growth of a 'race science' coincided with the emergence of the idea that humans were both naturally equal and equal before the law (Fredrickson 2002). Universal equality meant exclusion had to be justified, and this is where race science played a significant role. Inequalities such as those based on race and gender could be justified only by scientific evidence that human differences were found in nature. Scientists made race and sex objects of study for the purposes of establishing such evidence (Schiebinger 1993). In addition to this naturalisation of difference, the diversity of humankind was understood historically in terms of the progressive development of people from primitive to civilised. Thus, all those who occupied the highest rungs of the evolutionary ladder – Europeans, and especially men – were both the same and equal, while those who were by nature and by history different – Africans, Asians, women, etc. – were unequal.

Race – understood biologically in terms of genetic inheritance, descent, and physical features – and culture – understood as behavioural characteristics, as an expression of race, and in terms of the progress of civilisation – both became markers of primordial human superiority and inferiority. Inequalities were thus presented as found and rooted in nature rather than made by humans in the context of the politics and power relations of states and empires. The racial violence of colonialism, the Nazi genocide of the Jews, and the racial terror of apartheid, all derived their logic from these ideas.

In Europe challenges to race science, hitherto marginal, took centre-stage after the Second World War when mainstream scientific conceptions of race were turned upside down: race was demoted from being a biological fact or truth to a meaningless falsity. Scientists declared race scientifically invalid and went as far as suggesting that the term be 'dropped altogether' (Montagu 1964: 9). In its place came the anti-typological idea of permeable, adaptable, natural populations defined by 'gene pools' as a way of understanding human variation. Although the idea of human populations moved away from the notion of race as 'type', the discourse of biological science – rather than politics – continued to provide the framework for understanding human difference and development. Furthermore, objections to the biological category were not necessarily always accompanied by challenges to the assumptions underpinning the idea of race, many of which continued to circulate under new guises (Boonzaier 1988: 58).

As with all new ideas, the anti-typological idea of race took a while to filter into social practice. Despite this shift and contrary to the process of decolonisation that took place in most of the rest of Africa in the 1960s, South Africa followed an almost diametrically opposite route by setting up 'the most comprehensive racist regime … the world has ever seen' (Fredrickson 2002: 133). Twentieth-century South African thinking about racial segregation and apartheid was strongly influenced by nineteenth-century scientific ideas of race and human difference. Apartheid ideology drew on an often contradictory synthesis of race science, German ideas of cultural nationalism, and the quasi-religious notion that God had created diverse peoples or nations each blessed with a unique culture, though some were 'more developed' or 'more civilised' than others (Dubow 1995; Fredrickson 2002).

Until the 1920s the idea of race in South Africa was shaped by the experience of the South African War. While divisions between settlers and 'natives' were couched in racialised language, at the same time 'race', as a synonym for nation, was used to refer primarily to divisions among white British and Afrikaner settlers (the 'white races'). But with the Depression of the 1930s and increasing industrialisation and urbanisation in the 1940s, working-class white Afrikaans-speaking people felt threatened by the movement to the cities of African jobseekers, and by their growing resistance to white oppression. In this context, the idea of race as a reference to divisions between white and black people grew strongly, and the need for apartheid (separateness) became a major rallying cry of the emerging Afrikaner nationalist movement. Race, class and cultural nationalism all intersected in the apartheid project and, in the 1960s and 1970s, they shaped the Bantustan policy in which ideas of culture and nation came to do the work of race.

The apartheid government used race to classify South Africans by law into a general hierarchy of 'types' with correspondingly differential access to human rights and freedoms. While those classified 'white' were full citizens, and those classified 'coloured' and 'Indian' were partial citizens, 'Africans', who were at the bottom of this structure, were considered for the most part tribal subjects.[3] By this logic, Africans were also subdivided into separate cultural categories of 'ethnicity' – Xhosa, Zulu, Tswana and so on – each destined to evolve into an independent nation. Apartheid discourse thus merged race, culture and nation. It made race 'real' materially – by entrenching unequal access to housing, employment, remuneration, education, health and other social services – and also non-materially, by defining where one could live, what one could aspire to be, and whom one could love.

Apartheid race categories were thus based not only on who one's ancestors were and 'what one looked like' but also on 'how one lived', what language one spoke and whom one associated with, making race and culture inseparable. In this context, race became normalised and naturalised not only through its taken-for-granted visibility, but also through assumptions about culture, understood as an expression of race and as a given essence.

Lived reality defied apartheid's 'pure types', though in the same breath people sometimes resorted to using and manipulating the system of racial classification to pass for 'white' or 'coloured' in order to access the rights and opportunities associated with these legal categories. In general, classification and reclassification had profound and painful consequences for people's everyday lives. Among these were the splitting of families and the renouncing of kin of a darker skin because of fear of exposure. The story of Sandra Laing, the dark-skinned daughter of a 'white' couple who was reclassified as 'coloured' and later as African (Thomas 1977), and Zoë Wicomb's recent novel *Playing in the Light* (2006), attest to these consequences.

Furthermore, apartheid's race categories created clearly defined places for people in the material and social world and, at the same time, specific ways for people to be in the world. For the most part, people came to see themselves in terms of these categories, thus making them subjectively real. This history has meant that after apartheid, most South Africans' lived experiences continue to be shaped by racialised material and subjective realities. This can be seen in both the continued racialised inequalities and in the ways South Africans use the concept of race today.

Race after apartheid

While there was a close correlation between race and class during apartheid, these inequalities now intersect in more complex ways in South Africa post-1994. Wealthy black South Africans are mostly able to escape the brutal and material effects of race. In many cases, they continue to experience race discrimination but in more subtle forms (Steyn and Van Zyl 2001; Luhabe 2002; Soudien 2004; Erasmus 2006). Poor and working-class black people, on the other hand, still face the effects of race. For example, wages among rural and urban working people often remain ranked by race

(De Swardt 2003; Bezuidenhout 2003), and the poor remain predominantly black.

The violence of race, though, is often more direct. In January 2004, Nelson Chisale, a black farm worker, was tied to a tree, beaten unconscious and then fed to a pride of lions by his former white employer, Mark Scott-Crossley. Another black worker, Simon Mathebula, was an accomplice in this murder (*The Guardian*, 1 October 2005). This is but one example of the physical brutality of race faced by the poor.

To complicate matters, the arrival of increasing numbers of refugee and migrant Africans displaced by wars beyond South Africa's borders has led to the emergence of xeno-racism, a practice that fuses race, culture and nation (in a somewhat different configuration from the same fusion of apartheid ideology) for the purposes of excluding these other Africans, often with violent consequences (Valji 2003; Landau 2004). Finally, although most white South Africans today continue to benefit from the legacy of legally guaranteed race privilege during apartheid, whiteness no longer confers automatic privilege. These changes have not unmade or de-centred race. Instead, they show that while race remains a key factor shaping inequality and vulnerability, it is now reproduced and spoken about differently.

In the post-apartheid era, discourses of race have taken on various forms, often comprising contradictory beliefs. Here I outline two predominant ways in which South Africans use race. One sees race as nothing and nowhere, an approach social scientists refer to as 'colour-blindness'; the other sees race as everything and everywhere, commonly known as an essentialist approach.

Race: nothing and nowhere

Some colour-blind approaches draw on mid-twentieth-century scientific ideas dismissive of race, arguing that race as a biological concept is invalid, an illusion, and hence should be dropped completely. Others assert the validity of race as a biological category while subscribing to a colour-blind position when arguing against employment equity policies and black economic empowerment. For the most part, those who subscribe to these approaches insist that since the end of apartheid, race is no longer politically significant, and therefore any use or recognition of the concept is itself a racist practice harking back to apartheid. Proponents of this view argue that the concept should be abandoned in the interests of building a society in which race no longer matters. From this perspective, it is futile to consider the ways in which ideas of race have shaped formal and commonsense thinking, institutionalised practices, as well as material and subjective realities in the present.

This thinking underlies the position of the Democratic Alliance (DA), the official opposition party. Soon after a debate on race in parliament between President Mbeki and DA leader Tony Leon in June 2003 it was reported that 'the DA ... believes government policies have raised racial consciousness and led to the re-racialisation of South Africa ... that compliance with the requirements of the Employment Equity Act ... necessitates racial-head-counting and race-labelling and, consequently, the reclassification of South Africans according to race' (*Cape Times,* 9 July 2003). More recently, Professor David Benatar has argued that 'affirmative action perpetuates two fundamental errors of Apartheid – an insistence on classifying people by "race", and distributing some benefits ... by using race as a proxy [for disadvantage, which he likens to] a kind of racial profiling' (*Cape Times,* 12 April 2007).

In this view the current government's attempts to address past inequalities by making race a political matter amount to nothing less than apartheid race classification in a new form. Although there are limits to and problems with current government policy on redress (Erasmus 2005), it is inaccurate to equate them with apartheid race classification. Furthermore, while it is important to question the continued use of apartheid categories in current policies (Maré 2001), it is naïve to assume that abandoning the concept of race will automatically lead to a society in which race no longer matters.

To clarify my argument, it is important at this point to distinguish between two understandings of race: essentialist and constructionist. An example of the former is the use of race as a biological and scientific category to refer to something given and fixed in human nature. As we have seen, since World War Two the consensus of scientists is that race is not a scientifically valid category. This does not, however, make race an illusion. Instead, we should see race as a social construct, embedded in history and politics, with fluid and changing rather than fixed and given meanings. This kind of understanding draws our attention to the meanings we attach to (real or imagined) biological and cultural markers and enables us to recognise the hierarchies of power and privilege located within racialised structures of meaning. These meanings have shaped people's material lives, their perceptions of themselves, of others and the world around them, as well as institutionalised practices. It is in this sense that racialised meanings have real effects on people's lives.

Dropping the scientific category of race does not, however, address the continued historical inequalities, brutality and power relations for which it stands. From the examples of persistent racialised inequalities and brutality after apartheid, we can see that colour-blindness ignores the continued impact of race, through the history of colonialism and apartheid, on our present lives.

Besides its use as a scientific category, there are other essentialist positions on race that are still current today. As we shall see in the next section, these rely heavily on the assumption that race is socially, rather than (as before) biologically, natural. Such uses of race do not help us to move beyond racialised meanings and their effects, any more than dropping the use of the term as a scientific category. As I argue throughout this essay, the only way to address these inequalities is to lift our conception of race out of the realms of biological and social essentialism and to place it in the realm of politics and power (Gilroy 2005; Fanon 1986).

Race: everything and everywhere

The main alternative to colour-blindness in South Africa is an approach that uses race as *the* predetermining and all-determining element of social life and self; in this sense race predetermines everything we do, are and can be. Accordingly, race always is and always will be a central social fact in South African society. Proponents of this view map people's political interests, cultural characteristics, and assumptions about community and collective action on to racial 'kinship' or membership, explaining the former in terms of the latter.

In the aftermath of the national elections in 2004 for example, political analyst Nhlanhla Ndebele claimed that most black people who had voted for the opposition DA were 'rural, illiterate and not psychologically free and they still [saw] a white man like [Tony] Leon as a saviour' (*This Day,* 2 April 2004). Had they been urban, literate and free, Ndebele assumed, they would have voted for a black politician. Underlying this essentialist thinking, which draws on the metaphor of the (racial) family, is an assumption of black loyalty and community based on racial 'kinship'. Its suggestion that 'backward' members simply need to be brought into the fold reflects a use of 'race' as socially fixed.

Similarly, use of the terms 'coconuts' and 'dusty crusties' by post-apartheid black youth implies that culture is a fixed expression of race. 'Coconuts' – considered white people (socially and culturally) wrapped in a black skin – are reviled for having forsaken their black 'roots' by, for example, speaking English with a 'white' accent – though they are also revered for their apparent linguistic and social ease when negotiating white worlds. 'Dusty crusties', a term signifying people who embody a 'backward', rural, un-'hip' blackness, are on the other hand revered for their imagined preserved 'roots' in 'authentic', 'original' blackness.

Underlying these examples is an assumption that racial and cultural identities are timeless, given essences that can be found among those assumed to 'have' rather than live blackness. This language of roots and origins implies a use of race and culture which places lived realities outside historical change. Not unlike the modern idea of race, these ideas draw on socially and, more indirectly, biologically natural origins as all-determining, and understand culture and political interests as expressions of authentic or inauthentic connection with these origins.

Although many who hold essentialist views are often vehemently opposed to the idea of race as a biological fact, they nevertheless continue to treat both race and culture in much the same way: as all-determining, fixed and immutable. In this view race is everything. But it obscures significant class, gender and rural–urban inequalities and political differences among these racial or cultural communities, thereby erasing various political factors that shape race and its social place.

Concern with roots and origins is often expressed in the question 'Where are you from?' In a discourse that treats race and culture as fixed, this question often legitimates or denies belonging. A politics of belonging is at the heart of post-apartheid xeno-racism against refugee and migrant black Africans, who are derogatorily referred to as *makwerekwere*.[4] This xeno-racism draws on a racialised and gendered conception of the nation as a family, using citizenship rights and a synthesis of biological and cultural characteristics to exclude refugee and immigrant Africans from the South African national 'family'. Peberdy (2001) notes that local people and state officials often identify these Africans by racialised physical markers. These include skin colour (foreign black Africans are seen as darker than South Africans) and cultural markers such as ritualised scarification, forms of dress and language.

As Landau (2004) shows, many South Africans attach negative meanings to these markers by constructing non-South African Africans as the cause of unemployment, disease, inequality and crime. Warner and Finchilescu (2003) point to the gendered nature of these constructions by noting how these migrants are accused of 'stealing' South Africa's (black) women, while Sichone (2003) alerts us to a gendered economy in which local women often value foreign men more than they do local men. The real effects of these meanings are manifested in discrimination and violence. Post-apartheid xeno-racism illustrates the continuing close connection between ideas of race, culture and nation, and the gendered politics of these ideas, in constructions of non-South African Africans as inferior, 'undeserving outsiders' (Nyamnjoh 2006: 43).

The new science

In an earlier section we have seen that nineteenth-century science was much preoccupied with ideas of roots, origins, kinship, lineage and descent. Behind these ideas, as Haraway reminds us (1989, 1996), lay the metaphor of the human family (as opposed to the human polity), providing ready proof of human sameness, an assumed basis for community, cooperation and collective action. Not only is the modern idea of race tightly bound to these notions of origins, lineage and descent but they remain central to new scientific discourses on genetics, though now in a different form.

The recent South African documentary *So, Where Do We Come From?*, a popularised version of this discourse, invited viewers to see themselves in terms of the narrative of roots and origins. In the midst of persistent use of the term 'race', it claimed that genes 'provide an unbiased record of the history of our country' and tell 'an unbiased story of us being related to one family'. While this discourse challenges racialised hierarchies within the South African population, the recurring assumption that the 'family' is the only means through which we can imagine a sense of unity obscures possibilities for bonding premised on ties other than blood and 'kinship', like friendship, hope, a sense of shared mortality and, more mundanely, what we do (Haraway 1996: 265). This documentary subtly implies that DNA *makes* one African or not, and suggests not only that 'African' is a biologically determined rather than historically formed identity but, in an almost religious sense, that the human genome is the unbiased One who has the final say over who one *is*. It further declares that 'you might even say that differences between races are all merely cosmetic', implying that such differences have no real political and material effects on people's lives. This is despite its reference to the racial violence of apartheid.

There is no doubt that genomics challenges the old idea of race as different biological types and confirms the predominant biological likeness among humans. This is an important first step toward undoing ideas of race. At the same time, though, as Haraway argues (1996: 348), the genome has become in the late twentieth century *the* 'blood tie' among humans. She warns that while the modern idea of race reduced concepts of humanity, sameness and difference to biological nature by positing the notion of separate human species, genomics reduces the concepts of human nature, sameness and difference to DNA as an informational structure. As a result the concept 'human life' is removed from its messy lived contexts and encased in artificial ones: clinical laboratories, statistical databases and computer programs. These places of 'hard' science are often understood to be outside politics. This conception, Haraway argues, resonates with modern ideas of race in the way it places concepts of race and humanity outside history and politics.

From essentialist conceptions to race as a social construct

This chapter started off with an exposition of the modern idea of race – at the time a sign of what it meant to be human – understood as a primordial difference based in nature. In this paradigm, race is already there waiting to be discovered, making it something that exists *before* politics and history. I have argued that essentialist uses of race and culture work with these concepts in similarly fixed ways. As we have seen, colour-blind arguments against race as well as some discourses on genomics divorce race and humanity from history, lived reality and the politics of social inequality. What would it take to bring politics back into what it means to be human, and what it means to be racialised?

We need to start thinking about unmaking race. Race is not found either in nature or in society. In other words, race is not given. The idea that race is biologically given was produced by modern science, which did not stand outside but rather was intricately shaped by the complex matrices of thought and culture, and by the politics of imperialism of the time. Rather than already there, race is a socio-historical and political construct that is culturally contextual and situation specific. Race is made and remade over time as a learned way of seeing ourselves and the world. This view of race challenges the idea that it has any biological or cultural basis. Race is not a fixed and tangible thing we can find in our blood or DNA; nor is it something we are born with because of our culture or heritage.

Race is not about roots and origins, but about how particular ways of seeing the world and humanity have shaped who we have become. This way of seeing and using race opens a path away from questions about 'where we come from' towards questions about 'where we are going' and 'who we are becoming'. It opens a path for unmaking race by revealing the possibility for unlearning racialised ways of being in the world.

People play a part in constituting themselves as racialised. In making ourselves and our realities at a particular time, the resources on which we draw are historically formed. Apartheid has shown that the possibilities open for the kinds of persons we can be are shaped and limited by a particular historical conjuncture. At the same time, we are not trapped in history. As agents capable of reflecting on the limits of the past, we can open up new possibilities for being a person, possibilities outside race, and create new tools with which to make ourselves and our realities.

This agency was reflected in the lives of at least some South Africans under apartheid. For example, pockets of everyday life in Sophiatown, Johannesburg, in the 1950s held the promise of living outside apartheid's rigid rural, 'tribal' identities. This was revealed in local appropriations and modifications of urban black North American cultural styles in processes of making cosmopolitan identities (Nixon 1994). Furthermore, until the 1990s, most South Africans and anti-apartheid supporters across the world never thought they would live to see the end of apartheid. Sadly many did not. Fortunately, many more did. This was made possible by leaders like Steve Biko and Nelson Mandela who were able to imagine a South Africa without apartheid because they refused to be prisoners either of history or of the apartheid present. They dared to imagine and live towards a different future. That future, now our present, was shaped by the politics and practice of Mandela and others, not by their genetic make-up or the essence of their cultural heritage.

Understanding race as a social construct allows one to see that meanings of race change. Beyond the fluidity of its meanings, this conception of race allows one to be open to the possibility of its demise. Politically and philosophically, this approach implies that instead of conceiving ourselves as a family of natural beings, there is space to view ourselves as political beings constantly struggling toward becoming 'new[ly] human' (Fanon 1986). From this perspective, the future of race and of humanity does not lie entirely in the hands of science and biology, but partly, if not mostly, in the political choices we make. It is important to remember that these choices are contextual. For example, for the vast majority of South Africans, everyday life continues to be deeply ordered by a racialised fragmentation of humanity, often placing beyond grasp possibilities outside such a fragmented condition. In this context, a post-racial future is most definitely not one in which race no longer matters in the liberal humanist sense (Eze 2001). Instead, it is one in which the continued material, subjective and physically brutal effects of race are actively and politically confronted with a view to creating a more humane and egalitarian society.

Endnotes

1 The writing of this chapter was enabled by funding from the Thuthuka Programme supported by the National Research Foundation and the University of Cape Town's University Research Committee. To remind us of its offensive and derogatory nature, I put the word 'race' in quotation marks at first use. Hereafter I mostly eliminate the quotes to facilitate reading and rely, instead, on the reader's continued vigilance. Writing 'race' is a political choice. It signifies awareness of the tension between re-inscribing the idea, and acknowledging the inequalities it stands for in one's efforts to eradicate both these inequalities and the idea itself.

2 Mainstream social science uses the term 'modernity' to describe a particular period in the history of social relations, dating approximately from the end of the eighteenth century in Europe. It is said to mark a shift from feudal relations to relations enshrined in formal declarations of equality. This period is characterised by large-scale, globalising networks often counterposed with small-scale, traditional social formations. Some of the central characteristics of modernity are said to include the development of ideas of democracy; processes of industrialisation; colonial expansion; the growth of bureaucracy; and the increasing role of science and technology in society.

3 Mamdani (1996) points to the racialisation of citizens and the ethnicisation of subjects in the context of colonial rule.

4 *Makwerekwere* is a hostile, derogatory term imbued with power. Its meaning is similar to the colonial equivalent of referring to Khoi languages as a 'clucking of turkeys' (see Joris van Spilbergen 1601 cited in Raven-Hart (1967: 28)). It means that the Other, in this case refugee and migrant Africans, make only unintelligible noises and are incapable of language.

References

Abrahams, Y. 1997. 'The Great Long National Insult: "Science", Sexuality, and the Khoisan in the 18th and Early 19th Century', *Agenda*, no. 32, pp. 34–48.

Bezuidenhout, A. 2003. 'Post-Colonial "Colour Bars" in the South African Engineering Industry', Paper presented at the South African Sociological Association Conference, University of Natal, July 2003.

Boonzaier, E and Sharp, J (eds.). 1988. *South African Keywords: The Uses and Abuses of Political Concepts* (Cape Town: David Philip).

De Swardt, C. 2003. 'Unravelling Chronic Poverty in South Africa: Some Food for Thought', Paper presented at the conference Staying Poor: Chronic Poverty and Development Policy, University of Manchester, 7–9 April 2003 (www.chronicpoverty.org).

Dubow, S. 1995. *Illicit Union: Scientific Racism in Modern South Africa* (Johannesburg: Witwatersrand University Press).

Erasmus, Z. 2005. 'Race and Identity in the Nation' in Daniel, J, Southall, R and Lutchman, J (eds.), *State of the Nation 2004–2005* (Cape Town: HSRC).

Erasmus, Z. 2006. 'Living the Future Now: "Race" and Challenges of Transformation in Higher Education', *South African Journal of Higher Education,* vol. 20, no. 3, pp. 51–63.

Eze, E. 2001. *Achieving Our Humanity: The Idea of the Postracial Future* (New York: Routledge).

Fanon, F. 1986. *Black Skin, White Masks* (London: Pluto Press).

Fredrickson, GM. 2002. *Racism: A Short History* (Princeton: Princeton University Press).

Gilman, S. 1985. 'Black Bodies, White Bodies: Toward an Iconography of Female Sexuality in Late Nineteenth-century Art, Medicine and Literature' in Gates, Henry L Jr (ed.), *Race, Writing and Difference* (Chicago: University of Chicago Press).

Gilroy, P. 2005. 'Race is Ordinary' in *There Ain't No Black in the Union Jack* (London: Routledge).

Gould, S. 1985. 'The Hottentot Venus' in *The Flamingo's Smile: Reflections in Natural History* (Harmondsworth: Penguin).

Haraway, D. 1989. 'Remodelling the Human Way of Life: Sherwood Washburn and the New Physical Anthropology, 1950–1980' in *Primate Visions* (London: Routledge).

Haraway, D 1996. 'Universal Donors in a Vampire Culture: It's All in the Family: Biological Kinship Categories in the Twentieth Century United States' in *Modest-Witness @ Second-Millennium: Femaleman Meets Oncomouse: Feminism and Technoscience* (London: Routledge).

Landau, L. 2004. 'The Laws of (In)Hospitality: Black Africans in South Africa', Paper prepared for the colloquium The Promise of Freedom and Its Practice: Global Perspectives on South Africa's Decade of Democracy, Wits Institute for Social and Economic Research, 17–21 July 2004.

Luhabe, W. 2002. *Defining Moments: Experiences of Black Executives in South Africa's Workplace* (Pietermaritzburg: University of Natal Press).

Magubane, Z. 2001. 'Which Bodies Matter? Feminism, Poststructuralism, Race, and the Curious Theoretical Odyssey of the "Hottentot Venus"', *Gender and Society,* vol. 15, no. 5, pp. 816–34.

Maré, G. 2001. 'Race Counts in Contemporary South Africa: "An Illusion of Ordinariness"', *Transformation,* no. 47, pp. 75–93.

McGrane, B. 1989. *Beyond Anthropology: Society and the Other* (New York: Columbia University Press).

Montagu, A. 1964. *The Concept of Race* (New York: The Free Press).

Nyamnjoh, F. 2006. *Insiders and Outsiders: Citizenship and Xenophobia in Contemporary Southern Africa* (Dakar: Codesria Books; London: Zed Books).

Peberdy, S. 2001. 'Imagining Immigration: Inclusive Identities and Exclusive Policies in Post-1994 South Africa', *Africa Today,* vol. 48, no. 3, pp. 15–32.

Raven-Hart, R. 1967. *Before Van Riebeeck: Callers at South Africa from 1488 to 1652* (Cape Town: Struik).

Schiebinger, L. 1993. *Nature's Body* (Boston: Beacon).

Sichone, OB. 2003. 'Together and Apart: African Refugees and Immigrants in Global Cape Town' in Chidester, D (ed.), *What Holds Us Together: Social Cohesion in South Africa* (Cape Town: HSRC Press), pp. 120–40.

Soudien, C. 2004. '"Constituting the Class": An Analysis of the Process of "Integration" in South African Schools' in Chisholm, L (ed.), *Changing Class: Education and Social Change in Post-apartheid South Africa* (London: Zed Books).

Steyn, M and Van Zyl, M. 2001. '"Like That Statue at Jammie Stairs": Some Student Perceptions and Experiences of Institutional Culture at the University of Cape Town in 1999', Research report, Institute for Intercultural and Diversity Studies of Southern Africa, University of Cape Town.

Strother, ZS. 1999. 'Display of the Body Hottentot' in Lindfors, B (ed.), *Africans on Stage* (Bloomington: Indiana University Press).

Thomas, Antony (producer). 1977. *The South African Experience: The Search for Sandra Laing* (film).

Valji, N. 2003. 'Creating the Nation: The Rise of Violent Xenophobia in the New South Africa', Research report for the Centre for the Study of Violence and Reconciliation, www.queensu.ca/samp/

Warner, C and Finchilescu, G. 2003. 'Living with Prejudice: Xenophobia and Race', *Agenda*, no. 55, pp. 36–44.

Wicomb, Zoë 2006. *Playing in the Light: A Novel* (New York: The New Press).

RIGHTS

Steven Robins

WHILE DRIVING PAST the Cape High Court building in Cape Town in January 2007, a colleague and I came across a small demonstration by young men with scrappy handwritten cardboard placards that referred to the murder of one Xolani. It turned out that Xolani Zodwana was a teenage street child who had allegedly been shot dead by the owner of a strip club on 16 May 2004 in downtown Cape Town (*Cape Times*, 31 January 2004). The protesters told us that if the man who they claimed shot Xolani was to be acquitted, the street kids of Cape Town would be extremely angry and there would be trouble. 'Justice must be done. We also have rights,' they told us. As one of them asserted, 'If Xolani had been a white boy from Camps Bay [a wealthy suburb], the murderer would be in jail already.' They believed that Xolani was killed because the murderer assumed that this young boy was responsible for smashing the window of his silver Mercedes-Benz.

This account of Xolani's death seemed to resonate with the all too familiar accounts of death squad killings of Brazilian street kids, who are killed because some middle-class Brazilians believe they are the prime source of urban crime and violence. But the difference here was that these Cape Town street youths spoke repeatedly about their rights as citizens. They told us that they belonged to One Love, an NGO that works with 'street children' in Cape Town. Clearly, 'rights talk' was more than simply an elite language of educated, middle-class citizens; it was also being spoken by youth living on Cape Town's dangerous streets.

'Rights talk' is of course pervasive among the more powerful sectors of South African society. During the first decade of democracy, cultural rights claims took varied and fascinating forms. For instance, shortly after the arrival of democracy in 1994, delegations of middle-class white Afrikaners converged on UN-sponsored indigenous rights meetings in Geneva and elsewhere claiming to be an indigenous people just like the Inuit, San, Aborigines, Maoris and so on. At roughly the same time, similarly minded Afrikaners established the all-white *volkstaat* (homeland) of Orania in an attempt to live out their ideals of ethnic self-determination in a post-apartheid constitutional democracy that protected language and cultural rights. In January 2007, animal rights activists from the Society for the Prevention of Cruelty to Animals (SPCA) contested the right of senior ANC politician Tony Yengeni to spear a bull at a family ritual. Vigorous public debates ensued in the media about Yengeni's 'cruel spearing' of the bull before being slaughtered at a cleansing ceremony after the four months that he spent in prison for defrauding parliament (*Cape Times*, 24 January 2007).

In response, Mongezi Guma, chairman of the Commission for the Promotion and Protection of the Rights of Cultural, Religious and Linguistic Communities, claimed that criticism of this age-old Xhosa ritual violated the Constitution. As Guma told the press, 'It is ethnocentric and undermining to hide behind animal rights and deny human beings their rights to uphold and practise their cultures and religions. Even more serious is the temptation to violate the Constitution, which protects the cultural and religious rights of all who live in South Africa.' Another commissioner explained that Yengeni had not speared the bull but merely 'prodded' it with a spear to make the bull bellow to indicate that the ancestors had accepted the ritual slaughter (*Cape Times*, 26 January 2007).

Meanwhile, a Ministry of Arts and Culture spokesperson reiterated the Constitution's protection of the right of all indigenous people to perform rituals that connected them with their ancestors. The Minister of Labour responded by extending an invitation to the SPCA 'to join us as we will be slaughtering a bull without [anaesthetising] it ... We want the bull to bellow – and then we'll sing the praises of our ancestors' (*Cape Times*, 29 January 2007).

Following initial criticism of these ritually prescribed slaughter methods, the SPCA's executive director, Marcelle Meredith, decided to accept the invitation to attend the ceremony, stating that 'we are assured there is no suffering, if the slaughter is carried out in the traditional manner by a skilled person, taking into account the transport, handling and restraining of the animal' (*Cape Times*, 31 January 2007). Cultural rights, and 'rights talk' more generally, had clearly become an integral part of public discourse in the new South Africa.

South Africa's relatively peaceful transition to a rights-based constitutional democracy has been praised internationally as a 'miracle'. The larger-than-life figures of former President Mandela and Archbishop Tutu came to embody the possibility of peaceful democratic transitions in even the most violent and conflict-ridden societies. South Africa's Truth and Reconciliation Commission became a popular export to countries struggling to overcome legacies of violence, brutality, and authoritarianism.

Similarly, South Africa's 'state-of-the-art' Constitution, with its emphasis on socio-economic and cultural rights and sexual and gender equality, has been touted as one of the most progressive on the planet.

A decade after democracy, however, the gap has widened between this bright vision of a 'rights paradise' and the grim everyday social, economic and political realities experienced by the majority of South Africa's citizens. This chapter tracks the twists and turns of 'rights talk' within South Africa's liberal democratic revolution. It identifies 'rights' as one of the important keywords of this transition to democracy. It discusses the limits and possibilities of rights-based politics and forms of mobilisation, as well as post-apartheid and postcolonial tensions between questions of 'rights' and 'culture'. The chapter illustrates how ambiguous and contradictory liberal democratic discourses on 'rights' and 'culture' circulate within the post-apartheid public sphere by focusing on three case studies: (1) the rights-based AIDS activism of the Treatment Action Campaign (TAC); (2) the sexual politics surrounding the rape trial of former Deputy President Jacob Zuma; and (3) the identity politics that surrounded the ≠Khomani San land claim in the Kalahari district of the Northern Cape Province.

From revolution to rights: the limits and possibilities of 'rights talk'

During the course of the ANC's dramatic transformation from liberation movement to ruling party, there was a seismic shift in its political lexicon. Radical keywords and concepts such as socialism, national liberation, class struggle, people's revolution, and resistance to racial capitalism and colonialism-of-a-special-type were replaced with 'tamer' words such as rights, citizenship, liberal democracy, nation-building, transformation, Black Economic Empowerment (BEE) and so on. This dominant language of liberal 'rights' and citizenship is, however, regularly challenged by the revolutionary rhetoric of the popular Left in the trade union movement and the South African Communist Party (SACP).

Whereas the militant language of national liberation envisioned the revolutionary seizure of state power, the ANC government was soon rudely reminded of the limits of political power in a country characterised by centuries of social and economic inequality and racial domination. During the anti-apartheid struggle, Left scholars had described apartheid as a system of racial capitalism whose overthrow would require more than simply taking racially based legislation off the statute books. Addressing the raw facts of deeply entrenched race and class inequality, it was argued, would require nothing less than a socialist revolution. Nevertheless, with the break-up of the former Soviet Union, socialism was no longer on the cards for a liberated South Africa. These constraints became increasingly visible as the ANC took over the mantle of political power.

Left critics of South Africa's liberal democratic order also argue that the global hegemony of neoliberal capitalism, along with the ubiquitous model of the self-interested and autonomous rights-bearing citizen, undermines radical class-based politics in South Africa and elsewhere. As John Comaroff has remarked, in the contemporary era class action seems to have replaced class struggle (see also Brown 1995). Similarly, Professor Ben Turok, an ANC MP, has noted: 'We did not say our struggle against apartheid was a civil rights struggle. We said it was a liberation struggle. There is actually a difference ... A liberation struggle includes socio-economic issues, it includes power relations. It includes structures of society, etc. Whereas civil rights [is] quite a limited, legalistic formulation' (2005: 14–15). From this perspective, liberal democracy's 'rights talk' is incompatible with radical politics and the structural transformation of highly unequal societies.

Left critics also argue that liberalism's celebration of the 'freedom to choose' all too seamlessly slides into the 'postmodern' spectre of the depoliticised consumer citizen whose search for meaning and identity is reduced to ceaseless shopping. Nonetheless, with ideas such as class, socialism and revolution virtually absent – or having 'disappeared' – from post-Cold War academic and popular discourses, 'rights', 'civil society' and 'citizenship' have become notable keywords in South African political discourse.

All the same, the actual realisation of rights has not lived up to expectations. For instance, although there have been considerable gains in terms of 'first-generation' human rights – political and civil rights, such as freedom from discrimination on the grounds of race, gender, sexual orientation, religion – the same cannot be said about the realisation of 'second-generation' socio-economic rights. Despite these limits, celebrations of South Africa's 'political miracle' continue to focus on political and civil rights, often glossing over limited delivery on socio-economic transformation. Meanwhile, external and domestic economic and political constraints, as well as state capacity problems, have stymied state and civil society attempts to address these systemic inequalities, and post-apartheid South Africa, like Brazil, remains one of the most unequal countries in the world. For example, recent studies reveal that the poorest 50% of the population are worse off economically than they were under apartheid (Terreblanche 2002).

As the shortcomings of the post-apartheid state have been revelaed in the realm of socio-economic transformation, jobs, housing and social services, civil society organisations, including NGOs and new social movements, have stepped into the breach. Post-apartheid NGOs and social movement activists have increasingly recognised the emancipatory potential of rights-based approaches. Since the early 1990s, a number of militant social movements have flexed their muscles throughout South Africa. While the movements include anti-globalisation and popular Left movements that challenge neoliberalism, they also include rights-based social movements that have sought to use the Constitution and the courts to leverage access to state resources such as land, housing and health care.[1] The formation of these movements can be seen as 'civil society' responses to perceived failures of the post-apartheid state to address issues of HIV/AIDS, land redistribution, job creation, housing, poverty, indigenous land rights, and language, religious and cultural rights. In the next section we shall discuss the 'rights versus culture' conundrum in relation to the transition to democracy in postcolonial Africa and, in particular, post-apartheid South Africa.

'Rights versus culture': a postcolonial conundrum?

Notwithstanding attempts by international donors to promote liberal democracy and rights-based constitutions throughout the global South, cultural and language rights, tradition and ethnicity remain potent keywords and political rhetorics in many postcolonial African countries. In South Africa, millions of rural people in southern Africa live under the patriarchal regimes of traditional leaders who do not necessarily subscribe to the gender and sexual equality clauses enshrined in the South African Constitution.

Similar 'rights versus culture' conflicts surfaced during the 2006 public hearings on the Civil Union Bill, which granted gay and lesbian couples the right to participate in same-sex marriages. While political, religious and traditional leaders vigorously attacked the Bill at these hearings, citing homosexuality as 'unAfrican', 'immoral' and 'sinful', gay activists from numerous organisations in turn registered their anger at what they perceived to constitute homophobia, hate speech and a violation of their constitutional rights as citizens. Speaking at Heritage Day celebrations in KwaZulu-Natal Province on 24 September 2006, former Deputy President Jacob Zuma told a large crowd of supporters: 'When I was growing up an *ungqingili* [a gay] would not have stood in front of me. I would knock him out.' Zuma was also quoted as saying that same-sex marriages were 'a disgrace to the nation and to God'. Yet, as a result of an avalanche of criticism from human rights and gay and lesbian activists, Zuma apologised for his statements, saying that the 'Constitution clearly states that nobody should be discriminated against on any grounds, including sexual orientation, and I uphold and abide by the Constitution of our land' (*Mail & Guardian*, 26 September 2006).

Zuma's response reflected his own ambivalence and unease in relation to the tensions between sexual rights and sexual culture. The public debates surrounding the Civil Union Bill revealed widely held homophobic and patriarchal attitudes that were sanctioned and promoted by conservative religious, political and traditional leaders. This has contributed towards reinforcing a set of problematic binaries of rights versus culture, citizens versus subjects, and modernity versus tradition.

These binaries recently made a return to political theory on Africa through the work of Mahmood Mamdani. In his acclaimed book *Citizen and Subject* (1996), Mamdani argued that in colonial and contemporary Africa, the majority of the rural population can be understood as ethnic subjects living under the despotic rule of traditional authorities. By contrast, urban Africans have been able to make claims as autonomous rights-bearing citizens. This African scenario, Mamdani argued, is a product of the late-colonial legacy of indirect rule. His analysis draws a neat and categorical line between the liberal individualist citizens of the African city and the ethnic subjects of the countryside, and in the process, reproduces timeless binaries. Mamdani also argued that the problem with democratisation in postcolonial Africa has been that it left intact the late-colonial legacy of indirect rule. Mamdani's model – with its urban–rural and citizen–subject binaries – cannot accommodate the complex, hybrid and situated subjectivities of postcolonial citizen-subjects. In its quest for symmetry and conceptual clarity, his account sacrifices the more ambiguous and 'messy' forms of everyday life in the postcolony.

The relationship between liberal individualist notions of citizenship and collectivist conceptions of 'culture' and communal belonging have been extensively debated by donors, policy-makers and academics (Cowan et al. 2001). Numerous ethnographic studies reveal that the conception of the citizen as an atomised and autonomous rights-bearing subject is generally at odds with African realities where intersubjectivity and interconnectedness are highly valued (Werbner 2003; Nyamnjoh 2003; Von Lieres 1999, 2005). These studies demonstrate that it is precisely the extreme vulnerability and uncertainty of everyday life in many parts of Africa that demands that postcolonial subjects negotiate their subjectivity through relationships with others. At the same time communitarian forms of citizenship, conviviality and sociality may also be valued precisely for their capacity to hold powerful state actors, traditional leaders and patrons accountable in terms of the delivery of material and social goods.

But this does not mean that people in the Third World do not respond to rights-based and state-centred discourses when these offer possibilities of access to redress and resources. People often live their lives as both citizens *and* subjects. What appears to be an autonomous rights-bearing citizen in one setting may, in another context, morph into an 'ethnic' subject invoking indigenous values, traditional beliefs and forms of sociality based on family, clan and community. This situational politics takes place in local as well as national politics in South Africa.

Everyday political realities like these question the standard binaries of modern and traditional; liberalism and communitarianism; and rights and culture (Ong 1999; Cowan et al. 2001). Yet outmoded modernisation paradigms continue to draw on timeless conceptions of self-reproducing African traditional systems, which are regarded as obstacles to progress and development. One implication of this line of thinking is that, with time, Africans will ultimately become just like the liberal citizens of 'the West'. These examples of linear and binary thinking remain present in contemporary scholarly and policy writing on Africa notwithstanding a burgeoning literature on 'alternative modernities' (Chakrabarty, 2000; Gaonkar, 2001), African and Asian modernities (Ong, 1999; Deutsch et al. 2001), and 'alternative democracies' (Paley 2002: 484).

A rejection of these dichotomies can begin to clear the ground for the recognition of the particularities of diverse and situated forms of belonging, rights, citizenship and subjectivity. While scholars still struggle to grasp these hybrid postcolonial realities, activists and citizens face them close-up in daily life.

Case study 1: Treatment Action Campaign (TAC)

Whereas critics of liberalism and 'rights talk' are acutely aware of the economic limits of liberation (Bond 2000; Marais 1998; Robins 2005), a growing number of South African activists, NGOs and social movements have identified opportunities for extending the liberal democratic envelope through rights-based mobilisations. The Treatment Action Campaign (TAC), for example, was founded in South Africa in 1998 at a time when AIDS treatment was not available in public health facilities. TAC deployed rights-based approaches as well as collective mobilisation in the courts, streets, the media and global forums in their struggle for treatment and better health care.

The TAC also drew on the political culture of the anti-apartheid struggle in its efforts to engage with, and at times challenge, the state and the global pharmaceutical industry (Robins 2004). It creatively reappropriated locally embedded political symbols, songs and styles of the anti-apartheid struggle. Its civil disobedience campaigns resonated with the historic anti-*dompas* (pass law) defiance campaigns. TAC mobilised township residents, especially working-class and unemployed black women, and brought the trade union movement on board, thereby challenging 'AIDS dissident' critics who claimed it was simply a front for international drug companies seeking to market their products in Africa. In the process, TAC activists created a new discursive space for critical engagement with the ANC government, while simultaneously calling for new conceptions of 'health citizenship' and forms of rights-claiming and political agency that have been referred to as 'biomedical', 'therapeutic' and 'biological' citizenship (Nguyen 2005; Petryna 2002). These developments have raised important questions about the changing nature of democracy in South Africa.

TAC's rights-based politics were profoundly shaped by the experiences of its members who had participated in the United Democratic Front (UDF) in the 1980s. Such an activist legacy also found expression in songs at marches, demonstrations and funerals, and the regular press releases and conferences, website information dissemination, television documentaries, and national and international networking. This political style was a sophisticated refashioning of 1980s political rhetorics and modes of activism, drawing on the courts, the media, and local and transnational advocacy networks, along with grassroots mobilisation and skilful negotiations with business and the state. This multi-stranded approach to AIDS activism culminated in the government's eventual decision to 'roll out' AIDS treatment in the public health system.

TAC's modes of political engagement revealed the empowering possibilities for deploying rights, together with social mobilisation, to leverage access to state resources. It also drew attention to some of the limits of rights-based approaches to improving health care for poor people. For example, scientists, NGOs, AIDS activists and government had to acknowledge and respond to 'local' and 'lay' interpretations of AIDS that prevented people from accessing health care. These included the blaming of AIDS on witchcraft, as well as a variety of AIDS conspiracies: 'whites' who want to contain black population growth; 'white doctors' who inject patients with AIDS when they go for tests; the CIA and pharmaceutical companies who want to create markets for drugs in Africa; the use of Africans as guinea pigs for scientific experiments with AIDS drugs; beliefs that sex with virgins, including infants, can cure AIDS.

But perhaps the most daunting problem for AIDS activists and health professionals was President Mbeki's flirtation with AIDS 'dissident' theories. The President's position, along with a plethora of popularly held 'AIDS myths' and the stigma and shame associated with AIDS, contributed towards defensive responses and AIDS denial amongst both the general population as well as the President's inner circle. These cultural and political obstacles had serious negative implications for TAC's rights-based struggle to improve access to health care. It soon became clear that stigma, denial, AIDS myths and cultural beliefs prevented many South Africans from accessing HIV prevention and treatment programmes.

Case study 2: 'The Zuma affair': another case of rights versus culture?
In the Johannesburg High Court in May 2006, during the rape trial of former Deputy President Jacob Zuma, South Africans witnessed a televised 'postmodern' spectacle in which Zuma, a tribal elder-cum-liberation struggle icon, performed 'Zulu traditional masculinity' (Butler 1990) for consumption by both the court and the broader citizenry. According to Zuma's version of 'African masculinity', in Zulu culture 'leaving a woman in that state [of sexual arousal]' was the worst thing a man could do. 'She could even have you arrested and charged with rape,' he told the attentive court. In other words, he would have in effect violated and disrespected her had he not had sexual intercourse with her. Addressing the judge as *nkosi yenkantolo* (the king of the

court), Zuma referred to his accuser's private parts as *isibhaya sika bab'wakhe* – her father's kraal. He conceded that he entered 'the kraal' without *ijazi ka mkhwenyana* – the groom's or husband's coat, i.e. a condom. These Zulu idioms (themselves hybrid amalgams of Zulu, English and Afrikaans words) are usually associated with 'deep' rural KwaZulu-Natal. To those attending the Johannesburg High Court hearing, and millions of others following the trial through the extensive media coverage, these words signified that Zuma was indeed a 'real' Zulu man: '100% Zulu boy' as his supporters' T-shirts put it. They sought to normalise his sexual behaviour. After all, he was simply being a normal Zulu man. This representation of Zulu masculinity was also part of a broader national political discourse of African re-traditionalisation.

It was in his discussion of *lobola* (bridewealth) that Zuma publicly performed his 'Zulu masculinity' most vividly. In response to questions about two 'aunts' who had attempted to initiate *lobola* negotiations with the complainant, Zuma answered that he 'had his cows ready'. As he put it, 'Lobola is an issue between the girl ... and the family. Should [the complainant] have told these two ladies that "Yes, I want Zuma to pay lobola," I would definitely do it.' Here again, a discussion on *lobola* sought to valorise traditional Zulu masculinity and thereby normalise and redeem his sexual behaviour.

Zuma's court statements suggested that he was indeed an authentic Zulu traditionalist. This representation of Zuluness was mediated to South Africans and the wider world via television, radio, the Internet, and a local and international press fascinated with primordialist fantasies of Zulu culture. Such a representation of the '100% Zulu boy' was strategic and effective in making the case that the sex had indeed been consensual. Zuma's behaviour was, after all, how Zulu men are meant to act, so this patriarchal argument went. This particular understanding of Zulu masculinity was self-consciously fashioned and situationally deployed by Zuma in the Johannesburg High Court as a sign of a revitalised Zulu traditionalism.

Zuma's performance of unblemished, virile Zulu masculinity in court mirrored popular perspectives on sexuality, gender and masculinity. This also partly explains Zuma's popularity across a variety of constituencies, social classes and ideological camps including 'traditionalists', the ANC Youth League and the popular Left. What united Zuma's diverse constituency was the linking of African populism with 'traditional' masculinity and conservative sexual politics. This distinguished Zuma's brand of Zulu traditionalism from the liberal modernism of President Mbeki, a man who was seen to be promoting sexual and gender rights, including same-sex marriages for gay and lesbian couples. Such a traditional–modern binary was rhetorically and politically highly productive. It contrasted Zuma's virile Zulu traditionalism with the image of President Mbeki as the (Xhosa) modernist architect of South Africa's rights-based constitutional democracy, a political order which was widely perceived to challenge 'African culture' by undermining patriarchal traditional institutions and cultural practices.

Case study 3: Indigenous rights and cultural identity

In the early 1990s, South Africa witnessed the emergence of new forms of ethnogenesis in which indigenous identity and 'community' were reconstituted through cultural and intellectual property rights. These new forms of 'ethnic' mobilisation included the successful ≠Khomani San land claim that was concluded in 1999. Prior to the land claim, most of the members of the ≠Khomani San had been living in conditions of dire poverty and unemployment on farms and small towns in the Northern Cape. The land claim created the conditions for their emergence as a ≠Khomani San community.

Following the claim, the ≠Khomani San's lawyer Roger Chennells, together with the South African San Institute (SASI), also entered into negotiations over the sale of indigenous San knowledge concerning the use of the *Hoodia gordonii* plant to a global pharmaceutical company interested in marketing it as a natural appetite suppressant and weight-loss product. Both the land claim and the *hoodia* deal contributed towards the creation of a community of people who more actively identified themselves as ≠Khomani San. These developments also had the effect of exacerbating intra-community divisions between those deemed to be 'traditional Bushmen' and those considered 'modern' and thus less authentic (see Robins 2001).

This example reveals how the land claimant community, together with their lawyers and NGO allies, used the ANC government's Land Restitution Act to claim land rights and at the same time reconstitute themselves as primordial 'Bushman' hunter-gatherers. The San land claim also played a part in the growth in southern Africa of a globally connected indigenous rights movement. And it encouraged South African anthropologists to engage critically with debates on indigenous rights and culture (Boonzaier and Sharp 1994; Wilmsen and McAllister 1996; Sharp and Douglas 1996; Robins 1997, 2005). The ≠Khomani San story reveals the complex ways in which local responses to 'development' and rights-based interventions, as well as local constructions of indigenous identities, are influenced by state, NGO and donor discourses on both rights and 'cultural survival'.

One of the key challenges that emerged following the ≠Khomani San land claim was how to give substance to the strategic fictions of community solidarity and cultural continuity that were produced by claimants, their NGO lawyers and the media during the land claim process. After being awarded the R15 million land settlement, the San community and the NGOs supporting it faced the dilemma of having to create viable community structures and livelihood strategies in a province characterised by massive unemployment and poverty. The case illustrates the tensions and contradictions that arise when donors and NGOs deploy essentialist indigenous discourses of 'traditional Bushmen' alongside 'rights talk'. It also draws attention to the creative agency and hybrid repertoire of strategies used by 'Bushman' citizen-subjects who are constituted as 'beneficiaries' of national and global donor and NGO programmes.

While the land claim itself did not generate significant income, Chennells's negotiation of the *hoodia* deals certainly has. These forms of the commodification of culture and indigenous knowledge can be aptly described as Ethnicity, Inc. Another example of this phenomenon is the case of the Bafokeng kingdom of North West Province which, in 1999, won a legal battle for royalty payments from Impala Platinum Holdings (Implats). The Bafokeng have used their massive deposits of platinum, the largest outside Russia, to reinvent and reproduce 'tribal' traditions and build infrastructure including schools, clinics, hospitals, sports and recreation facilities, and a major Science and Technology Academy. It would seem that access to these resources – indigenous knowledge about *hoodia* and platinum deposits – have facilitated the 'reinvention' of these indigenous communities. Rights-based struggles such as those forged by the San are thus not necessarily incompatible with cultural reinvention and collective forms of social reproduction.

Conclusion

Until the 1980s, anti-apartheid activists and progressive intellectuals and academics, including anthropologists, did not see much revolutionary potential in cultural and ethnic politics. In fact, a stress on cultural and ethnic difference was seen to play into the apartheid state's strategies of 'divide and rule'. The state's establishment of authoritarian regimes in the Bantustans (the 'homelands') seemed to provide concrete evidence of the inherently reactionary nature of these forms of 'tribal' and ethnic-based politics. Many anti-apartheid intellectuals and activists hoped that the overthrow of apartheid would usher in a new, non-racial modernist state characterised by socialist or liberal democratic principles rather than African traditionalism. Yet, as the case studies in this chapter have highlighted, 'culture' and 'ethnicity' have proved to have a much longer shelf life than anticipated. Together with 'cultural rights', they have indeed become keywords in public life in post-apartheid South Africa.

Endnote

1 Since 1994, some of the social movements that have come into existence include the following: the South African Homeless People's Federation (1994), the Treatment Action Campaign (1998), the Concerned Citizens Forum (1999), the Anti-Eviction Campaign, the Anti-Privatisation Forum, the Soweto Electricity Crisis Committee (2000), the Landless People's Movement, the Coalition of South Africans for the Basic Income Grant (2001).

References

Bond, Patrick. 2000. *Cities of Gold, Townships of Coal* (Trenton, NJ: Africa World Press).

Boonzaier, E and Sharp, J. 1994. 'Ethnic Identity and Performance: Lessons from Namaqualand', *Journal of Southern African Studies*, vol. 20, no. 3, pp. 405–15.

Brown, Wendy. 1995. *States of Injury: Power and Freedom in Late Modernity* (Princeton, NJ: Princeton University Press).

Butler, Judith. 1990. *Gender Trouble: Feminism and the Subversion of Identity* (London: Routledge).

Chakrabarty, Dipesh. 2000. *Provincializing Europe: Postcolonial Thought and Historical Difference* (Princeton, NJ: Princeton University Press).

Cowan, JK, Dembour, M-B and Wilson, RA (eds.). 2001. *Culture and Rights: Anthropological Perspectives* (New York: Cambridge University Press).

Deutsch, J-G, Probst, P and Schmidt, H (eds.). 2001. *Perspectives on African Modernities* (Oxford: James Currey).

Gaonkar, DP. 2001. *Alternative Modernities* (Durham, NC: Duke University Press).

Mamdani, M. 1996. *Citizen and Subject: Contemporary Africa and the Legacy of Late Colonialism* (Princeton: Princeton University Press).

Marais, Hein. 1998. *South Africa: Limits to Change* (New York: St. Martin's Press).

Nguyen, Vinh Kim. 2005. 'Antiretroviral Globalism: Biopolitics and Therapeutic Citizenship' in Ong, A and Collier, S (eds.), *Global Assemblages: Technology, Politics, and Ethics as Anthropological Problems* (Oxford: Blackwell).

Nyamnjoh, F. 2002. '"A Child Is One Person's Only in the Womb": Domestication, Agency, and Subjectivity in the Cameroonian Grassfields' in Werbner, R (ed.), *Postcolonial Subjectivities in Africa* (London: Zed Books).

Ong, Aihwa. 1999. *Flexible Citizenship: The Cultural Logics of Transnationality* (Durham, NC: Duke University Press).

Paley, Julia. 2002. 'Towards an Anthropology of Democracy', *Annual Review of Anthropology*, vol. 31, pp. 469–96.

Petryna, Adriana. 2002. *Life Exposed: Biological Citizens after Chernobyl* (Princeton: Princeton University Press).

Robins, Steven. 1997. 'Transgressing the Borderlands of Tradition and Modernity: "Coloured" Identity, Cultural Hybridity and Land Struggles in Namaqualand (1980–94)', *Journal for Contemporary African Studies*, vol. 15, no. 1, January 1997, pp. 23–44.

Robins, Steven. 2001. 'NGOs, "Bushmen" and Double Vision: The Khomani San Land Claim and the Cultural Politics of "Community" and "Development" in the Kalahari', *Journal of Southern African Studies*, vol. 27, no. 4, pp. 833–53.

Robins, Steven. 2004. '"Long Live Zackie, Long Live": AIDS Activism, Science and Citizenship after Apartheid', *Journal of Southern African Studies*, vol. 30, no. 3, pp. 651–72.

Robins, Steven (ed.). 2005. *Limits to Liberation after Apartheid: Citizenship, Governance and Culture* (Oxford: James Currey).

Robins, Steven 2006. 'From Rights to "Ritual": AIDS Activism and Treatment Testimonies in South Africa', *American Anthropologist*, vol. 108, no. 2, pp. 312–23.

Sharp, John and Douglas, Stuart. 1996. 'Prisoners of Their Reputations? The Veterans of the "Bushman" Battalions in South Africa' in Skotnes, Pippa (ed.), *Miscast: Negotiating the Presence of the Bushmen* (Cape Town: University of Cape Town Press).

Terreblanche, Sampie. 2002. *A History of Inequality in South Africa, 1652–2002* (Pietermaritzburg: University of Natal Press).

Turok, Ben. 2005. 'Editorial', *New Agenda*, no. 19, pp. 14–15.

Von Lieres, Bettina. 2005. 'Marginalisation and Citizenship in Post-apartheid South Africa' in Steven Robins (ed.), *Limits to Liberation after Apartheid: Citizenship, Governance and Culture* (Oxford: James Currey).

Werbner, Richard P. 2002. *Postcolonial Subjectivities in Africa* (London: Zed Books).

Wilmsen, Edwin and McAllister, Pat (eds.). 1996. *The Politics of Difference: Ethnic Premises in a World of Power* (Chicago: Chicago University Press).

TRADITION

Emile Boonzaier and Andrew D Spiegel

THE GLOBALISED WORLD in which we live is one where rationality and free choice are celebrated, where individuals are expected to make decisions after weighing up the pros and cons and not simply follow pre-ordained rules. That same globalised world includes a wide variety of appeals to tradition that assert that if people are to maintain their social-cultural identities, they must accept that certain behaviour patterns are required of them. At first glance, then, it seems that we live in a world marked by a contradiction. But do such appeals to tradition really contradict the neoliberal principles that have come to dominate modern social life? Is tradition really just an anachronism, an outmoded carry-over from the past, an inappropriate relic that flies in the face of ideas about rationality, progress and modernity. All too often today we recognise that all that is modern is not necessarily good, and that many traditional practices and values are indeed worth preserving. We feel very strongly that traditions and heritage can be a source of pride, a means of establishing social identity, of responding to the environmental crisis marked by global warming. Our goal in this chapter is to demonstrate that, despite appearances, appeals to tradition in today's modern world are actually part and parcel of that world. They are themselves outcomes of people's efforts to adapt to the contestatory and competitive demands of the world, and to ensure that they gain and maintain access to the resources they need to sustain themselves with dignity.

The apparent contradiction between modernity and traditionality has prompted concern, widely felt and publicly debated in the media, about the persistence and re-emergence of a range of traditional ideas and practices that, some argue, are singularly out of place in contemporary South Africa. Newspapers, magazines, radio and television regularly report on and debate issues such as circumcision rituals, bridewealth, virginity testing, reed dances, traditional leaders and indigenous healers.

The debates generally crystallise into two opposing viewpoints: one supportive, the other condemning. For example, December 2006 newspaper headlines reported the revival of a ritual involving the bare-handed killing of a bull by a group of young men in KwaZulu-Natal. Those who defended the practice argued that 'this is the African continent and you must bear in mind that we as Zulus are practicing our culture as Africans' (Mthembu 2006). And, in a somewhat more measured piece, Ndela Ntshangase (2006), a lecturer at the School of isiZulu Studies, University of Natal, pointed out apropos of the Zulu king's approbation of the practice:

> The king is doing this because he realises that, during the years of colonialism and apartheid oppression, many important concepts and aspects of life – from which Africans derived their pride – were discontinued. As a result, Africans were denuded of their essence; their ceremonies and beliefs were distorted. By reviving some of these ceremonies and customs, the king hopes to re-imbue us Africans with our pride and self-confidence.

In contrast, opponents of the ritual have argued, as did journalist Fred Khumalo (2006), that it is an outmoded and barbaric practice:

> Over the past few days I've listened to self-appointed experts on Zulu culture explaining why it was necessary to revive the custom of killing a bull with bare hands. It was possibly relevant and apt to indulge in this practice in the past as a way of expressing the warriors' gallantry and strength. But time marches on, dear people. Cultures evolve and some customs get jettisoned along the way. Today there are many other ways of expressing one's gallantry rather than killing a beast with one's own bare hands.

And, more strongly, a reader's letter commented:

> The word culture has taken on a new meaning in South Africa. 'It's our culture' has become a phrase top leaders in the ANC use to justify their sexcapades. Now so-called Zulu warriors spend 20 minutes torturing a bull to death with their bare hands in the name of culture (R. Becker 2006).

Such exchanges, besides raising significant questions about cultural relativism and authenticity as well as social power and identity, serve to highlight a point often overlooked: that the contestation over tradition and culture is itself very much part of a modern, global reality. If no cultural options were available, we would not be faced with choices; if marginalised people did not feel threatened by cultural and political-economic imperialism, culturally constructed social identity would have little currency for them; if there was no shared notion of free speech, we would have difficulty debating contentious issues; and if liberal notions of cultural relativism and equality had not risen to prominence, we would simply have to accept the impositions of the powerful.

Contrary to some popular wisdom, rapid increases in the global spread of goods, people, technologies, images and ideologies do not necessarily mean that the world has become homogenised in accord with a neoliberal model of modernity. In fact, ample evidence suggests that modernity takes on different forms at different times and places; that everything that is new is no longer universally viewed as progressive and better; and that, in a range of diverse locations, people are actively resisting globalisation's homogenising tendency by recalling and reconstituting what they regard as their traditional or indigenous ways.

Globalisation has thus not promoted just one model of the world. Part of its own rhetoric has simultaneously stimulated the idea that alternative models are conceivable, valid and perhaps more worthy than those that have come out of Europe's Enlightenment experience. In other words, globalisation has created a space in which new possibilities can be aired and explored. Not surprisingly, the quest for 'new' alternatives does not preclude looking to the past for inspiration. But the past is now being reconceived in two senses.

Firstly, the negative connotations of the past that associated it with the primitive, the backward or the conservative (in contrast to the civilised, the modern or the progressive) have been thrust into the background as Western modernity is felt to be failing to meet its promises and as the natural environment is seen to be increasingly threatened as a consequence. Those negative connotations have thus made way for the emergence of the past as something that deserves respect as a source of wisdom and a resource for new possibilities. Secondly, the past is being reinterpreted. New histories, from different perspectives, are being written, not only as an antidote to previous histories produced by the powerful, but also in recognition that *all* history is interpretation – an imperfect reconstruction of what happened in the past.

Just as history is best understood as interpretation rather than unmediated fact, tradition, too, is less about a real or authentic past and more, indeed always, about interpretations and reconstructions. Recognising this raises an important question: How should we, as critical social scientists, understand and assess such reconstructions?

Beyond culture: tradition, civilisation, heritage, indigeneity

The old idea of culture, promoted and accepted by anthropologists throughout most of the twentieth century, has come under much criticism in recent decades. Edward Tylor's persistently cited definition of culture as '*that complex whole* which includes knowledge, belief, art, law, morals, custom, and any other capabilities acquired by man [*sic*] as a member of society' (1873: 1, our emphasis) paved the way for culture to be viewed as a coherent package associated exclusively with a distinctive population. In the process, culture became much more than a concept to explain the differences within and especially between human societies.

When conceived as a stable, coherent and shared system of values, beliefs and knowledge, culture readily mutates into a view that cultures are bounded, homogeneous and static entities. In supposed contrast to the dynamic and progressive 'Western society' governed by so-called rationality, people in other societies were transformed into anthropological objects ruled by their culture. The Other became frozen in time and space, exoticised and represented in stereotypical cultural caricatures. And its respective traditions were, equally, seen to be static and useless for supporting any progressive processes as these Others were impressed into the modern world.

This view of culture (and tradition) became entrenched in popular thinking (and unfortunately in various social sciences) during the middle of the twentieth century and has proved to be particularly resilient, notwithstanding numerous subsequent critiques from anthropologists themselves (see, for example, Wright 1998; Borofsky 1994). The old idea of culture assumes that it is learnt from parents and grandparents rather than from, for example, the media or one's peers. In other words, it views culture as old and unchanging: hence the ease with which culture and tradition are used interchangeably. And, unfortunately, it is this understanding of culture that is implicit in anthropology's celebrated idea (also now widely, albeit crudely, adopted) of cultural relativism and in policies of multiculturalism.

Not surprisingly, the idea of culture as an unchanging package has also permeated and percolated through to the non-Western populations to which it has been applied. Here it has come to be used as a self-conscious marker of identity, and as a way of differentiating between 'us' and the dominant (often global) political majority. Thus we find that in South Africa today many blacks argue that, in contrast to themselves, whites have neither culture nor traditions nor customs, since their lives are thought to be guided by principles that have no sense of time-depth. The same has been pointed out of people in other parts of the previously colonised world such as New Guinea, where, Sahlins (1994: 374) reports, a local person explained to an anthropologist that 'If we didn't have *kastom*, we would be just like white men'.

But there are indications that the currency of the old understanding of culture *is* beginning to change. Today the term is being used in a variety of different ways, causing understandable confusion. For example, various countries have ministerial portfolios labelled 'Cultural Affairs' or 'Arts and Culture' (as in South Africa), whose business has little, if anything, to do with distinct cultural groupings. Similarly, the term has come to be used in new settings, such as 'corporate culture', or as a shorthand label for any widespread behaviours or values, such as 'the culture of violence' or 'the culture of entitlement'.

Much more significantly, in many parts of the world, but especially in those countries with multiculturalism policies, minority populations have been impelled to conceive of themselves in terms of fixed cultural identities – to claim their own cultural distinctiveness and to practise their own 'authentic' culture (Rapport and Overing 2000: 100–1). Liberal multiculturalism stands in stark contrast to forced cultural integration, such as was most clearly exemplified by past policy in Australia where the children of Aborigines were removed from their parents so that they could be brought up in a manner thought appropriate to life in modern Australia.

But multiculturalism can be a mixed blessing for those whose rights it supposedly protects. It has, as Povinelli (2002) has argued for Australia, often simply perpetuated unequal power relations by demanding that minorities identify with an *impossible* standard of cultural authenticity. This scenario has been played out in other parts of the world, and has been especially evident in the context of land disputes. Traditional land rights and claims involving first nations have tended to depend on the claimants being able to establish that they still practise their authentic culture. Thus, for example, it was noted that in the US land claim by the Mashpee Wampanoag Tribal Council, Inc.: 'An unprecedented trial ensued whose purpose was not to settle the question of land ownership but rather to determine whether the group calling itself the Mashpee Tribe was in fact an Indian tribe, and the same tribe that in the mid-nineteenth century had lost its lands through a series of contested legislative acts' (Clifford 1988: 277). Not surprisingly, 'surviving pieces of Native American tradition' had to be offered as evidence of such continuity.

In southern Africa, similar expectations of proof of traditional culture in the present have been witnessed in cases involving the Nama of the Richtersveld and the ≠Khomani San of the Kalahari. The recent case of the Basarwa in Botswana provides an interesting counterpoint. Here it was not the Botswana government that promoted or sought the idea of traditional culture in the present, but NGOs (especially Survival International) that used this argument to justify the special status accorded the Basarwa. In its efforts towards nation-building, the Botswana government has been actively promoting a policy of integration of the Basarwa, which some of those people as well as an international consortium of NGOs have resisted – ostensibly in favour of a multicultural option that recognises the Basarwa as culturally distinctive.

Yet multiculturalism policies often demand adherence by minorities to cultural norms unattainable in contemporary conditions. It is therefore no surprise that there is a perceptible shift away from culture to other ways of conceptualising difference and the past. The use of tradition, and closely related notions such as heritage and indigeneity, represents such a step. Although tradition may be associated with its own conceptual baggage and indeterminacy, it does have the potential to escape two problems associated with culture: it clearly signifies some reference to the past; and it does not suppose that people necessarily incorporate a whole package of cultural elements. Moreover, tradition (and especially heritage) can, at least in principle, be used in ways that place both global Northern and global Southern societies on an equal footing, since it is something to which both can lay claim.

While Tylor's (1873) notion of culture fostered the idea of static, timeless cultures, tradition necessarily implies a time dimension. In other words, it is acknowledged that tradition is a resource drawn from the past; and thus its contemporary relevance is open to negotiation. When Nelson Mandela, in his *Long Walk to Freedom* (1995), recounts his experiences of traditional manhood initiation with positive nostalgia, he is singling out one particular custom from the past. He shows how the experience benefited him personally and in so doing argues the case for its retention. This is neither an instance of blind conservative adherence to the past, nor cause to accuse him of not being modern and progressive.

Muslim outrage, spurred by cartoons depicting the Prophet Mohammed, published in Denmark in early 2006, has been a topic of much comment in the global North's media. Somewhat surprisingly, however, the vehement response has not been attributed to the usual 'Muslim fundamentalism'. Instead, it has been widely discussed in terms of two contradictory value sets: Muslim religious sensibility on the one hand, and liberal 'Western' notions of free speech on the other. And, lest religious values trump secular ones, these two sets of values are pitted against each other on an equal footing by conveniently labelling the conflict as a 'clash of traditions'. Of course, one might well question to what extent unbridled free speech is in fact a Western value of either the distant or recent past, especially considering recent restrictions on free speech introduced in response to the 2001 attacks on New York's World Trade Center. But doing so merely introduces another dimension to the issue of tradition – that of authenticity.

Authenticity and the invention of tradition

In 1983, Eric Hobsbawm and Terence Ranger edited an influential book, *The Invention of Tradition*. As the title suggests, they argued that things labelled traditions or traditional were actually the product of just so much myth-making. They showed that a variety of different traditions – in both Western and non-Western contexts – were neither very old nor very true to any original.

In retrospect, the lessons taken from the book were disappointing, and Ranger (1993) himself has since significantly modified the argument. For a while after its publication, the book's argument enabled social scientists to take what they understood as the intellectual high ground (they knew the 'truth' about traditions; others – those who claimed traditions to be authentic – did not). In doing so, the argument spawned numerous additional debunkings and questions about the authenticity of anything that anyone anywhere claimed to be traditional. A leading anthropologist, Marshall Sahlins, has complained: 'Unfortunately a scholarly air of inauthenticity hangs over this ... The academic label "invention" already suggests contrivance, and the anthropological literature all too often conveys the sense of a more or less counterfeit past, drummed up for political effects, which probably owes more to imperialist forces than to indigenous sources' (2002: 3). The corollary of the argument, however, was that social scientists needed to recognise precisely that if tradition is invented, one has also to realise that it is a political resource and therefore inevitably the site of contestation by competing interest groups. And that insight continues to provide social scientists with an important means to understand the notion of tradition and its salience in political contexts where appeals are made to tradition as a means of justifying action or mobilising people.

What the original idea of the invention of tradition suggested was that anthropology, history and other social sciences had come to position themselves, perhaps unwittingly, on the side of those who opposed any appeals to tradition. The problem with this lies not in the fact that one is choosing sides as such, but rather that, by apparently exposing inauthenticity, one is effectively prejudging the *effects* of appeals to tradition. Another way of talking about those effects is to ask: How is tradition *used*? Or, what *functions* do appeals to tradition serve? Two common themes that emerge in this regard relate to the way in which appeals to the past are used to promote group identity, and to validate gender relationships. We deal with each in turn.

Tradition and social identity construction
Group identity comes in many different forms: people can identify with kinship groups (e.g. clans), political groups (e.g. tribes or political parties), church groups (e.g. Zionist Christian Churches), sports teams (e.g. Orlando Pirates or Manchester United), nations (e.g. Germany or South Africa) and so forth. But in South Africa today *cultural-ethnic* identity has come to loom particularly large. And it is here that tradition and images of the past can play such a significant role. Consider the following examples.

Some white South Africans today seek to establish an identity for themselves by rediscovering their European roots. For example, Afrikaans-speaking Du Plessises, Du Toits and Labuschagnes have begun travelling to France to visit the regions from which their forefather Huguenots fled. Some white Afrikaners have also sought to preserve 'pure' Afrikaans as the language symbolic of their exclusive identity. And most recently, a pop song about the Boer leader General De la Rey has recalled his leadership in the struggle against British oppression and thereby struck an intense emotional chord among a significant section of the white Afrikaner population.

Certain coloured South Africans have similarly begun drawing on various images of the past to legitimate their distinctiveness: their history as South Africa's first nation (the Khoisan – itself a highly contested historical category), the history of slavery and of the apartheid-era forced removals from District Six (now permanently encapsulated in a museum of that name). Similarly, some South African Indians have sought to commemorate their history as descendants of indentured labourers, and their more recent history of forced removals from areas such as Durban's Cato Manor. And, of course, African culture and African tradition, along with powerful images of warriors from the past – and especially great leaders such as Shaka – can and do evoke a strong sense of group solidarity and identity.

These examples highlight the role of tradition and history in the creation and perpetuation of certain kinds of social identity; a relationship that we have all come to recognise. But what is perhaps less recognised is the way different images of culture and tradition can (or cannot) appeal to different groupings. While promoting a sense of community, tradition can at the same time also heighten divisions and difference.

President Thabo Mbeki's now famous 'I am an African' speech was clearly an attempt to seed the unity of all South Africans, irrespective of race or cultural association. It did so by drawing on images of a pan-African past to promote a sense of a common future. But the seeds he broadcast seem to have fallen on ground not yet fertile enough to germinate them. Public and media debates have scrutinised the notion of the 'African', and many blacks have denied whites the right to identify as Africans on racial or cultural grounds.

Similarly, Mbeki's concept of an African Renaissance has not resonated with many South Africans. Part of his message has been the notion that Africa has a proud precolonial history, including a tradition of writing. To emphasise this, the government has given its financial support to the preservation of the famed manuscripts of Timbuktu. Yet there is no evidence that this gesture has had any impact on South Africans' perception of their history. Nor does it seem to have done anything to reduce the rampant xenophobia towards refugees and immigrants in South Africa from the rest of Africa, or to have changed the opinion of those critics who question why Mbeki spends so much time in the rest of Africa when there are pressing problems at home.

White South African journalist Hans Pienaar's derision of the Timbuktu project, in the *Weekend Argus* in 2005, probably echoes the sentiments of many white South Africans. In a set of articles he argued that the initiative is no more than an effort at 'disseminating propaganda'; that Timbuktu is too remote and lacks the necessary infrastructure for tourists; that there are better examples of African advancement in Spain; and that the history being presented is sanitised and stripped of any reference to the city as a hub of the Arabic slave trade. In fact, he points out, 'slavery is still being practised in areas not so far from Timbuktu' (Pienaar 2005).

Timbuktu may indeed be too distant to resonate positively with ordinary South

Africans. But not so the traditional cleansing ceremony performed for ex-chief whip of the ANC, Tony Yengeni, after his release from prison. The details of what became known as the 'Tony Yengeni saga' have become commonplace: having pleaded guilty to defrauding parliament by failing to declare a significant discount on a luxury vehicle (amid suspicions of bribery involving a state arms deal), he was sentenced to four years' imprisonment. When Yengeni was released on parole after serving only four months, a ceremony, 'part of normal Xhosa culture', was performed at his father's home in Gugulethu to 'wash away the prison curse and integrate him spiritually and physically with his family' (Gophe 2007). One may be inclined to see this merely as Yengeni's right to practise his own culture, as protected in South Africa's Constitution, and there can be little doubt that the ritual also served to reaffirm his social identity as a member of his clan, as a Xhosa, and as a member of society.

But clearly the episode represents much more than this. For many in Gugulethu, it demonstrates that Yengeni is still one of them: even though he wears natty clothes and lives in Milnerton, a predominantly white suburb, he has not forgotten his roots. At another level, support for his action as a traditional Xhosa man amounts to tacit support for the view that he should not have been jailed in the first place, while criticism implies outrage at his having been released after serving only four months. And then there was the outrage expressed, not at the ritual as such, but at the fact that it involved the slaughter of a bull after it had first been stabbed by Yengeni, who, his supporters pointedly explained, had used 'his family's traditional spear'.

This furore (it even included threats of prosecution by the SPCA under animal protection legislation) suggests that practices said to be traditional are not merely about solidifying Xhosa social identity. Rather, the event seems to have provided an arena within which a whole range of different allegiances and divisions could be played out. In all this Yengeni has come across primarily as a traditionalist – in stark contrast to the corporate executive style of President Thabo Mbeki – and this has no doubt helped to define and mobilise a particular support base within the ANC.

We should also remind ourselves of the important part that the media have played in this whole process, for the media perform a crucial globalising role in making salient the diverse appeals to tradition that are used to mark differences. Perhaps, if Yengeni had not been seeking publicity (and confrontation), he might not have allowed the media (including photographers) on to his father's property where the ritual took place. Nor, however, would he have so readily been able to mobilise supporters from among those inclined to resist attacks on what they regard as their authentic culture or traditional customary practice. In other words, he would not have been able to use the power of an appeal to tradition to mobilise such people.

The Yengeni case not only indicates the extent to which appeals to tradition are integral to the social construction of identity, and to reinforcing social identity boundaries. It also displays the emotional depth with which people regard symbols that mark social identity. Moreover, in doing so it reveals how readily popular notions of culture raise emotions about identity – and about the traditions appealed to in the process of its construction and maintenance – to the level of the spiritual. Yet doing that overlooks its essentially sociological and personal-psychological character.

This is particularly evident in the Department of Arts and Culture's comment that tradition is about 'man's [*sic*] ... relationship with the cosmos, God and his ancestry' (quoted in Saunderson-Meyer 2007) – a comment that suggests that tradition, and by association identity too, are fixed, beyond challenge and impossible to foist on people or to abandon: one has one's identity, it is God- or ancestor-given, and one cannot choose any other. Holding such a position means that those who do not conform are misfits and traitors to their culture and tradition – as in the common disparaging notions of 'oreo' or 'coconut' and of *volksverraaier* ('traitor to one's people' amongst Afrikaans-speaking whites).

Tradition and the dynamics of gender relations

Tradition also very commonly provides an arena within which gender divisions are played out. What is salient here is that tradition can be invoked by either men or women, depending on context; that traditions in any one context are interpretable in various ways; and that, except in strictly authoritarian contexts, there is, rightly, always space for tradition to be contested.

In the Thongaland area of northern Natal near Kosi Bay, it was the women who invoked tradition to support their interests in the domestic sphere (Webster 1991). There, however, the competing scripts were not African traditionality and modernity but local people's perceptions of Zulu and Thonga traditions about gender relations, particularly between spouses, and the expected behaviour of wives in their affines' presence. People in this area had long experienced successive waves of political authority washing over them, lending weight, authority and enlightened self-interest to the espousal of one set of cultural practices and identities or another, with the ebb and flow of Thonga and Zulu influence.

Women presented themselves as Zulu when it came to public occasions to do with the apartheid-era KwaZulu bantustan authorities – such as on pension payday – and its national cultural movement, Inkatha. But in the domestic domain, women preferred to regard themselves as Thonga while men continued to consider themselves as Zulu. Why was this? As Webster pointed out, it is ethnographically puzzling that men have spurned the Thonga heritage while their own sisters and wives embrace it. His answer to the conundrum, which is the issue of significance here, was that it was in women's interest to appeal to Thonga traditions of domesticity and wives' expectations, while men preferred the Zulu ways – or the local rendering of these

– because they legitimated patriarchy and male dominance.

Thonga tradition was understood to give wives much greater independence than did Zulu tradition. It was understood to allow women to keep their own patronymics; to rise to positions of great status as father's sister and mother-in-law in their affinal groups; to maintain an independent dignity with regard to their fathers-in-law which, in their eyes, the Zulu tradition of *hlonipha* (elaborate rules of respect) undermined; and especially to obtain a divorce. Furthermore, Thonga women were said to have various rights not commonly recognised for Zulu women. Their husbands could not maltreat them; they had the right to sexual gratification and to luxury items, not just subsistence; and they were allowed to dissolve their own marriages if, for example, a husband failed for a long period to support his wife (Webster 1991: 256–9).

Another example of tradition being played out in gender relations comes from Namibia. There, as in many other postcolonial countries, the state has been keen to promote neoliberal notions of democracy and equality, and has entrenched these in its Constitution. It has thus attempted to introduce legislation in line with these values. For example, the Traditional Authorities Act (No. 17 of 1995) and the Married Persons' Equality Act (No. 1 of 1996) were deliberate efforts to promote women's rights. Yet opponents claimed that the Acts were contrary to African tradition. Indeed, many Namibians, albeit not any significant women, came to believe that 'the Government destroys tradition' (H Becker 2000) – even though the legislation's supporters argued that only oppressive elements of culture and tradition were being abolished. Showing how opponents of the Married Persons' Equality Act appealed to both African *and* Christian tradition to support their arguments, Heike Becker reminds us how this reflects a similar conspiracy in the past when colonial administrators, Christian missionaries and male traditional elites connived to entrench 'an image of an allegedly ancient, immutable tradition, which defined authority in the family, the community and the State as exclusively male domains' (2000: 195).

This example illustrates how tradition can be invoked to promote contemporary agendas. It also indicates how tradition itself is open to diverse and sometimes contradictory revisions and reconstructions. In this regard, two further points are noteworthy. In other contexts, women have been able, especially where their age or elite status is valued, to contest the dominant image of precolonial African tradition as necessarily oppressive of women. And, as Becker adds, the abstract notion of gender equality has stimulated, at the local level, an on-going process of renegotiation of all aspects of tradition and the way it translates into practice (2000: 196).

The point of our various examples about the dynamics of tradition and gender relations is not simply to show that tradition is invented or manipulated. Rather, it is to stress that tradition is a constituent part of more general processes of adaptation and survival in the modern world where contestation and competition are central and widely fêted. Moreover, once renegotiations and contestations over what constitutes tradition become part of a public debate, it seems that there is indeed room for compromise in so far as the more oppressive elements of this tradition become susceptible to amendment.

In South Africa there has recently been much media coverage of the continuation (or possibly revival) of a virginity testing ritual (*inkciyo*). Debate about the traditionality of the practice seems to have shifted away from emotional appeals to an assumed immutable authority of tradition towards consideration of the *contemporary* costs and benefits of the practice. Those in favour argue that it is a way to revive morality and protect girls from abuse – issues that are particularly relevant to the current human devastation associated with HIV/AIDS.

And the Children's Bill, currently under consideration, offers a compromise in relation to the ritual, not only between tradition and modernity, but also between urban and rural and, as some have claimed, between black and white values: the practice will be banned for children under 16; it will only be allowed if done with the girl's consent and after appropriate counselling; her status may not be made public without her consent; and her body may not be marked (Edmunds 2006). Similar legislation applies to male circumcision and is aimed at protecting boys, especially from being abducted against their will, and from surgical complications and practices that might lead to the spread of HIV.

Conclusion: using tradition in modern contexts

When he critically reassessed the idea of invented tradition, Ranger (1993) – one of its early protagonists – suggested that we should reconceptualise uses of tradition as just part of general processes of imaginative and creative drawing on cultural resources – not all of them necessarily tradition. Writing specifically about the postcolonial Zimbabwean state's use of tradition, he noted that that state 'claims simultaneously to be the heir of African tradition and colonial modernity … [and that] … Its imaginings and uses of an array of traditions, customs, and identities are challenged and contested by others' (1993: 106–7). The 'others' to whom he referred included local-level and popular social and political interest groups. By recognising their role in this field, he highlighted the extent to which tradition, along with other cultural resources, has come into a field of contestation and competition which the postcolonial state may attempt to control, but without effectively being able to do so.

Ranger's point – as well as all the examples we have offered above – demonstrates that contestation over tradition occurs in a space where values, relationships and practices can be negotiated and reconstituted in new ways, and where the principles of cultural relativism have become common currency. This shows that tradition, and appeals to it, have become central to the processes of adaptation and survival in the modern world, a world where a hegemonic liberal ideology decrees that all is relative and should therefore be open to negotiation.

Yet in this world the idea that difference should be respected is acceptable only until the point where such difference challenges other dominant values. At that point, commitment to those values consistently trumps relativism, demonstrating only too clearly that the interests of the globally powerful always tend finally to prevail even when their rhetoric suggests otherwise. It also shows, therefore, that when the globally powerful take it upon themselves to claim that tradition is something fixed and unchallengeable, there is the danger that they will either sideline it for its inability to fit into the global scheme of things, or monopolise it and use it as a resource for their own ends. But as the Zimbabwe case reveals, no postcolonial state can ever be so powerful to be able to do that.

Acknowledgement

We are grateful to Richard J Spiegel for his critical comments on an earlier draft of this chapter.

References

Becker, Heike. 2000. 'A Concise History of Gender, "Tradition" and the State in Namibia' in Keulder, Christiaan (ed.), *State, Society and Democracy: A Reader in Namibian Politics* (Windhoek: Gamsberg Macmillian).

Becker, R. 2006. 'A Load of Bull about Culture' (Reader's letter to the editor), *Sunday Times,* 17 December 2006.

Borofsky, Rob. 1994. 'Rethinking the Cultural' in Borofsky, R (ed.), *Assessing Cultural Anthropology* (New York: McGraw Hill), pp. 243–9.

Clifford, James. 1988. *The Predicament of Culture: Twentieth-Century Ethnography, Literature and Art* (Cambridge, MA: Harvard University Press).

Edmunds, Marion. 2006. 'The Politics of Virginity', *FairLady,* March 2006, pp. 54–60.

Gophe, M. 2007. 'Washing Away the "Prison Curse"', *Weekend Argus,* 20 January 2007.

Hobsbawm, E and Ranger, T (eds.). 1983. *The Invention of Tradition* (Cambridge: Cambridge University Press).

Khumalo, F. 2006. 'Killing a Bull with Bare Hands to Show Bravery Is … a Lot of Bull', *Sunday Times,* 17 December 2006.

Mandela, Nelson. 1995. *Long Walk to Freedom: The Autobiography of Nelson Mandela* (London: Abacus).

Mthembu, LS. 2006. 'Tired of Whites' Domination' (Reader's letter to the editor), *Sunday Times,* 17 December 2006.

Ntshangase, NN. 2006. 'Ancient Ceremonies Help Us to Rediscover Ourselves', *Sunday Times,* 17 December 2006.

Pienaar, H. 2005. 'Is Timbuktu the Right Place for a Renaissance?', *Weekend Argus,* 4 March 2005.

Povinelli, Elizabeth. 2002. *The Cunning of Recognition: Indigenous Alterities and the Making of Australian Multiculturalism* (Durham, NC: Duke University Press).

Ranger, Terence. 1993. 'The Invention of Tradition Revisited: The Case of Colonial Africa' in Ranger, T and Vaughan, O (eds.), *Legitimacy and the State in Twentieth Century Africa* (Basingstoke: Macmillan).

Rapport, Nigel and Overing, Joanna. 2000. *Social and Cultural Anthropology: The Key Concepts* (London: Routledge).

Sahlins, Marshall. 1994. 'Goodbye to Tristes Tropes: Ethnography in the Context of Modern World History' in Borofsky, R (ed.), *Assessing Cultural Anthropology* (New York: McGraw-Hill).

Sahlins, Marshall. 2002. *Waiting for Foucault, Still* (Chicago: Prickly Paradigm Press).

Saunderson-Meyer, William. 2007. 'Getting in Touch with the Ancestors and Cosmos –or Load of Bullocks', *Weekend Argus*, 27 January 2007.

Tylor, Edward. 1873. *Primitive Culture* (New York: GP Putnam's Sons).

Webster, David. 1991. '*Abafazi Bathonga Bafihlakala*: Ethnicity and Gender in a KwaZulu Border Community' in Spiegel, AD and McAllister, PA (eds.), *Tradition and Transition in Southern Africa* (Johannesburg: Witwatersrand University Press).

Wright, Susan. 1998. 'The Politicization of "Culture"', *Anthropology Today*, vol. 14, no. 1, pp. 7–15.

TRANSFORMATION

Thiven Reddy

SINCE 1994 MANY WORDS have been used to motivate for and describe the changes from the old apartheid order to the new social relations and practices ushered in by democratic elections. Among the words in the languages of post-apartheid politics are 'revolutionary', 'reformist', 'broad-based', 'elitist', 'grassroots', 'human-rights-driven', 'participatory', 'just' and 'de-racialised'. Topping the list is 'transformation', which denotes a change from one qualitative state to another, and usually implies 'improvement'. As used in South African politics, the term embraces diverse meanings in competing discourses of social change. It arguably occupies centre-stage of the contemporary political terrain and, as to be expected, is the locus of intense contestation.

After apartheid some would reasonably say that it is quite impossible to be against 'transformation'; racism can no longer be easily expressed in the old discourses of white supremacy. After all, as Derrida (1985) suggests, apartheid represented 'racism's last word'. Once the institutional basis of organised state racism was finally overthrown, replaced by a government representing the majority, competing notions of 'transformation' surfaced. Conflicts arose over the grand visions and the minute details of addressing and reorganising historically sedimented power relations in institutional contexts and cultures and in everyday life. In democratic South Africa today, conflicts over power, its movements and distribution, express themselves through conflicts over the meanings of transformation. Why the word 'transformation' has taken centre-stage to represent a notion of social change, and not competing signifiers such as 'structural change', 'radical change', 'liberation' or 'revolution' – words that traditionally resonate with the language of the struggle against apartheid – is an interesting question. A possible explanation is that it is easily incorporated into many diverse, and often conflicting, discourses of politics and conceptions of social change.

In the formative period of its acceptance into South Africa's language of politics, transformation was more popularly associated with resistance discourses, yet these days even opposition parties schooled in Afrikaner nationalist and conservative liberal frameworks rely on its power to make their utterances 'reasonable', understandable and legitimate. Used like this, the word 'transformation' suggests and defines the limits of the 'acceptable' in post-apartheid political language. State and civil society actors invoke it to serve various purposes. In official and popular discourses of social change, it is frequently used to indicate an ongoing process as well as an end to strive for, the two aspects assuming different meanings depending on audience, ideology and the political moment. If there is something of a consensus, it is in the reference to some broad notion of societal change away from apartheid (as in 'a break with the past'). In opposition circles, the word is increasingly used to criticise the ANC for failing to adhere to a democratic ethos in its implementation and practice.

This chapter examines the meanings and functions of transformation in the discourses of social and political change after apartheid. The following sections discuss notions of transformation in the ruling party, the ANC, and government policies and practices as they relate to 'empowering black business' and affirmative action. It also discusses key oppositional views on the ruling official definitions and interpretations of transformation.

Notions of transformation in the ANC

As the ANC is the dominant party in the post-apartheid political system and the leading anti-apartheid organisation, its conceptions of change permeate society. Established to fight the discriminatory laws and practices confronting Africans, the ANC views itself as defined by the goal of liberation. The key term denoting social change before the transition period was 'liberation struggle'; the opening of negotiations ushered in a new terrain, and in this context of greater uncertainty and fluidity of outcomes, the signifier 'transformation' became more prominent (Singh 1992). Although the ANC has always been an organisation advocating political change, the precise elements requiring change in the existing society, the way change should be brought about, and the form an ANC-controlled society should take were naturally subjects of debate and intense contestation. Broader societal changes in various historical periods influenced these internal debates. And given that the relationship between whites and blacks, the dominant and the subaltern, involved collaboration as well as resistance, an ambiguous intermingling played itself out in the ANC, too.

For heuristic purposes, we can identify four strands of 'transformation' in the discourse of the ANC: modernist, traditionalist, radical and reformist. These derive from the dominant ideological influences – liberalism, Marxism and Third World ideologies of nationalism – that found expression in the organisation. In its formative period, two contrasting visions of opposition framed debates, both a response to the 'modernising' imperative of colonialism. The first, modernism without radical change, is best associated with the Christian educated elite and some 'non-traditional' chiefs who formed the ANC in 1912 (Karis and Carter 1972). They demanded the extension of the restricted franchise of the Cape to Africans residing in the three remaining provinces of the new Union of South Africa. They saw their role as a reformist political opposition working within the avenues of protest permitted by the ruling political order, reflecting a partially accommodative recognition and acceptance of the political structures imposed by colonialism. This strand remained influential throughout the organisation's history, adapting to different conditions facing black society and advocating a pragmatic political practice that sought compromise rather than an 'all or nothing' approach.

Later, in the aftermath of World War Two, this modernist quest was accompanied by a far-reaching, more radical democratic agenda. However, the pragmatic and accommodationist stance remained. Within the ANC the dominant view embraced 'modernist' political practices and structures and explicitly rejected 'tribalism' and any return to precolonial political structures though not all of its myriad cultural manifestations. The metaphors and images of the precolonial past and the wars against the colonial state and the Boer armies served as nostalgic reminders of a 'free' and independent past. Consider Mandela's ambiguous navigation between modernist and 'tribal' interpretations that could perhaps be read as conforming to Orientalist framings of colonial situations. Reflecting on popular participation in the society in which he was brought up, he observed:

> Everyone who wanted to speak did so. It was democracy in its purest form. There may have been a hierarchy of importance among the speakers, but everyone was heard … At first I was astonished at the vehemence and candour with which people criticised the regent. He was not above criticism – in fact, he was often the principal target of it … The meeting would continue until some kind of consensus was reached. They ended in unanimity or not at all … As a leader, I have always followed the principles I first saw demonstrated by the regent at the Great Place. I have always endeavoured to listen to what each and every person in a discussion had to say before venturing my own opinion … Oftentimes, my own opinion will simply represent a consensus of what I heard in the discussion (Mandela 1994: 20–1; Nash 1998).

In a similarly essentialising move, he emphasised the importance of genealogical roots in Xhosa identity, the organic harmony of such communities, their consequent 'unchangingness', and his attraction to a tradition of curiosity and 'inquisitiveness' associated with 'white culture'.

The Xhosa are a proud and patrilineal people with an expressive and euphonious language and an abiding belief in the importance of laws, education, and courtesy. Xhosa society was a balanced and harmonious social order in which every individual knew his or her place. Each Xhosa belongs to a clan that traces its descent back to a specific forefather … Like all Xhosa children, I acquired knowledge mainly through observation. We were meant to learn through imitation and emulation, not through questions. When I first visited the homes of whites, I was often dumbfounded by the number and nature of questions that children asked their parents – and their parents' unfailing willingness to answer them. In my household, questions were considered a nuisance; adults imparted such information as they considered necessary … My life, and that of most Xhosa at the time, was shaped by custom, ritual and taboo. This was the alpha and omega of our existence, and went unquestioned. Men followed the path laid out for them by their fathers; women led the same lives as their mothers had before them (Mandela 1994: 11).

This accommodative, adaptive response to domination accounts partly for the ANC becoming the leading body representing the interests of the black majority during the transition to democracy.

A second strand in approaches to social change within the ANC – a militarist and Africanist outlook – stemmed from identification with the Bambatha Rebellion of 1906 and the wars fought against colonial armies by independent African polities during the latter part of the nineteenth century. Although the ANC was formed as a response to the failure of such resistance, this strand contributed to ANC 'tradition' and influenced those who cherished the folk values of precolonial society. It rejected elements of the modernising project associated with colonialism and apartheid. Remaining less visible in the formal organisational positions, especially after World War Two and the expulsion of Africanists from the ANC in 1958, this strand emphasised a continuity of struggle with the heroic battles of the past, which functioned as an important ideological element of pride and mass mobilisation. This viewpoint has been echoed in the Mbeki years, particularly in his 'I am an African' and 'Two Nations' speeches, and has also strongly influenced some conceptions behind the implementation of affirmative action and black economic empowerment policies.

During its exile years following the party's banning in 1960, the ANC drew on this militarist tradition of anti-colonial African wars, but under conditions inspired by nationalist 'revolutionary' struggles in the Third World and particularly southern Africa. This is the third, arguably 'radical' strand of transformation discourse in the ANC. For a number of reasons – the hardened posture of the apartheid state, the isolating, alienating and fragmented conditions of exile politics, dependence on Soviet support and the popularity of Marxist-inspired national liberation victories in China,

Vietnam and Cuba, as well as the influence of the first-wave decolonisation movements in Africa – the strand displayed some centralist and authoritarian tendencies. Key ANC documents of this period – such as 'Strategy and Tactics' and 'No Middle Road' – spoke of 'radical', 'fundamental' or 'socialist' transformation (ANC 1969). In the 'Strategy and Tactics' programme adopted at Morogoro, Tanzania, in 1969, the ANC argued that even though 'national liberation was the chief content of the struggle' in Africa, the global and regional context showed that everywhere there was a 'transition to socialism' (ANC 1975).

The ANC saw itself as a national liberation movement fighting the first stage of a 'national democratic revolution' aimed at replacing apartheid with a democratic, majoritarian system. Naturally, this stage would entail the goal of de-racialisation, preparing the conditions for a post-apartheid socialist society, the final and desired stage of transformation. In the stage of national democratic revolution, all oppressed 'racial groups' under apartheid and progressive individual whites would come together to form a united anti-apartheid bloc. The ANC's core constituency consisted of the mass of African poor and exploited, the workers and peasants. At the same time, despite recognising South Africa as a relatively developed capitalist formation, the ANC in exile decided that armed struggle for national liberation – as exemplified by struggles in China and Vietnam and, later, Mozambique, Zimbabwe and Namibia – served as an important model for the struggle against apartheid.

The fourth strand in the ANC's thinking about transformation derives from the radicalisation of its understanding of social protest, influenced as it was by the long tradition of socialist struggle in South Africa. This Marxist tradition, emphasising working-class struggles and mass resistance, certainly did not contradict the militarist tradition prevailing in the organisation though, perhaps because it was advocated largely by the more 'non-racial' Communist Party, sat uneasily with the Africanist view. It was a strand derived from the historical changes in the social organisation of black society from the 1940s onwards, the increase in rural-to-urban movement and the emergence of a settled working class in and around South Africa's growing cities. Marxist-influenced bodies, some cooperating with the ANC, such as the Communist Party and the trade unions, increasingly challenged the elitist notions prevalent in the ANC at the time. They demanded the active participation of the urban working poor, focused on the capitalist and imperialist causes of black exclusion from the political system, and envisioned a socialist society as the goal of mass struggle.

Thus, the ideology that took the masses most seriously within the ANC followed rather than led the way for increased mass participation and mobilisation. Already in the 1920s the Communist Party of South Africa, under pressure from the Communist International (Comintern), began to look towards black rather than white workers as its main constituency for socialist revolution. The All African Convention and later the largely Cape-based Unity Movement served as other sources of pressure and influence on the ANC. The trend towards radicalisation in the ANC was assisted by a number of events: the 1946 mineworkers' strike, the victory of the National Party in the 1948 elections, and the increasingly militant approach of the ANC Youth League. In 1955 the ANC adopted the Freedom Charter, which brought together some of the radical demands then in currency. In recent years, radical critics within the ANC have come to believe that the goals of the Freedom Charter have been ignored by the government, and trade unions and the Communist Party have been marginalised in the ANC-led Alliance in favour of big business, an emerging black business class and a state elite. They have waged a concerted campaign to shift the balance of influence back to the concerns of organised labour.

Post-1994 programmes of de-racialisation

Under Thabo Mbeki the ANC government embraced a disappointingly technocratic framework of governance, influenced no doubt by the context of the negotiated settlement and the constraints of the global economy exerted by the IMF and World Bank. It found itself in the contradictory position of implementing an austere macro-economic policy, one decidedly neoliberal and favouring business interests, while also aiming to accommodate the expectations of its supporters for far-reaching redress. Faced with a deeply racialised social formation and white dominance of the economy, it set out to de-racialise social relations by relying on affirmative action and black economic empowerment (BEE). The next section of this chapter discusses the narrow BEE policy aimed at changing the composition of the business class. This is followed by an analysis of the diverse notions of 'transformation' and the debate surrounding them.

Black economic empowerment

Despite the government's intention to present a single meaning of BEE in its policy, there are multiple meanings in relation to particular paradigms. The conflict over the precise meaning of the term is ultimately a political fight, both within and outside the ruling ANC, about the direction of South Africa's economic development and the nature of its democracy. While the voices in the debate are often those of old allegiances – nationalists and socialists – there are also voices that articulate a variety of overlapping positions.

In 2005 Blade Nzimande, general secretary of the Communist Party, characterised BEE as 'white captains of industry and finance … [lending] an aspirant upwardly mobile elite the membership fees to the country club and the keys to the Porsche' (Nzimande 2005). He distinguished between 'narrow' and 'broad-based' BEE, the former being the high-profile transactions witnessed since the mid-1990s, involving a small elite of beneficiaries, and the latter, which he advocated, being the transformation of material conditions for the mass of the unemployed and poor, with a far-reaching redistribution of wealth and resources.

To date, BEE has largely involved 'black-owned consortiums' buying equity shares in one or other of South Africa's larger corporations or state enterprises; or the appointment of prominent black businessmen to senior positions in company management. This type of BEE has brought many criticisms. The 'black-owned consortium' of investors is often a small group of individuals made privately rich by such transactions. Those selected by white capital are members or former members of the ANC or have close ties to it (thus revealing the underlying logic as political rather than market-driven or merit-based). The transactions do not demonstrate how they will benefit 'disadvantaged South Africans' more broadly nor do they make a dent in established patterns of ownership in the national economy. Many questions remain about the transparency of the deals. Ultimately, questions are raised whether this kind of BEE constitutes 'de-racialisation' in the wider society to any significant degree or addresses the real transformational challenges facing South Africa. Similar criticisms of BEE have been made by former Archbishop Desmond Tutu, the media and many academics. Heribert Adam (Adam et al. 1998) labels BEE as 'crony capitalism', similar to developments in the South Asian countries of Singapore, Malaysia, Indonesia and South Korea.

BEE of this kind has had its defenders within the ANC. Saki Macozoma (2005), a member of the then ANC executive, accused critics of expecting BEE to usher in socialism, an outcome that BEE was not designed to accomplish. 'Many critics of BEE accept the need to de-racialise the economy, but they think that the process has "elitist consequences". It is not alleviating poverty, but enriching the few ... What did they expect? Where have you ever seen a capitalist system producing socialist results?' There was a need and a challenge, he maintained, to encourage black people to take up the opportunities offered by BEE. Even without significant shifts in class relations, BEE represented at the very least the 'de-racialisation' of the business class; it has helped create a bigger black middle class and more black businesses. In his view, blacks in management will make a company more sensitive to black interests and such companies will represent themselves in ways that address a broader, historically marginalised community. And certainly, he argued, de-racialisation of any sector of South African society was a step forward from a segregated 'racial' monopoly.

Macozoma was correct in saying that those who criticise BEE have another political agenda. Their socialist paradigm views BEE as amounting to a series of partial reforms, leaving intact the exploitation of the majority of people, a situation inherited from the apartheid era. For them, BEE constitutes a 'sell-out' when it comes to the real demands of transformation – a more egalitarian society, not a market-driven capitalism. While BEE has had some limited success on the de-racialisation front, it is not making any significant dent in the income distribution inherited from apartheid and it is unlikely to do so in its present form. After more than a decade, we see a failure to narrow the inequality gap; rather, inequality has increased.

From several quarters have come increasing demands for a 'broad-based' BEE that includes more people (outside narrow ruling-party networks), is more transparent and is implemented differently so as to benefit the marginalised sectors of society. It will have to encourage active community participation, a grassroots democratic movement from below, and well-established structures that will hold potential elites accountable.

Affirmative action and its contradictions

After 1994 the new democratic government faced the immediate challenge of changing the composition of the state and its related structures. In the course of negotiations prior to the settlement the ANC had conceded a 'sunset clause', which protected the white civil service from immediate retrenchment, after which affirmative action policies would apply. Despite this clause, the President had the power to appoint the senior management in the civil service, and those appointed after 1994 invariably came from the ranks of the ANC.

In 1996, the government passed the Employment Equity Act, establishing a legal framework compelling employers to meet affirmative action targets that would reflect the 'demographics' of the broader society. This Act defined those previously disadvantaged as 'designated groups' – Africans, coloureds, Indians, women and the disabled – who qualified for affirmative action policies. Employers would incur penalties if they failed to meet the requirements of the Act, and enterprises would be assessed on the basis of annual reports submitted to the Department of Labour.

In their own domains, various state departments defined transformation in broad enough terms to include as many features and criteria as possible, often leading to quite unintended and contradictory outcomes. Take, for example, the definition used by the South African Police Service, which emphasised change in institutional culture as well as an approach to policing itself, leaving very little out:

> the overall process of change includes rationalisation and amalgamation. It further includes the transformation of policing styles, approaches, priorities, policies, cultures and attitudes whereby the South African Police Service (SAPS) becomes a community service-orientated police service aligned with values and principles such as transparency, accountability, impartiality and professionalism. It thus entails not only the transformation of the nature of the organisation, but of the very essence of policing (Lue 1995).

While transformation has often been motivated and promoted by ANC spokespeople in broad, far-reaching terms (see Motlanthe 1998), in practice most state departments and civil society organisations have understood and implemented transformation through a focus on numbers, securing representative additions of people who had previously been excluded under apartheid. Since all the institutions of apartheid society were exclusively dominated by whites and resources and opportunities distributed on the basis of a hierarchy of identities – whites, Indians, coloureds and Africans – the new government implemented personnel change by relying on apartheid racial classification. The result has been a source of tension and has given rise to a great deal of debate.

The debate about transformation has been multi-dimensional and has assumed many forms, depending on issues specific to the institution or sector involved, its political dynamics, and its role in the overall 'trench warfare' between different social forces. We will highlight a few examples – in sport, higher education and job hiring – to map the contours of the debate.

In the arena of sport, where the raw emotions around transformation seem to be most immediately felt, the key issue has been the selection of national teams. Because of deep historical and cultural affiliations between particular sports and particular racial and ethnic identities – cricket and rugby with whites (and coloureds and some Indians), and soccer with Africans and coloureds – team selection has been highly politicised. Though the national soccer team includes a few white players, the cricket and rugby national teams have remained largely white, the proportions not in keeping with the racial demographics of the country. The Department of Sport and Recreation and the ANC-controlled parliamentary committee on sport have on many occasions voiced their disapproval of the minimal number, or even absence, of black players in national sports, threatening to impose state intervention and penalties.

In opposing ANC policies, the sporting federations, media commentators and sports fans have contributed to a highly charged, ongoing battle. Many critics have spoken of government interference, blaming the government for poor performance at the international level, and echoing the apartheid-era response to international sports isolation: governments should leave sport out of politics. Some point out the importance of government intervention at grassroots level rather than the media-grabbing international level. The ANC and its supporters have responded by emphasising the importance of 'representivity', the need to address past discrimination, and the role of sport in nation-building.

Issues of transformation in higher education have resulted, as expected, in wide differences of opinion about current policies. The extensive legislation governing higher education demands that the sector and individual institutions address issues of equity, democratisation, development, quality, academic freedom, institutional autonomy, and effectiveness and efficiency (DoE 1996).

At the historically white universities, there have been dramatic increases in black student numbers. Historically, the low numbers of African students admitted to the universities of Cape Town and the Witwatersrand, which were considered more open and liberal under apartheid than others, were shocking. At the University of Cape Town, 39 African students registered in 1959; the number dropped to 18 in 1961, and then to 5 in 1965, at the height of the apartheid era. At the University of the Witwatersrand, African student numbers decreased from 74 in 1959, to 38 in 1961, and then to 10 in 1965. In the 1980s, though, black student numbers rose steadily, and in the last decade black students have constituted nearly a half of the total student body, in evident contrast to the numbers of academic staff. Among the issues causing widespread tension and disagreement are student numbers, admissions and quotas, staff composition and the promotion of black staff to senior positions, course offerings, Eurocentric curricula content and institutional culture.

While some of these issues have cropped up in the transformation debate at the University of Stellenbosch, the predominant question here is the language of instruction. This has a direct bearing on non-Afrikaans-speaking black students. The change from Afrikaans as the predominant medium of instruction to a 'dual medium' system, allowing for English and Afrikaans undergraduate lectures – the proposal of university reformers – would enable more African students to attend the university. However, 'traditionalists' have waged a well-organised campaign to retain Afrikaans as the only language of instruction, arguing that Stellenbosch has an historical and cultural obligation to protect Afrikaans from the 'threats' it faces in the new South Africa. In their view, African students ought to learn Afrikaans; there are enough coloured Afrikaans-speaking students who already make the university sufficiently non-racial; and an Afrikaans-language university should be encouraged and supported by the state as it promotes a multilingual society.

There are numerous cases, daily reported or spoken about, relating to the issue of transformation in job hiring procedures. One recent controversial case illustrates the tensions caused by affirmative action within communities oppressed under apartheid. An appropriately qualified man classified as 'coloured' was not given a job in the parastatal company Sasol. Instead, another employee with lesser qualifications, classified as African, was appointed. The case was taken on appeal to the Labour Court, where the judge ruled in favour of the company, reasoning that since Africans were the most oppressed under apartheid, affirmative action practices should give preference to Africans over coloureds and Indians in job hiring. Among those who protested, a struggle activist, Zenzile Khoisan, familiar with struggles in the Western Cape, countered that there was no basis to compare 'degrees of oppression' under apartheid, that coloureds had suffered as much as Africans, and that they could trace their indigeneity to the Khoi and San communities at the Cape, which predated the arrival of white settlers in South Africa.

The opposition to affirmative action has been extensive. Compared to the criticisms of BEE, which have been made mainly by the old 'struggle' Left, the backlash against affirmative action as a form of transformation comes from diverse sectors of society. These include the Solidarity trade union which represents Afrikaner workers in former parastatal companies, some coloured and Indian people who believe that in practice affirmative action benefits only 'indigenous Africans', and opposition parties. The Democratic Alliance, the main opposition party, aims partly to garner electoral support from those dissatisfied with ANC affirmative action policies (or 'racial quotas', as the party calls them), and the Independent Democrats, another opposition party, has sought to win support specifically from alienated coloured voters.

Opposition to affirmative action assumes various and sometimes contradictory forms, drawing on the political discourses and symbols of the new democratic dispensation. In any situation of social change, of course, vested interests will fight to secure positions of dominance. Common arguments include the fear of falling standards or the importance of 'tradition'. It is said that jobs are given to unqualified people and principles of merit are sidelined to satisfy government targets or win the favours of the ruling party; as a result the employing institution is compelled to invest further in outside consultants, which leads to greater inefficiency, increased costs, wastage and corrupt practices. Critics also claim that the efficient 'service delivery' needed to address the backlog inherited from apartheid is unachievable because the employment of unqualified staff has produced capacity problems for the state. Notions of 'standards', 'excellence' and 'efficiency', meritocratic criteria and neoliberal values come together, often in ambiguous configurations, to present a powerful counter to ANC practices claiming to redress past wrongs.

For the ANC, while a discourse of 'the apartheid past' organises its approach to post-apartheid politics, as government a depoliticised discourse of policy, inputs and outputs, systems, measuring indicators and evaluation permeates its policy and practice. The focus on a change in personnel is quite clearly a necessary stage of the decolonisation process, and hardly avoidable. Fanon pointed out that this was a messy and antagonistic process as it involves 'simply the replacing of a certain "species" of men by another "species" of men ... To tell the truth, the proof of success lies in a whole social structure being changed from the bottom up' (1963: 35).

In the main, however, the ANC has conformed to, rather than broken with, decolonisation projects elsewhere; transformation at this stage is viewed as a 'numbers game', in which 'representivity' is the key term. This is the idea that all public institutions ought to have roughly proportional numbers of the different 'race' groups in the whole society. The degree of transformation is thus evaluated according to how 'representative' the institution is, and this is done by the simple method of counting heads, with 'representivity' being considered more important at the level of leadership than among the ordinary members of the institution. While companies sometimes make their overall employment equity targets by hiring more white women, in everyday applications the dominant perception is that the practice is to count how many people of African descent work in a particular institution. Fanon would have criticised the ANC government for conforming to the narrow, elitist programme of change he railed against, where the nationalist bourgeoisie uses popular ideas of Africanisation or nationalisation merely to promote its own class interests.

If the struggle against apartheid was also the struggle against race classification and the creation of a normative order free from race, the re-encroachment of a language of race identification has made many uncomfortable. In a democratic South Africa, even though not by law but by convention, race classification remains paradoxically alive because it is reinforced by dominant state ideology, civil society practices, and various acts encouraging 'transformation'. This is a difficult issue, morally and politically, in post-apartheid South Africa, and it has been the source of the ongoing 'trench warfare' surrounding transformation. Liberal critics argue that the practice reproduces the racial divisions of the past and amounts to a 'reverse racism'. Radical critics, on the other hand, demand a more thoroughgoing transformation of everyday material conditions that will benefit the masses rather than a narrow elite, or else propose that the categories be 'problematised' to demonstrate the fluidity and relational character of identities. But the government, the ANC and perhaps many beneficiaries want to see no other way of correcting and reversing the racial hierarchies of the past. To evaluate progress, they contend, there is a need to classify and count heads – it is a necessary evil.

A more nuanced stance would challenge the politics of reducing transformation to merely personnel changes rather than effecting the deeper structural relations and consequent cultural manifestations inherited from apartheid. In one such framing, it has been argued that the ANC under Mbeki has over-elevated race to a position that undermines the consolidation of a non-racial ethos, which was embryonically developed during the anti-apartheid struggle. Having abandoned its ethical foundation of a non-racial politics, the ANC has replaced it with a narrow African nationalism, emphasising a discourse of indigeneity (Chipkin 2007). These policies promote the interests of conservative elites rather than the masses of poor. All transformation has amounted to is a change from an Afrikaner elite to a black elite with ties to the ruling party. The dominance of the ANC in the political system produces a patronage system in which the ruling party dishes out offices and goods to key societal actors in exchange for support. Even the ANC's attempts to redress the inequities of the past have come under fire. Some on the Left criticise the notion of 'service delivery', arguing that it creates a technocratic conception of politics where citizens assume the role of passive recipients of state goods, leaving state bureaucrats, consultants and experts to dominate decision-making, minimising active and critical citizen participation, and failing to produce any significant changes in development, planning and service delivery.

The examples suggest the difficulty of achieving change beyond the conquest of state power by the majority. They are about struggles for hegemony, since transformation means different things to different societal actors. One side of these debates broadly criticises transformation in terms of 'standards' and, at times, 'tradition' and the undermining of merit and efficiency; the other bewails the lack of transformation, alluding to the continuing prevalence of white racism and new forms of racism that feed on old networks, double standards in applying institutional rules and procedures, and the resilient interconnection between the institutionalised racism of the past and liberal and Afrikaner ideologies. On each side there are different ideas about what is ethically defensible in terms of the content, goals and practices of implementation. But at the very least communication appears to remain open because both sides are talking about transformation – a term which, because of its generality in referring to social change, allows for many different interpretations.

Conclusion

The ANC-led government received an explicit mandate to 'correct' past wrongs and, if possible, reverse the effects of institutionalised racism. The notion of 'transformation' functions variously: to describe, to mask, justify or vilify, or to preserve or mobilise the narrow interests of a few or the broad interests of the many. Conflicts over its content – what should be transformed, by how much, in whose interests – and the way it should be implemented, define the contemporary political terrain. How could it be otherwise, given that apartheid's demise came about through a protracted process of compromise and negotiation, rather than the outright overthrow of the previous order of things? It is a matter of debate as to 'who won'; ongoing battles are the order of the day, and change often commingles with continuity, and sometimes, in a confusing mixture, new elites rely on old conservative discourses. The success of the frontal assault on the apartheid state has been followed by this terrain of trench warfare; in everyday politics, the new democratic society unfolds with much reluctance. The nature of this post-apartheid terrain, an outcome of ongoing struggles, will depend on what meaning of 'transformation' sticks (to borrow from Gramsci) and becomes common sense.

References

Adam, HF, Slabbert, F van Zyl and Moodley, K. 1998. *Comrades in Business: Post Liberation Politics in South Africa* (Cape Town: Tafelberg).

ANC. 1969. *Strategy and Tactics: Morogoro* (Johannesburg: ANC).

ANC. 1975. *Declaration of the ANC Executive Committee: Morogoro, March 1975* (Lusaka: ANC).

Chipkin, I. 2007. *Do South Africans Exist? Nationalism, Democracy and the Identity of 'The People'* (Johannesburg: Wits University Press).

Derrida, J. 1985. 'Racism's Last Word' in J Henry Louis Gates (ed.), *'Race', Writing and Difference* (Chicago: University of Chicago Press), pp. 329–38.

DoE. 1996. *National Commission on Higher Education: An Overview of a New Policy Framework for Higher Education Transformation* (Pretoria: Department of Education).

Fanon, F. 1963. *The Wretched of the Earth* (New York: Grove).

Karis, T and Carter, GM (eds.). 1972. *From Protest to Challenge: A Documentary History of African Politics in South Africa 1882–1964*. Vol. 1: *Protest and Hope 1882–1934* (Stanford, CA: Stanford University Press).

Lue, M. 1995. 'No Easy Route from SAP to SAPS', *SASH*, vol. 37, no. 3.

Macozoma, S. 2005. 'Can a Capitalist System Produce Socialist Results?', *Umrabulo*, vol. 22.

Mandela, N. 1994) *Long Walk To Freedom: The Autobiography of Nelson Mandela* (New York: Random House).

Motlanthe, K. 1998. *ANC on Transformation of State Institutions* (Johannesburg: ANC).

Nash, A. 1998. 'Mandela's Democracy', *Monthly Review*.

Nzimande, BC. 2005. 'Black Empowerment Should Be about the Workers and the Poor', *Umrabulo*, vol. 22.

Singh, M. 1992. 'Transformation Time!', *Transformation*, vol. 17, pp. 48–60.

Trauma

Christopher J. Colvin

Is South Africa post-traumatic?

Is post-apartheid South Africa 'post-traumatic'? Are its citizens 'traumatised'? Is its history a 'traumatic history'? On one hand, the answer to these questions may seem obvious. Three centuries of external and internal colonial rule have left South Africans with a vast archive of suffering. This violent record – of stolen land and children, of murdered families and villages, of slavery, torture, discrimination, rape, detention, arson and exile – is found not only in the many written accounts but also in the traces left on bodies, memories, communities, landscapes, stories, images and songs, traces that document and give texture to the many violences that populate the South African past.

On the other hand, the South African past is populated not only by these sombre ghosts but also by stories of resistance and reconciliation, moments of furtive border-crossings and novel compromises, by flashes of innovation and creativity, and by the constant birth and rebirth of people, of ideas, of communities and cultures, and of world-historical icons and social movements.

But the question I am interested in here is not whether the South African past was a violent and painful one or a creative and heroic one. It was clearly both. Instead, I am interested in what happens when we use the word 'trauma' to name an important part of this complex past. The word 'trauma' has, by now, acquired a fairly generic meaning, as any form of serious violence or suffering. An event that sufficiently disturbs us – a violent crime, a car accident, a flood, a bombing, a failed marriage, a lost job, a missing child, a burglary, a hijacking – may be called a 'traumatic' event in popular discourse, an event that 'traumatises' its victims and witnesses.

But 'trauma' is a fairly recent term, at least in popular discourse, and it was originally a narrow, technical term within psychiatry. It is only in the last twenty years, in South Africa and in the rest of the world, that this term has become widely known and used to name and explain those experiences of suffering and disorder that shake us out of our daily lives.

So what does it mean to describe South Africa's past as 'traumatic'? Why use a psychiatric concept to account for the many social, cultural, political and economic dimensions of the South African past? Is a country like a psychiatric patient? Do its citizens experience the broad sweep of their troubled history as primarily a medical problem?

This chapter tackles these questions by examining the recent origins of the 'trauma discourse' in Western psychiatry and politics, its early use in South Africa in the fight against apartheid, and the recent uses and transformations of this concept in post-apartheid South Africa. It also considers what is gained and what is lost when we use this medical term to describe the suffering of South Africa and its citizens, both past and present. What is this term's ideological baggage? What ways of looking at the world are bound up in this little word?

Global origins of the trauma discourse

As an official diagnostic term within Western psychiatry, trauma only appeared in 1980 as part of a new anxiety disorder called Post-Traumatic Stress Disorder (PTSD) (McNally 2003). In this model, a trauma is an event so extreme that its meaning cannot be fully comprehended. Victims aren't able to interpret the event in terms of the everyday stories they tell themselves about who they are and how the world works. Unable to confront or understand the memory of the unspeakable event, victims repress these memories. These repressed traumatic memories inevitably fail to remain buried, though, and instead erupt into the present in the form of anxiety attacks, flashbacks, hypervigilance, detachment, avoidance and a general inability to distinguish the past from the present. Repressed traumatic memories, thus, produce a 'disorder of time' in which the traumatic past continues to invade the post-traumatic present.

The therapist's task is to help patients become more fully aware of the often forgotten details of the traumatic event and, in doing so, realise that the event is indeed over. To do this, the patient is asked to 'relive' every detail of the traumatic experience. Retelling the traumatic story allows the trauma to be reinserted into its proper place in the day-to-day narrative framework that was torn apart by the traumatic secret. This reliving is sometimes accompanied by a 'catharsis'. Catharsis is often understood as evidence that the traumatic event has been fully relived and that the violent effects of the trauma have finally been appreciated. 'Closure' is supposed to happen when patients have integrated the newly recognised traumatic secret into their own self-narrative. By narrating the traumatic event back into its rightful place in the narrative – in the past – the ability of the past to impact further on the present is reduced (Leys 1996).

The diagnosis of PTSD grew largely out of attempts in the 1970s by American psychiatrists to understand and treat the growing population of psychologically disturbed veterans of the Vietnam War (Young 1995). There were, of course, prior attempts within psychiatry to account for the ways violent and shocking events could disrupt the minds of those who experienced them. Soldiers in the US Civil War who were unable to handle the rigours of the battlefield were said to suffer from 'combat fatigue'. In World War One, this condition came to be known as 'shell shock'. Within psychoanalysis, the term 'trauma', originally meaning a physical wound, came, under Freud's and Janet's guidance, to describe early childhood experiences of sexual abuse or emotional conflict that were thought to be the root cause of later neurotic and hysterical behaviour.

It wasn't, however, until the designation of PTSD as an official psychiatric diagnosis that the ability of certain events to induce a debilitating and persistent form of anxiety disorder was formally accepted and theorised within biomedicine. Until then, those suffering from combat fatigue, shell shock, or plain and simple 'nerves' after violent events were more likely to be thought of, even within psychiatry, as weak-willed and of a poor or nervous 'character', than to be seen as innocent sufferers of a psychiatric condition.

This proved useful, in one way, to the many women and men who had returned from their violent experiences in Vietnam to a disappointed and angry home country. Many of them were treated badly on their return and the psychological suffering they endured because of their time in Vietnam was rarely recognised, much less treated. More often than not, expressing this suffering only brought them further moral and political condemnation. To have a psychiatric diagnosis, however, offered them a less problematic route for their suffering to be recognised. It gave them a way to frame their suffering in a more morally neutral idiom, not as the regrets of a guilt-ridden soldier back home, but as the predictable psychological effects of external experiences of 'traumatic stress'.

Allan Young (1995) has described this new model of traumatic stress as an 'invention'. He does not mean that the suffering of Vietnam veterans was – and is – not real. Instead, he argues that the discourse of trauma gave veterans a way to label and interpret their experiences that was previously unavailable. This new discourse proved to be a double-edged sword, though. Veterans could now claim a new status as victims of a medical – rather than moral – disorder, but in the process they risked being turned into 'patients' as well. Their anger and frustration at what they experienced in Vietnam, and upon their return, could now be portrayed as symptoms of their medical condition rather than as valid moral and political complaints. Their protests and marches could be seen as failures to cope with a mental health disorder rather than conscious acts of political critique.

Since the establishment of PTSD as a psychological diagnosis for returning soldiers, it has been applied to more and more classes of victims. Victims of incest and sexual abuse were the first to adopt this new language, then victims of domestic violence, of terrorism, of criminal violence and, eventually, of natural disasters. There has also been a parallel geographical expansion of the use of the trauma discourse around the world. It is not unusual to hear about trauma counsellors being dispatched to far-off scenes of natural disasters or civil war; or to hear the basic principles of traumatic stress and its treatment in radio and TV talk shows in Cape Town, Osaka and Caracas. In fact, this discourse of trauma is now part of a global cultural complex, reflected in both professional mental healthcare and in global popular culture.

The trauma concept has also become a significant political term in the last two decades. Campaigns for the protection of human rights, victim empowerment programmes, claims for reparations, and identity politics grounded in what Wendy Brown (1995) has called the 'politics of injury' have all mobilised the trauma discourse in their political activity. The medical language of trauma gives victims and activists an ability to name their suffering and the suffering of others in a way that cannot be so easily dismissed by their political opponents. Even the work of writing history has been suffused with this therapeutic language, with many scholars and politicians paying renewed attention to the 'traumatic' elements of their ethnic and national pasts rather than just to their heroic and victorious moments.

Trauma in South Africa

During apartheid, the term 'trauma' was used principally by progressive mental healthcare activists. They wanted to use this new psychiatric model of trauma to prove that victims of apartheid – both of its physical violences and of its daily forms of discrimination and oppression – were suffering from a real psychiatric condition. They hoped that this would force those who defended apartheid to recognise its genuine pathological effects on individual minds.

For many in South Africa, the first time they came into regular contact with the word 'trauma' was probably with the Truth and Reconciliation Commission (TRC). Those engaged in the TRC, as well as those commenting on its work, often used a therapeutic vocabulary to describe the Commission's brief. They said that testifying at the Commission's hearings was a chance for people to 'work through' and 'debrief' some of their 'traumatic memories' and achieve some kind of 'catharsis' and 'closure' in the process. They said these memories had been 'repressed' during apartheid, but now victims had the chance to 'open their wounds in order to cleanse them' (Tutu 1999). This language drew both from general psychoanalytic principles about the usefulness of the 'talking cure' and from more recent theories about psychological trauma.

It wasn't only through its vocabulary that the TRC promoted this model of traumatic memory. Trauma counsellors – psychologists who had special training and experience in treating traumatic stress – were involved in designing the Commission, in training the 'briefers' who offered support to victims during testimony, and in providing counselling after the hearings to victims who were still in need of support. Many of these counsellors worked for non-profit 'trauma centres', some of which have continued to offer services to victims of traumatic violence in the years after the TRC. There is, in fact, a national network of these trauma service providers called Themba le Sizwe, or 'Hope of the Nation'. These centres offer debriefing, counselling and other services not only to victims of apartheid-era political violence, but also to victims of sexual, domestic and other forms of criminal violence as well.

Since its early appearance in progressive mental health circles during apartheid, and its debut on the wider national stage with the TRC, the trauma discourse has since travelled more broadly in popular discourse and practice. It has moved out of the clinic and the TRC hearing, and into community healthcare clinics, police stations, newspaper articles and talk shows, and beyond. In local clinics, patients can now find informational posters that describe the list of symptoms associated with PTSD and urge patients to contact their doctors or nurses about these symptoms and about the possibilities of securing disability grants if their experience of PTSD is sufficiently debilitating.

In these same clinics, though, the language of trauma jostles, sometimes uncomfortably, with the language of 'nerves'. This idiom of nerves is a longer-standing language of complaint among South Africans and is used to describe a wide variety of feelings of nervousness, anxiety, tension, stress, unease and irritability (Swartz 1998). It is a 'folk idiom' for distress, used and understood by doctors and nurses in their conversations with patients, but not part of the official biomedical language of disease and treatment. In some important ways, to 'have nerves' or for one's nerves to 'be up' is a lot like being 'traumatised', and in many situations either term could be used and be equally sensible to sufferers and healers alike. 'Trauma' has an advantage over 'nerves', however, in that it is an accepted term within psychiatric medicine with clear symptoms and treatments, whereas 'nerves' is not.

The trauma discourse has also moved into some police stations in middle- and lower-middle-class areas as these stations have opened up 'trauma rooms' to offer victims a safe place to sit and talk in the moments just after their experiences of violent crime. Often the product of lobbying efforts from local community mental health workers, victims advocates and interested individuals, the trauma rooms are intended to offer victims a chance to 'debrief' about their experiences and be offered support as soon as possible after their violation. They are often staffed by volunteers from the area and from local mental health NGOs.

Finally, the language of trauma has moved into popular culture as well. Newspaper articles frequently describe the victims of crime as 'traumatised'. Radio and television talk shows encourage people to call in and talk about what has traumatised them and how they have been able to work through the effects of that trauma. The word 'trauma' has also been easily borrowed into local African languages as well. I have heard a number of people, outside the context of the TRC or local trauma centres, using *i-trauma* (noun form of 'trauma') or *uku-trauma-taisa* ('to be traumatised') when recounting events they had experienced or witnessed.

The first time, though, that I ran across the term 'trauma' in South Africa wasn't at the TRC or with victims of political or criminal violence, but in an ad for the Edgars Club Card that I saw on the day I arrived in Cape Town in 1999. Among the many benefits of membership that this poster listed – including special discounts, guarantees, early admission to sale days, newsletters, free card replacement, and low interest – was free access to a 24-hour trauma counselling telephone hotline. It is a good sign of an idea's widespread acceptance and importance when it shows up as a perk on a store credit card.

The spread and acceptance of 'trauma' as a way of framing and treating suffering hasn't been completely even in South Africa. The rural areas in particular have not been quick to take up this new language. This is partly because there is a general lack of basic services and access to media and urban discourse in these areas. The language and practice of trauma counselling simply haven't reached these areas in the way they have in the cities. However, even when trauma centres have tried to do limited outreach in these areas, they have found it very difficult. Very few people in rural South Africa have ever met a psychologist, their more immediate survival needs are often felt to be more pressing, and, for many, trauma therapy's approach to healing – talk therapy about your most private feelings and experiences once a week in a small room with a person you don't know – is culturally foreign (Colvin 2004).

Promises and pitfalls of the trauma discourse

In thinking critically about the use of the concept of trauma in popular and political discourse, we have to consider both its advantages and disadvantages as a way of describing, explaining and responding to suffering. In the discussion that follows, I have focused more attention on the possible disadvantages of the trauma model, but this is not because I don't acknowledge its real benefits. But given the wide acceptance of this discourse, and the easy way in which so many seem to have incorporated it into their everyday ways of thinking about suffering and recovery, I want to spend more time on the pitfalls than the promises.

But let's consider the promises first. The principal benefit of this new way of thinking medically about the effects of extreme stress is that it recognises that violent events do sometimes produce real and debilitating psychiatric disorders. These disorders can thus be recognised as something other than the product of a malingering, weak-willed or hypochondriacal personality. Until the development of the trauma model, psychiatry did not have an effective way to understand or treat the effects of traumatic events. Instead, when people came undone because of the terrible things that happened to them, their symptoms were more often seen as reflections of underlying 'deep' personality or anxiety disorders, or repressed memories of earlier sexual and violent abuse, or perhaps simply bad characters.

In all these cases, victims of traumatic stress were more likely to be stigmatised and sidelined rather than taken seriously and treated for a medical condition related to the traumatic event itself. Armed with a diagnosis of PTSD, however, they could now demand a wide range of possible treatments – psychotherapy, medication, cognitive-behavioural therapy, eye-movement desensitisation therapy – and have a better chance of having some of their suffering alleviated.

This new development was not only of immediate medical benefit for the victims. It could also be of broad legal, political and financial benefit as well. Victims who could link their medical symptoms to specific events – rather than to their own underlying psychopathologies – could now claim compensation and recognition from those responsible for the event, from the courts and from the political arena more generally. Trauma theory offered a number of new classes of individuals a status as 'real' victims in a way that had not been possible before. Vietnam veterans, victims of racial abuse and sexual violence, battered wives, victims of incest – all now had a medical condition that legitimated their suffering and connected their symptoms directly to things that were done to them by others rather than to their own characters and personalities.

The advantages of the psychiatric model of trauma to these many, previously unrecognised and stigmatised, victims are not to be discounted. The trauma model proved to be both psychologically healing and politically empowering for many people. As with any social practice, however, it has its pitfalls as well, pitfalls that often reflect the particular political ideologies and cultural assumptions on which trauma theory and Western psychiatry more generally are based.

The most common complaint about the idea of trauma is that it is an event-centred and individual-centred model of suffering. In terms of the psychiatric definition, a trauma has to be an 'event' that occurs to an individual. And the individual is where the experience of trauma takes place, where the effects of traumatic stress manifest, and where the solutions to overcoming traumatic stress are to be found. But what about those causes of mental anxiety and distress that are not 'events' *per se*, but could still be considered 'traumatic' in their effects. What about chronic poverty? Or sustained police harassment? Or persistent discrimination and humiliation?

Those trying to use the idea of trauma to fight apartheid came to realise that many of the violences of apartheid were systematic and structural, lived everyday as part of the basic conditions of 'normal' life, rather than as an unusual event that shook one out of daily life. There were recommendations that PTSD should be complemented by something like 'continuous traumatic stress disorder' or 'ongoing traumatic stress disorder'. But these new formulations never took hold within psychiatry because they challenged the core assumption that a 'trauma' was a discrete event that happened to an individual person rather than a structure of oppression that happened to a community or group of people.

The problem here is not so much that these kinds of individual-specific events don't happen. They do, and it is good and necessary that psychiatry can recognise them. But psychiatry has not been able to 'see' these other forms of violence and suffering as easily, forms that are just as powerful in their ability to cause psychological harm and, thus, just as necessary to respond to on both a psychological and a political level. Psychiatry's inability to recognise – to name, theorise, and treat – 'ongoing' forms of stress is not a simple oversight or failure of the scientific imagination; it reflects the fact that conventional psychiatry is politically more disposed to recognise and legitimate some kinds of problems and not others.

Another related critique of trauma is that it 'medicalises' and 'privatises' suffering. When responding to violent and disruptive events, and the suffering these events produce, the trauma discourse makes this suffering the target of specialist medical interventions and makes individuals the objects of these interventions. Again, the point here is not that serious medical consequences are not suffered by individuals who experience violent events. Rather, the problem is that traumatic events are never *only* medical problems faced by individuals. They also represent social, moral, political, economic and even spiritual problems for both individuals and communities.

To medicalise a problem is to turn it first and foremost into a medical problem when it is in fact much more. Similarly, to privatise suffering is to understand suffering as a problem only of the individual sufferer, rather than of some broader community as well. In both cases, suffering is depoliticised, removed from the world of political and moral debate, and isolated safely in the realm of technical, individual medical intervention. Furthermore, in this realm, it is the responsibility of the victim-patient to learn to cope with the sources of their suffering. Thus, while traumatic stress has been diagnosed in a wider and wider set of victims, there has been a parallel tendency to make all the many problems these victims face – often as a group – into medical problems faced only by each individual alone.

Just as the trauma discourse has a tendency to turn individuals and communities, who are struggling with complex forms and sources of suffering in their lives, into passive, autonomous clients of technical medical interventions, it also has the tendency to neglect the agency, resistance, resilience and creativity of these same individuals and communities as they work to improve their lives. In the conventional model of traumatic stress, events come from the outside and 'happen' to individuals who then experience a range of negative psychological consequences. Little mention is made – and little formal theorising has been done – about the fact that the majority of people who experience traumatic events do not in fact suffer symptoms of traumatic stress. Most people experience short-term symptoms of shock, disbelief, anxiety, anger or helplessness, but, for most, these symptoms soon disappear. Even in cases when victims do experience more persistent symptoms, most people have a range of coping strategies and resources that can help them to mitigate or even alleviate their symptoms without medical intervention.

In some cases, people channel their experiences of suffering into social and political activism. Others turn it into art or recreation. In short, the ways that people find to cope and work through their psychological suffering vary widely. For those who do find the effects of traumatic events too difficult to deal with, the targeted, specialist intervention of a psychiatrist or psychologist can make all the difference in the world. For the rest, however, the over-eager attention of mental healthcare professionals is more likely to short-circuit their own forms of coping and healing and deny the many active, creative and resilient aspects of their engagement with the problems of suffering (Emmerik et al. 2002).

Finally, some critics have argued that the whole idea of trauma and how to treat it is based on very specific cultural assumptions – about the role of narrative in healing, about what the mind is and how it works, about the confidential client–therapist relationship, and about the meaning of certain symptoms and of the problem of suffering more generally – that are foreign to the great majority of the world. They argue that the idea of trauma, and the popular discourses and therapeutic practices that it has inspired, better reflect the cultural and political moment of the late modern West (Farrell 1998).

Suffering has, of course, been with all people at all times, but the particular model of suffering and recovery at work in trauma theory is more a reflection of the confessional, individual, mediatised, medicalised, litigious and commodified character of a globalising Western culture than a simple and neutral description of a universal medical condition. Conventional trauma therapy tends to ignore both local meanings – about the body, about god, goddesses and spirits, about witchcraft, about the purpose of suffering – and also local resources for coping with and transforming suffering in whatever ways possible (Honwana 1999).

Conclusion: trauma as metaphor

One of characteristic uses of the trauma discourse in post-apartheid South Africa has been to imagine the South African nation as a whole as if it is like a person who has been traumatised and must now submit to a range of treatments to alleviate its traumatic stress. The country is said to have repressed its traumatic histories. It must now, through mechanisms like the TRC, unearth and work through its violent past, hoping to achieve some kind of closure that will allow it to move unimpeded by the past into the future.

When the word 'trauma' is used in this fashion, as a metaphor that treats groups in the same way as individuals, do we confront the same kinds of promises and pitfalls? Many of the promises are the same. The idea of trauma can usefully focus our attention on the human toll of violent conflicts rather than on the conventional heroes and villains that are typical of nationalist histories. It thus may prevent the development of at least one form of historical fiction after conflict – the kind that erases the deep but hidden suffering of those on all sides of the conflict in favour of the heroic suffering of a few individual national figures. Paying attention to trauma – either individual or collective – can also signal a commitment to human rights on the part of the nation. And many hope that paying attention to lingering traces of hurt and resentment in individuals and communities can help to break cycles of trans-generational violence that seem to plague some countries in the world (Volkan 1997).

There are dangers, though, in too easily allowing the trauma discourse to frame the way we understand the challenges of post-conflict societies. Much of trauma therapy, for example, revolves around getting patients to accept the fact that the traumatic event is truly in the past and can no longer harm them. This makes sense when the traumatic event is a car accident, but when we are thinking about deep histories of religious conflict or racial prejudice, it makes less sense to speak about them as if they were magically 'over', without the power to cause harm in the present. The South African government has made energetic use of this idea of drawing the line between past and present. While there is a universe of difference between the pre- and post-1994 political and legal environments, when it comes to social and economic divisions within society post-apartheid South Africa doesn't look so 'post' apartheid.

Treating the nation's past suffering as a problem of traumatic stress also tends to limit the scope of what we understand as the sources and forms of historical and contemporary suffering. In the same way trauma therapy can medicalise the problems of individuals, it can reduce the many social, economic and political problems confronting a post-conflict state to problems of the repressed memories of victims of violence. The solution – getting victims of trauma to speak out publicly about their experiences – is an important but limited response to the complex challenges on many fronts facing new nations.

This process of public testimony, as we have seen at the TRC, can also be damaging to individual victims who are trying to deal in their own ways with the effects of the past (Walaza 2000). Putting your own traumatic memories on display in front of the nation, with little follow-up or support in the process, is not a good recipe for individual psychological recovery. Though many people did find the TRC process helpful in their own journey to understand and overcome their violent memories, there were also many who felt undone by the process, people whose own processes of coping and recovery were interrupted by the request to testify on stage as part of the recovery of the 'nation'.

To critique the use of the term 'trauma' at either the individual or the sociopolitical level is not to deny the very real suffering of individuals and communities. But the language in which we describe our suffering, explain its causes, and attempt to end it is never neutral. Even an explicitly medical discourse like the trauma discourse brings with it a host of cultural assumptions and political implications. This is not to say that the trauma discourse is in reality a ploy to promote certain political or cultural perspectives under the guise of scientific neutrality. Rather, every discourse that tries to account for our suffering and the suffering of others inevitably reflects a particular perspective. Trauma, in its ubiquity, may seem like a generic term, a simple synonym for suffering or pain. But it brings with it, sometimes subtly and sometimes not, a certain way of looking at the world, a perspective that makes some kinds and causes of suffering harder to see than others.

References
Brown, Wendy. 1995. *States of Injury: Power and Freedom in Late Modernity* (Princeton, NJ: Princeton University Press).
Colvin, Christopher J. 2004. 'Performing the Signs of Injury: Critical Perspectives on Traumatic Storytelling after Apartheid', PhD diss., Department of Anthropology, University of Virginia.
Emmerik, Arnold AP van, Kamphuis, JH, Hulsbosch, AM and Emmelkamp, PM. 2002. 'Single Session Debriefing after Psychological Trauma: A Metaanalysis', *The Lancet*, no. 360, pp. 766–71.
Farrell, Kirby. 1998. *Post-Traumatic Culture: Injury and Interpretation in the Nineties* (Baltimore, MD: Johns Hopkins University Press).
Honwana, Alcinda. 1999. 'Negotiating Post-war Identities: Child Soldiers in Mozambique and Angola', *Codesria Bulletin*, no. 2, pp. 4–13.
Leys, Ruth. 1996. 'Traumatic Cures: Shell Shock, Janet and the Question of Memory' in Antze, P and Lambek, M (eds.), *Tense Past: Cultural Essays in Trauma and Memory* (New York: Routledge), pp. 103–45.
McNally, Richard J. 2003. *Remembering Trauma* (Cambridge, MA: Belknap Press).
Swartz, Leslie. 1998. *Culture and Mental Health: A Southern African View* (Cape Town: Oxford University Press).
Tutu, Desmond. 1999. *No Future Without Forgiveness* (New York: Doubleday).

Volkan, Vamik D. 1997. *Bloodlines: From Ethnic Pride to Ethnic Terrorism* (New York: Farrar Straus and Giroux).

Walaza, Nomfundo. 2000. 'Insufficient Healing and Reparation' in Villa-Vicencio, C and Verwoerd, W (eds.), *Looking Back, Reaching Forward: Reflections on the Truth and Reconciliation Commission of South Africa* (Cape Town: University of Cape Town Press), pp. 250–5.

Young, Allan. 1995. *Harmony of Illusions: Inventing Post-Traumatic Stress Disorder* (Princeton: Princeton University Press).

TRUTH AND RECONCILIATION

Fiona Ross

IT IS NOW A LITTLE MORE than a decade since South Africa's Truth and Reconciliation Commission (TRC) commenced its innovative, internationally acclaimed and extremely contested work of recording gross violations of human rights,[1] offering a limited amnesty and attempting reconciliation in a country that the Constitution describes as 'deeply divided'. Frequently described exaggeratedly as one of South Africa's most successful exports, the Truth and Reconciliation model has become important in transitional justice processes around the world, most recently having been recommended by US President George Bush as an intervention process for reconciliation in Iraq. The Commission's work has generated an enormous literature, both critical and adulatory (see Verdoolaege 2006; the bibliography at http://cas1. elis.ugent.be/avrug/trc), and interest in its assumptions, process, outputs, and effects has scarcely waned, despite the fact that a large proportion of its work was completed in 1998.

Truth commissions are investigations into past violence, often drawing on a human rights model, and have become a popular measure in transitional justice processes as countries democratise. Priscilla Hayner notes that by 2001, there had been 21 commissions around the world, commencing with a commission of inquiry into disappearances in Uganda in 1974 (2001) and the most recent being conducted in Sierra Leone. These have varied in their success. Most have been predicated on the assumption that knowing the truth of violations committed in the past is important, not least to the establishment and legitimation of new political dispensations in the present (Wilson 1996). Commissions may be established by presidential decree, legislation, or non-state and civil society interventions in the aftermath of political violence. The best-known examples prior to the South African Commission were those of Argentina and Chile, which employed a rhetoric of truth-telling to promote catharsis and healing.

The South African experiment

South Africa's TRC was initiated as part of the negotiated settlement of 1993 that brought an end to minority rule. In comparison to prior commissions, it was unusual in that it linked 'truth' with 'reconciliation', the latter being considered necessary to overcoming division and creating a new national identity. One of several interventions designed by South Africa's first parliament elected by universal franchise to redress apartheid and colonialism, the Commission was established by an Act passed by parliament in 1995 (the first truth commission to have been so mandated), and tasked with promoting national unity and reconciliation 'in a spirit of understanding which transcends the conflicts and divisions of the past'. In popular interpretations, South Africa was understood to be traumatised and in need of healing (see Ignatieff 1996 for critical assessments). This was to be achieved by 'establishing as complete a picture as possible of the causes, nature and extent of the gross violations of human rights' committed between 1960 and 1994; facilitating amnesty for those who qualified in terms of the Act; establishing the fate of victims and restoring their dignity 'by granting them an opportunity to relate their own accounts of the violations of which they are the victims' and devising reparation measures; and compiling a full report including recommendations as to how to prevent future violations (Promotion of National Unity and Reconciliation Act No. 96 of 1995).

The Commission undertook this work through three committees; on human rights violations, amnesty, and reparation and rehabilitation. After seven years of work, these committees produced a seven-volume Report (TRC 1998, 2003), granted a total of 1167 full amnesties (a further 157 people received amnesty for some but not all actions for which they had applied; see http://truth.wwl.wits.ac.za/cat_descr.php?cat=3), identified some 22,000 victims of gross violations of human rights, and made recommendations for reparation, some of which have been implemented.

The Commission is widely considered to have been extremely successful, yet at the tenth anniversary celebrations in April 2006, its chair, former Archbishop Desmond Tutu, expressed dissatisfaction at its results. He is reported as having said that reparations offered to victims had been 'ungenerous', that victims had been unfairly treated, that amnesties had been granted too quickly, and that the Commission had failed to reveal the full truth (Breytenbach 2006). In other words, that neither truth nor reconciliation had been achieved.

His opinion has been borne out by others who recognise the shortcomings of the much-lauded Commission and the assumptions that underpin it. In his National Reconciliation Day speech of 2005, at which he commemorated the signing into law of the Promotion of National Unity and Reconciliation Act a decade previously, President Thabo Mbeki commented that notwithstanding the important work done by the Commission and by the state in trying to implement some of its recommendations, 'real reconciliation and nation-building can only happen when the South African people, black and white, through their own initiative, without any prompting from government, take visible and decisive steps to break down the racial walls that still define us'. In other words, he recognised that the Commission could not achieve reconciliation alone: that it remains a societal process yet to be completed.

These assessments are not without precedent. The debate about truth and reconciliation and the relationship between them in South Africa has raged for almost a decade and a half now. Indeed, in an early assessment of the effectiveness of truth commissions, Michael Ignatieff (1996) noted that, contrary to much of the literature which posits that they are significant in ensuring social change and democratic process, 'A truth commission cannot overcome a society's division. It can only winnow out the solid core of facts upon which society's arguments with itself should be conducted. But it cannot bring these arguments to a conclusion. All that a truth commission can achieve is to reduce the number of lies that can be circulated unchallenged in public discourse.'

If this is indeed all that the South African Commission did achieve, it is still an important contribution. So, let us examine this more closely by focusing on the Commission's work and effects in a single site. I draw from research conducted between 1996 and 2000 in Zwelethemba (Ross 2003a), the 'African' township attached to Worcester, a town in the fruit-growing region of the Western Cape, and an area that had long been a site of resistance to the apartheid state.

The Commission's report on events in Zwelethemba

In June 1996, the Commission's human rights violations committee held hearings on gross violations of human rights in the area. Let us then begin with the Commission's findings (Vol. 3: 427–9).[2] The report focuses on the mid-1980s and presents events in Zwelethemba as typical of those in other small rural towns at the time:

138 In Worcester the spark was provided by the killing of Mr Nkosana Nation Bahume, after which a cycle of deaths and injuries took place until the end of the year.

139 On 16 August 1985, student activist Nkosana Nation Bahume [CT00547], aged twenty-one, was shot dead by the security forces. On 30 August, the local magistrate issued restriction orders on the funeral of Bahume, who was to be buried the following day. At the funeral, police fired at mourners, killing Mr Mbulelo Kenneth Mazula [CT00528], aged twenty. An eyewitness testified that 'police dragged his body to the vehicle and took him to the mortuary'. People were assaulted, shot and detained by security forces in the uproar.

140 Mbulelo Mazula was buried on 8 September without incident. However, on 21 September 1985, Mr Andile Feni [CT08402] and two others were shot and injured by a policeman in Zwelethemba after a crowd had thrown a petrol bomb at a police officer's house after a mass meeting that had resolved to chase all police from the area following the killings.

141 On 1 October 1985, Mr Thomas Kolo [CT08400], age eighteen, was shot dead by security forces. He was buried on 11 October and the funeral was restricted by the magistrate. The following day, security forces shot Mr Zandisile Ntsomi [CT00320]. Ntsomi's leg was amputated and he was discharged from hospital back into police custody the following day …

142 Ntsomi was then driven in the van to Cape Town and back to Worcester …

143 On 13 October, Douglas Ndzima [CT00821] was shot twice by police in Zwelethemba. That day Ms Martha Nomathamsanqa Mooi's house [CT03026] in Zwelethemba was petrol-bombed by UDF [United Democratic Front] members. Mr Mpazamo Bethwell Mbani (Yiko) [CT03026], her brother-in-law, was shot dead and his body set alight.

144 On 2 November 1985, Mr Cecil Roos Tamsanqa van Staden [CT00132] was shot by police and died two days later. The following day, Mr William Dyasi [CT00823] was shot dead by police in Zwelethemba. An inquest was held and Constable Michael Phillip Luff was found responsible for the murder but he was not prosecuted. At the intervention of the Commission, the case was reopened, following which Luff applied to the Commission for amnesty [AM3814/96].

145 On 9 November, at the night vigil of one of the victims, Mr Buzile Fadana [CT00131] was shot dead after police arrived and an 'armed encounter' resulted. His death marked an end to this cycle of killings and injuries that year.

146 By November 1985, an extreme environment [sic] of repression existed in Zwelethemba, which was declared out of bounds to all except residents. Roadblocks were set up and residents were only allowed to go to their homes on producing identity documents. There were twenty-four-hour foot patrols, and searchlights swept the streets at night. Residents reported a heavy presence of Zulu-speaking policemen. Funerals of unrest victims were restricted to only fifty people and the family of the deceased. In one instance, forty young people were detained whilst participating in a funeral vigil.

THE COMMISSION FINDS THAT THE KILLING BY POLICE OF MR NKOSANA NATION BAHUME ON 16 AUGUST 1985 TRIGGERED A SEQUENCE OF VIOLENCE, IN WHICH NUMEROUS RESIDENTS OF WORCESTER WERE KILLED OR INJURED BY POLICE AND A NUMBER OF PERSONS AND BUILDINGS WERE ATTACKED IN RETALIATION. THE DRACONIAN RESPONSE OF THE AUTHORITIES, INCLUDING CURFEWS, ROADBLOCKS AND SWEEPING DETENTIONS, ONLY AGGRAVATED THE SITUATION.

The report pays scant attention to the long history of oppression and resistance in the area. Although the Commission was mandated to conduct its research from 1960, in Zwelethemba, as elsewhere, the struggle against apartheid and oppression predated the 1960s. During the 1960–1 pass law protests, people burned their passbooks in public. Many were arrested for violating apartheid's laws, both petty and grand. Men and women were involved in strike action at various factories in the area from the 1960s and young people joined the nationwide youth protest against Afrikaans as a medium of instruction in 1976. Protests against Bantu education were sustained in the area. By 1985, most of the senior leadership of local struggle activities – trades unionists, members of the UDF, underground ANC operatives – had been jailed or were in exile. The mantle of leadership fell on the youth (see Reynolds 2005).

The Commission's account of events in Zwelethemba offers a litany of male death and damage, to the exclusion of women's activities, the harms they suffered and the ways in which people tried to create meaningful lives for themselves and others. An emphasis on gross violations of human rights – individual experiences of torture, abduction, killing or severe ill-treatment – thus generates a biased account of the past which holds experiences that were mainly masculine to be the norm. Only one woman is included in the events and that because during the incident, her brother-in-law was killed.

Many of the women with whom I worked in Zwelethemba had participated in struggle activities and were present, some being injured, during the events described in the Report (see Ross 2003a: 77–161). None of this is included in the Commission's report on Zwelethemba. The Report clearly holds the state responsible for much of the violence experienced in Zwelethemba at the time. Yet there is scant account of the brutality of a range of different police, military, and para-military interventions or of the structures of power and command that enabled them to act with virtual impunity. The Commission offers no record of the bravery of the young or the complex work of making and remaking everyday life that is so often undertaken by women. It offers little account of the complexity of anti-apartheid struggle, the tensions that existed between residents of Zwelethemba, or the betrayals of some by others, the effects of which endure into the present and shape interpersonal relations (see Reynolds 2005; Ross and Reynolds 2004).

Why has this somewhat biased account of the past happened? It is clearly not from ill intent on the Commission's part. Instead, I suggest, it arises from an insistence on documenting events rather than processes, a focus on gross violations of human rights rather than systemic relationships, a reflection on damage and a lack of attention to how people make relationships in fraught circumstances, and the assumption that truth exists independent of social contexts. Let us explore some of these in more detail.

The past in the present

The Commission's model assumed that one could talk immediately and directly of pain and, indeed, many people were able to do so (although, as I show later in the chapter, speech was shaped by powerful conventions to do with gender and age). It also assumed that speaking of suffering was in some measure cathartic and would give rise to interpersonal and national reconciliation.

Most of those with whom I worked had made substantial efforts to overcome past divisions with those within their communities and outside them who may have caused them harm (see also Reynolds 2005). Some worked alongside those who had betrayed them, or interrogated, tortured or taunted them. In the post-apartheid period, people have made enormous efforts to overcome histories of harm. However, despite careful tending to control their destructive capacities, old hurts may sometimes erupt into everyday interactions. Focusing on a small event allows us to consider the work that goes into holding anger at bay.

Take, for example, an event during Women's Day celebrations in 2005, when members of the ANC Women's League in Zwelethemba attended a celebration at the prison from which Nelson Mandela was released in Paarl. Two women there, let's call them Phakama and Zoleka, had long been opposed to one another, each accusing the other of having betrayed comrades to the police during the tense times of the mid-1980s. The two women had never fully patched up their differences. At the Women's Day celebration, Phakama overheard Zoleka commenting about her in a derogatory fashion. She in turn made equally snide comments. As is so often the case, the comments were elliptical and their import may well not have been understood by bystanders unfamiliar with the idiom in which insults are offered or the history that lay behind them. For example, Zoleka commented that Phakama had suddenly become rich with her children's life insurance money, implying, for those who surrounded them, that Phakama was a witch who had killed her children in order to profit from their deaths. Phakama asked out loud why Zoleka was so slender; was it perhaps her African potato diet? She followed it up with a question about why Zoleka always dressed in such fancy modern clothes, wearing a different 'traditional' style for each day of the week.

Writing is deceptive. Absent the tone of voice in which they were uttered, the comments might even be read as compliments, but bystanders understood Phakama to be implying that Zoleka had HIV/AIDS (the potato diet being the local way that HIV is referred to after the Health Minister suggested that seropositive people use African potatoes as part of their healing repertoire), and that she was so estranged from her own customs that even her clothing reflected her lack of grounding in culture. The comments, innocuous to an outsider, enraged the two women so severely that bystanders had to separate them.

Here, events long past in chronological time haunt the present. It is worth noting that this was one of the first times that overt conflict had erupted between the two women; although working in the same political organisation, they had managed to avoid direct confrontation for many years. Each had exercised a great deal of restraint. However, the visit by a group of women to a site of strong emotional resonance in Paarl brought long-suppressed angers to the surface. The language that draws them to anger is elliptical, subtle, and makes no reference to either the events of betrayal or to the period from which the angers stem, although bystanders all attribute the confrontation to these events. Instead it is metaphoric, interpretable only from within a particular speech community. What appear to an outsider to be simple or obscure comments are in fact loaded, full of reference to death, witchcraft and the undoing of social relations at every level – individual, familial and cultural.

It is hard for outsiders to make sense of intimations of this kind. They work to disguise direct conflict at the same time as fomenting it. The Commission assumed that one's 'story' about the past existed intact, waiting to be told, and that the ordinary language of 'who did what to whom' was adequate to the telling and sufficient for truth. Yet as the incident illustrates, talk can be dangerous and reference to the past is often disguised. This is not to say that it is impossible to speak directly of pain, but merely to point out that sometimes the language within which suffering is related is opaque and rests on local idiom and familiarity with events long past. Part of what this story also illustrates is a truth too – that it takes concerted individual and social effort to overcome old tensions, and that notwithstanding the supposedly cathartic effect of testifying before the Commission (as Phakama had) and the impetus to reconciliation that this is supposed to release, some hurts do not heal and avoidance may be a coping mechanism through which individuals manage past hurts.

Truth be told?

The account told above should give some indication of the complexity of truth-telling. I explore this further now through an assessment of the forms of silence that shaped the Commission's 'truth'.

There were clear age and gender patterns in speaking about violence before the Commission. At the Human Rights Violations hearings that were held across the country between 1996 and 1997, men and women spoke differently of the harms they experienced during the apartheid era. Men spoke directly of their physical and psychological suffering whereas women usually testified about damage to others, mainly men; sons, husbands, brothers and other male kin. Women's testimonies were generally broader in scope than men's: they were more likely than men to describe the effects of violence on family and community life. They were also more likely to testify to the reverberations of suffering through generations and down time. Much to the Commission's concern, and despite encouragement, women across the country gave scant account of their own suffering or experiences of violence, least of all of sexual violation.

The Commission's model of truth was such that it expected that women could and should testify about such violence. It consistently underestimated the dangers to women of testifying about violence in public. Drawing from a model that holds that speech is cathartic and that persons are autonomous individuals with the capacity to choose freely how to engage in institutional processes, it read the absence of women's testimony of direct harm as silence caused by reticence, propriety or lack of education about rights, or, as a few people told me, as evidence that women had not been as directly affected by apartheid as had men, a claim which is easily refuted but which continues to hold some sway in masculinist discourses of the past. Notwithstanding evidence that demonstrates very clearly that women's safety cannot be secured when certain kinds of experience is made public (I am thinking here particularly of the horrifying violence sometimes visited on women who publicly disclose their HIV-positive status), there is still a normative assumption that silence is intrinsically damaging and speech healing.

There is little recognition of the complexity of silence or of the costs of being called to speak of personal experience. For young women, in particular, the costs may be high, and indeed very few young women gave statements to the Commission or testified about their experiences of violence. Indeed, the chapter on women in Volume Four of the Commission's Report and Volume Seven, completed some four years after the first five volumes had been presented to parliament, are explicit in their recognition of the Commission's failures in respect of women – in relation to both sexual violence and women's experiences more generally. None of the young women with whom I worked in Zwelethemba spoke publicly, and those few who made statements to the Commission did so with some reluctance, usually after prompting by senior women in the community or by their families. The women were afraid that deeply hurtful experience might become public and thereby expose them to judgement and censure. In contexts in which young women are often blamed for the harm they experience, especially when that harm is sexual, it ought not to be surprising that many would prefer not to speak.

A few young women who did testify publicly elsewhere told me that they had been humiliated in speaking of intimate matters publicly; one woman halted her testimony midway, two others were protected from public scrutiny by testifying from behind sheets, and another young woman explained that she was glad that her experience of violation had emerged in a friend's testimony so that she would not have to expose herself to the well-meaning but heavy-handed approach of Commissioners.

When particular experiences are considered to be defiling or polluting, as violence, incarceration and death often are, silence may be a means of protection of the self and others, holding experience at bay or within so that its harm cannot extend outwards. We do not yet know fully what happens to people when dangerous words have been uttered. The assumption that truth is neutral belies the complex processes of interpretation and entextualisation that go on in real life (Ross 2003a and 2003b; Gready 2003). Accounts that exonerate or explain experience in one context may undermine it in another, as different interpretations are brought to bear.

My work (Ross 2003a and 2003b) shows that testimonies were reinterpreted in the light of local knowledge and gendered codes of conduct. Often these reinterpretations were less than generous and were in fact sometimes cruel, especially where these concerned women's activities that stood outside the registers of local conventions of propriety. Thus young women who had been actively involved in political resistance to the state, or who had borne children out of wedlock, or who had been detained, raped or tortured, were particularly vulnerable to accusations of impropriety and, unless they were widely acknowledged to have been leaders in struggle, they tended not to speak of the past lest it invite negative assessments.

Entrenched patriarchies and local understandings of gender relations may undermine women's attempts to speak of violence. As is evidenced in so much public talk about rape in South Africa, powerful conventions continue to hold women responsible for the violence they experience. Beset by forms of power that hold them responsible for the actions of others, the worlds women inhabit are fragile and the power that shapes them is not always easily put into words. Given this, it is unsurprising that in some contexts contestation over the past or conflicts that are informed by prior histories of distrust should take the elliptical forms that I have described above. This is not to say that people do not speak directly of violence or harm or betrayal, but to caution that often the way in which the past is manifested in the present is metaphoric, circuitous, and allusive. Truth-telling may depend on symbolic registers and gestures which may not be immediately open to scrutiny and analysis.

Material consequences

The stakes of truth-telling and silence can be high and can have material consequences. In Zwelethemba, for example, some people who testified about their experiences of gross violations of human rights qualified for reparations (a one-off amount of R30,000). Others, for a variety of reasons, did not. Among the reasons some did not qualify was that they made statements too late in the process for consideration. Their reasons for doing so often rested on the fact that they were unsure of what would happen to the material – the 'stories' – they offered and were afraid to reveal aspects of their experience that might implicate others as either victims or perpetrators. Some did not offer statements because they strongly resisted the idea that they were victims, seeing themselves as having contributed to the struggle against apartheid and to its eventual political demise. Proud of their achievements, they were concerned not to be labelled victims; as a result, however, they did not qualify for reparations when these were eventually forthcoming.

Most were not rewarded for their roles as activists in ending apartheid either; although young, many felt too old to return to school after 1994, and most were unable to complete their education. The Special Pensions Act implemented by the new state explicitly excluded them from its ambit, and most did not qualify for other forms of state support. As a result, there was a great deal of dissatisfaction when some people received reparation grants and others, whose suffering had been as great or greater, did not.

In other words, the truth that has emerged about Zwelethemba through the Commission's Report and the forms of reparation available to those who suffered do not fully acknowledge the scale of harm. They also do not recognise that the historical record – both that created by the Commission and that held in diverse forms in communities of sentiment – is shaped by absences and elisions as much as by what is actually said.

Truth and reconciliation?

Earlier in the chapter, I described Archbishop Tutu's evaluation of the failures of the Commission, particularly his disappointment with the treatment of victims and the Commission's failure to reach the whole truth. While he blamed the latter on the apartheid state's destruction of documents (as did the Commission Report – see Vol. 1: 201), the question of finding and telling the truth is more complex. The Commission was aware of this perspectival dimension, eventually identifying four different kinds of 'truth' (Vol. 1: 110–14). Factual truth referred to that which can be corroborated by data. In many instances, this simply was not possible: documents did not exist, events were not recorded, materials had been destroyed. The Commission also worked with the notions of personal, social and healing truths. Personal or narrative truth was composed of the testimonies, offered in deponents' languages of choice (see Ross 2003a for analyses of early testimonies and patterns in testimony); social truth referred to the process of truth-telling; while healing truth was considered to be 'the kind of truth that places facts and what they mean within the context of human relationships' (Vol. 1: 114). It is shaped not only by the availability of documentation as corroborating evidence but also by what it is permissible to say within a specific discourse and by local patterns of speech, propriety and (dis)trust.

In other words, I have argued that what is presented as 'truth' depends on the discourse in circulation at the time; and that all four kinds of truth are made complex by the ways in which local discourses enable or disallow talk of the past and by the ways that people are able to listen or attend to such talk. The Commission's 'truth', its archive of the past, is made up of silences and absences as much as it is of data. These constitutive gaps are significantly patterned by age and gender. I have shown too that the past arises unexpectedly in everyday life, and reconciliation and national unity may not necessarily have a bearing on how people conduct their ordinary lives. Instead, people may guard against coming into contact with those who have hurt them, avoiding their polluting presence.

Putting the past behind us?

The Commission frequently claimed that its aim was 'to deal with the past', 'to put the past behind us'. However, as philosophy has long reminded us, the past has a way of haunting the present and the notion of chronological time, in which past, present and future are neatly separated, is a fiction. The Commission was a social process, an intervention in social life, and, as such, has consequences that endure. These include the on-going anger around the lack of sustained reparations, the unequal distribution of reparation, and the lack of recognition of people's roles as activists in a struggle against a system of oppression. Many of the people with whom I worked in Zwelethemba are members of the Western Cape branch of Khulumani, a victim support group that, together with Jubilee South Africa, has, since the Commission ended, brought cases in New York courts against companies that did not disinvest from South Africa during the period of international sanctions (see www.khulumani. net). They seek more broadly based reparation for those who were oppressed by the processes of capitalist accumulation in South Africa; something that the Commission explicitly refused to investigate.

In other words, far from putting the past behind us, critiques of the Commission's work and assumptions have stimulated further investigation into the apartheid years, investigations that are broader than those the Commission was mandated to pursue. By using international law to challenge the actions of corporations during apartheid, 'victims' have taken the question of reparation beyond the limited terrain of the Commission's work. In so doing, they challenge what is meant by human rights violations, and extend the definition of harm from the narrow purview of violations of bodily integrity. They also challenge conventional definitions of victimhood, which understand 'victims' as passive. The tragedy is that the onus again rests on those who have already experienced harm, to continue to challenge existing power structures.

Endnotes

1 Defined as torture, disappearance, killing and severe ill-treatment.
2 The Report refers to the area as Worcester but in fact reports almost exclusively on Zwele-themba.

References

Breytenbach, K. 2006. 'TRC Failed to Meet Needs of Victims – Tutu', *Cape Times*, 21 April 2006.
Coalition of NGOs. 1996. *Submission to the Truth and Reconciliation Commission Concerning the Relevance of Economic, Social and Cultural Rights to the Commission's Mandate*, Cape Town.
Gready, P. 2003. *Cultures of Political Transition* (London: Polity).
Hayner, P. 2001. *Unspeakable Truths: Confronting State Terror and Atrocity* (London: Routledge).
Ignatieff, M. 1996. 'Articles of Faith', *Index on Censorship*, no. 5, pp. 110–22.
Mbeki, T. 2005. Address on the Occasion of the 10th Anniversary of the Establishment of the Truth and Reconciliation Commission and Celebration of National Day of Reconciliation, Freedom Park, Tshwane, 16 December 2005. Full text of speech accessed online at: www.dfa.gov.za/docs/speeches/2005/mbek1216.htm on 5 June 2006.

Reynolds, P. 2005. 'Imfobe: Self-knowledge and the Reach for Ethics among Former, Young, Anti-apartheid Activists', *Anthropology Southern Africa,* vol. 28, nos. 3 and 4.

Ross, FC. 2003a. *Bearing Witness: Women and the Truth and Reconciliation Commission in South Africa* (London: Pluto Press).

Ross, FC. 2003b. 'Measuring Wrongs with Rights: Method and Moral in the Work of the South African Truth and Reconciliation Commission' in Mitchell, J (ed.), *Human Rights in Global Perspective: Anthropological Studies of Rights, Claims and Entitlements* (London: Routledge), pp. 163–82.

Ross, FC and Reynolds, P. 2004. 'Voices Not Heard: Small Histories and the Work of Repair' in Villa-Vicencio, C (ed.), *To Repair the Irreparable: Reparation and Reconstruction in South Africa* (Cape Town: David Philip), pp. 106–14.

TRC. 1998, 2003. *Report of the Truth and Reconciliation Commission,* 7 vols. (Cape Town: Juta).

Verdoolaege, A. 2006. 'The Debate on Truth and Reconciliation: A Survey of Literature on the South African Truth and Reconciliation Commission', *Journal of Language and Politics,* vol. 5, no. 1, pp. 15–35.

Wilson, R. 1996. 'The Sizwe Will Not Go Away', *African Studies,* vol. 55, no. 2, pp. 1–20.

Writing Africa

Achille Mbembe in conversation with Isabel Hofmeyr

COULD WE BEGIN WITH the biography of your book On the Postcolony? *How would you characterise the intellectual genealogies and pathways that shaped the text?*

I wrote most of *On the Postcolony* at night. It was in the early 1990s, as the deep shadow of Afro-Marxism was receding. Then, to many of us, it seemed as if the study of Africa was caught in a dramatic analytical gridlock. Many scholars were peddling increasingly useless maps of the present at the very moment new dramas were taking shape.

As the crisis in the social sciences was intensifying, innovative trends, even a new kind of thinking, quite creative and radical, were emerging in fields as disparate as fiction, fashion, painting, music, dance, the arts, and the domain of aesthetics in general. In all these disciplines, something of a reconciliation between so-called African identity and a certain idea of cosmopolitanism was in the making.

But a proper biography of *On the Postcolony* is impossible without a direct reference to African music. During my days as a student in Paris, I had started listening to Fela Anikulapo Kuti's vocal and instrumental expression, Pierre Akendengué's songs of the forest and Ray Lema's experimentations with classical music. It was in the late 1980s that I 'discovered' Congolese music. First, I was struck by the fact that in spite of its mixture of pain and suffering, this was a music of rare emotional sublimity. It could easily be characterised as a practice of jubilation.

What I also found in this music was a deep stream of a particular strand of social memory – the social memory of the present. In this expressive practice, a drama was unfolding – the drama of African self-realisation. A good reader of texts can hear the sounds of Congolese music late in the night behind many a chapter of *On the Postcolony*. Some days, while writing this book and listening to this music, I could literally feel the transitory rhythms of earthly life in Africa.

Congolese musical imagination taught me how indispensable it was to think with the bodily senses, to write with the musicality of one's own flesh if we are to say anything meaningful about life in contemporary Africa. Not only could I feel with this music the movement of power, but I could also hear in it WEB Du Bois's injunction: 'Life is not simply fact.' Indeed, life is also the rendering of fact into song, sound and thought. Congolese music helped me to descend into the African world of the senses so I could write a book in which the song carries with it the flesh that gives it life. That is why, underneath the developments concerning violence, brutality and death, *On the Postcolony* keeps alive the possibility of a redeemed body of Africa at the Day of Resurrection.

The other direct biographical element of this book is the African novel. From the late 1980s onwards, while many analysts were locked in sterile debates about the prospects of Africa's development, the francophone African novel was already celebrating the demise of the nationalist project and of the claim of Africa's post-independent states to stand for the 'Father'. At the same time, the novel was alerting us to the apparition on the horizon of new, uncommon forces that we did not quite yet grasp and that could not quite be said in the then dominant conceptual languages.

During my last years as a student in Paris in the late 1980s, I had begun studying the work of the late Congolese writer Sony Labou Tansi. I was struck by the way in which, contrary to the then dominant African nationalist or even anti-imperialist discourse, his thinking and writing were putting 'experimentation' before 'ontology'. Whether in *La Vie et demie*, *L'État honteux*, or *La Parenthèse de sang*, reason and language were always bifurcating, new styles and themes were ever evolving, and unexpected bridges were constructed between abstraction and concreteness, the conscious and the unconscious. It was as if in his writings, art and thought were made to come alive and to resonate with one another. I also noticed that for him, contingency and ephemerality appeared to offer a vast reservoir of freedom and free play.

In these works, time always appeared as heterogeneous and unpredictable. There was an element of anti-systematicity, immediacy and directness in these works that appealed to me. For instance, I liked very much what Sony Labou Tansi taught me about the openness to encounters with what we can neither yet determine nor fully describe nor agree upon since we do not yet even have the words for it and therefore we have to keep trying to invent a name for it. I also liked Labou Tansi's idea of an agreement constantly deferred in order for new questions to be introduced, and the necessity to expand the 'dictionary' for a rethinking or reinvention to happen, or for difference to become productive. I also noticed the importance Labou Tansi was giving to the human sensorium as a privileged, if dangerous, archive of the present – an archive that constantly threatens to overwhelm and suffocate the subject.

It seemed to me that this new *écriture* was succeeding where the social sciences had failed to formulate new problems and to invent new concepts with cultural, political and aesthetic implications. When it came to Africa, the crisis in the social sciences could be dealt with if the social sciences were to work through, with and against the arts. That is what got me on the road, in search for a social science discourse free from the dogmas of 'developmentalism' (left and right) – a discourse that would unashamedly be a political, philosophical *and* aesthetic practice.

The book's title, On the Postcolony – *why the 'postcolony' rather than 'postcolonial'?*

This book is an attempt to negotiate the problem of time. To be more precise, it is written in the belief that in order to provide a radically new interpretation of what it means for an African to be alive in the present, we must take very seriously the task of interpreting time or, more specifically, the *durée* (duration).

The term 'postcolony' is an attempt to experiment with a different dictionary of representation – a lexicon in which to pose different questions about the 'now', its course, the different ways in which it passes away and comes along at the same time. The concept of the 'postcolony' also allowed me to keep my distance from 'postcolonial theory' *per se*. No one can deny the role played by this current of thought in the deconstruction of imperial knowledge and in the critique of every form of universalism hostile to difference and, by extension, to the figure of the Other.

But by insisting too much on 'difference' and 'alterity', certain strands of this current of thought have lost sight of the weight of the fellow human without whom it is impossible to envisage the possibility of a common world, of a common humanity. On the other hand, in so far as postcolonial theory has considered the struggle between Father and Son – that is to say, the relationship between coloniser and colonised or native and settler – to be the most significant political and cultural paradigm in formerly colonised societies, it has tended to overshadow the intensity of the violence of 'brother' towards 'brother' and the status of the 'sister' and the 'mother' in the midst of fratricide.

More fundamentally, and without doubt as a consequence of its relative philosophical poverty, this current of thought has hardly been able to account for the fact of abjection and the impossibility of signification – essential marks historically assigned to the African sign in the theatre of the world. I refer to the impossibility of signification, not so much because the African sign resists every process of symbolisation, but because Africa has been, for so long, the name of the irreducible outside, an impossible remainder whose meaning and identity cannot be spoken about except by way of an originary act of expropriation. This originary confinement in primitive difference – it is this that Senghor, Césaire and Fanon and others tried hard to refute, at times no matter what it took, according to the means available to them.

But contrary to Senghor, Césaire and Fanon, *On the Postcolony* aimed at revisiting this archive of abjection, no longer in the context of the call to murder the settler, but at a time when 'brother' and 'enemy' have become one, and in an age in which the sovereign right to kill is exercised against one's own people first. In so doing, the book was trying to prolong an African tradition of critical reflection on the politics of life.

By the politics of life, I meant the conditions of possibility for the African subject to exercise his or her own sovereignty and to find in this relationship with oneself the fullness of his or her happiness. Yet, contrary to an approach typical of certain strands of postcolonial theory or nativism, I critiqued the solipsism of the Western *logos* only in order to open a path to the critique of the self, to a genealogy of responsibility. Indeed, any serious critique of the West and any serious critique of freedom entails, of necessity, a revisiting of our own fables and the various grammars that, under the pretext of authenticity or radicalism, prosaically turn Africa into yet another deadly fiction.

One of the ways in which you define the postcolony is via time. By the postcolony, you do not simply mean those societies that have become independent after colonial rule as though we can somehow divide time into a 'before' and 'after'. Rather, the postcolony is the place in which past and present are intertwined and entangled in hydra-headed ways. What do these views of time as defining the postcolony mean for the practice of history as a discipline?

Frankly, I do not know. Although I was trained as an historian (and political scientist), the method used in *On the Postcolony* has not been that of a classical historian. For example, I do not believe that time is uniform, homogeneous, irreversible and divisible into verifiable units. Nor do I believe that history and memory can be situated in two different systems haunted by gaps and discontinuities. It is largely because of the historical process of dematerialisation, calculation and abstraction that fuels capitalism that we have come to view time as eminently divisible. Now, the societies I am writing about are not, *stricto sensu*, capitalist societies. To be sure, they are commercial civilisations. But this does not make them capitalist in the proper sense of the term.

I would argue that structures of temporality in colonial and postcolonial conditions are thoroughly entangled with the vicissitudes of the affective; with the subjective play of desire and uncertainty, fear and terror, trauma and unpredictability. In such contexts, we can only refer to the abstraction of time as a rhetorical figure. For many people caught in the vortex of colonialism and what comes after, the main indices of time are the contingent, the ephemeral, the fugitive and the fortuitous – radical uncertainty and social volatility. Radical changes go hand in hand with various other gradual and subtle shifts, almost invisible, imperceptible. Sudden ruptures are entangled with structures of inertia.

To account for change (which I understand as one of the tasks of the historian) is therefore to account for simultaneity, multiplicity and concatenation. Social life is shaped and reshaped in the midst of instability. For me, the historian's practice is one that helps us to think philosophically about the very precariousness of life and of the social; the various ways in which events coexist with accidents. What Africa teaches us is that our lives are always-in-the-making. They do acquire a certain unstable consistency, including in the midst of uncertainty. To a large extent, human life is always a potentiality, a process of fragile actualisation.

Most readers will have encountered some of the ideas in the book from your widely cited article 'Provisional Notes on the Postcolony' which appeared in English in 1992. Here you pioneered a new understanding of postcolonial power that departed from traditions of Marxist, nationalist and nativist frameworks that rely on romantic narratives of domination and resistance. Your book jolts us out of these narratives by examining the dramaturgy of power in the postcolony and the way in which ordinary people are drawn into these spectacles. They project themselves into power, wanting that power to reflect their own greatness. Tyranny, then, is always intimate: 'those who command and those who are assumed to obey are so entangled as to render both powerless'. What we see is 'mutual zombification', to use another of your phrases that has assumed a wide currency.

The most controversial thesis of the book has to do with the sensory life of power and the logic of mutual corruption and conviviality uniting rulers and their subjects in one and the same episteme. Whereas a large part of the social theory of the last decades of the twentieth century preoccupied itself with the phenomena of identity, social control and resistance, the central chapter of the book in effect affirms that the underlying force of postcolonial brutality and venality is the fact that the political relationship between the rulers and their subjects is inscribed in a deeply shared symbolic matrix.

Today, I would add that this order is governed by two kinds of drives: on the one hand, the unlimited desire to acquire wealth – what the Greeks called chrematistics – and on the other hand, the stupefaction experienced in pleasure (pleonexia). These drives encircle power, devitalise it, weigh it down, and participate in its dissipation. In the same way, they dispel the possibility of its overthrow since, as I argue, these drives are deeply shared by the ruled. The entanglement of rulers and subjects is constantly masked, sanctioned and reiterated by way of both a ceremonial type of civility and the banality of ritualised modes of coercion. The inequality produced in this way is experienced by both sides as a form of exchange and as a form of the gift.

Your discussion of power frequently invokes the history of the senses. Power, as you note, is tangible: 'The fact is that there is no power other than that which offers itself for touching, and in turn, touches its subjects' (Mbembe 2001: 166–7). The book engages constantly with the senses: pain, laughter, religious ecstasy, death, the sights and smells of everyday life. Why do you consider a history of the senses integral to an understanding of power?

I take the postcolony to be a figure of a fact – the fact of brutality, its forms, its shapes, its markings, its composite faces, its fundamental rhythms and its ornamentation. The book takes brutality in its matter-of-factness, as a domain of representation that tends to circumscribe and to obscure the very conditions of its representation. I attempt to read colonial and postcolonial brutality as a workmanship that requires virtuosity, creativity of the imagination, extravagance in expenditure, manufacturing of marvels as well as superstitions – in short, what the Greeks called a *phantasia*.

One powerful theme in the book is a Fanonian concern with the psychic structures inaugurated by colonialism and their aftermath where the colonised must always be a thing, a 'no-thing', or an animal, and how these return in nightmare form in the postcolony. The citizen of the postcolony hence exists in a state of doubleness, of constantly having to become another person, to assume another identity as authority switches and changes. Such doubling reminded me of the figure of the trickster and the hustler.

At the time the book was written, I did not have in mind the figure of the trickster and the hustler as such. I was interested in questions of symbolisation and figuration of power. My main concern was with processes of production of power that could not be captured in the categories of classical political economy and development studies.

On the other hand, I was struck by the quasi-impossibility of revolutionary practice in the continent. There are social upheavals, to be sure. Once in a while, things break loose. But the latter hardly translate into an effective, positive, transformative praxis. It is almost always as if what ensues is a continuation in the void.

I therefore wanted to be attentive to the multiplicity of holes that constantly eat away at power, penetrate it, drain it, dry up its flows without this necessarily resulting in any enhancement of life potential. I wanted to write about this most miserable and fragile struggle, its zones of intensity and its vibrations in the senses. This was to be a history of power that would be inseparable from the history of the senses.

I was fascinated by the structure of the book, which is a wonderful compendium of different genres: philosophy, theology, pavement ethnography, excerpts from novels, cartoons, dense and almost prophetic writing. The final chapter seems particularly apt as it returns us to the religious basis of sovereignty and, in doing so, sends us back to the beginning of the book all over again to consider what we have read thus far in light of the final chapter. In this structure, the book asks the reader to experience many different orders of reality in rapid succession. It is as if, if we are to understand anything about power, we need to encompass as many realms of reality as possible. Complex topics can never be grasped without effort. We need to read again if we are to understand. Do you have any comments on the structure of the book itself and what work you think this requires the reader to do? Also it is clear that the book has a lot to say about the relationships between history and fiction. Any comments?

The structure of the book is borne out of a combination of aesthetic and political concerns. This is the reason why I resorted to various archives and modes of thinking – the historico-economico-political (Chapters 1 and 2), the literary, the fictional and the psychoanalytical (Chapters 3, 5 and 6), the theologico-political (Chapter 6), and the philosophical, everyday life creativity, including the pictorial (Chapter 4).

The last chapter, 'God's Phallus', was written as an allegoric dialogue with Frantz Fanon. The question raised by Fanon's considerations on the politics of life is the following: Can one seriously consider the history of human freedom as fundamentally governed by the unique, compulsory and unavoidable law – that of the generalised circulation of death? Fanon's response to this question is the following: To give one's own life for the sake of freedom, or still to kill the settler, is to be born in freedom. For him, this human ascension to freedom is an intrinsically moral act. There are moments in Fanon's narrative of freedom when this upsurge takes up the appearance of an orgiastic mystery.

The last chapter of *On the Postcolony* suggests that in order to exit the Fanonian cul-de-sac – the dead-end of the generalised circulation and exchange of death as the condition for becoming human – it is important to examine in what way, in a context of a life that is so precarious, disposing-of-death-itself could be, in fact, the core of a veritable politics of freedom. A politics of freedom is a politics in which the old practice of human sacrifice is exceeded, surmounted and sublimated. It is this radical utopia that runs throughout *On the Postcolony*. In this chapter, I indicate that one can only express the unconditionality of such a utopia in a poetic, even dreamlike, form. Because disposing-of-death-itself is precisely the kind of difference that can be neither eradicated nor integrated nor overcome, the radical utopia of disposing-of-death-itself cannot be read literally. It can only be read figuratively, poetically. It can only be left to the difficult and never completed labour of decipherment. And in this absence of closure lies a politics of life and freedom that would not be a simple repetition of the originary murder.

The conclusion of the book I found very powerful. Here you set out again the difficulties of writing about Africa in a field that has been overburdened by centuries of formulaic representation. You note: 'Thus, we must speak of Africa only as a chimera on which we all work blindly, a nightmare we produce and from which we make a living' (Mbembe 2001: 241). In this place of shadows, the method you seem to favour is that of 'the glimpse', 'truths that flicker out like fireflies' (242), something between 'the visible and graspable'. The section captures the difficulties of trying to bring something new into being when our academic senses are so numbed by the existing formulaic discourses. Can you give us your views on language and expression in academic writing?

For me, to write about Africa is not only to write about a trial (*une épreuve*), but also to write from a rift (*la faille*). I find it necessary to find a way of writing about this trial in a language that allows its pulse to be felt. Faced with the cul-de-sac of the many discourses on Africa, it seems to me that a means for escaping the trap of the name can be found through experimenting with the deconstitutive and propitiatory force of language. This is why my own way of writing is always an attempt to explode received language altogether.

In *On the Postcolony* (especially in the original French version of the book), I attempted to carry out this labour of deconstitution through shortcuts, repetitions, inventions, a manner and rhythm of narration or description at once open, hermetic, and melodious, made up of sonorities – in the tradition of Senghor's 'shadow song' (*chant d'ombre*) – a song that can only be captured and truly understood by the entirety of the senses, and not by hearing alone. But these encounters with the senses only interested me in so far as they were fragmentary, evanescent and even sometimes unsuccessful. As far as I was concerned, it was a matter of encountering those zones of contemporary African life overloaded with memory, remembrance and debt – regions of knowledge irreducible to those of the classical social sciences. This explains why I granted such a place in the book to philosophy, religion, literature and psychoanalysis.

This mode of writing was intimately linked to a manner of reading, notably the reading of everyday life, that privileged sites where the subject experiences her or his own history as present past. I insist on this relationship between writing, language and experience. Over the last quarter of the twentieth century, African life has taken various forms. The real and the fictitious have been reflected in one another, provoking radical forms of uncertainty and the loss of any stable reference, since each thing thereby is always refracted in several others, in a relationship that could be described as proliferating but also falsifying. It is this power of the false that gives to the experience of the postcolony, if not its unique character, then at least its share of originality.

Reference
Mbembe, Achille. 2001. *On the Postcolony* (Berkeley: University of California Press).

XENOPHOBIA

Owen Sichone

Xenophobia is the deep dislike of non-nationals by nationals of a recipient state. Its manifestation is a violation of human rights. South Africa needs to send out a strong message that an irrational prejudice and hostility towards non-nationals is not acceptable under any circumstances. Criminal behaviour towards foreigners cannot be tolerated in a democratic society.

– Braamfontein Statement on Xenophobia, South African Human Rights Commission, 15 October 1998.

XENOPHOBIA, IN THE PSYCHOLOGICAL SENSE, is an irrational and debilitating anxiety induced by fear of strangers, foreign things and places. Like other phobias it afflicts individuals and can be treated or cured by therapists. A somewhat different kind of xenophobia is the racist or nationalist sentiment that sometimes grips entire countries and is expressed more as hatred of, or contempt for, rather than fear of foreigners and foreign things. More often than not, it results in violence against foreigners or war against neighbours. In this latter sense, xenophobia has become a buzzword in discussions of the hostile attitudes and actions that have been taken in South Africa towards foreigners, especially those from other African states. What lies behind this expression of xenophobia is the subject of this essay.

South African xenophobia

Xenophobia in South Africa varies from the benign 'Proudly South African' campaign promoting locally made consumer items (because local is *lekker*) to the more sinister 'mass action' against foreigners in violent forms of political mobilisation that some have labelled ethnic cleansing and even genocide. When 'xenophobic violence' exploded, in May 2008, into shocking pogroms that initially targeted Zimbabwean refugees in

Alexandra, Johannesburg, and rapidly spread like a veld fire to the rest of the country, many government officials claimed that they were taken by surprise and even blamed it on a 'third force'. However, tensions and actual violence against foreigners had in fact been simmering for more than fifteen years. Around Johannesburg mass action against foreigners dates back to the last, very violent days of the apartheid regime. In Alexandra in December 1994 and early 1995, over a period of several weeks, marauding gangs used violence to try to evict alleged 'undocumented migrants' from the township, after blaming foreigners for increased crime, sexual attacks, economic deprivation, unemployment, disease and all manner of social ills. The mobs claimed to belong to the ANC, the South African Communist Party, and the South African National Civic Organisation – although the ANC–SACP–Cosatu alliance has always officially condemned xenophobia and, in the case of Cosatu, actively fought for the rights of migrant workers. The 1995 pogrom was called *Buyelekhaya* or 'Go back home' (Minnaar & Hough 1996: 188; Cox 1995). It was not the first time that such mass action had been organised against African migrants residing in the black townships and informal settlements, and of course it was not the last.

In March 1998 Human Rights Watch published a report entitled 'Prohibited Persons: Abuse of Undocumented Migrants, Asylum-Seekers and Refugees in South Africa', which alerted the world to the abuses suffered by African migrants at the hands of the South African authorities. In the same year the Southern African Migration Project (SAMP) of Queen's University, Ontario, and Idasa published their own report 'Challenging Xenophobia'. Probably in response to the two reports, the Human Rights Commission, the United Nations High Commissioner for Refugees (UNHCR) and other human rights groups launched the Roll Back Xenophobia Campaign in later 1998. Since 2005 newspapers have recorded a number of murders of Somali shopkeepers, probably by criminals, especially in the Eastern and Western Cape. As a result the Premier of the Western Cape instituted a policy of getting immigrants and local people to teach each other skills and to work together in the townships and informal settlements that they shared. Nobody, therefore, should have been taken by surprise by the violent campaign to rid South Africa of African migrants in May 2008.

The Johannesburg township of Alexandra exploded in a wave of 'xenophobic attacks' on Zimbabwean refugees and Mozambican migrants more or less similar to those of 1994–5 and 2005. The campaign quickly spread from Alex to Diepsloot and other parts of Gauteng. Each new attack seemed more vicious than the last as mobs attacked, robbed and raped their way into the public eye demanding the deportation of foreigners. But soon, not just foreign migrants were under attack – 'They are killing Shangaans,' some residents of Ramaphosaville informal settlement on the East Rand shouted as they ran for their lives. The setting on fire of Mozambican migrant worker

Ernesto Alfabeto Nhamuave by a crowd in Ramaphosaville made the front page of the world's newspapers and reminded people of the necklace killings and attacks by mobs with traditional weapons which were common in the 1990s. It was as if South Africans were continuing where they left off when interrupted by Archbishop Tutu and the Truth and Reconciliation Commission. Here it seems was yet more evidence that South Africa is a very unwell, unhealed and unstable land, one that must yet confront the unfinished business of post-apartheid reconstruction.

Xenophobia has been defined as 'one among several possible forms of reaction generated by anomic situations in the societies of modern states' (Wicker 2001). The new South Africa is a good candidate for a society in a condition of anomie, given its state of permanent negotiation over basic values and norms, and we should therefore not be surprised to find unusual levels of moral confusion among the citizenry. The old South Africa was completely discredited long before its formal demise in 1994. The new South Africa, though filled with promise, came into being after prolonged violence and struggle, during the course of which systems of populist justice meted out punishment to the 'enemies of the people': witches, *askaris* (captured and turned ANC or PAC militants who then worked for the apartheid security forces), bantustan leaders, *impimpis* (informers) and township sell-outs. In the process the 'struggle' fell short of its own democratic ideals, especially those spelt out in the Freedom Charter.

By the time the new South African Constitution had been debated, negotiated and passed into law, apartheid was a thing of the past, but the ideals and values of the new democratic order which the Constitution enshrined had still to be fully realised and accepted in the life of the country. It is against this background of a new society emerging but still not fully developed, and of an old one rejected but still dying out slowly, that xenophobia became manifest in South Africa.

Ethnic identity and the poor

In an internally divided and highly unequal society like South Africa, it is very difficult to create a sense of belonging that cuts across the old apartheid-era fences and divides. Black townships are still black, a few Nordic tourists notwithstanding, and white suburbs are still white despite the presence of the black elites who have moved into them, some probably wishing them to remain that way, and keeping their distance from the black townships. In the turmoil of May 2008 the absence of the black elites from the scenes of crime exposed the extent to which the political leaders and the new black middle class have moved away, distanced themselves from and become alienated from their working-class roots. Like race and ethnicity, class is a basic category of mobilisation for political entrepreneurs both big and small. In South Africa it is the local-level, *induna-* (headman-) type political entrepreneur that has so far made use of xenophobia to mobilise poor people against migrants in the struggles for space, jobs and other resources. None of the populist local leaders has so far attained national prominence like France's Le Pen, and most national leaders refrain from championing a xenophobic nationalism.

Although it has been shown by SAMP surveys that South Africans of different backgrounds are equally xenophobic, there is a tendency to blame the racial intolerance and violent nationalism entirely on the poor. After the May 2008 pogroms, newspapers were full of letters from the educated elite condemning the violence and dissociating themselves from the senseless behaviour, which was thus blamed on the shantytown dwellers. While it is true that xenophobic violence usually bubbles up from below, we need to reinforce the finding of the SAMP researchers that it is not just the poor who are xenophobic. Whether we are talking about land or social welfare, in postcolonial Africa or post-Maastricht Europe, the recourse to ethnic devices for excluding others from resources is a well-established practice among both rich and poor. In the townships of South Africa, where livelihoods are difficult to sustain, the sense of ethnic identity among the poor has become sharper as their sense of civic identity and citizenship has been disappointed by the failure of the new state to deliver a 'better life for all'. Here, more than in any other African postcolonial society, wages and money are the main source of livelihood, land long having ceased to provide a peasant farming alternative to South Africa's working class. It is thus a matter of life and death when unemployable male youths in the townships declare that foreigners are 'taking our jobs and our women' because as far as they are concerned, their means of reproduction have been taken away. Since they were doomed under apartheid to provide migrant labour to the mines and farms and now lack the basic skills to function in wage labour and in the informal sector, they do not have the means to earn a living, get married and establish their own homes. As a result they blame their state of social death on the *makwerekwere*, or foreign Africans, in their midst, who provide a convenient scapegoat for their ills.

Post-apartheid South Africa emerged in a post-Cold War world where global and regional economic and global processes increasingly demand that individuals and firms must adopt creatively inclusive multiple identities. For the wealthy, multiple citizenships are just another commodity freely available on global markets. 'Foreign investors' have worked out ways whereby they cease to be natives of any land and cannot therefore be declared aliens unless they are arbitrarily deprived of their cosmopolitan documents. On the other hand, it is very difficult for working-class migrants to the South African cities, whether they are from KwaZulu or Malawi, to exercise their right to be citizens of the world because the global economy just does not grant them the means.

Indeed, it is difficult for the poor and unemployed in South Africa even to exercise their rights as South African citizens. Like other former colonies in Africa, South Africa still bears the legacy of its colonial past when the state differentiated between citizens and subjects. While white settlers were accorded the privileges of citizens, as Mamdani (1996) has argued, the 'natives' were excluded from this regime of rights and belonged not to any civic space but to native reserves – in short, ethnic space. Regardless of where they were born or lived, natives were said to come from an ancestral area, but beyond that they were always alien. The term *makwerekwere* belongs to the politics of homelands, tribal areas and neocolonialism and not to nationalism, regionalism, pan-Africanism or globalism. It explains why the native is in fact always an alien even in his homeland. Thus we can see that it is not only foreign Africans who are denied citizenship in the new South Africa; even the unemployed and permanently poor 'natives' from the bantustans and rural areas and their descendants are excluded from many of the benefits and rights of the new state.

Ironically, South African law attempts to be inclusive and to afford refugees and migrants the same human rights as citizens. Despite this, neither state officials nor the South African public has a positive opinion of immigrants; indeed, some nationalities are even less welcome than others. Whether they are perceived as job-takers or viewed as a threat to the 'better life for all' promised in post-apartheid South Africa, foreigners face varying levels of hostility. The media have also provided other fears, linking foreign Africans in particular to organised crime, drugs, diseases, guns and child abuse. It is thus now difficult to dissociate Nigerians from drug syndicates even though many of them are very visible in academia and in the arts as law-abiding role models. Mozambicans, who have been key players in the mining industry's migrant labour force longer than anybody else, are also perceived as gun runners more than mineworkers. Labelling foreigners as *makwerekwere* thus attaches to them a completely negative and pejorative name that pays no attention to the historical facts and is heavily influenced by the colonial legacy of regulating access to the cities and the economy, by distinguishing between insiders and outsiders, citizens and subjects.

The making of *makwerekwere*
The term *makwerekwere* is the key label by which South African ethnic discourse refers to African migrants. Though it is considered derogatory by the migrants, some South Africans insist it is merely descriptive. It centres on cultural differences between black South Africans and other Africans, especially language – *makwerekwere* is a term for babblers or barbarians. In South Africa, as in other anglophone African countries, though English is the chief official language, it is not the preferred language of personal communication in the townships. Consequently foreigners who use English as a means of communication mark themselves off from locals. Africans who cannot speak 'a black man's language' – in this case, a local language – are perceived with some suspicion in Swahili-speaking East Africa as much as in Sotho- or Nguni-speaking

southern Africa. But to their annoyance, African immigrants understand that South African languages are not unique. As multilingual as they are, South Africans are unaware that Nguni and Sotho languages are spoken north of the Limpopo, and that numerous other African languages share a substantial vocabulary with their own.

Apart from language, skin colour provides another criterion for distinguishing foreign Africans from locals. *Makwerekwere* are considered darker than South Africans. South Africans perceive the rest of the continent as hotter than their own country and are of the view that there is a connection between heat and dark skin. Although there are populations from the Sudan belt, for example, that are generally darker than southern Africans, all shades of black and brown can be found in the population. One woman, a refugee from Sudan who lived in Langa, Cape Town, recalled in an interview she gave to an Idasa radio production team how people would see her on the street and exclaim 'Yo, yo, yo! Mnyama' because she stood out in the crowd as unusually dark. Some would express open hostility and shout, 'You foreigner, you foreigner, go back to your country'. Others would approach her and ask, 'Where do you come from? Where are you living? Do you work?' Clearly, asking a stranger where she comes from is not necessarily a hostile act, but the refugees, especially, tire of answering it every day. Alan Morris (1999: 313), who has worked with Congolese and West African immigrants in Johannesburg, reports very similar sentiments expressed by African migrants in inner-city Hillbrow. One Congolese man said, 'Here in Hillbrow, people are not accepting us, especially black men. They think we are coming to take their jobs ... They think that white men are bringing jobs and black men come to take their jobs.' Although apartheid should have taught people that classifying identity by appearance is not a foolproof technique, the police continue to round up Africans of a dark complexion as suspected illegal aliens. Of course they usually arrest many angry South Africans in the process (see Madywabe 2000).

In the same Idasa radio programme on xenophobia, Halif, who used to be a mathematics teacher in Mogadishu but now survives by selling sweets at a train station, recalls his reply to a South African man who once asked him where he came from: 'There are so many whites who are from overseas, have you ever asked a white man?' When the South African admitted he hadn't and didn't know why, the Somali refugee explained, 'Because you are afraid of asking him. You are still afraid inside.' The suggestion that South Africans have not shed their colonial mentality is an accusation that one hears frequently from African expatriates, who, just like the South Africans they criticise, regard South Africa as a European enclave.

Pascal, a Tanzanian migrant who managed to incorporate himself into Cape Town society and has many South African friends, recalled in an interview with this author (11 July 1999) that he once asked a Xhosa-speaker what the meaning of *kwerekwere* was. The South African looked at him and said, 'Your appearance is not like a *kwerekwere*.' When asked why he replied, 'Because you are not so black.'

But neither skin colour nor language can distinguish between South Africans and non-South Africans, given that the latter is a legal rather than cultural or racial category. Nor does *makwerekwere* differentiate immigrants from refugees, tourists from guest workers, or illegal from legal migrants. In any case it is a dangerous term because it deprives people of their language and humanity, and because it can lead to violent attacks on others.

Migrancy

In their search for a better life, people have always resorted to migration and South Africa has played the role of destination country for centuries. People who felt limited by political oppression, low wages and unemployment set out to realise their dreams elsewhere. Everyone has their own aspirations but money is the key to obtaining higher education, raising capital for a small business venture or some other investment. According to the Report of the Global Commission on International Migration (2005), all countries are destination, transition and sending countries. Thus South Africa is not the place where the rest of the world wants to move, although it may appear that way. The Angolan diamond fields or the Congolese gold fields or the Ethiopian highlands are all places where some people go to make a better life for themselves.

The opportunities in the South African economy for foreigners are better than in most African countries and include professional football, industry, and even relatively menial work, e.g. subcontracting to Cape Town's small construction companies, which are mainly owned by Muslims. The range of work referred to as cheap labour includes work as security guards and petrol attendants. South Africans looking for cheap land and labour for agricultural purposes have migrated to Zambia, Mozambique and even the Congo. Opportunities can be found even in poor countries, and relations between migrants and host populations are not always characterised by violence, even in South Africa.

New arrivals in Cape Town's townships are usually provided with board and lodgings by women whom East African migrants call 'Xhosa mamas'. The women's role in providing shelter to the foreigners, even if it is not entirely out of charity, contrasts with the hostility of the men. The Xhosa mama provides a home for the migrants even though her house or shack may be overcrowded already. The East Africans observe that as long as they have money to pay the rent they are welcome, and that if they fall on hard times their hosts are not so supportive. Nevertheless, they seem to understand each other's plight. Local women also work as sales assistants for the more successful traders, and spend a lot of time in the company of foreign men.

Some of them get married to and have children with the immigrants. This side of the relationship between South Africans and migrants rarely receives coverage in the press; it is the violence of gangsters and policemen that gets reported (see Sichone 2008).

Migrants who are serious about getting on with the job of making money make an effort to learn Xhosa quickly by immersing themselves in the township community in order to learn the language and other survival tactics. This is not just to save themselves from harassment by policemen who use language to define illegal aliens, but also because the business deals that ambitious men are involved in require them to be fluent in local languages. Their attachment to South Africa can, however, be destroyed by one act of violence that reduces their economic resources to zero and tears them away from their wives and children.

Conclusion

This essay has highlighted the context in which xenophobia has emerged in South Africa and especially the lot of the poor and unemployed, their frustrations of waiting for the ruling elites in the new South Africa to deliver on their promise of a better life for all. In these circumstances, migrants in their midst from elsewhere in Africa provide a convenient scapegoat, despite the fact that in many cases foreign Africans actually create employment. This has, however, not made any difference as far as most South Africans are concerned, in part because it is South African women whom the Senegalese or Congolese street vendor is likely to employ, as assistants; South African men still prefer regular factory wage employment.

But we also need to look beyond economic problems and explanations. When asked why they were being attacked, many Somali and Mozambican immigrants mentioned jealousy. The only other context where the idea of jealousy is normally evoked is in witchcraft accusations. So we need to explore as well the sexual jealousies and the perceived anti-social threat that migrants pose in the eyes of the South African youth. What they see is not really an economic rival but an anti-social force that threatens their very existence; all evidence to the contrary is just ignored. In this sense we can speak of an irrational group hatred of foreign Africans. Looking to the future, we should expect that no simple apology will repair the damage that has been caused, because jealousy and witch-hunts require public confessions and cleansing rituals of both a spiritual and political nature.

Finally, as studies of neo-Nazi skinheads among the youth in the former East Germany suggest (Kurthen et al. 1997), ignorance and ethno-cultural distance are also key factors in xenophobia. The perception of most African migrants is that despite access to television and numerous newspapers, South Africans know very little about the rest of the continent. Papa Fall, a Senegalese trader who ran a restaurant at the Pan African Market on Long Street in Cape Town, joked in the Idasa radio programme that when he was called a *kwerekwere* he responded by saying, 'Call me brother: even Mandela married a *kwerekwere*,' referring of course to Nelson Mandela's wife Graça Machel, who is from Mozambique.

In all, the rolling back of xenophobia thus requires a multipronged solution: sustained economic growth that results in job creation; education to improve skills as well as general knowledge about Africa and the rest of the world; and the promotion of a non-exclusionary, human rights political culture that takes South Africans out of their narrow ethnic identities and into a more cosmopolitan and co-operative form of citizenship.

References

Cox, Anna. 1995. 'Armed Gangs Force Foreigners out of their Alexandra Homes', *The Star*, 25 January 1995.

Kurthen, H, Bergmann, W and Erb, R (eds.). 1997. *Anti-Semitism and Xenophobia in Germany after Unification* (Oxford: Oxford University Press).

Madywabe, Lungile. 2000. 'My Four Hours as an "Illegal Immigrant"', *Mail & Guardian*, 3–9 March 2000, p. 16.

Mamdani, M. 1996. *Citizen and Subject* (Cape Town: David Philip).

Mamdani, M. 1998. 'When Does a Settler Become a Native?' Inaugural lecture, University of Cape Town.

Minnaar, M and Hough, M. 1996. *Who Goes There? Perspectives on Clandestine Migration and Illegal Aliens in Southern Africa* (Pretoria: HSRC).

Morris, A. 1999. *Bleakness and Light: Inner City Transition in Hillbrow* (Johannesburg: Wits University Press).

Sichone, OB. 2003. 'Together and Apart: African Refugees and Immigrants in Global Cape Town' in Chidester, D (ed.), *What Holds Us Together: Social Cohesion in South Africa* (Cape Town: HSRC Press), pp. 120–40.

Sichone, OB. 2008. 'Xenophobia and Xenophilia in South Africa: African Migrants in Cape Town' in Werbner, P (ed.), *Anthropology and the New Cosmopolitanism: Rooted, Feminist and Vernacular Perspectives* (Oxford: Berg), pp. 309–24.

Southern African Migration Project (SAMP) and Idasa. 1998. *Challenging Xenophobia: Myths and Realities of Cross-Border Migration*, Southern Africa: Migration Policy Series no. 7, April 1998.

Wicker, HR. 2001. 'Xenophobia' in *International Encyclopedia of the Social Sciences* (www.sciencedirect.com/science).

LIST OF CONTRIBUTORS

Emile Boonzaier is a senior lecturer in medical anthropology and sociology at the University of the Western Cape.

Christopher J Colvin is a postdoctoral fellow in health and human rights at the School of Public Health at the University of Cape Town and a part-time lecturer in the Department of Social Anthropology at the University of Stellenbosch.

Jean Comaroff is Bernard E and Ellen C Sunny Distinguished Service Professor in Anthropology at the University of Chicago and director of the Chicago Center for Contemporary Theory.

John L Comaroff is Harold H Swift Distinguished Service Professor in Anthropology at the University of Chicago, fellow of the Chicago Center for Contemporary Theory, and senior research fellow of the American Bar Foundation.

Ben Cousins is director of the Programme for Land and Agrarian Studies (PLAAS) in the School of Government at the University of the Western Cape.

Zimitri Erasmus is a senior lecturer in sociology at the University of Cape Town.

Harry Garuba is an associate professor in the Department of English Language and Literature and in the Centre for African Studies at the University of Cape Town.

Lesley Green is a senior lecturer in social anthropology at the University of Cape Town.

Ruth Hall is a senior researcher at the Institute of Poverty, Land and Agrarian Studies (PLAAS) at the University of the Western Cape.

Thomas Koelble is professor of business administration at the Graduate School of Business, University of Cape Town.

Kai Horsthemke is a senior lecturer in the School of Education at the University of the Witwatersrand.

Thembela Kepe is an assistant professor in the Department of Geography and the Program in International Development Studies at the University of Toronto.

Achille Mbembe is a research professor in history and politics at the University of the Witwatersrand, a senior researcher at the Wits Institute for Social and Economic Research (WISER), and a visiting professor in the Department of English and the Department of Cultural Anthropology at Duke University.

Helen Moffett is a freelance writer, academic, editor, researcher and gender activist, formerly of the University of Cape Town's African Gender Institute and English Department.

Edgar Pieterse holds an NRF SARChI chair in urban policy and is based at the African Centre for Cities in the School of Architecture, Planning and Geomatics at the University of Cape Town.

Deborah Posel is a professor of sociology, and the founding director of the Wits Institute for Social and Economic Research (WISER) at the University of the Witwatersrand.

Sam Raditlhalo is a senior lecturer in the Department of English Language and Literature at the University of Cape Town.

Thiven Reddy is a senior lecturer in the Department of Political Studies at the University of Cape Town.

Steven Robins is an associate professor in the Department of Sociology and Social Anthropology at the University of Stellenbosch.

Fiona C Ross is an associate professor in the Department of Social Anthropology at the University of Cape Town.

Nick Shepherd is a senior lecturer in the Centre for African Studies at the University of Cape Town.

Owen Sichone is an associate professor in the Department of Anthropology and Archaeology at the University of Pretoria.

Andrew Spiegel is an associate professor and head of the Department of Social Anthropology at the University of Cape Town.

Jonny Steinberg is a journalist and prize-winning author, who holds a doctorate in political theory from Oxford University.

Kees van der Waal is professor of social anthropology at the University of Stellenbosch.

Bettina von Lieres is a lead researcher and convener for the Development Research Centre on Citizenship, Accountability and Participation at the Institute of Development Studies, University of Sussex, and teaches at the University of the Western Cape and the University of Toronto.

INDEX

Achebe, Chinua 42
Achmat, Zackie 53, 55
affirmative action 165, 216–21
African National Congress (ANC) 32, 51, 62, 70, 75, 143, 144, 149, 160–3, 184, 189, 210–21, 256
African Renaissance 19, 20, 21, 22, 202
AIDS 7, 8, 13–23, 30, 33, 47, 129, 165, 206, 240; see HIV
AIDS dissidents 15–16, 22, 53, 189
anthropology 3, 5, 36, 39, 66, 80, 136, 138, 139
apartheid 33, 159–61, 165, 171, 178
Appadurai, A 124
archaeology 118–20
Arendt, Hannah 5
Bafokeng 85–8, 192
Benjamin, Walter 99
Biko, Steve 41, 43, 107, 114, 118, 178
Black Consciousness 41, 107, 121
black economic empowerment (BEE) 63, 73, 74–5, 86, 164–5, 184, 214
Bond, Patrick 165
Boonzaier, E and Sharp, J 2, 10
Bushmen see San
Cabral, Amilcar 11, 42–3, 249
capitalism 60, 76, 92, 95, 100–1, 160–3, 167, 185, 250
Césaire, Aimé 249
citizenship 9, 40, 47–56, 124, 147, 171, 182, 258, 263
civil society 48, 50, 51–2, 64, 70, 71–2, 93, 185, 210, 217
class 163–5, 257
Coetzee, JM 25, 27
colonialism 5, 36, 40, 41, 83, 129, 170
Comaroff, Jean and John L 6, 124
Comaroff, John L 185
community 6, 60, 152, 175, 191
Constitution of South Africa 11, 56, 62, 67, 112, 183–4, 186, 203, 257
constructionism 1, 9, 37, 123, 125, 139, 174, 201; see essentialism
crime 25–33, 99, 101, 106, 176, 182, 256
culture 35–45, 79, 82, 85, 87, 88, 117, 125, 133, 134, 139, 170–2, 175, 177, 186, 191–2, 196, 197–200, 204
democracy 47–56
dependency theory 61
Derrida, Jacques 5, 209
development 6, 38, 58–67, 70, 144, 148, 191
District Six 121, 202
Dlamini-Zuma, Nkosazana 15

DuBois, WEB 248
Durkheim, Emile 93
economy 157–68
empowerment 59, 69–77, 100, 164–5; see also black economic empowerment
Enlightenment 36, 37, 38, 45, 92, 138, 169
entrepreneur 166–7
epistemology 7, 136
essentialism 174
ethnicity 3, 6–7, 79–88, 172, 186
Evangelicalism 93
faith 91–101
Fanon, Frantz 11, 42–3, 118, 178, 219, 252, 253
feminism 104–5, 107–8,
Foucault, Michel 59, 66, 76
Frank, AG 59
Freedom Charter 62, 149, 214, 257
Fukuyama, Francis 8
gender 104–14, 150, 176, 186, 204–6, 241–2
globalisation 6, 8, 37, 44, 45, 62, 96, 123, 125, 129, 133, 159, 167–8, 185, 197
Growth, Employment and Redistribution (GEAR) 62, 75, 162, 167
Hammond-Tooke, David 3
heritage 116–26, 195, 199
history 117, 197
HIV 30, 112, 129, 136, 165, 206, 240; see AIDS
Hobsbawm, Eric 200
hoodia 83–4, 88, 131, 191–2
hybridity 122
identity 6, 37, 41, 45, 50, 81, 82, 84, 87, 88, 106, 109, 114, 117, 122, 125, 145, 148–50, 175, 191–2, 195, 199, 201–4, 211, 258
indigenous knowledge 85, 117, 122, 129–40
intellectual property 84, 87, 96
International Monetary Fund (IMF) 59, 159, 214
knowledge 7, 37, 82
land 6, 87, 88, 143–54, 186, 199
Landless People's Movement (LPM) 143, 149, 165
landscape 120
Left intellectuals 7, 75, 77, 165, 184–5, 221
Madlala-Routledge, Nosizwe 14
makwerekwere 176, 258–61
Mamdani, Mahmood 40, 41, 124, 187, 259
Mandela, Nelson 26, 116, 178, 211
market, the 73, 92, 93, 97, 98, 101, 157–68
Marxism 3, 10, 59, 60, 107, 159, 210, 212, 213, 251
masculinity 111, 113, 189–90
Mbeki, Thabo 14–23, 30, 54, 116, 123, 135, 163, 189, 190, 202, 203, 212, 214, 220, 236
Mbembe, Achille 10, 247–54

Mda, Zakes 45
memory 122
modernisation 32, 58, 61
modernity 5, 92, 133, 139, 186, 195, 197
multiculturalism 37, 39, 45, 198–9
nation 42, 82
nationalism 210, 251
nativism 10, 251
Ndebele, Njabulo 11
neocolonialism 23, 259
neoliberalism 6, 35, 36, 61, 62, 67, 69, 73, 75, 77, 79, 92, 95, 96, 98, 99, 101, 158, 161, 163, 165, 185, 219
new South Africa 2, 8, 11, 18, 19
non-governmental organisations (NGOs) 64, 66, 151, 185, 191, 199
ontology 92, 97, 98
participation, citizen 51, 60, 65, 70, 72, 73, 121, 221
patriarchy 106, 107, 110, 112, 113, 124, 186, 243
Pentecostalism 93–5, 97, 98
poor, the 49, 69, 71, 100, 144, 147, 164, 165, 191, 213, 220, 258, 262
postcolony 9, 10, 40, 123, 124, 126, 187, 247–54
postmodernism 60, 99, 125
post-traumatic stress 113, 224–7
power 79, 132, 135 145, 150–1, 243
race 3, 27, 41, 81, 111, 134, 163–4, 169–79, 219, 220
racism 16, 33, 149
Ranger, Terence 200, 206
reconciliation 26, 44, 235–45
Reconstruction and Development Programme (RDP) 61–3, 69, 70, 77, 161
relativism 9, 11, 92, 97, 132, 196, 198, 206
rights 47, 62, 79, 87, 105, 108, 124, 151, 245, 263

Rostow, WW 58
Said, Edward 11
San 6, 82–5, 88, 119, 131, 146, 152, 169, 170, 183, 191–2, 199, 202
science 134, 136–9
Senghor, Léopold 41, 42, 249
service delivery 64, 71–3, 77, 97, 161, 219, 221
sex 23, 105–9
social movements 54, 55, 185
Sontag, Susan 18, 137
state 48, 49, 61, 66, 76, 87, 93, 98, 152, 159, 164
Thompson, EP 3
tourism 123
tradition 7, 41, 80, 87, 117, 124, 125, 134, 183, 186, 190, 195–207, 219
traditional healing 129, 131
traditional leaders 64, 124, 151, 186, 195
transformation 124, 209–21
trauma 223–33, 236
Treatment Action Campaign (TAC) 47, 52–5, 188–9
Truth and Reconciliation Commission (TRC) 118, 132, 183, 226–8, 232–3, 235–45, 257
Tutu, Desmond 183, 215, 236, 244, 257
Tylor, EB 197, 200
underdevelopment 59
violence 30, 31, 105, 110, 113, 173–4, 177, 183, 229, 256, 261
Weber, Max 79, 93, 95, 98, 100
Williams, Raymond 3–4, 10, 11, 37, 39, 41, 43, 44
World Bank 59, 65, 72, 159, 214
xenophobia 173, 176, 202, 255–63
xeno-racism see xenophobia
Yengeni, Tony 183, 203
Zimbabwe 143
Zuma, Jacob 7, 110, 112–13, 186, 189–91